MW00643314

Nonprofit Neighborhoods

Historical Studies of Urban America

EDITED BY LILIA FERNÁNDEZ, TIMOTHY J. GILFOYLE, AND AMANDA I. SELIGMAN

JAMES R. GROSSMAN, EDITOR EMERITUS

Recent titles in the series

Mike Amezcua, MAKING MEXICAN CHICAGO: FROM POSTWAR SETTLEMENT TO THE AGE OF GENTRIFICATION

William Sites, SUN RA'S CHICAGO: AFROFUTURISM AND THE CITY

David Schley, STEAM CITY: RAILROADS, URBAN SPACE, AND CORPORATE CAPITALISM IN NINETEENTH-CENTURY BALTIMORE

Rebecca K. Marchiel, AFTER REDLINING: THE URBAN REINVESTMENT MOVEMENT IN THE ERA OF FINANCIAL DEREGULATION

Steven T. Moga, URBAN LOWLANDS: A HISTORY OF NEIGHBORHOODS, POVERTY, AND PLANNING

Andrew S. Baer, BEYOND THE USUAL BEATING: THE JON BURGE POLICE TORTURE SCANDAL AND SOCIAL MOVEMENTS FOR POLICE ACCOUNTABILITY IN CHICAGO

Matthew Vaz, RUNNING THE NUMBERS: RACE, POLICE, AND THE HISTORY OF URBAN GAMBLING

Ann Durkin Keating, THE WORLD OF JULIETTE KINZIE: CHICAGO BEFORE THE FIRE

Jeffrey S. Adler, MURDER IN NEW ORLEANS: THE CREATION OF JIM CROW POLICING

David A. Gamson, THE IMPORTANCE OF BEING URBAN: DESIGNING THE PROGRESSIVE SCHOOL DISTRICT, 1890–1940

Kara Murphy Schlichting, NEW YORK RECENTERED: BUILDING THE METROPOLIS FROM THE SHORE

Mark Wild, RENEWAL: LIBERAL PROTESTANTS AND THE AMERICAN CITY AFTER WORLD WAR II

Meredith Oda, THE GATEWAY TO THE PACIFIC: JAPANESE AMERICANS AND THE REMAKING OF SAN FRANCISCO

Sean Dinces, BULLS MARKETS: CHICAGO'S BASKETBALL BUSINESS AND THE NEW INEQUALITY

Julia Guarneri, NEWSPRINT METROPOLIS: CITY PAPERS AND THE MAKING OF MODERN AMERICANS

Kyle B. Roberts, EVANGELICAL GOTHAM: RELIGION AND THE MAKING OF NEW YORK CITY, 1783–1860

Amanda I. Seligman, CHICAGO'S BLOCK CLUBS: HOW NEIGHBORS SHAPE THE CITY

Timothy B. Neary, CROSSING PARISH BOUNDARIES: RACE, SPORTS, AND CATHOLIC YOUTH IN CHICAGO, 1914–1954

Julia Rabig, THE FIXERS: DEVOLUTION, DEVELOPMENT, AND CIVIL SOCIETY IN NEWARK, 1960–1990

Aaron Shkuda, THE LOFTS OF SOHO: GENTRIFICATION, ART, AND INDUSTRY IN NEW YORK, 1950–1980

Mark Krasovic, THE NEWARK FRONTIER: COMMUNITY ACTION IN THE GREAT SOCIETY

Ansley T. Erickson, MAKING THE UNEQUAL METROPOLIS: SCHOOL DESEGREGATION AND ITS LIMITS

Andrew L. Slap and Frank Towers, eds., CONFEDERATE CITIES: THE URBAN SOUTH DURING THE CIVIL WAR ERA

Evan Friss, THE CYCLING CITY: BICYCLES AND URBAN AMERICA IN THE 1890S

A complete list of series titles is available on the University of Chicago Press website.

Nonprofit Neighborhoods

An Urban History of Inequality
and the American State

CLAIRE DUNNING

THE UNIVERSITY OF CHICAGO PRESS   CHICAGO AND LONDON

The University of Chicago Press, Chicago 60637
The University of Chicago Press, Ltd., London
© 2022 by The University of Chicago
Published 2022
Printed in the United States of America

31 30 29 28 27 26 25 24 23 22   1 2 3 4 5

ISBN-13: 978-0-226-81990-7 (cloth)
ISBN-13: 978-0-226-81989-1 (paper)
ISBN-13: 978-0-226-81991-4 (e-book)
DOI: https://doi.org/10.7208/chicago/9780226819914.001.0001

Library of Congress Cataloging-in-Publication Data

Names: Dunning, Claire, author.
Title: Nonprofit neighborhoods : an urban history of inequality and the American state /
    Claire Dunning.
Other titles: Historical studies of urban America.
Description: Chicago : The University of Chicago Press, 2022. | Series: Historical studies of
    urban America | Includes bibliographical references and index.
Identifiers: LCCN 2021050910 | ISBN 9780226819907 (cloth) |
    ISBN 9780226819891 (paperback) | ISBN 9780226819914 (ebook)
Subjects: LCSH: Neighborhood assistance programs—Massachusetts—Boston. |
    Federal aid to nonprofit organizations—Massachusetts—Boston. | Federal aid
    to community development   Massachusetts—Boston. | Community development—
    Massachusetts—Boston. | Urban poor—Services for—Massachusetts—Boston. |
    Segregation—Massachusetts—Boston.
Classification: LCC HT177.B6 D85 2022 | DDC 307.1/416097446I—dc23/eng/20211029
LC record available at https://lccn.loc.gov/2021050910

♾ This paper meets the requirements of ANSI/NISO Z39.48-1992 (Permanence of Paper).

Contents

Figures

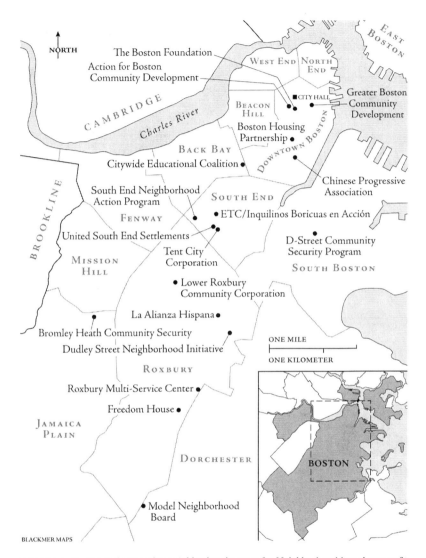

NORTH

The Boston Foundation
Action for Boston
Community Development

CAMBRIDGE

Charles River

WEST END NORTH END

■ CITY HALL

BEACON HILL

Boston Housing
Partnership ●

BACK BAY

Citywide Educational Coalition ●

DOWNTOWN BOSTON

EAST BOSTON

Greater Boston
Community
Development

BROOKLINE

South End Neighborhood
Action Program

FENWAY

United South End Settlements

MISSION HILL

Tent City
Corporation

SOUTH END

● ETC/Inquilinos Boricuas en Acción

Chinese Progressive
Association

D-Street Community
Security Program

SOUTH BOSTON

● Lower Roxbury
Community Corporation

La Alianza Hispana ●

Bromley Heath Community Security

Dudley Street Neighborhood Initiative

ROXBURY

ONE MILE

ONE KILOMETER

Roxbury Multi-Service Center ●

Freedom House ●

JAMAICA PLAIN

DORCHESTER

BOSTON

● Model Neighborhood
Board

BLACKMER MAPS

FIGURE 0.1. *Boston and some of its neighborhood nonprofits.* Neighborhood-based nonprofit organizations exist all over Boston and provide a wide range of services to residents. Depicted here are the organizations and neighborhoods most discussed in *Nonprofit Neighborhoods.*

Neighborhood Nonprofits

In 2014, the governor of Massachusetts made a headline-grabbing bet on social change. The bet took the form of an innovative public-private partnership known as a "social impact bond" or "pay for success" program that aimed to meet government goals via private financing, nonprofit service delivery, and third-party evaluation. The idea was simple: a government would contract with a local nonprofit organization with a proven track record of success and commit to reimburse for its services if a set of outcomes was achieved by a certain date. Until the results came in, private investors—of both the for-profit and philanthropic varieties—would front the money to cover the nonprofit's expenditures working in some of the region's toughest neighborhoods with some of its hardest-to-reach people. If the nonprofit's intervention hit goal targets of, say, a 40 percent reduction in recidivism among young men, the government would repay the lenders with interest and ultimately save taxpayer dollars that would have gone, in this example, to incarcerate repeat offenders. By minimizing the risk of experimentation for government and involving the expertise of trusted local nonprofits, the effort was what many called a win-win.

The state government in Massachusetts launched the social impact bond, but in practice it was an urban program targeting anew the very old problems of American cities. For even as many spoke of an "urban renaissance" in Boston, the seeming contradiction of poverty amid plenty continued to characterize the commonwealth's capital city and others like it.[1] The idea to structure public, private, and philanthropic financing into a social impact bond hailed originally from the United Kingdom, and the model's emphasis on prevention intrigued President Barack Obama. He imported the strategy to the United States and offered sizable federal grants to incentivize states and cities to experiment with it.[2] Massachusetts jumped at the opportunity, confidently launching three social impact bonds, the first of which addressed juvenile incarceration and reincarceration, followed by programs targeting homelessness and adult education and workforce training. The executive director at one of the local nonprofits involved in the effort framed it as finally "changing the odds" and "confronting . . . stubborn trends."[3] Hardly the first generation of public, corporate, and nonprofit leaders to voice concerns and take action on these issues, perhaps this constellation of partners would succeed where others had failed.

A January press conference announcing the first of three contracts in Massachusetts captured the widespread enthusiasm for data-driven results, business discipline, and cost savings that social impact bonds were supposed to deliver. "The Pay for Success initiative will help us marry smart financial solutions with programs proven successful," Governor Deval Patrick stated, while another administration official assured a focus on "government paying for demonstrated results, rather than simply the hope for success."[4] The ambitious and complex plan, anchored by $28 million, had financial support from the US Department of Labor, Goldman Sachs, and some of the nation's preeminent philanthropic foundations.[5] It also had the involvement of nonprofit community partners with stellar local and, increasingly, national reputations as well as strategic plans rooted in results and designed by consultants. Patrick's announcement made waves: newspapers reported, think tanks opined, Harvard's Kennedy School of Government launched a new lab to study and promote such arrangements, and a bipartisan group in Congress introduced legislation to fund social impact bonds on a larger scale.[6]

An important subtext, implicit in the public fanfare, was the contrast between these new reform efforts and the traditional social welfare programs that had drawn the ire of conservative and liberal critics alike. By the early twenty-first century, the political assumptions about the limitations of government and the potential of markets reflected in Patrick's rhetoric had become so ingrained in American politics and policy that few thought to question the broader implications of using philanthropic dollars to subsidize corporate lending, of financializing social welfare provision, or of using metrics to address issues rooted in structural inequalities based on race and income. Then again, when needs were high among both people living in poverty and the nonprofit organizations working to aid them, it was hard to critique dollars put forward with an earnest desire to see change.[7] Still, for all the talk of a new and better era of public problem solving, what was happening in Massachusetts might instead be understood as the culmination of political and policy trends decades in the making.

Social impact bonds were less a break with the past than a product of it. They reflected a governing approach that *Nonprofit Neighborhoods* traces back to the mid-twentieth century, when, in an earlier moment of inequality and instability, a diverse coalition of people—those with power and those without it, Black and white, elected and appointed, business and nonprofit—embraced the idea of government-nonprofit partnerships and of channeling public dollars through these private entities. Their choices followed a pattern in the United States of what sociologist Elisabeth Clemens calls the "coproduction of public goods" by state and nonprofit actors, but they also steered that coproduction in a new direction to address a vexing combination of deindustrialization, white flight, and grassroots protests that augured ill for American cities in the 1960s.[8] From there, grants, contracts, and, in time, loans, increasingly linked private nonprofits to public governments in every sector of American social policy, ranging from education to employment, health to housing, and arts to parks.[9] Though the precise form of the dollars shifted, as did the goals and strategies, the public funding of private, nonprofit activity has become a fixture of US policy and a primary tool for addressing urban problems.

These financial ties and the broader governing relationships they embody can be hard to detect and, among historians, have been underexplored as a node where the American state met urban neighborhoods and citizens accessed certain democratic rights, including the rights to participation, representation, and social welfare provision.[10] Despite the fact that in the twenty-first century, nonprofits receive more revenue from governments than from private donors, few know this to be true.[11] The notion of an independent, charitable, voluntary realm remains one of the country's greatest myths, and it obscures how intertwined government and nonprofit organizations have become and why this has been so consequential for US cities. The formal engagement of neighborhood-based nonprofits in urban governance constitutes one of the most profound, if hidden, transformations in the United States over the second half of the twentieth century.[12]

Nonprofit Neighborhoods follows the movement of government dollars into private nonprofits and positions the development of this public-private relationship at the center of postwar US history. To tell such a big story, this book follows a local one. Local granularity reveals how a new system of urban governance developed and sheds light on why, despite efforts to the contrary, it carried economic, political, and social inequalities present at midcentury into the new millennium. Rather than simply evaluating the outcomes of individual government grants, this book considers the political and administrative structures they reflected as a whole. It asks why solving public problems through private means and solving structural problems through local organizations became central tenets of US politics and policy. And through an analysis of how such efforts worked on the ground—in community meetings, government offices, storefront organizations, and pleas for more funding—it questions the ability of such arrangements to meaningfully address the inequality of American cities. For while government-nonprofit partnerships have improved individual lives and reduced the imbalance of American capitalism, they have proven ineffective at creating cities that are just, democratic, or equitable.

* * *

It made sense that Boston produced one of the earliest social impact bonds in the United States. Enthusiasm existed for such experiments in Washington, DC, but it took a particular combination of political inclination and local public and private capacity to turn concept into action; federal policy and local implementation are always two sides of the same coin. Boston claimed such a mixture by the twenty-first century thanks, largely, to decisions made in the twentieth. Though the history of relying on private nonprofits to solve public problems—especially those related to poverty—dates to the colonial era, those relationships have shifted over the centuries.[13] *Nonprofit Neighborhoods* argues that one such shift, a significant one, occurred after World War II, when, amid a flurry of protest and concern about poverty, policy makers and local officials responded to the so-called urban crisis by formally linking private neighborhood nonprofits to the American state and grantmaking to urban governance. Boston soon became part of the vanguard of social welfare experimentation and a bellwether of a new system of governance in the United States. There is perhaps no better place to trace how high economic and racial inequality and an extensive nonprofit infrastructure not only coexisted but grew in tandem over the twentieth century.

Boston never fully recovered from the Great Depression of the 1930s, and the city suffered further when wartime and postwar policies invested in suburban expansion that drained jobs, people, and tax revenue from the city in the 1940s and 1950s. It was a pattern familiar to other American cities—particularly those in the Northeast, where the previously dominant industrial and manufacturing bases that kept local banks capitalized and people employed faced extinction. The US political economy had begun its shift toward finance, real estate, and service provision, and the contemporaneous investment—of financial, cultural, and political capital—in highways and housing in the suburbs spelled disaster, many worried, for Boston.[14] The city's population hit a peak in 1950 and then lost 13 percent of its residents before the next census in 1960; this decline continued until 1980.[15] Beyond a loss in the number of residents, the composition of the city's population was shifting too. As African Americans escaped the violence of the Jim Crow South and migrated from Caribbean islands as part of what is known as the Great Migration, Boston's population became increasingly more racially and ethnically diverse. It was also becoming poorer, as Black residents encountered discriminatory policies that suppressed their incomes and wealth and placed 17 percent of Boston residents below the poverty line in 1960.

Metropolitan inequalities based on income, race, and job access portended financial and governance problems for Boston, and those at both the top and bottom of the income ladder knew it. For city officials, more residents in poverty meant both less tax revenue and higher demand for municipal services. For people experiencing poverty, it meant the inability to find adequate shelter or employment and health and safety risks for families. Inequality also posed a political problem. Poverty in Boston and in the larger metropolitan region was not equally distributed. It was, as in other cities, racialized and spatialized such that the capital city was becoming more racially and economically segregated. Those excluded from the postwar prosperity of the United States, of course, recognized the inequalities at hand. African Americans in urban areas organized, mobilized, and demanded their full set of rights and an end to the discriminatory policies and practices that continued to favor white middle- and upper-class families. In Boston, activists such as Ruth Batson and Mel King ran for the Boston School Committee to demand equal investment in schools with Black students, Otto and Muriel Snowden founded Freedom House as a community center to draw resources to Black neighborhoods, and grassroots entities organized a boycott of Wonder Bread until the local manufacturer hired more Black workers.[16] These actions and others like them for economic and racial justice seemed to those in power to threaten unrest and economic decline.

Many at the time claimed, not unfairly, that the federal government had abandoned American cities, but it had given mayors at least one powerful tool to reshape their physical and economic terrain. Urban renewal, famously reviled by urbanite Jane Jacobs for destroying the civic life of cities and by writer James Baldwin for its practice of "Negro removal," funneled millions of dollars to urban mayors to eliminate blighted slums, redraw city grids, and attract the investment of private developers to newly accessible hospitals, industrial complexes, and luxury housing.[17] The program physically and politically cast a long shadow over the twentieth century and ushered in a new era of public grantmaking that steadily drew neighborhood nonprofits into the state.[18]

Boston's initial success at winning federal grants under urban renewal created opportunities for both local municipal offices and community organizations. Appointed as the city's renewal leader in 1960, Ed Logue deserved much of the initial credit for drawing funding, attention, and energy to the city that then compounded over time. In federal funding applications, Logue harnessed the political desirability of the city's reputation for liberal politics, ties to the Kennedy administration, and prominent research universities and world-renowned hospitals. He also took charge of the Boston program under a mayor who promised, unlike his predecessor, to "plan with people" and include local residents in the planning and design of the so-called New Boston. The city might have been on the leading edge of renewal but was by no means unique. Federal legislation, Bostonians learned, encouraged local renewal agencies to make small grants to local community organizations—churches, neighborhood associations, and civic clubs—to smooth over the initial allegations of top-down planning and displacement that haunted urban renewal. Following suit, the Boston Redevelopment Authority issued grants to neighborhood groups, charging them with facilitating participation and mobilizing support for renewal in line with federal guidelines. Doing so addressed both the political problem of protest and the governance one of capacity. It also established the origins of an administrative infrastructure for government grantmaking that used neighborhoods as a governing unit and designated nonprofit organizations as spaces to mitigate the biases of government.[19] It proved a promising start, particularly in Boston's predominantly African American neighborhoods, and foreshadowed a new era of partnership in urban governance that would fully emerge under President Lyndon Johnson's War on Poverty and broader Great Society agenda.

Beyond the experimentation under urban renewal, government grant-making that linked private neighborhood nonprofits to the American state and urban governance arrived in the 1960s as a response to "the urban crisis."[20] Historians use the term as a form of shorthand to capture the particular intersections of economic, fiscal, social, and political challenges facing American cities that, this book argues, funding of neighborhood nonprofits aimed to ameliorate. Initially, observers used the term narrowly, as racially coded language to variously refer to the growing majorities of urbanites who were Black and poor, the problems they posed to municipalities, and the rebellions they launched in places such as Watts in 1965 and in Newark, Boston, and elsewhere in 1967 and 1968. Scholars have since identified the origins of the urban crisis earlier in the postwar period and expanded the time frame and meaning of the term, uncovering the white violence used to create and reinforce Black ghettos, highlighting the policy choices that created such unequal landscapes, contextualizing the shifting political-economic terrain of the United States, and drawing attention to the freedom movements of African American and Latinx urban residents that challenged the structural inequalities of democracy in the United States.[21] This more nuanced framing recognizes the urban crisis as neither inevitable nor natural and traces how it reshaped nearly every facet of American political, economic, and social life. *Nonprofit Neighborhoods* considers how the urban crisis also reshaped urban governance and the routes by which residents in cities accessed their rights and benefits of democratic citizenship.

The idea of working, either directly or indirectly, with private nonprofit entities was not new in the 1960s, but the decade did mark a pivot in a longer trend. Michael Katz has argued that "boundaries between public and private always have been protean in America."[22] However, he and other historians have noted key turning points when the relationships between public and private and between different tiers of government and different forms of private entities have shifted. The upheaval of wars, depressions, and natural disasters punctuate the history of how Americans have sought to solve public problems, and the responses to such immediate triggers often involved new forms of coordination between or reliance on public and private entities. More substantively, such responses produced wide-ranging consequences for what it meant to be a citizen and the shape of the American state.[23]

Often, governments expanded direct aid to individuals and grants to nonprofit organizations together. Consider how, during the Progressive

Era, settlement houses became recognized and, in some cases, subsidized as spaces that socialized new populations of women and immigrants at the same time that government aid to mothers with children expanded.[24] Even the New Deal, heralded for its expansion of the public sector in American life through federal aid such as unemployment insurance and social security, had its share of public-private provisions that ran through charitable organizations.[25] Following urban renewal, Johnson's War on Poverty expanded individual benefits related to health, education, and welfare and doubled down on the idea of working with nonprofit organizations. He put the weight of the federal government financially, administratively, and programmatically behind partnerships with nonprofits that had, until then, been mediated by state and local governments. Two features differentiated Johnson's version from its predecessors; both carried political and administrative consequences. First, his administration linked the federal government to neighborhood-based entities, circumventing, at least initially, lower tiers of government. Second, it used grantmaking as a policy tool to not just reduce poverty but also find new ways for traditionally excluded groups to participate in governance.[26]

As under programs that preceded and followed it, a good share of these War on Poverty dollars made it to Boston, where federal designs took local form as an uneasy and shifting coalition of bureaucrats, politicians, business leaders, social welfare professionals, civil rights activists, and residents. These were coalitions united in a desire to bring in dollars and divided over who should control them. Public funds granted to neighborhood-based nonprofit organizations supported new programming and services, covered rent for community agencies, and paid staff salaries in well-established entities and in the fledging ones popping up in neighborhoods around the United States. These grants carried clear expectations for program delivery and reporting requirements to account for the use of funds. At the same time, grants allowed degrees of flexibility not typically possible in government bureaucracy, which nonprofit organizations embraced and learned to stretch to their advantage, using funding to pursue alternative visions for Boston's neighborhoods not always shared by those in power.

Boston was—and, in the eyes of many, remains—a city boastful of its liberalism but resistant to naming the racial inequalities in its mix, and the influx of government grant funding became a new terrain for the politics of race as white officials and Black residents vied for decision-making authority. The enmeshing of private, neighborhood-based organizations into the apparatus of the state was a governance revolution fought in store-front offices and community centers. People of color, who saw at once the theoretical and practical implications of what government funding for nonprofits might mean for their organizations, neighborhoods, and futures, pursued that goal most vociferously. It was, in the end, on the ground where policies passed in Washington came alive, where local politics animated contests over funding, and where the consequences of funding programs were actually felt.[27]

Government grants created valuable, meaningful opportunities for neighborhood-based nonprofits, but there was another side to this grass-roots story that helps explain not just their inclusion in urban governance but also their persistence therein. Whether funding of nonprofit organizations by government grants would merely ease the pains of discrimination, disenfranchisement, and deindustrialization or actually begin to dismantle the oppressive structures sustaining them was not an abstract question. It animated demands for community control in the 1960s, the politics of busing in the 1970s, the waves of displacement and gentrification in the 1980s, and the desire for capital investment in the 1990s. It was enumerated on the agendas of community agencies such as the Roxbury Multi-Service Center, written into the speeches of protesters at a tent city, and debated in correspondence between funders and grantees in Dudley Square. Yet, as people fought for a better future, traditional interests twisted demands for inclusion into new forms of exclusion. Financial payments to neighborhood-based entities enabled a rhetoric of compassion and a veneer of inclusion among elites but also held community organizations responsible for their own uplift and reified the private sector as the route to the full rights of citizenship. As neighborhood nonprofits mediated, for some, access to public goods and services, participation, and representation, they also facilitated a form of privatized inclusion, simultaneously making urban governance more decentralized, diverse, and participatory, and more insulated from the structural changes African American and Latinx residents had been calling for.[28]

Some say that by the new millennium, Boston had emerged from the urban crisis to experience an urban "renaissance."[29] Such boasts had merit: the city's population had rebounded to steadily increase since the 1980s, property values had soared, and urban living had become desirable to those with the ability to choose where to live. As such boasts often do, however, the notion of Boston's renaissance masked a deep and widening inequality based, still, on race and income. A startling 2015 report by the

Federal Reserve Bank of Boston found that white households in the city had a median net worth of $247,500, while Black households had a meager $8.[30] Boston, it turned out, had not solved its problem of crisis and inequality; it had just found in government grants new tools for managing it.

*   *   *

The tension between managing and reducing poverty and inequality has been *the* challenge of American cities in the postwar era. Although this book is grounded in a local study of Boston, the political pressures, policy frameworks, and public funding programs shaping the story were national in origin and in reach. Grants are often hiding in plain sight and exist as powerful tools not only for policy but also for analysis. They reveal the preferences of those distributing funds and the goals of those seeking them, and, in the case of government grantmaking, they show how state power functioned on the ground in urban America.[31] *Nonprofit Neighborhoods* aims to offer a template or a methodology for others to mine archival collections as well as the scholarship on American cities for further evidence of how government grantmaking reshaped places and the people who lived in them. Readers interested in specific portraits of how neighborhood nonprofits reshaped governance in other cities already have a rich literature on postwar urban history to turn to. Even if others have not placed government grantmaking at the center of their analyses, historians of the postwar period populate their accounts of social movements, political contests, and urban development with local nonprofit organizations and grantmaking programs.

As anyone who has ever applied for a grant knows, grantmaking is an expression of power by those with resources over those seeking them. Almost by definition, a grant exists as a privilege to be won rather than an obligation to be fulfilled; it represents the rewarding of some and the denial of others. When Johnson's administration launched the War on Poverty, it invited nonprofits to apply for a slice of the federal pie by submitting piles of application materials and projected budgets. These submissions then competed against applicants from other cities proposing slightly different projects and budgets based on a combination of what they wanted to do and thought government evaluators wanted to hear. Federal bureaucrats then decided which places and which programs to support, and at what level and with what amount of oversight, setting in motion structures for monitoring and discipline that would grow in importance over the following decades. When the Obama administration sought to encourage social impact bonds, it engaged in a similar process, just as every administration since Johnson's had. Private foundations issue grants in a similar way.

Though as an administrative tool, grants are, in theory, ideologically and politically neutral and broker partnership arrangements between entities with shared goals, they do not put parties on equal footing.[32] Neighborhood nonprofits' choice to apply for government funding or enter into a partnership with government is not equivalent to government bureaucrats' choice to select or deny the proposal. The element of choice for the grant maker is what defines grantmaking and, as a result, renders grants a poor vehicle for delivering rights. This might not be a problem for a philanthropic foundation, itself a kind of private corporation, but ought to prompt questions—if not concerns—when the state increasingly governed through grantmaking.[33] Power differentials in public grantmaking became one of its defining features; they helped make the governing tool popular and productive but also prevented it from achieving its highest democratic ideals.

From a research standpoint, grants produced reams of useful materials: funding applications, financial records, correspondence around grant terms and changes to them, annual reports, and programmatic data. These sources give evidence to the concept, particularly familiar among legal scholars, that more than just money changes hands when the government extends a grant.[34] In particular, grants gave governments, as funders, new visibility into private organizations and power to dictate their futures. As neighborhood nonprofits became increasingly dependent on public funds for their continued operations amid budget crises of the 1970s, government grant programs shaped what these entities did and how, often just on the mere prospect of a government grant or the hope to be competitive for one. In exchange for the possibility of financial resources and, perhaps, a glimpse at the governing table, neighborhood nonprofits abided by new standards of bookkeeping and accounting, limitations on political engagement, requirements for board composition and hiring, expectations about data collection and evaluation, and programmatic guidelines—all of which were set by legislation and the bureaucratic rulemaking that followed to ensure the proper stewardship of public resources. Even as both grantor and grantee benefited from these transactions, these were not relationships of equals nor ones removed from the racial hierarchies of power in the United States.[35] With each grant, the distinction between public and private blurred and lines of democratic accountability and representation became harder to trace.

The turn to grantmaking as a governing strategy represented, at a more abstract level, the growing reach of the American state in the postwar period.[36] Characterizing the American state has been notoriously challenging. Scholars describe it as strong and weak, centralized and decentralized, hidden and visible, robust and hollow. And scholarly attention has shifted from a focus on the state to questions of political ideology and policy.[37] In part, this ambiguity signals the vastness of the scale of US governance—at home and abroad—and the manifold spheres of its activity. It also suggests the reality that the American state is rife with contradictions, often simultaneously strong and weak, centralized and decentralized. Grants from the federal government to neighborhood nonprofits and the broader administrative world they created fit this framing, positioning neighborhood nonprofit organizations as simultaneously agents of and appendages to the state, and as extending and reducing state capacity.

The federal government's reliance on grantmaking to manage problems of US cities altered the state itself, shifting its internal operations and extending its reach. At a practical level, grants and the outsourcing of certain activities to neighborhood nonprofits turned at least some government activities from doing to monitoring.[38] Evaluating grant applications, negotiating contracts, ensuring compliance, enforcing austerity, assessing outcomes, and reporting results required new bureaucratic infrastructures, staffing organizations, and procedures. These capacities developed in fits and starts over the entire postwar period, as each administration in Washington designed its own models for deploying funds and as each lower tier responded in turn. Though the precise forms varied, these state structures existed under both Democratic and Republican administrations, who share credit for building a postwar state able to monitor, choose, and outsource, predicated on competition and austerity and cloaked in the language of meritocracy and innovation.[39]

At a conceptual level, the grants that *Nonprofit Neighborhoods* follows from Washington into Boston's neighborhoods to reduce poverty and improve poor places occupy the intersection between the welfare state and the associational state. To help make sense of the American state, scholars have segmented and named various slices of it based on shared governing logics, state structures, and policy arenas. The welfare state is perhaps the most familiar of these segments, but scholars have productively traced, among others, the carceral state, administrative state, and associational state as spheres with shared functions such as the provision of a safety net or the enforcement of law or, in the case of the associational state, shared approaches to blend civil society and state institutions.[40] In addition to defining these distinct spheres, scholars productively note their intersections: how the punitive nature of the welfare and carceral states, for example, share roots in racism, sexism, and surveillance.[41] Indeed, analyses of the various states through the lenses of gender, race, sexual orientation, and other identities have enriched how historians understand the unevenness of the American state and its various manifestations.

Of the various slices or segments of the state, certain features of the welfare state have garnered the most attention. In his seminal treatment of welfare in the United States, Michael Katz frames a public and a private side of welfare provision, each of which contains two tracks. The public side consists of public *insurance*—such as unemployment insurance and social security—to aid workers, the elderly, and others deemed deserving of such support as well as public *assistance*—such as Aid to Families with Dependent Children, now known as Temporary Aid for Needy Families—which targets poor people with aid that is restricted, punitive, and stigmatized.[42] Gendered and racial categories map neatly onto these "good" and "bad" sides of public welfare.[43] The private side consists of workplace benefits—such as health insurance—which tend to flow through the corporate sector, and private services, which tend to flow through the nonprofit sector.[44] The latter rely on nonprofit organizations, frequently use grants to steer them, and overlap with the associational state as it deals with issues of poverty. This shared, and often overlooked, slice has tended to be analyzed through national studies conducted by scholars trained in political science, sociology, or public administration rather than history.[45] For example, few have applied to this slice of the welfare and associational states the racial analyses that have so productively been used to explore direct aid to individuals.

Nonprofit Neighborhoods attends to this neglected terrain of state-funded, nonprofit-provided social welfare with analyses of race and of space, and finds here, too, the unevenness of citizens' access to rights, services, and goods. From this conceptual understanding of how the welfare and associational states overlap, this book recognizes that they did so in a particular place: the segregated neighborhoods of postwar cities. Even as public funding of private nonprofits was not exclusively an urban phenomenon—anti-poverty grants went to rural areas as well—it skewed quite urban and carried consequences for cities as a result. New approaches to urban governance made the state simultaneously more present in the lives of city residents, particularly Black and later Latinx residents, and also less visible. Grants expanded the state's reach into the day-to-day operations of privately incorporated nonprofit entities, even as the bureaucrats managing them retreated behind a veil of paperwork; and grants enabled increasing participation in governance, even as the funding mechanisms behind them remained outside democratic processes. From their origins in the urban crisis, these instruments of state power became a preferred means of meeting the demands of those long denied the full rights of citizenship and channeled their access to social welfare goods and their rights to deliberate, participate, and express democratic preferences through the nonprofit sector.

The history of Boston recounted here reveals how a state that operated on the power to choose and that fostered competition among organizations, neighborhoods, and local governments could not and did not deliver the level playing field policy makers promised. Selective grantmaking could not undo legacies of withheld spending and racial exclusion. By nature of being selective and rooted in scarcity, grantmaking enforced continued precarity among neighborhood organizations and disciplined them to stay within what funders deemed appropriate, nonpolitical activities.[46] This was true even as designated funds improved the lives of some, as bureaucrats made choices that extended authority and resources to grassroots groups, and as nonprofit organizations used government funding to pursue progressive programs.[47] Attending to this segment where the welfare and associational states overlapped in urban space makes visible the unevenness of citizens' experiences of the state, the inadequacy of the aid they received, and their unequal ability to engage in democratic rights of participation and representation under such a governing regime.

* * *

As the American state increasingly targeted neighborhood nonprofit organizations as a means to manage the urban crisis, it delivered resources to structurally disadvantaged places and people, creating what I call *nonprofit neighborhoods*: places where neighborhood-based nonprofit organizations controlled access to the levers of political, economic, and social power and mediated the local manifestations of the state and market.[48] The term *nonprofit neighborhoods* places analytical emphasis on the neighborhood as the dominant unit of governance and on the role of nonprofit organizations in those activities. It spatially grounds in place what some have called the "nonprofit industrial complex" in order to look beyond individual organizations and beyond distinct policy arenas of housing or social services to underscore the structural embedding of nonprofits in urban governance.[49] Nonprofit neighborhoods were places where nonprofits took in funding and churned out services across policy domains, where they facilitated community meetings and represented local interests, and where they occupied storefronts and purchased property. In Boston, these were often overlooked and underserved places such as Grove Hall, Dudley Square, and Villa Victoria. They are the product of what happened when the American state assigned democratic processes of deliberation, representation, and participation to nonprofit entities, and the consequences of submitting those private entities to the whims of politics and the pressures of scarcity.[50] Nonprofit neighborhoods became spaces of simultaneous inclusion and exclusion, where precarity was more often replicated than reduced.

Nonprofit neighborhoods depended on a state apparatus of government grantmaking, but their construction and maintenance over the second half of the twentieth century equally reflected the changing political landscape. Not all urban neighborhoods became nonprofit neighborhoods during the postwar period, nor did they emerge whole cloth. Instead, successive generations of executive directors, elected officials, and residents built them grant by grant and meeting by meeting.[51] It was an uneven transformation in Boston and elsewhere as political pressures steered grantmaking decisions at the federal and local levels, and as political ideologies on the left and right increasingly preferred nonprofit service provision as an alternative to government. These were deliberate, if not contested, political projects and policy products and, often, desired ones.[52]

The emergence of nonprofit neighborhoods as governing spaces in the postwar US city cannot be disentangled from the racial politics of the Black freedom movement. Nonprofit neighborhoods constituted an organizational, administrative, and governance legacy of those struggles for equality.[53] Certainly protests and petitions were among the most visible activities of the freedom movement, but activists also sought full, lived equality through the acts of applying for, negotiating, and complying with government grants and claiming a visible role in local governance.[54] For neighborhoods long ignored and exploited by governments at all tiers, the grantmaking inaugurated by the War on Poverty presented an opportunity to benefit from state resources and spend them in ways prioritized, at least to an extent, by the community. Still, it took local mobilization to ensure some dollars flowed through grassroots or Black-led entities and built up the capacity and authority that made nonprofit neighborhoods possible over the long run.[55] That they were able to do so indicated the political power community mobilization tactics achieved and the desirability, at least in theory, of government grantmaking to those living and working in predominantly Black neighborhoods.

At the same time, the extension of grants to neighborhood organizations also served to constrain Black residents and stamped nonprofit neighborhoods as new manifestations of an old discrimination. There were certainly those in policy-making circles and in neighborhood organizations who hoped government grants could deliver a better future, and their labors pushed the administrative apparatus of grantmaking in that direction. On balance, however, government grants created new routes for minority residents to participate in urban governance without actually undoing the structures of their exclusion. Mediating public goods and participation through neighborhood-based, financially vulnerable, and politically constrained organizations, and subjecting them to the competition, cuts, and cycles of grantmaking, fundamentally weakened the access residents of nonprofit neighborhoods had to full citizenship. Indeed, this circumventing of actual political power in favor of a version mediated by private, nonprofit organizations was precisely what enabled nonprofit neighborhoods to exist. The United States has a long history of pairing expanded access to public institutions with new forms of inequality, and nonprofit neighborhoods emerged as another chapter in that saga.[56]

Building nonprofit neighborhoods began in predominantly non-white neighborhoods as a way for those in power to mitigate, often reluctantly, the demands for civil rights and community control, but it did not end there. As the twentieth century continued and freedom movements expanded, neighborhoods that were home to residents with minority status based on ethnicity, language, and sexual orientation recognized nonprofit incorporation as a means to access resources from a government unwilling to restructure but eager to appease.[57] Over the 1970s, 1980s, and 1990s, policy makers and local bureaucrats distributed grants to recognize a range of communities, and government grantmaking intersected the spatial segregation of urban America to produce Latinx, Asian American, and LGBTQ+ nonprofit neighborhoods. As it had for African Americans, this practice extended degrees of power without changing the fundamental power relations at the root of their position. These political, social, and spatial dynamics of nonprofit neighborhoods meant that predominantly white neighborhoods typically did not become nonprofit neighborhoods, or at least not to the same degree as others. Even as neighborhood organizations served useful roles in both rich and poor white neighborhoods, their residents did not rely to the same extent on those entities for rights, benefits, and privileges.

If ties to freedom movements helped build nonprofit neighborhoods, the growing popularity of neoliberalism as both a political ideology and governing practice helped sustain them. Questions of how to define neoliberalism and how to locate its emergence temporally have animated recent scholarship in US history, rousing scholars to look locally and globally at the actions of free-market ideologues and pragmatists addressing immediate problems and in the rhetoric of those who embraced the "neoliberal" label and those who abhorred it.[58] Some scholars avoid the term altogether, seeing little value in a word at once so bloated and devoid of meaning. Scholarly debates aside, these inquiries share the desire to understand how and when finance and markets came to structure American political, economic, and social life and, for many, to confront the inequality and precarity that resulted by the end of the twentieth century.

Nonprofit Neighborhoods engages these questions, taking neoliberalism as a set of principles and practices that steered US governance away from investing in state institutions in favor of bolstering financial markets and private entities to secure individual rights, profits, and labor. In analyzing public-private partnerships and competitive grantmaking programs — two hallmarks of neoliberal governance — that linked government and neighborhood nonprofit organizations, this book looks where few have. Even as many urbanists have, of late, begun to root the emergence of neoliberalism in the uneven transformations of the postwar American city and in the choices of mayors, boosters, and community activists, few have recognized nonprofit organizations as both unwitting and purposeful sites of neoliberal governing arrangements, and, in time, neoliberal ideologies.[59] In arguing just that, this book aligns with those who frame "neoliberalization by default" and see it as an on-the-ground response to a set of fiscal, social, and political pressures that did not burst on the scene in the 1980s but instead developed over a longer stretch of the postwar period alongside elite ideological preferences.[60] Eager to extract whatever funding they could from the hodgepodge of government and philanthropic programs available to them, neighborhood nonprofits sought out, participated in, and helped justify governing arrangements that many of the participants would have rejected politically and ideologically.

When nonprofit neighborhoods funneled government funding, democratic processes, and public responsibilities through private entities, they became, perhaps surprisingly, manifestations of neoliberalism. Federal

grantmaking programs lay critical groundwork in the 1960s with a governing regime under the War on Poverty reliant on what would later be identified as core tenets of neoliberalism: partnerships, competition, scarcity,
choice, monitoring, and market expansion.[61] Yet, while governing tools consistent with a neoliberal political economy emerged in the 1960s, the motivations behind and ideological interpretation of them shifted as critiques
of welfare spending and hostility to government mounted over subsequent
decades and cities saw their budgets shrink, needs grow, and interest in urban living rise. Grants to nonprofits became a politically expedient means
of distributing aid through channels that amplified private-sector involvement, decentralized delivery, and financialized forms of assistance that many
hoped would stretch limited public dollars. Even Boston's African American and Latinx leaders became early champions of financialized forms
of assistance for nonprofits in the 1970s—often loans or loan guarantees
instead of grants—seeing in these new funding forms a means to translate demands for community control into ownership. Nonprofit neighborhoods made strange bedfellows of bankers, bureaucrats, and activists, who,
while differently motivated, shared a concern about US cities, a skepticism
of government's ability to address them, and an enthusiasm for local nonprofit action.

The growing role of private, nonprofit organizations in urban governance over the postwar period did not indicate the complete absence of
municipal institutions or public aid from these neighborhoods. Direct allocations via Aid to Families with Dependent Children, social security,
Medicare/Medicaid, and housing vouchers kept families afloat, while institutions of public housing, public schools, public parks, public welfare,
police departments, and public works remained essential elements of nonprofit neighborhoods. What distinguished nonprofit neighborhoods, then,
was that the shortcomings of these public institutions—their patterns of
discrimination, their inadequate budgets, their slow bureaucracies—were increasingly addressed through nonprofit supplement or substitution rather
than through policy reform or public investment during and after the 1970s.
(This was done selectively, of course, as growing investment in policing
and law enforcement makes clear.)[62] Charter schools, tenant management
corporations, community-developed housing, and neighborhood park cleanups became common features of the urban landscape by the end of the
twentieth century and were welcomed for all the ways they appeared to
contrast with government: responsiveness to community needs, racially and
ethnically diverse leadership, flexibility to experiment, and the ability to
fundraise philanthropic and charitable donations. Governing tools initially

designed to draw neighborhood organizations into the state and local government and thereby expand governing capacity had become a means to further shed government capacity and cede ground to the private for-profit and nonprofit sectors.

Outsourcing responsibility for improving broken systems via grants, loans, or contracts to eager neighborhood nonprofits remained politically and administratively desirable, fueling a neoliberal vision for the city that solidified a fundamental misalignment in both scale and capacity between the source of a problem and those designated responsible for solving it. In fact, misalignment is what made nonprofit neighborhoods persist. Activism on the ground successfully positioned nonprofit organizations as important partners to city government and business elites, but the benefits of involving such entities still accrued to those at the top and outpaced the actual benefits to organizations and communities increasingly vulnerable to displacement and budget cuts. And as cities began to gentrify and see new investment in luxury housing in the 1980s, arrangements purportedly designed to attach poor and racially segregated neighborhoods to the growing economy at best accommodated, and at worst accelerated, continuing investments in real estate, financial services, and a knowledge economy that magnified economic inequality.[63] Neighborhood nonprofits as individual organizations and nonprofit neighborhoods as geographically and economically constrained spaces could not compete with the broader forces of finance capitalism, service-sector employment, and evaporating safety-net programs despite the rosy rhetoric surrounding arrangements that, in time, included social impact bonds.

Inequality, inadequacy, and scarcity defined nonprofit neighborhoods and were what enabled them to grow into the dominant mode of urban governance by the twenty-first century. For those with power in cities, much of the appeal of grantmaking, lending, and partnering with neighborhood-based nonprofits lay in their ability to extend degrees of authority to marginalized residents while insisting such power move through private organizations. Such privatized inclusion revealed the limits of pursuing democratic goals through antidemocratic processes and of expecting nonprofit neighborhoods to deliver equity and justice to those repeatedly denied it.

*   *   *

The seven chapters that follow move chronologically, as well as thematically, from urban renewal of the 1950s to the present. They follow the people, money, and programs that linked federal policy to local implementation,

showing how Bostonians shaped a new regime of urban governance. Together, the chapters trace the building, altering, and cementing of nonprofit
neighborhoods that in turn reshaped the lives and participation of many in
Boston.

Chapter 1 introduces Boston in the postwar period, highlighting the
challenges the city faced in an age of suburbanization and the activities
it undertook to remain financially solvent. Federal urban renewal programs enabled the physical and, many hoped, economic redevelopment of
blighted neighborhoods in Boston, but they also shifted the political and
administrative terrain of the city. As residents mobilized in the face of displacement, city authorities turned to private, neighborhood organizations
to facilitate the participation mandated by federal regulations. In particular, Freedom House, a neighborhood nonprofit founded by local civil rights
leaders, took on a governmental role to solicit input, represent opinions,
and distribute information in the predominantly Black neighborhood of
Washington Park. Contracting with nonprofit agencies raised questions
about accountability but also set political expectations and administrative
infrastructures that readied Boston for the 1960s, when federal policies expanded funding programs for private nonprofits in US cities.

The next two chapters cover the origins of nonprofit neighborhoods.
Chapter 2 analyzes how policy makers, philanthropic funders, and political elites in Boston designed grantmaking programs and built a network
of neighborhood-based nonprofit agencies to manage the increasingly visible problems of poverty. Working through the experimental organization
of Action for Boston Community Development initially appeared more
responsive to community concerns and more participatory than the entrenched formal politics of the city. In areas as wide-ranging as education,
social services, economic development, health care, job training, youth
development, and neighborhood planning, Bostonians in poor neighborhoods gained access to new services and programs as well as a degree of
decision-making power over them through their roles as board members,
staff, and volunteers. Such decentralized delivery of social welfare goods
and services proved expensive, bureaucratically cumbersome, and, as chapter 3 details, politically fraught as residents demanded greater control over
the private organizations performing public roles in their communities.
The emerging infrastructure of nonprofit neighborhoods might have been
designed by policy, but it was shaped by social movements on the ground.
Specifically, the Black freedom movement infused a language of community control, attention to racial identity, protest tactics, and political rela-

tionships into the seemingly mundane administrative aspects of running organizations. In so doing, Black Bostonians proposed an alternative vision of what a nonprofit-government partnership might look like, and the more equitable city it might produce.

Chapters 4 and 5 examine changes to the grantmaking that underlay nonprofit neighborhoods. Though an interest in delivering social welfare via nonprofit organizations persisted throughout the 1960s, the funding channels that transferred public monies to private agencies began to shift in the second half of the decade and over the 1970s, as did the form that funding took. Before Richard Nixon's administration further decentralized social welfare into block grants in 1971, the Johnson administration responded to urban revolts and pressure from city mayors eager for more control over incoming funds by inserting municipal and state-level governments into the distribution patterns of federal grants via the Model Cities program and the Law Enforcement Assistance Administration. Chapter 4 describes the ways that municipal agencies shifted their structures, responsibility, and activities following their new role as local grant makers, and found new utility in doing so in the years of court-mandated busing. Chapter 5 then examines the changing forms of public aid amid a more general turn to the market in US policy. For neighborhood nonprofits, this meant an increasing use of loans and loan guarantees in the 1970s and the development of intermediary nonprofit organizations to broker deals and provide technical assistance. These financialized tools were designed to help neighborhood nonprofits access the capital needed to develop affordable housing and support local businesses. An increase in loans from philanthropy and government helped make nonprofit organizations more competitive for commercial loans, though doing so replaced calculations of justice and need with those of market viability and return on investment.

The final two chapters explore the cementing of nonprofit neighborhoods in urban governance and the widening appeal these arrangements found. Chapter 6 considers the rhetorical and political embrace of neighborhood nonprofits by elite Bostonians in the 1980s as a means of responding to new manifestations of urban crisis. They crowed about the triumphs of public-private partnerships amid the shifting policy and political landscape of the decade, forging a new political reality in which neighborhood nonprofits gained elite partners and a publicly celebrated role in governance while remaining dependent on the preferences of those at the top of the economic and political ladder. By the 1990s, the partnerships forged in Boston during a conservative era served as a model for Democrat Bill

Clinton's campaign and presidency. Chapter 7 demonstrates how central nonprofit organizations had become to urban governance by this time, when Boston launched a series of place-based coalitions led by neighborhood nonprofits representing the full racial, ethnic, and sexual diversity of the city. These efforts produced visible results, but census data collected at the start of the new millennium showed poverty and inequality to be deeply entrenched in the very neighborhoods boasting new housing, retail stores, after-school programs, and bus routes.

Boston entered the twenty-first century as a city of contrasts. The city had rebounded from the suburban age to become a desirable place to live. A robust knowledge economy of high-tech start-ups and biomedical firms kept the city's world-class universities and hospitals flush with talent and resources. Local nonprofit organizations continued to win federal funding and earned awards for innovative partnerships between nonprofits, local funders, and city government. This approach to urban poverty carried political weight and yoked previously isolated organizations to institutions of government across nearly all policy arenas and activities of municipal government. In their everyday efforts to improve the city, Bostonians reshaped the practice of urban governance to be more private, decentralized, and market-driven as well as more participatory, diverse, and wide-reaching. Neighborhood nonprofit organizations went from being on the outside of city governing to being deeply entangled in it with a clear seat at the table. Yet, and not unrelatedly, Boston was also a place of growing inequality, where categories of race, ethnicity, income, gender, and citizenship continued to dictate where and how people lived, worked, and learned. Many of the challenges that Bostonians faced in the 1960s persisted despite and because of strategies pursued in the intervening decades. Even as anti-poverty efforts and the nonprofit neighborhoods that delivered them had improved the lives of many, they had been ineffectual at structurally altering the political-economic conditions facing Boston residents. As a result, poverty rates as a whole were higher in Boston at the new millennium than they had been in 1960. On this measure, Boston did not stand out from the crowd but instead exemplified a national trend that it had helped create.

*   *   *

Nonprofit organizations perform visible and vital roles in cities around the United States. They have become such a ubiquitous presence in the urban landscape that it can be difficult to envision a time when private, nonprofit organizations were fewer, smaller, and more limited in their role. Still, the roles that neighborhood nonprofit organizations have taken on and the development of nonprofit neighborhoods was neither inevitable nor smooth. That recognition means that another way was—and is—possible.

This book asks readers to neither valorize nor dismiss the new housing and after-school programs that neighborhood groups produced, and to instead recognize the policy choices, state structures, and racial politics that defined this system and continue to do so. There is no denying that past efforts have bettered the lives of many, but improving outcomes is not the same as eliminating causes. Intertwining community organizations with the American state since World War II opened up new spaces for inclusion and participation and served simultaneously as new means of exclusion and partial citizenship. As cities continue to be sites of nonprofit activity and economic, political, and social inequality, it is worth considering what government grantmaking as a whole has produced over the past half century, what inequalities it has reproduced, and what injustices remain. Those will be the defining questions of the twenty-first century, just as they were of the twentieth.

CHAPTER ONE

The City

In March 1963, a new flag billowed over Boston, proudly proclaiming it an "All-American City." Shocking even locals, a jury for the National Municipal League and *Look* magazine's annual contest had looked favorably on Boston's submission and advanced it to the pool of finalists. For a city that had been on the brink of bankruptcy just a few years earlier, the award offered a welcome opportunity to showcase "the New Boston" Mayor John Collins had promised on the campaign trail in 1959.[1] As any politician would, the mayor likely saw the all-American city designation as a marker of the city's rebirth and a feather in his cap for the next election cycle. It also highlighted the city's status as one to watch, exemplifying both the pressures facing US cities in the 1950s and 1960s and the demonstration of new approaches to those challenges. Boston had not yet rid itself of blight, poverty, or fiscal crisis, but it had begun a transformation that many hoped might ensure Boston lived up to its new designation.

At the award ceremony, Mayor Collins hoisted the flag alongside the two city representatives who had accompanied him to Washington, DC, to present the city's submission: Carl J. Gilbert, chair of the local Gillette Corporation, and Muriel Snowden, cofounder of the nonprofit Freedom House in Roxbury. As emissaries, Gilbert and Snowden embodied the image Collins and his renewal administrator, Ed Logue, hoped to project as friendly to business and responsive to residents. Gilbert's presence, and the elevation of corporate leadership more broadly, came as no surprise. Urban renewal planners in Boston, as elsewhere, put together attractive packages of land and financing to retain business investment in cities.[2] It was Muriel Snowden, a petite woman nearly blocked by the wheelchair Mayor Collins used after a bout of polio, who stood out in an otherwise all-male and all-white crowd.[3] As an African American woman, Snowden's

FIGURE 1.1. *Flag raising commemorating Boston as an "All-American City" (1962).* Muriel Snowden of Roxbury's Freedom House became a key figure in the urban renewal program for Washington Park and in Boston's renewal efforts more generally. She is pictured here standing behind Mayor John Collins as he raises a flag declaring Boston an "All-American City." (John Lane, "All-American City Award (1962) Ceremony in Front of Boston City Hall. Mayor John Collins center with flag and Muriel Snowden center behind Mayor," Image A004224, box 72, folder 2881, FH, NU. Image courtesy of Northeastern University Archives and Special Collections.)

gender and race almost always worked to undermine her authority, yet in this role as a representative of Boston's renewal program, her identity lent additional weight. Snowden had told the contest jury of the "genuine citizen effort" and of an "apathy and deterioration transformed into enthusiasm and determination to rebuild our great city."[4] At a time when urban renewal often went by the moniker "Negro removal," Snowden's endorsement of Boston's program and characterization of it as genuinely participatory set the city apart.[5]

Such a portrait had not always characterized urban renewal in Boston, nor did it accurately portray the renewal program when Collins hoisted the celebratory flag. Like most cities at the time, Boston felt the effects of demographic and economic shifts in the immediate postwar period.

Linked processes of deindustrialization, migration, and suburbanization reshaped the metropolitan landscape of the Boston region, segregating the city and suburbs along economic and racial lines. Early attempts in the 1950s to use the new federal redevelopment program to strengthen the city's bottom line became an infamous example of top-down planning and wholesale clearance.[6] Celebration of Boston as an all-American city and the prominence of Muriel Snowden in such celebrations belied the poverty and racism that increasingly characterized Boston in the 1960s. Snowden's depictions of an eager, approving citizenry similarly flattened the ongoing discord—and often open hostility—in residential neighborhoods over efforts to rebuild Boston's physical and economic infrastructure. Still, Snowden's presence at the flag raising hinted at changes afoot in the city's renewal program and in urban governance more generally: Black residents could have a voice in renewal, and that voice was heard via neighborhood nonprofit organizations.

Urban renewal began as a federal program targeting the urban built environment, but its impact on the United States went far beyond bricks and mortar to include the social, organizational, and governing landscape of American cities.[7] The expansive reach of urban renewal was due, in part, to the federal legislation authorizing the program that mandated comprehensive planning, encouraged partnerships with for-profit and nonprofit private entities, and established new ties between federal and municipal government agencies. Legislation, however, was not solely responsible for the expansive changes wrought by urban renewal. Credit is also due to those involved in the program on the ground—residents, planners, politicians, and investors—who, despite their shared interest in strengthening cities, disagreed in their visions of an improved urban future and how to get there.[8] Local contests over development shaped not just which buildings got bulldozed or built but the processes by which such decisions were made.[9] Increasingly, those processes involved neighborhood nonprofits. Friendly relationships and formal contracts drew these private entities into the work of governing during renewal that set administrative, policy, and political precedents for the remainder of the 1960s—an era of increasing federal attention to poverty and civil rights activism around racial equality.

The movement of billions of dollars into renewal programs around the United States served as a powerful incentive for cities struggling to survive the suburban age but also necessitated a new approach to urban governance that rethought local decision-making, citizen participation, and administrative systems. As Boston sought to shed its reputation for renewal's failures, city leaders positioned nonprofit entities on the forefront of that effort. The testing of new approaches, perhaps more so than the actual results, affirmed Boston's status as an all-American city.

The Golden Road

As a former colonial outpost designed for carts and horses, Boston struggled to keep pace in a modern world. Even before postwar investments built up American suburbs at the expense of urban centers, Boston suffered under the weight of an aging housing stock, departing manufacturing, and declining municipal revenue that never fully recovered from the Great Depression decades earlier. Corrupt politicians and entrenched patronage networks, as well as a rivalrous political scene dominated by Yankees and the Irish, made for an unwelcoming and often violently hostile environment by the mid-twentieth century, when new generations of African American, Puerto Rican, and Afro-Caribbean migrants moved north. Perhaps Boston would return to its status as a backwater as attention shifted to the suburbs and the Sun Belt, or perhaps it would once again stand as a city upon a hill, as one of Massachusetts's earliest colonial governors had hoped in the 1630s. After World War II, the former seemed far more likely than the latter, particularly as the construction of a new circumferential highway around Boston both literally and figuratively provided a means to ignore the once fabled city.

The construction of Route 128 during the 1940s signaled the arrival of a new era for Boston and reorganized people and capital throughout the metropolitan region. State Public Works Commissioner William Callahan first proposed the construction of Route 128 in the early 1930s, but in a time of limited automobile ownership and general economic depression, such plans were mocked.[10] By the time construction began in 1948, however, federal investments in highways, housing, and research made real the economic growth Callahan had envisioned. The suburbs surrounding Boston had existed as separate entities from the city since the nineteenth century but had not yet become home to urban commuters until the automobile, and then Route 128, made that possible.[11] Estimates that the road might carry as many as fifteen thousand cars per day were quickly surpassed, as initial counts put the average daily usage at twenty-two thousand cars in 1951.[12] Use of the route continued to increase, and only seven years after opening, the number of lanes doubled, from four to eight. The newly expanded road offered suburban drivers both access to downtown and an ability to avoid urban congestion. Even the *Boston Globe*, which had once dubbed the project the "Road to Nowhere," admitted that Route 128 had become the "Hub of Everything." Some even called it the "golden road" to capture the optimism surrounding suburban growth and the wealth to be amassed from it.[13]

The number of cars driving on new pavement indicated the speed with which both industry and residents flocked to the now accessible suburban towns. Many of the firms along Route 128 had decamped from Boston in search of space to expand, taking with them future tax revenue and job prospects for those who could access them.[14] Even more valuable were the new firms that capitalized on Cold War–era government investments in defense-related research and manufacturing and benefited from close ties to area universities such as the Massachusetts Institute of Technology.[15] Often, the jobs created by these firms called for highly credentialed knowledge workers and engineers and paid salaries that enabled the suburban lifestyle increasingly en vogue and, for some, increasingly within reach. As historians Kenneth Jackson and Lizabeth Cohen have argued, the preferences Americans expressed for suburban living reflected federal housing policies that made homeownership a realistic possibility for more families as well as changing patterns of consumption that framed suburbia as the epitome of freedom, privacy, and success.[16] These patterns played out in cities around the United States, and in the Boston metropolitan region, they were accelerated by the opening of Route 128, which enabled both residents and industry to relocate from the city and tap the prosperity that lay beyond its borders.

Opportunities for fortune and picket fences, however, went overwhelmingly to white families, shaping a metropolitan region characterized by economic and racial segregation. Some ongoing patterns, including the rapid influx of returned GIs bearing homeowner benefits, knowledge professionals seeking employment in the new office parks, and the displacement of Bostonians through slum clearance programs, might, in theory, have produced a more racially integrated metropolitan landscape. In practice, however, legacies of racism that extracted wealth from Black Americans and prevented its accumulation via real estate foreclosed that possibility early. Black GIs, for example, often were denied the educational and homeownership benefits promised in the 1944 GI Bill, and those that received them struggled to find sellers, lenders, or schools willing to accept the credits.[17]

Though some African American families called towns along Route 128 home, nearly 98 percent of residents in Boston's suburbs were white by 1970.[18] On investigating the area, the Massachusetts Advisory Committee to the US Commission on Civil Rights dubbed the golden road the "road to segregation."[19]

Such racial sorting also reflected local choices, as zoning and tax policies of suburban town governments discriminated against renters and Black home buyers. Complex tax policies and zoning procedures accompanied the highway's construction to simultaneously attract industry and maximize revenue while maintaining a high standard of living, competitive real estate markets, and low population densities.[20] Though the state would eventually pass "anti-snob zoning" laws in 1969 that required a meager 10 percent affordable housing in cities and towns, at the height of suburban growth in the 1950s and early 1960s, no financial incentives existed for creating affordable units in a real estate market saturated with buyers, mortgages, and jobs.[21] Policies enacted to maintain a certain physical environment of detached single-family dwellings had the desired effect of maintaining the extreme whiteness of Boston's suburbs.[22] Though the language employed was race-neutral, the protected whiteness of the suburbs had been a deliberate goal, facilitated in Boston, as elsewhere, by federal mortgage regulations, local zoning policies, and practices of real estate agents that tied whiteness to wealth and higher property values.[23]

As the suburbs along Route 128 became whiter and wealthier, demographics in Boston shifted as well, as African American, Afro-Caribbean, and Puerto Rican families moved to the city.[24] Historians estimate that over the twentieth century, eight million African Americans left the South as part of the Great Migration to escape the violence of Jim Crow segregation.[25] In the 1920s and 1930s, a wave of Black immigrants to Boston came from the British West Indies and Cape Verde.[26] Over the next several decades, migrants from the South made their home in Boston too, and the number of Black residents tripled between 1940 and 1960.[27] By that time, Boston's Black population comprised 9.1 percent of the city's total population. As the absolute number of Black Bostonians rose to over 100,000 by 1965 and white Bostonians left the city for the Route 128 suburbs, that percentage rapidly grew to 17 percent of the city's population.[28] Amid a rapidly changing demographic landscape, white Bostonians maintained a remarkable commitment to racial segregation.

In Boston, Black migrants encountered a small but present Black community and what one report from the 1960s called a long-standing

"paradox of liberalism and discrimination."[29] Thanks to both the existence
of slavery and a prominent free Black community, from the start, Black
Bostonians were, one report noted, "interwoven into the very fabric of
Boston and American Revolutionary history."[30] After all, Crispus At-
tucks died at the Boston Massacre of 1770 and William Lloyd Garrison
launched the *Liberator* from his office at 6 Merchants Hall in 1830. In a
city that prided itself as the home of freedom, liberty, and independence,
the Brahmin elite typically took a paternalistic approach to race relations
that enabled both Black achievements and unequal status in the centuries
following independence. Black Bostonians established middle-class communities in the South End and Roxbury during the late nineteenth century that often, researchers found, shared Brahmin political and cultural
values, such as the "importance of family lineage, pride in local origins and
superiority toward outsiders, and political and social conservatism."[31] This
delicate coexistence of white paternalism and Black conservatism continued, albeit strained, as waves of white immigrants from Europe moved
to the city in the early decades of the twentieth century and as racial violence began to increase nationally following World War I. By the 1950s and
1960s, a select few Black leaders rose to positions of prominence in the
city—including justice of the Roxbury District Court, deputy superintendent of the Boston police, and chairman of the Boston Finance Commission—but on balance, the status of Black people in Boston eroded in
the same decades their numbers increased.[32]

After World War II, Black Bostonians encountered an urban landscape
that was unequal and becoming more so. As African Americans moved
north and west during the Great Migration, they encountered in Midwest-
ern cities of Chicago and Detroit and mid-Atlantic cities of Baltimore,
New York, and Philadelphia, as well as in Boston, a Jim Crow of another
variety. Though not subject to the same de jure segregation characteristic of former Confederate states, northern cities and states devised their
own forms of discriminatory policy, unequal resource distribution, and
violent enforcement of segregated spaces.[33] In Boston, as was typical elsewhere, schools attended by Black students received less funding and saw
more teacher turnover; neighborhoods that were home to Black families
had infrequent street cleaning and trash pickup; wards with Black voters were gerrymandered to stifle electoral power; jobs held by Black men
and women frequently lacked the protections of unions or seniority; and
houses owned and rented by Black families cost more to insure and more
frequently needed repairs.[34] Black activists fought such conditions in the

courts, at the checkout counter, in the streets, and in the voting booth. The blighted conditions in Black neighborhoods that white observers often attributed to individual behavior reflected, in fact, structural disadvantage. Despite laws mandating equality on the books, local and federal policies created conditions far from it.

The concentration of Black residents in a handful of Boston neighborhoods did not, on its own, stand out from the broader patterns of social life in a city where residents felt more affinity for their neighborhood or district than for the city as a whole. Earlier waves of immigration from Europe had produced a map of Boston's neighborhoods and a political landscape dominated by battles between Irish, Italian, and Yankee enclaves. The identification of South Boston and Charlestown as predominantly Irish, East Boston as Italian, Back Bay and Beacon Hill as home to Brahmins, and Mattapan to the Jewish community certainly echoed patterns of earlier discrimination and exclusion. Still, by the 1950s and 1960s, these white residents had attained degrees of choice over where in Boston to live and whether to decamp to the increasingly prosperous suburbs. In contrast, African Americans and Black migrants from the Caribbean faced constrained choices where unequal treatment systematically disadvantaged the neighborhoods where they could live and the health, welfare, and futures of those living in them. Black Bostonians—poor and middle class, recent arrivals and those with deep roots in the city—found themselves increasingly limited to a handful of neighborhoods stretching from the South End to Roxbury thanks to various mechanisms in the racially discriminatory domain of real estate. A local social service agency found in 1961 that only fifteen hundred African Americans in Boston lived outside these two neighborhoods. Further data revealed that 80 percent of Black Bostonians lived in twenty of the city's 156 census tracts.[35] The Urban League of Boston began referring to these neighborhoods as the "Black boomerang" because of the shape of the census tracts.[36]

Observers and activists at the time recognized the construction of what was rapidly becoming a ghetto in Boston, and they drew attention to it. In a 1961 report on the Roxbury–North Dorchester neighborhood, civil rights leader Whitney Young Jr. warned of the creation of a "ghetto . . . and the problems of human isolation, economic waste and potential breeding grounds for tension and violence." Though he did not invoke the "urban crisis" by name, Young's reflections signaled the near crisis conditions created, he noted, not by accident but by choice. These were not neighborhoods without assets; rather, they were ones that those whom Young called

Census Tracts in Which African Americans
Were 50% or More of Total Population in 1960

Source: U.S. Census of Population, 1960

FIGURE 1.2. *The Black boomerang (1963)*. Boston, like most cities in the United States, developed deep patterns of racial segregation in the postwar period. Researchers with the Massachusetts Advisory Committee to the US Commission on Civil Rights mapped the "Black boomerang," depicting the 15 of the 156 census tracts in Boston in which Black residents comprised at least 50 percent of the population. These tracts accounted for over 70 percent of all Black Bostonians. (Map redrawn from original in Massachusetts Advisory Committee to the United States Commission on Civil Rights, "Report on Massachusetts: Housing in Boston," December 1963.)

"downtown interests" had repeatedly exploited and denied opportunities. He noted the possibility of a different future, with active financial and political investment, to bring the Black neighborhoods "in relation to Boston's other communities."[37] Such possibilities for change, however, lay not within the neighborhoods themselves but with those who controlled the private and public resources that flowed into and out of Boston neighborhoods. To that end, civil rights activists mounted (largely unsuccessful) campaigns for seats on the Boston School Committee and steered the local NAACP chapter to advocate equality in schools, housing, and jobs.[38]

By the end of the 1960s, a report from the National Commission on Urban Problems likened the development of American suburban areas to a "noose around the inner city." The metaphor—in Boston's case, mapping onto the so-called golden road—purposely highlighted the racial segregation of white suburbs and Black cities and invoked the violence of both action and policy that retained such strict boundaries. The Douglas Commission, as the group was often called, was not specifically referring to Boston, but it might as well have been. If any doubt lingered, a report on Route 128 and its effects on the city directly identified the new highway as a noose choking Boston.[39] The economically and racially segregated metropolitan landscape tied people to place in ways that proved detrimental to Boston's bottom line and, as a result, problematic for its mayors as they embraced urban renewal to keep the city afloat.

Urban Economics in the Suburban Age

In the 1950s, Boston struggled to compete against the promises of low taxes, open tracts of land, and accessible transportation of its suburban counterparts. While the bulk of postwar federal policy favored suburbia, Congress had recognized the problems facing US cities and provided a powerful tool for mayors in the form of urban renewal. As mayor, John Hynes saw in renewal an opportunity for "major surgery" and seized the chance to physically and economically redesign Boston for the modern age.[40] After all, he faced a city with rising tax rates, declining tax revenue, and increasing municipal costs. In both process and planning, however, Hynes's renewal activities permanently scarred the city and set an example of how not to govern.

As Route 128 drew capital and white residents from Boston, it also drained tax revenue from municipal coffers already on the decline. The

stock market crash of 1929 and the Great Depression that followed wiped
out the savings of Boston families and devastated real estate values across
the city, spelling near disaster for the city's operating budget. In Boston,
taxes on property accounted for between 60 percent and 70 percent of
the total revenue used for basic city services such as schools, government
operations, and public safety.[41] Ideally, the city would have diversified
its revenue streams such that a blow to property values could be more
easily absorbed. The Commonwealth of Massachusetts, however, statu-
torily limited the levies the city could impose, rendering taxes on property responsible for the vast majority of the city government's annual
income.[42] Mayor Hynes's predecessors had nearly doubled the tax rate
and artificially inflated property assessments, but revenue could still not
keep up with their pre-Depression numbers when counting for inflation.[43]
Property value was destiny for Boston as tax policy yoked the city's built
environment and economic prospects, incentivizing efforts to squeeze
more and more value out of land.[44]

To generate revenue for the city, Hynes planned to add value to the
city's property base via construction. Speaking to a group of business
elites, the mayor assured them that, "with a broader tax base most of Boston's troubles would evaporate into thin air."[45] Federal urban renewal
policies gave him the financial backing and legal authority to pursue such
a plan. The Housing Act of 1949 passed under President Harry Truman's
Fair Deal agenda was a compromise between public housing advocates,
who saw a need for more affordable and safe housing, and the real estate
lobby, which favored private developers.[46] In particular, a new program
under Title I of the Housing Act called "urban redevelopment" allocated
$1 billion for loans to municipalities and allowed cities to acquire land
designated as blighted or slum for either public or private housing redevelopment. The federal government also gave municipalities the tools
of clearance and zoning to redesign the physical layout of the city while
also providing financial support to do so by committing to pay two-thirds
of the cost for redevelopment projects, provided that local municipalities
put up the remaining third. Title I signaled a significant change in federal-
city relations as the federal government footed the bill and assumed some
responsibility for large-scale changes to city infrastructure.

Despite such optimism, the initial urban redevelopment program
failed to attract private investors in Boston and elsewhere, prompting
Congress to loosen regulations.[47] A series of amendments followed, starting in 1954, that rebranded "urban redevelopment" as "urban renewal"

and offered concessions to both housing advocates and private developers to encourage activity. Private developers, who had seen little profit in the construction of low-income housing in so-called slum areas, now had more opportunities for non-housing redevelopment—and therefore more opportunities to reap profits—on land cleared with federal financing. For balance, the amendments also included requirements for a "workable program" of comprehensive planning by municipalities to ensure a smooth and participatory process.[48] Taken together, the lowered requirement for post-renewal housing and the expectation of a comprehensive plan successfully enlarged the housing-centric program of urban redevelopment into the broad program for physical and economic transformation of urban renewal.

As the ink dried on the new federal program in 1954, Mayor Hynes pitched his plan for a revived Boston tax base that took full advantage of the reduced emphasis on housing. Several projects of urban redevelopment had been in the works in Boston since 1950, with an estimated twenty-seven hundred acres slated for clearance and redevelopment.[49] Now an opportunity existed to shift the direction of those projects to dedicate more land to business and other high-value types of development. The first phase of this massive undertaking targeted two residential neighborhoods: the West End and New York Streets. City reports on the neighborhoods painted a bleak picture that invoked disparaging tropes of poor areas and poor people as dirty, diseased, and beyond repair.[50] Hynes described the New York Streets, a racially diverse immigrant section of the South End, as "a congested, disease-breeding section of the city," while planning documents described it as "disfigured," with "down grade" housing and "squalid" buildings and "dirty streets . . . [that] swarm with children and adults too."[51] By this logic, the problem was not that poor people lacked safe and sanitary places to live, but that such otherwise desirable land was being wasted in ways, planners attested, "harmful to the City, and detrimental to society as a whole."[52]

Urban renewal offered a means to wipe the slate and repurpose neighborhoods with uses deemed financially beneficial to the city. Residential buildings comprised about 75 percent of the New York Streets—a figure considered "unfortunate" by municipal investigators, to whom such use "constituted a barrier to the most useful development of good downtown industrial land."[53] Instead, Hynes planned to clear "all but a few structures" in the neighborhood and transform it for "light industrial and commercial use," complete with a "new street pattern" and access to major

FIGURE 1.3. *Urban renewal in the New York Streets (1958).* In the late 1950s, the Boston Redevelopment Authority cleared the residential neighborhood known then as the New York Streets section of the South End to make way for industrial and commercial uses, including the headquarters of the *Boston Herald Traveler* newspaper. The site has more recently been converted to luxury apartments in the trendy SoWa (south of Washington Street) district. (Urban Redevelopment Division, Boston Housing Authority, "Boston Herald Traveler Site from Corner of Broadway and Albany Street," May 23, 1958, in Boston Redevelopment Authority photographs, Collection 4010.01, BCA. Boston City Archives Digital Photograph Collection.)

highways, railroads, and port areas.[54] By contrast, the West End's proximity to downtown and Massachusetts General Hospital suggested to city planners the area might be better suited to luxury housing designed for "young married Hospital interns, laboratory specialists and doctors with small children."[55] Plans also called for a significant reduction in the number of housing units in the West End, effectively eliminating any possibility for current residents to return to the neighborhood.[56] Accomplishing these transformations required government action and investment to foot the bill of seizing, clearing, and rezoning the land; displacing residents; and consolidating parcels into larger tracts for private developers. Such a role seemed appropriate for city government, which, with the financial aid and endorsement of the federal government, took on a larger role in coordinating the economic activities and physical infrastructure within its boundaries.

What city planners called poorly used land, however, working families called home. The once thriving community of the West End has been memorialized in works such as Herbert Gans's *Urban Villagers* as a prime example of the failures of urban redevelopment.[57] Mel King, who would later go on to become one of the city's most prominent community activists and politicians, recalled growing up in the New York Streets in his book *Chain of Change*, with vivid descriptions of what was lost: a community with street baseball, neighbors that organized a reception for a local woman's wedding, and a public elementary school nicknamed the "Little United Nations" for the diversity of children from Albanian, Chinese, Greek, Irish, Jewish, Lebanese, Lithuanian, and Syrian families.[58] Residents, King wrote, "endeavored to make their neighborhoods viable communities while city planners sought to remove them."[59]

Though Congress required cities to consider residents as part of comprehensive planning, Boston families slated for displacement found little aid. Mayor Hynes developed some participatory mechanisms in compliance with the renewal amendments of the 1950s, but the flexibility and uncertainty of the federal standard created a low bar easily cleared by the involvement of urban elites looking to benefit financially from a reconstituted Boston.[60] Municipal authorities made half-hearted attempts to solicit input from residents in the West End but did so at such a late stage that objections and protests had little effect.[61] After learning about renewal plans in the newspaper, most families had already moved out while their property still held some value or before landlords stopped maintenance.[62] Residents in both neighborhoods were overwhelmingly poor and low-income, and the vast majority qualified for public housing. At the time, many saw public housing as a step up in quality from apartments with no running hot water and welcomed the opportunity to move into the newly constructed public housing developments around Boston.[63] So little tracking occurred, however, that it is unknown how many families from the West End and New York Streets actually ended up in public housing or where they went.[64] That uncertainty was replicated around the country in cities large and small, with data on displacements vague and nearly absent for where people went.[65] What is clear is that in Boston, as elsewhere, displacements from renewal served to disrupt long-standing communities and further segregate the urban landscape in both public and private housing.[66]

For all the promises Hynes attached to his clearance of the West End and New York Streets, these renewal projects actually worsened Boston's financial and economic position in the short term. Planning for renewal moved so slowly that as he neared the end of his term in 1959, Hynes had little to show for the highest-profile initiative of his mayoralty.[67] Research in the 1960s by the National Commission on Urban Problems confirmed the slow progress of renewal, noting "the unconscionable amount of time consumed in the process."[68] One conference summarized these frustrations as follows: "First seen as a 'planner's paradise,' redevelopment has rapidly assumed the aspect of an administrator's hell!"[69] It was also becoming a politician's nightmare. While federal funds covered the majority of renewal costs, cities still had to cover a portion of them, and cash-strapped municipalities had little recourse to financing. Hynes had nearly doubled the effective tax rate, and Moody's Investors Service ranked Boston bonds lower than any other major American city in 1959.[70] Hynes's city sat on the brink of bankruptcy and receivership.[71] Even accelerating the value of urban land—as urban renewal tried to do—fell short of rewriting the revenue formula for cities. With wealth increasingly built in suburban development and later in the transactions of finance capitalism, cities faced few prospects for financial stability without significant resources from public federal aid and private philanthropy.[72]

The West End and New York Streets projects achieved notoriety as examples of renewal done wrong. The clearance of the predominantly white neighborhood of the West End has been immortalized in books such as Jane Jacobs's *Death and Life of Great American Cities* published in 1961 and Gans's *Urban Villagers* in 1962, which drew attention to the limitations of renewal as a theory and the human consequences of it as a practice of urban improvement.[73] Less is remembered about the New York Streets area, which renewal erased from Boston maps and decades later rebranded as the trendy SoWa district. Residents might not have stopped the federal bulldozer in the 1950s, but when they started to vocally question the merits of large-scale planning and the modernization schemes of top-down renewal activities, they shifted the politics of renewal moving forward.[74] As the 1960s unfolded, the politics of housing, control, and participation became visible issues around which to organize communities and demand both material and procedural changes. On their own, these were already substantial changes from the 1950s and served as the foundations of Boston's nonprofit neighborhoods.

"Planning with People"

Hynes's version of renewal failed to live up to its promise, but it did not signal the end of renewal as a whole. It was not renewal per se that had gone wrong, many surmised, but the way it had been applied in Boston and elsewhere in the 1950s: with too much bulldozing, too much cater- ing to business interests, and too little community input. Hynes's succes- sor, John Collins, campaigned in 1959 and won the mayoralty on prom- ises to end what he called "top down power politics" by "planning with people instead of planning for people" and using renewal to improve, not eliminate, residential neighborhoods alongside the downtown business districts.[75] Collins and his renewal administrator, Ed Logue, expanded urban renewal from a project focused mainly on economic and physical change to one that incorporated at least some attention to the human or social side of renewal. Doing so more faithfully followed federal guide- lines mandating a comprehensive workable program and responded to local demands but also raised new questions about the boundaries of mu- nicipal government and the mechanics of citizen participation. These were as much political questions as administrative ones, and they were issues that would move Boston's mayor to embrace community organizations as partners in the work of urban improvement.

The mayoral election of 1959 functioned as a referendum on urban renewal in Boston, producing what one observer called "one of the most stunning upsets in the history of the city."[76] Hynes's announcement that he would not seek a fourth term as mayor left the race wide open. At the time, few mentioned probate officer John Collins as a candidate, because most assumed John Powers would easily take over from Hynes. After all, as president of the Massachusetts senate and a former mayoral candidate against Hynes, Powers won endorsements from all major leaders and built a well-organized and well-funded political machine. He had over a decade of prominent political experience, while Collins had bounced between the Massachusetts house and senate and then moved to the city council—a seat he won while sick with polio and his wife campaigned on his behalf. In an era of frustration and anger about the direction Boston was headed, however, Powers's experience became a liability.[77] Collins positioned him- self as the outsider candidate, running television advertisements telling voters to "stop power politics: elect a hands-free mayor."[78] And in Novem- ber 1959, the people did. After coming in second in the primary, underdog Collins defeated Powers by capturing 55 percent of the vote.

For Collins, who had run on a platform of involving everyday Bostonians in the planning and processes of urban renewal, turning campaign
rhetoric into governing reality meant reinventing Boston's entire program.
To fulfill his pledge, the newly elected mayor dubbed the effort Operation
Revival.[79] Collins himself had little experience in urban planning, so he
courted one of the country's leading experts, Ed Logue, who had gained
a name for himself after managing a renewal program for the city of New
Haven, Connecticut, that attracted significant federal assistance and incorporated both downtown and neighborhood improvements. A former
labor organizer and army bombardier, Logue credited his bombing runs
over Italy during World War II with helping him see cities as whole units.[80]
To entice Logue, Collins prepared an attractive package of top salary and
consolidated powers in a reorganized and enlarged Boston Redevelopment Authority. Logue came to Boston as a part-time consultant before
assuming the position full-time in late 1960.[81] He devised a new plan for
Boston that would eventually dwarf earlier projects in the West End and
New York Streets in size, scope, and expense. "Big projects," he hinted,
"are no harder to do than little ones," and his vision for the city blended
social justice ideals of racial and economic integration with a confidence
that urban renewal, if properly implemented, could be a means to achieve
it.[82] Boston soon rose from seventeenth to fourth among recipients of federal renewal aid.[83]

In September 1960, the mayor released Logue's provisional plan for
Boston, boldly named the "90 Million Dollar Development Plan." It proposed renewal programs in two downtown districts and eight residential
neighborhoods with an emphasis on rehabilitation over clearance and
promises of participation. Stunning maps captured the proposed expansion of renewal, now encompassing neighborhoods home to over half of
Boston residents. The plan called for immediate attention to the Charlestown and South End neighborhoods—two areas that differed in demographics but shared a legacy of inadequate housing, neglect, and poverty.
Accompanying statements from Mayor Collins invited neighborhood
groups into a "key partnership role" with the city, given both the rich history of such religious and civic groups in the city and his promises for
"planning *with* people."[84] The phrase became somewhat of a mantra for
the Boston program, setting a political expectation of a new participatory
approach linking the physical, economic, and social sides of urban governance.[85] Logue embraced this rhetoric and, to the extent that participation
would move renewal projects forward, put it in practice too. He placed

faith in an ever-growing roster of planners and experts on his staff but also read the political landscape with enough experience to know that participation meant buy-in from residents whose endorsement was increasingly essential to renewal progress.[86] After all, citizens would be voting on renewal plans prior to federal approval and investing their sweat and dollars in rehabilitation plans to buoy the renewal property values.

To manage participation, Logue turned to community organizations. The choice exemplifies, Lizabeth Cohen notes in her biography of Logue, a puzzle throughout his career about how to incorporate democratic processes and citizen input into renewal and how to balance public good and private interest.[87] In Boston, Logue had a wide array of organizations to choose from, including religious congregations, settlement houses, block associations, civic clubs, and civil rights groups—only some of whom accurately represented the interests of those slated for renewal.[88] Strategically reaching out to local nonprofits made good political sense, as it had in New Haven, to build consensus around renewal plans and include private entities in the governance process. It also responded to demands from community groups, many of whom, particularly Black homeowners, actively courted the investments promised by renewal as a means of shoring up declining property values.[89] Finally, the approach also followed advice increasingly floated in federal guidelines and academic publications about renewal that positioned nonprofit organizations as entities able to, in the paternalistic words of one federal publication, aid in "interpreting the program to neighborhood families."[90]

In the professional social workers often at the helm of local organizations, Logue saw kindred spirits to urban planners with middle-class sensibilities about uplift, stability, and family structure. Even before he had officially accepted the position in Boston, Logue had consulted with Charles Liddell, the social worker and executive director of the United South End Settlements, about renewal plans for the South End.[91] Those conversations set the groundwork for Logue's approach to renewal in that neighborhood, and to participation around the city more generally. With both informal authority and, soon, formal contracts, community organizations liaised between the Boston Redevelopment Authority and neighborhood residents in such tasks as surveying local preferences, presenting draft plans, hosting forums, representing local interest, and, in the end, counting votes to ensure a green light for urban renewal.

In addition to facilitating participation in urban renewal, community organizations offered a vehicle to incorporate what Logue called the "human side of renewal." Early in his time in Boston, Logue conceived the Boston Community Development Program as an analogue to the Boston Redevelopment Authority (BRA). Where the municipal agency, the BRA, coordinated and planned for the physical and economic development of Boston, this other entity would manage the city's social and cultural development as part of a two-pronged attack on poverty. Put simply, the BRA would handle the physical blight, and the Boston Community Development Program would help the people living in the decrepit housing. Logue envisioned a prominent role for area universities, and he sketched a plan to court private philanthropic funding.[92] After hearing Logue outline his ideas at a roundtable in Cambridge, a consultant to the Ford Foundation called the proposal "the most promising thing so far."[93] Collins endorsed the idea as well, and in early 1961, he appointed an advisory committee with members from the city's civic and educational elite, including representatives from Harvard University, New England Merchant's National Bank, the Boston Finance Commission, the BRA, and United South End Settlements.[94] Funding from the local Permanent Charity Fund—later known as the Boston Foundation—and official incorporation as a nonprofit in 1962 established the newly renamed Action for Boston Community Development (ABCD) as a coordinating body for human renewal. In addition to "help[ing] neighborhood leaders and residents participate in planning," as the charter noted, ABCD would oversee social science research into poverty in Boston and coordinate a program of services to address it.[95]

Partnering with community organizations to manage participation in renewal produced a range of outcomes across the city. For many, that was the aim. In the language of renewal chronicler Langley Keyes Jr., community organizations were key players in Boston's "planning game," mediating between residents and the Boston Redevelopment Authority while pursuing their own organizational interests. Initial efforts for facilitating participation involved the formation of federations of local organizations, such as block clubs, church groups, settlement houses, and business associations. In Charlestown, a predominantly white and working-class community highly suspicious of renewal after watching the experiences of the West End, tensions between a federated group and a more grassroots one erupted at a public hearing on renewal in 1963 that threatened to derail the entire project.[96] In the South End, initial facilitation by a group dominated by the United South End Settlements produced an affirmative community vote on renewal plans in 1965, though that was after several adjustments to the BRA's strategy and before historic protests against renewal in 1968.

It was Washington Park—a district artificially constructed by BRA planners and home to the city's Black middle class—that delivered Logue's desired outcome and became the model for participation in Boston. Before and even during the 1950s, when urban renewal earned the reputation of "Negro removal," residents of what was known then as Upper Roxbury actively sought attention from the city for improved schools, cleaner streets, and urban renewal investments. Home to the Black professional class in Boston as well as a long-standing, though shrinking, Jewish community, residents responded to neglect from city services and a discriminatory housing market in the 1950s by taking their own initiative.[97] At the helm of this effort were Otto and Muriel Snowden, two African American social workers who founded Freedom House in 1949 "to improve the civic, educational, recreational, and general welfare" of Upper Roxbury.[98]

The couple founded Freedom House as a response to worsening conditions in their neighborhood. The organization started in the Snowdens' living room, where they invited seventeen neighbors over to talk, they later wrote, "about ways of keeping the Roxbury section of Boston, in which all of us lived, from becoming another slum." The group decided to incorporate as a nonprofit, armed, initially, "with nothing but enthusiasm, faith in their community's potential, and sheer determination."[99] As the volunteer directors, the Snowdens infused Freedom House's activities with a civil rights agenda, offering job application workshops for Black students and organizing petitions to the city for increased police protection, repaved streets, and recreational facilities in the neighborhood.[100] The mix of services cemented Freedom House as a typical settlement house–type nonprofit popular at the time, whereas the advocacy agenda and civil rights focus set it apart in Boston but aligned it with strategies deployed by African American urbanites in other cities, such as Chicago, seeking a better life in the shadow of a neglectful municipal government.[101] Once secure with a building of its own in 1952 and some modest funds, Freedom House hosted a regular coffee hour, where women discussed topics such as juvenile delinquency and the civil rights movement, and evening programs with local dignitaries and candidate forums.[102] In such settings, Freedom House neighbors debated such questions as "whether we lived in Roxbury from choice or necessity; *would* we move if we could?" and hoped to ensure people answered in the affirmative.[103]

During the second half of the 1950s, Freedom House mobilized to get Upper Roxbury included in renewal plans. It started by helping launch nearly thirty block associations in the neighborhood and took a more assertive stance in 1959 to attract federal government resources. For all that community-initiated efforts could achieve through street cleanups and tree plantings, Black neighborhoods still needed government attention and investment to compensate for decades of neglect and to counteract an exploitative housing market.[104] Property values in Upper Roxbury had started to decline due largely to discrimination from redlined insurance providers, lenders, and speculators.[105] For working families who had invested their life savings in their homes, such decline suggested a worrisome future for Upper Roxbury and the Black community that called it home. In a 1959 letter to local block associations, Muriel Snowden urged residents to attend a public forum, saying "it means so much to us as property owners, taxpayers, and citizens, that the city . . . support the efforts which we are making ourselves to keep it the kind of place where our property investments are protected and where we can feel proud to live."[106] Showing up, Snowden argued, was the best way "Roxbury citizens can *show* that they are alert and that they *care*."[107]

To residents, urban renewal presented an opportunity not to rid Upper Roxbury of a slum but to prevent it becoming one by economically, physically, and socially integrating the neighborhood into the city and region more broadly.[108] When Collins released Logue's "90 Million Dollar Development Plan," however, the project dubbed "Washington Park" did not include Upper Roxbury and instead only included Middle Roxbury, an adjacent neighborhood with more dilapidated housing and working-class Black residents.[109] Otto Snowden fired off a furious telegram to the mayor, claiming "citizens here pioneered [the] Boston movement for citizen participation in urban renewal and resent seeming exclusion. . . . [We] cannot understand this constant bypassing unless it is a matter of racial discrimination."[110] Logue responded, "Give me a chance," beginning a formal collaboration between Freedom House and the renewal czar that inaugurated a new role for the nonprofit as a private space for the public inclusion Snowden and others in the neighborhood sought.[111]

For the city's first attempt at rehabilitation over clearance and for meaningful participation, Washington Park presented an attractive opportunity to implement "planning with people," where the people were predominantly Black and the planning palatable to white audiences. In time, the BRA added the predominantly middle-class Upper Roxbury to enlarge the Washington Park renewal area from 186 acres to 502 acres and appointed Freedom House to facilitate participation in the expanded district. The selection of Freedom House was not a foregone conclusion, as many expected the Roxbury Community Council to take the lead, but Logue preferred Freedom House and extended a formal BRA contract accordingly.[112] Doing so made good political sense given the prominence the Snowdens had begun to build, including hosting Dr. Martin Luther King Jr. and the Kennedys at Freedom House. It also made good economic sense according to the logic that including a more prosperous neighborhood in renewal would help stop what was imagined as the creep of blight.[113] In the words of one BRA consultant, "The superior quality of the residential structures and the existing leadership and community organizations in the Seaver-Townsend area [of Upper Roxbury] contribute material economic and social resources to the effectuation of the total program."[114]

Freedom House mounted an impressive campaign in partnership with the BRA and on its payroll as a contracted partner.[115] In March 1961, Freedom House signed a yearlong contract with the BRA worth $27,000, which was renewed the following year for an even higher amount.[116] The BRA had signed similar contracts for community agencies in other neighborhoods to manage the relocation of displaced families, but the Freedom House contract transferred far more responsibility for managing renewal to the Snowdens' organization, including planning and ratifying neighborhood designs and managing aspects of implementation. These dollars represented a significant influx of funds to the organization, enabling Freedom House to hire a staff expressly for urban renewal, including five Black women from the community.[117] Totaling the efforts, Muriel Snowden later counted 114 meetings, four public hearings, sixteen thousand community notices, thousands of informational bulletins, and "countless professional conferences" in which residents in the Washington Park renewal zone offered input and vision for their neighborhood.[118] Freedom House kept its doors open into the evenings and on weekends to accommodate working people and displayed on its walls large-scale prints of plans for Washington Park.[119] The organization's space was transformed, Muriel Snowden remarked, into "a temporary center for renewal information . . . able to coordinate and centralize the entire renewal operation."[120] As a private entity with a public charge, Freedom House tread a careful line between representing the interests of an economically diverse community and moving renewal forward to satisfy the Snowdens' goals and Logue's.

After soliciting input from neighbors, Freedom House delivered an

FIGURE 1.4. *Renewal planning at Freedom House (1961).* On a contract with the Boston Redevelopment Authority, nonprofit Freedom House managed the approval process for the
Washington Park renewal project. To solicit resident input, Freedom House kept its offices
open for extended hours, presented drafted plans, hosted community meetings, and organized
local conferences. (Irene Shwachman, "Presentation to Public of Boston Redevelopment Authority Maps at Freedom House, 14 Crawford Street," Image A004214, box 72, folder 2880,
FH, NU. Image courtesy of Northeastern University Archives and Special Collections.)

official community approval to the BRA that unlocked federal funds for
urban renewal in Washington Park. Freedom House hosted public forums and readied testimonies from residents at hearings before the BRA
board, city council, and mayor as Washington Park's renewal plans moved
through the approval process. At a time when other renewal projects in
Boston encountered protest, negative publicity, and significant pushback,
Washington Park in the early 1960s provided a welcome victory. When the
neighborhood voted on the final plans in 1962, *Boston Globe* coverage
reported "near unanimous approval," noting that "so overwhelming was
the reaction from proponents . . . that when BRA Vice Chairman Stephan
McCloskey cut them off after an hour and a half to hear opponents it
took less than fifteen minutes to hear the opponents."[121] The contrast to
a similar meeting in the predominantly white neighborhood of Allston
could not have been stronger. Where the Roxbury representatives were

"well organized" and "able to present their case and demands quietly and orderly," the Allston meeting featured "angry residents, hurling threats, shouting accusations and insults."[122] Disagreements and tensions among Washington Park residents had arisen over the previous years of planning but had been worked through in private.[123] The final step for Washington Park occurred in January 1963; at a public forum in Roxbury convened by the BRA board, Freedom House mobilized a "long parade" of twelve hundred citizens vocalizing support for the plans for Washington Park and eager to signal their approval.[124] Quickly and loudly, city officials heralded Washington Park's renewal plan for its participatory process and emphasis on rehabilitation.[125] They had Freedom House's careful management of the process and ties to the community to thank.

Collins and Logue never missed an opportunity to highlight Freedom House's partnership with the BRA, and in Muriel Snowden, they found an ideal spokesperson: a petite, well-dressed woman bearing degrees from Radcliffe College and New York University School of Social Work. She was the epitome of respectability who spoke a language of racial uplift, self-help, and racial cooperation in a manner amenable to white liberals in Boston. Muriel Snowden approached the politics of image carefully and strategically, becoming one of the most visible supporters of Boston's renewal program. She understood that as a Black neighborhood, Washington Park's renewal program would always be under strict scrutiny and that such scrutiny often carried economic implications, whether through business investment, government attention, or housing values.[126] She also lent credibility to the new renewal program in Boston and to its desired image as modern and inclusive. At every turn, Snowden made sure to credit the mayor and Logue for their "determination and dedication" that gave "the sense that we are truly *partners* not *pawns* in urban renewal."[127]

Both in Boston and to national audiences, Muriel Snowden touted Freedom House's approach to participation and helped set it as a model. She spoke about renewal at booster events for local advertisers and, with her husband, Otto, published in *Journal of Housing* a guide to citizen participation.[128] She posed for photographs chronicling Boston's renewal program, often as the only woman or the only African American person in the image, and hosted federal renewal authorities at Freedom House, including Robert Weaver, administrator of the Housing and Home Finance Agency and future secretary of Housing and Urban Development.[129] In the spring of 1964, when Boston hosted the annual meeting of the American Society of Planning Officials, attendees enjoyed a bus trip to

Washington Park and special exhibit at Freedom House.[130] Local coverage noted the planners' skepticism of "planning with people" quickly evaporated, quoting planners from Nashville, Detroit, Toronto, and elsewhere on the "tremendous participation" achieved and recording their vows to bring Freedom House's approach back to their home cities.[131] To these planners, how or for whom Washington Park improved mattered far less than Freedom House's ability to move a renewal process forward.

The image of Freedom House's renewal program and its role as a vehicle for citizen participation often exceeded its reality, though it took time for the tensions latent in Washington Park's plans and process to surface. Though the Snowdens saw their role as a "community broker," they later admitted that many in the community suspected they were agents of the BRA working merely to win approval for renewal to move forward.[132] Although unfounded, such criticisms nonetheless pointed to the economic and funding politics at play alongside the racial ones. With Freedom House in charge, renewal plans favored the preferences of the Upper Roxbury middle class even as it shaped the future of an area twice its size. Priorities elevated home rehabilitation over clearance, and commitments for new public facilities of schools, parks, playgrounds, and libraries were important concessions from the city that reflected the expanded version of neighborhood planning Black Bostonians had been advocating for years.[133] Still, such promised facilities mattered little to those Black families who were unable to afford housing and reaffirmed dominant theories that poverty, especially among Black Americans, indicated cultural or behavioral failings solved by schools and libraries.[134] Indeed, one of the rare votes against the BRA in Washington Park vetoed thirty units of public housing in the Upper Roxbury area, with Otto Snowden leading the opposition. As the 1960s wore on, Black power politics informed a new generation of local leaders who openly critiqued Freedom House's integrationist vision and middle-class orientation.[135] Implementation did not go as smoothly as hoped either, with promises of new schools and park facilities unfulfilled and higher rates of displacement than anticipated. By then, however, the question of whether a government agency could or should partner with a community organization had already been judged a good practice, even as people on both sides continued to question the details of doing so.

Outsourcing responsibility for participation in urban renewal, such as the BRA had done with Freedom House, reflected competing democratic and antidemocratic impulses. On the one hand, drawing independent voluntary associations into decisions about communities mirrored the very processes Alexis de Tocqueville had celebrated in his famous 1815 treatise as core to the American democratic experiment. Black Bostonians found that Freedom House amplified their concerns and helped solicit and shape city plans for the neighborhood when they had few avenues through which to do so. On the other hand, relying on the private entity and its unelected leadership to represent the diverse perspectives and needs of neighborhood residents placed public deliberations outside formal governance channels. Renters in Washington Park, for example, had little recourse in the privatized inclusion of the BRA–Freedom House partnership to combat plans put forward by Freedom House that favored property owners. As those tensions played out in halls and meetings across Roxbury, city and BRA officials learned a powerful lesson about the political benefits of such arrangements: the city got to reap the rewards of appearing responsive to residents while also abdicating responsibility for the results.

Legacies of Renewal

The legacies of Boston's renewal program can only partially be measured by the physical changes to the built environment. The new street grids, corporate headquarters, public housing developments, rehabilitated two-family houses, bulldozed lots, and government buildings in both downtown and residential neighborhoods undoubtedly reshaped the city and how people moved through it. Nevertheless, a visual scan of the Boston landscape tells an incomplete story. Renewal had another legacy as well— one grounded in the administrative processes of implementing such a program and shaped by the political demands for participation. It laid critical groundwork for nonprofit neighborhoods.

First, urban renewal made neighborhoods into governing units. The expectations of planning and the flow of significant federal dollars required strict boundaries around each renewal project. Yet, as the experiences of renewing the West End and New York Streets made clear, drawing lines on a map to shape the physical and economic futures of a district without consideration of the social connections or political opinions in that place did not work. Instead of the smooth process planners in Mayor Hynes's administration anticipated, their initial forays created political backlash, threatened future renewal programs, and furthered economic and racial segregation. The mayoral election of 1959 gave John Collins a clear mandate to approach renewal differently, with a more participatory ethos and comprehensive scope than his predecessor. The problem he and renewal administrator Ed Logue faced, however, was that no governing unit existed to meet these new demands. Such designations are quite common in other arenas of urban governance—police departments divide into precincts, census data into tracts, electoral representation into wards, and elementary schools into districts—but no parallel yet existed to manage the social considerations raised by renewal. In already established neighborhood nonprofit organizations, such as Freedom House, the city found ready and willing partners. Perhaps these entities, with their grounding in social work and trust in the community, would meet the political and practical needs of a renewal program vowing "planning with people."

Where federal renewal policy had raised the possibility of local renewal authorities working with community nonprofit organizations, the partnership between the BRA and Freedom House turned it into reality. This marks the second legacy established by renewal: contracting with nonprofit entities to manage democratic processes of citizen participation, policy implementation, community representation, and information distribution. Similar experiments unfolded in other cities across the nation as municipalities tried to address fiscal gaps, respond to public pressures, and consider the economic, racial, physical, and social dimensions of poverty in the era of renewal. Thanks to ongoing work by Freedom House, Boston's Washington Park project got out of the renewal gate quickly in the early 1960s and did so with a compelling story that countered renewal's declining national reputation. Working with the community agency gave the BRA practical experience in outsourcing parts of neighborhood governance and insight into the potential benefits and drawbacks of doing so. The BRA experienced, for example, dual shifts in governance that simultaneously decentralized planning and centralized oversight. As Freedom House gained an official platform to shape renewal plans and represent the Washington Park neighborhood, the BRA retained the governing and financial authority to select the agency.

That Freedom House and the Washington Park renewal project emerged as a model for citizen participation cannot be separated from the racial politics that elevated this Black-led organization in a majority white city. The third precedent renewal established in Boston was the particular utility of partnering with nonprofit organizations in neighborhoods typically excluded from city government. Decades of neglect in Black

neighborhoods and increasing ghettoization during the 1950s spurred organizing activities among Black Bostonians that boosted organizational
capacity, political savvy, and community networks in Upper Roxbury that
the BRA could capitalize on. Discrimination in city services, housing policies, and employment also rendered Freedom House particularly eager for
BRA funding and Upper Roxbury particularly eager for the investment
that accompanied renewal. Racism in policy and city administration had
made Washington Park a captive audience, motivated to participate yet
strategic in how it did so. The BRA had entered into similar contracts
with community agencies in other neighborhoods, but it was the one in a
predominantly Black neighborhood that moved the quickest, produced a
positive vote, and gained the most acclaim. Not without shortcomings or
disagreements, the BRA–Freedom House partnership nonetheless served
as a model of responsive governing during a period of increasing civil
rights activism.

For all the usefulness of these partnerships, they also had their problems, as Bostonians would continue to discover during the 1960s, when
such practices became even more common and prominent under the War
on Poverty. Nor had renewal in either of its manifestations fully addressed
the problems of racism, segregation, and poverty that increasingly characterized the city during an age of suburbanization and urban crisis. As the local NAACP office highlighted, designation of Boston as an all-American
city rang hollow for African Americans excluded from jobs, housing, education, and city services.[136] The fiscal problems facing Boston's municipal
government remained into the 1960s and beyond, even as federal resources
poured into the city. What residents in Washington Park, mayoral staff in
city hall, planners in the BRA, and staffers at Freedom House had forged
in renewal was a governing process more private and more participatory
that, at least for the moment, responded to the political problems renewal
had revealed.

CHAPTER TWO

The Grantees

While still living in Connecticut and sending correspondence on City of New Haven letterhead, Ed Logue approached the Ford Foundation about funding a new nonprofit entity he envisioned for Boston. It would be, he waxed, closely tied to municipal government, with citywide oversight and neighborhood-based partners. Logue called it the Boston Community Development Program, though it would later incorporate as Action for Boston Community Development, and saw it as a socially oriented analogue to his physically and economically oriented Boston Redevelopment Authority.[1] Logue drafted an outline for this new organization in 1960, giving one copy to Boston's mayor and the only other one to the Ford Foundation.[2] At the time, Ford Foundation staff shared Logue's assessment that urban renewal had failed to address poverty in US cities, and they were planning a grantmaking initiative to support the kind of experiments that Logue proposed for Boston.

As the Boston proposal made the rounds at the Ford Foundation, staff appended notes and memos to the growing file on the city, remarking on the notable aspects of Logue's concept and penning clever comments for colleagues. The program officers liked Logue's boldness, even if they mocked it among themselves, and resolved to keep a close watch on Boston as their own plans evolved.[3] Lester Nelson, head of the foundation's education portfolio, praised the "attention to purpose and to process" in the document, paying more heed to *how* Boston's human renewal agency planned to operate than to what it planned to do. He appreciated the attention to neighborhood "autonomy within city-wide purposes," and especially the "availability of an appropriate grant-receiving agency."[4] As a nonprofit organization, ABCD would legally be able to receive funding from the Ford Foundation in ways prohibited for municipal agencies such as the Boston Redevelopment Authority or Boston School Department. Nelson's colleague David Hunter agreed and offered brief comment on Boston's possible alignment for the foundation's new Gray Areas program. No actual content about Boston's proposal made it into Hunter's notes, but he singled out one crucial advantage: "There are some other resources there, too," he wrote.[5] To program officers well versed in the powers of philanthropy, the availability of local dollars in Boston signaled material support for the proposed entity as well as political buy-in from government, business, and civic leaders. Support from the Ford Foundation and, in time, federal funders, could similarly undergird ABCD with financial and social capital; the question was whether it would.

In the form of letters, memoranda, and official proposals, significantly more documents circulated within the Ford Foundation and between the foundation and ABCD in the years before any dollars changed hands. It was the kind of exchange and power imbalance that ABCD would come to know well, both in its role as a grantee and, later, as a grant maker in Boston. Ford Foundation program officers pushed the men behind ABCD—and they were, with one exception, all men, mostly bearing elite degrees—to refine their proposal and clarify their activities. The Boston team did so willingly to please the prospective funders and responded similarly to local foundations interested in poverty and federal bureaucrats overseeing the growing number of government programs offering grant dollars to address social problems. Pursuing funding in this ad hoc and, at times, frantic manner, shaped ABCD as a malleable organization that bridged various midcentury policy programs, from urban renewal to the War on Poverty, as well as a durable one that persisted far beyond its anticipated five-year life span.[6] Each new initiative, grant, and program at ABCD expanded the local nonprofit infrastructure and cemented it deeper in the governance of the city while also making what happened in Boston increasingly dependent on the preferences of and choices by those outside the city looking in.

ABCD existed in Boston as an organizational embodiment of popular ideas about poverty and racial inequality, and of how best to address them. Logue, and those he drew into the effort, designed ABCD around their expectation that better coordinated and more extensive social services in Boston would lift individuals experiencing poverty into the economic mainstream and remedy racial inequities. It was a move calculated to appeal politically locally and attract funding nationally. Liberals in the Ford Foundation and in the Kennedy and Johnson administrations shared

Logue's faith in community-based action and confidence in the broader US economy, and they held the professional positions that enabled them to back such ideas about change with material resources. To that end, several public and private funding schemes were launched in the early 1960s that continued older traditions in the United States in which the charitable realm supplemented the welfare state and served as a laboratory for experimentation.[7] Nonprofit organizations appeared innovative, inclusive, and responsive in ways attractive to midcentury liberals, who used the tools of an expanding federal state to build a system of local, private, nonprofit service providers.[8] Just as government support underwrote a voracious military-industrial complex during this era, so too did simultaneous financial and political support grow what some call the "nonprofit industrial complex."[9] Though unlike its military analogue, flush with resources, the nonprofit industrial complex was characterized by precarity, scarcity, and instability given its reliance on term-limited grants and competition.

Even as public and private grantmaking programs emphasized local service delivery, state and philanthropic influence shaped nearly every facet of the programs and the organizational and governing infrastructure behind them. Transferring funds, particularly from the federal government, to city- and neighborhood-based nonprofits did more than distribute dollars. So great was the need for federal support and so pressing the issues of urban poverty that even the mere possibility of funding shaped the local nonprofit landscape. Indeed, the real value of 1960s-era grantmaking programs lay not in the actual dollars transferred—though those shaped individual lives and organizations in material, lasting ways—but in the expectations, powers, authorities, and potential resources dangled before cities struggling to survive a period of urban crisis. Public grantmaking practices solidified in policy during the early 1960s laid the administrative, organizational, and intellectual groundwork for nonprofit neighborhoods, where financial resources, standardized practices, authority, democratic participation, and undemocratic power flowed in numerous, sometimes contradictory, directions.

Action for Boston Community Development

For all the political and financial investments in urban renewal in the 1950s and early 1960s, it quickly became clear that physical renewal alone could not solve the myriad problems facing American cities. Indeed, to many, renewal was the problem. In Boston, as elsewhere, growing attention to the poverty of urban residents raised questions that municipal governments seemed unwilling and unable to answer. The kind of relationships the BRA forged with a handful of neighborhood nonprofits represented one manifestation of a broader pivot in American urban governance to rely on private agencies to address the problems made visible during urban renewal. That pivot indicated both an ideological faith in the role of social services in addressing poverty and a pragmatic effort to win outside resources during a time of declining municipal revenue. In Boston, elite leaders launched ABCD, a new nonprofit entity that, in its scramble for funding, evolved quickly, becoming an organizational hub in Boston with resources, authority, and an expanding list of program areas.

Logue's description of "human renewal" as a complement to urban renewal offered a useful slogan but no clear institutional model. He might have framed this new coordinating body as a city department or built it into his already expanding BRA, as one consultant suggested—either of which would have, at least in theory, imbued the entity with more democratic accountability.[10] From the start of his time in Boston, however, Logue envisioned what became ABCD as a nonprofit organization and, with the support of Mayor John Collins and a handful of the city's prominent social work professionals, incorporated it as such in 1961.[11] It was, as Logue wrote in a funding application, "a new approach, a new organization, a new method."[12] The motivations and approach seemed obvious at the time. First, the existing landscape of charitable organizations in Boston was already consolidating in the 1950s, as small settlement houses in the South End and Dorchester began to merge into federations to pool funding and increase programming.[13] Second, the fixing of problems that were seen as *social*—as poverty was typically understood at the time— had traditionally been the realm of charity and private organizations, even as the government had increased social welfare insurance programs in earlier decades.[14] Third, Logue, ever the pragmatist, considered a private nonprofit "removed both from politics and red tape" as both more nimble and insulated, able to be firmly guided by expert hands.[15] These reasons nudged ABCD toward private nonprofit incorporation, but it was the financial opportunities that solidified the decision.

At a time of declining municipal revenue, the city government simply could not afford a new department, so ABCD's future—and in the minds of some, Boston's future—hinged on its ability to attract outside grant funding. Incorporation as a nonprofit qualified ABCD to win funding increasingly available from private foundations and the federal government, which intentionally relied on nonprofit agencies like ABCD to circumvent the entrenched political structures of city governments known for their patronage schemes and exclusion of non-white constituents.[16] The mighty Ford Foundation and its emerging interest in urban America enticed those behind ABCD, who had been willing to redraw the street grid of Boston following the availability of federal urban renewal funds and proved equally willing to take action in the social sphere following the availability of foundation funding. Local grants from Boston-based funders helped launch ABCD but were insufficient to implement the citywide agenda Logue and others had in mind. That would require resources at a far larger scale, which the Ford Foundation seemed able and, the Boston team hoped, willing to supply. After World War II, the foundation's grantmaking had focused internationally on the promotion of democracy and peace, but in the mid-1950s, staff on the domestically focused public affairs department built funding initiatives around problems of urban blight and poverty.[17] Before he left New Haven, Logue pitched ABCD to Paul Ylvisaker, a program officer at the Ford Foundation who considered Logue's letter "one of the most dazzling sales documents in urban renewal history" and weighed whether the Boston program might align with the foundation's new Gray Areas initiative.[18]

Launched officially in 1961 but in the works for several years beforehand, the Gray Areas grant program responded to the perceived inadequacies of urban renewal by supporting community-level and nonprofit-led activities. In particular, Ford Foundation staff embraced leading social scientific theories that diagnosed poverty as rooted as much in the social, psychological, and political lives of urban residents as in the economic and physical infrastructure of cities. This understanding of poverty acknowledged the role of racism in making people poor while still embracing individual uplift and improvement as a remedy.[19] The foundation planned to fund proposals pursuing coordination in municipal or metropolitan governance, increased citizen participation in urban programs, and the promotion of social scientific research to test and inform local efforts.[20] These three strategies targeted government reform in the long term, but did so on the belief that governments would more readily adopt solutions proven by nonprofits, and so invested financially and politically in nonprofit service provision as a means to that ultimate end. They also rested on the idea that solving the problem of urban poverty required new knowledge, not new political or economic power.[21] Even if Ford Foundation staff envisioned such investments as a short-term demonstration phase, the weight the foundation carried—what one observer likened at the time to "the fat kid in the boat"—shaped choices by those in hopeful nonprofits such as ABCD and liberal allies in government.[22]

Similar concerns and ideas about poverty inspired the incoming Kennedy administration to commit new federal resources to community action activities, particularly those focused on juvenile delinquency. During the 1950s, juvenile delinquency emerged as a hot-button issue, and social science research pointed to the maladjustment of boys who saw no future for themselves and lacked opportunities for societal advancement as a root cause of both poverty and crime. Using racially coded language, white elites identified African American teenagers in urban neighborhoods as psychologically stunted rather than as victims of discrimination and structural disadvantage.[23] Early in 1961 President Kennedy appointed a Committee on Juvenile Delinquency and Youth Crime, which soon became staffed with men linked closely to the Ford Foundation and their new domestic agenda and Gray Areas program.[24] The committee subscribed to many of the same theories as the foundation, most famously the "opportunity theory" of Columbia University faculty members Richard Cloward and Lloyd Ohlin, which positioned the political economy of the United States as fundamentally sound and asserted that those on its margins needed greater opportunity.[25] That such opportunity might come via community-level services such as job training or improved school curricula eschewed an approach to poverty rooted in antidiscrimination laws or other economic measures. Still, the idea of redesigning service provision was for some a novel proposition and necessary action, as Cloward had become a vocal critic of traditional charitable agencies for discriminating against the most destitute.[26] Thanks to legislative action, the president's committee gained its own pot of grant funding that, in both purpose and structure, forged a new path for US governance.[27] The legislation not only committed federal resources to an issue not previously considered part of the federal government's purview but did so via a new, direct connection between the federal government and local nonprofit entities instead of via state or municipal governments, as had been the case under urban renewal.

The existence of such prominent pots of private and public dollars by no means guaranteed support for Boston, because competitive grantmaking programs designed to encourage innovation put the burden on entities like ABCD to appeal to funders. Rather than propose their initial concept on citizen participation and urban renewal—activities that were already ongoing and therefore risked looking stale in the eyes funders bent on innovation—the leaders behind ABCD strategically expanded its mission to better align with funder goals. ABCD soon added school-related programs and "the improvement of community life in Boston" to its agenda.[28] Such pivoting for the sake of funding likely daunted Logue and the coterie of high-ranking university, social welfare, and government officials on ABCD's board of directors from a logistical perspective, but the approach remained intellectually consistent with their understandings of poverty and its remedies.[29] These predominantly white, credentialed men operated in the same political and ideological climate as program officers at the Ford Foundation and federal appointees on the president's committee.[30] As such, they shared beliefs core to midcentury liberalism, including the need to expand opportunity rather than restructure society, a faith in social scientific evidence and the replicability of experimental findings, and a concern that urban renewal alone was insufficient to address the poverty in American cities.[31] They also had similar blind spots: the assumptions that local solutions could address structural problems, that increasing participation via private routes could substitute for a sharing of public power, and that improved programs or services could reduce poverty.[32] The institutional arrangement of a private nonprofit organization tied to the government with funding offered the Boston supporters of ABCD the perfect avenue by which to express their concern for poverty without threatening the political-economic status quo.

Instead of repeating the familiar language of their funders, ABCD's backers might have listened to the growing cadre of activists in Boston espousing a different set of conclusions that connected racism and economic exclusion to poverty. In a time of municipal austerity, however, the choice to appeal to funders made sense even as it focused attention on a narrow set of activities. Funder interest in unemployment aligned with what was a growing problem in Boston, where unemployment among white youth sat at 12 percent and among Black youth topped 20 percent.[33] Researchers and local social workers recognized a labor force no longer anchored in manufacturing, but proposed to train individuals for the emerging service economy rather than create jobs or bolster wages. Early in his career, Mel King, for example, worked at a local nonprofit supporting teenagers looking for work. He lamented the only jobs he could match youth with were poorly paid and low-skilled positions in restaurants or hospitals and spoke directly of racism in employment. He advocated the creation of more

FIGURE 2.1. *Mel King at South End House (1963)*. Mel King ran a youth employment program at the United South End Settlements. The program received federal funding via ABCD starting in 1963 that expanded in 1964 under the War on Poverty. King's dismissal from that position in 1967 prompted protests in the South End neighborhood. (Bob Dean, "Melvin H. King, South End House," for *Boston Globe*, July 26, 1963, Collection 214: Boston Globe Library Collection (hereafter BGLC), NU. Image courtesy of Northeastern University Archives and Special Collections and the Boston Globe.)

jobs, protections of better pay and stability in the service industry, and the opening up of apprentice programs to Black teenagers.[34] King continued to work, however, at the individual level and kept an eye on incoming funds to ABCD, knowing that they would bring resources to his neighborhood even if the funder's goals differed from his own. Perhaps even a program that trained teenagers for jobs as supermarket clerks, maintenance workers, waiters, and machine operators would be better than nothing.[35] Then again, the choice was neither King's nor that of the teenagers in his program. The choice of what funding to seek, what programs to run, and what strategies to deploy rested with those holding the dollars and those writing the applications to win them.

Boston was not alone in seeking federal funding from President Kennedy's committee on juvenile delinquency and joined a crowded applicant pool of municipalities promising demonstration projects to test new solutions to old problems. Chicago, Philadelphia, Los Angeles, and Cleveland were among those putting forward proposals for local initiatives—all of which offered different administrative models of pairing public and private agencies to align with federal interest in "the widest possible involvement of all local agencies, public and private."[36] Boston's initial proposal in 1962 put forward a coalition of nonprofit and public agencies, including ABCD, the Boston School Department, the Massachusetts Division of Youth Services, and the city's Youth Activities Bureau, among others.[37] This plan, however, appeared "administratively unsound" to the federal review committee, which insisted that "one agency has to be the leader."[38] That ABCD emerged as the head of Boston's coalition reflected the multiple submissions Boston had under consideration and the hope that Ford Foundation funds would arrive. Keeping ABCD as lead agency under both the Ford and federal juvenile delinquency programs revealed strategic positioning more than a consensus on the organization's fitness for the task.[39] Motivations aside, the choice satisfied the federal reviewers, who awarded ABCD one of sixteen national planning grants to develop a strategy to reduce juvenile delinquency and improve education in Boston.[40] The funds were modest—a little over $150,000—but the grant solidified ABCD's standing in the city. A Ford Foundation grant of nearly $2 million for three years to ABCD soon followed as part of an informal pact between the foundation and federal bureaucrats to leverage their resources and fund the same projects.[41] Coverage of the grant announcement in the *Boston Globe* hailed Boston as the first "major" city to receive such funds, dismissing outright earlier grants to New Haven, Connecticut, and Oakland, California.[42]

Government and philanthropic grant programs translated the political ideology of midcentury liberalism into organizational form via their grantees, ABCD being a prominent example. Both the funding programs and their local enactment via nonprofits functioned as a bridge between urban renewal programs of the 1950s and the more expansive social agenda of the 1960s. For all the financial and political investment in new grant programs, staff at the Ford Foundation and in the Kennedy administration did not necessarily see their funding programs as ends in themselves, but they also remained resistant to more redistributive efforts such as tax reform or a federal jobs program. Even Boston's mayor considered ABCD "a great laboratory for solving human problems" in which problems could be studied and remedies tested, though he showed little interest in reforming the exclusionary and racist policies of city departments at the root of such problems.[43] Instead, grant dollars steadily fashioned the nonprofit sector as a site of planning, managing, and delivering social welfare goods and services and what was designed as temporary or transitional quickly became permanent.

Building the Nonprofit Sector in Boston

With major grants from the Ford Foundation and the federal government, ABCD gained significant responsibility as well as the authority and resources to act. Over the next few years, ABCD had committed to facilitate participation in ten neighborhoods undergoing renewal, launch a citywide program of research and evaluation, and manage a youth opportunity initiative with nineteen separate projects, including preschool, counseling, summer camp, tutoring, and job training.[44] ABCD's staff, however, would perform few of these tasks themselves. Instead, the nonprofit positioned itself as a funnel, drawing in resources from national competitive funding pools and redistributing them within Boston in ways that administratively cemented the agency in city governance and helped projects begin.[45] This left the organization, staff realized, "with a unique and awkward function" but one that also enabled it to partner with agencies around the city and exchange resources, ideas, and information.[46] This was the epitome of the coordinated response Logue had envisioned. The mere prospect of grant dollars, and the actual winning of them as ABCD had, developed capacity, experience, and relationships in Boston that over time became a fixture of American urban governance.

The influx of funds to ABCD enabled a hiring spree highlighting the agency's focus on planning and oversight rather than program delivery. In the fall of 1963, Joseph Slavet joined ABCD as the permanent executive director on Logue's recommendation and expanded a seven-member staff to forty-five.[47] Slavet had been responsible for seeding the initial idea of Logue coming to Boston and, as a result, had good relationship with the mayor that Logue thought useful for ABCD.[48] Consistent with ABCD's emphasis on testing and demonstration, Slavet came from the world of research, having previously overseen the Boston Municipal Research Bureau. He brought this orientation to his new post, where the majority of new staff worked in planning and research capacities, mimicking as well the reliance on expert planners and researchers at the Boston Redevelopment Authority.[49] The prioritization of social science approaches at ABCD, as evidenced by its hiring patterns, and the work those researchers performed ensconced at the city level ideas about poverty that were prominent in intellectual circles at the national level. ABCD's staff spent time in meetings and conducting field research, reading about the latest trends in preschool education, and securing space at summer camps for area youth. Across these initiatives they sought to translate lofty grant promises into concrete programs with curricula, partnerships, research agendas, and measurement tools. The growing corps of researchers at ABCD were not technically city employees, but public and private funds placed these private staff into public governance positions of decision-making and with administrative oversight.

Tasked only with coordination and planning per the terms of their grants, ABCD relied on neighborhood-based nonprofit organizations to deliver the experimental programs. This meant that ABCD staff selected the community agencies that would receive funds and what activities they would pursue. Following the announcement of Boston's participation in the Ford Foundation's Gray Areas program and the federal juvenile delinquency program, requests for a share of the grant dollars flooded ABCD from local churches, community centers, settlement houses, and city departments. Suddenly ABCD held the power of choice and monitoring in grantmaking. Conceptually, these partnerships aligned with the Ford Foundation's support of community-based action but in practice rendered ABCD, in the words of one foundation adviser, "a community grab-bag, where a host of community groups converge and compete over limited funds granted for uncertain durations."[50] As it outsourced programmatic responsibility for a variety of community organizing, educational, and anti-poverty programs, ABCD retained a fiduciary responsibility to monitor how community partners spent the regranted dollars and ensure a growing network of neighborhood-based organizations followed a standardized system of accounting, auditing, and services.

Through formal and informal partnerships, ABCD transferred its inflowing financial and human capacity to neighborhood entities around the city. These engagements, and the grant funds that followed, enabled groups such as the Cooper Community Center to launch a program welcoming migrants to Dorchester from the rural South and Puerto Rico and the St. Marks Center in the South End to develop a street-corner program for preteens as delinquency prevention.[51] ABCD contracted with Freedom House and the United South End Settlements to hire community organizers and with the Boston Legal Aid Society to open satellite offices in residential neighborhoods. When ABCD won a grant from the US Department of Labor to run a youth training and employment program, it partnered with four existing community agencies and helped cover the salaries of seven people at each of the four sites. Where its staffers saw gaps in nonprofit infrastructure, ABCD helped create new neighborhood nonprofits to fill them. ABCD pitched the idea of starting new nonprofits to the Ford Foundation as building "literally, centers in the sense that the hub of a wheel is its center with spokes extending in every direction" and planned to start with the Charlestown, Roxbury, and South End neighborhoods to parallel Boston's physical renewal activities.[52] Individually, these actions strengthened community organizations and supported the growth of new ones; collectively, they established Boston's nonprofit sector as a vehicle of service delivery and poverty reduction and framed grantmaking as the means of doing so.

As Boston's principal recipient of incoming federal and philanthropic dollars, the private organization ABCD also gained a degree of authority over municipal departments. One of its largest—and least successful— initiatives involved the Boston School Department, wherein funds from both the Ford Foundation and the President's Committee on Juvenile Delinquency and Youth Crime underwrote various education programs, including tutoring programs, a preschool initiative, a guidance program for middle school students, and an elementary school reading program. These programs varied in size from a single classroom to a few thousand students and imbued ABCD with responsibility to fix the structural problems of the public school system through supplemental programs. This approach reflected the faith of ABCD's leaders in the power of education and the general soundness of public schooling but also demonstrated the nonprofit's ability to circumvent the political gridlock that surrounded the Boston School Committee. Despite initial optimism in this initiative, ABCD reported to the Ford Foundation that working with the school department proved incredibly frustrating, slow, and, at times, counterproductive.[53] Municipal regulations, particularly around equity in hiring, irked ABCD for moving too slowly, while ABCD's insistence on standardized practices for the sake of research integrity angered teachers eager to adapt programs to meet the needs of students.[54] From ABCD's reports, Ford Foundation program officers concluded that "neither in design nor in execution has full potential of these limited efforts been realized."[55] Even as both funder and grantee expressed an abstract faith in government, staff rejected many of the democratic principles essential to it, preferring instead the flexibility and independence of the private voluntary realm.

Partnerships with city agencies proved administratively frustrating but rewarded ABCD with access to city data that further imbued the agency with public authority. To support their research agenda, ABCD staff gained access to the records of over fifty thousand public school students in over seventeen hundred classrooms, despite the fact that ABCD programs actually involved a fraction of that number of students. The collection of this data—including demographic data, personal information, and the performance records of children—took a reported "200 man-days of work" and was followed by another "245 man-days" to process, sort, and set up new data-processing equipment. ABCD also took the Boston Police Department to court in pursuit of data on arrests and police actions, perhaps expecting such information to be useful in reducing juvenile delinquency.[56] The amassing of this data and the tools to examine it enhanced ABCD's capacity to know and plan while also legitimating the organization's quasi-state authority with the transfer of information confidentially held by municipal agencies. It also strengthened ABCD's grant applications and reports.

ABCD's involvement with public agencies, most notably the Boston public schools, provided political flexibility for the mayor, particularly in navigating issues of segregation and inequality in the city. Mobilization by Black parents and area activists publicly connected discrimination in housing to widespread segregation in the public schools, while investigatory committees published reports documenting patterns of segregation supporting these claims.[57] A traditional policy of assigning students to schools based on residency produced thirty-five elementary schools in Boston with enrollments of over 90 percent white students and seven schools with enrollments of over 90 percent non-white students. The schools with predominantly African American students were more likely to be overcrowded, have fewer resources, and employ less experienced teachers.[58] The close ties between the city government and ABCD enabled Mayor Collins to claim credit for securing substantial resources and prominence for the city while not bearing the responsibility for the outcomes. When activists drew attention to segregation in the Boston school system, Collins merely highlighted ABCD as an "important social study agency" working on new programs particularly targeting Black students.[59] Supporting ABCD rhetorically and with a degree of authority through targeted government collaboration gave the mayor a means of appearing responsive to problems in his city but not responsible for their remedies. Coverage in the *Boston Globe* repeated this refrain in its coverage of the Boston schools as well as in its coverage of public housing and renewal.[60]

ABCD managed its reputation carefully too, at times distancing itself from city agencies and reinforcing its status as a private organization. Hostility toward the Boston School Department and the Boston School Committee was so strong—and grassroots activism so successful—that ABCD issued a press release separating itself from one particularly controversial school department program designed to ameliorate Black parent demands.[61] Instead of amplifying the issue of racial segregation in the city's schools, however, ABCD offered a color-blind value statement and stepped back from high-profile municipal partnerships to preserve its own credibility when things got tricky.[62] For the most part, these tactics worked. ABCD's harshest critics, who accused the organization of not meeting a federal standard for participation and called out the inadequacy of ABCD's programming, still saw the nonprofit's offerings as something better than nothing.[63] A series of reports released in spring 1965 on segregation in Boston's schools vigorously debated whether the school department held responsibility for remedying racial "imbalances," but all agreed on the value of "compensatory programs" from ABCD.[64] The very nimbleness of ABCD that Logue had envisioned in his initial draft was, in many ways, coming to fruition as the agency emphasized its public and private aspects as the situation dictated.

ABCD's biggest and most visible experiment was not in the content of programming it supported but in the administrative apparatus it built. Between 1962 and 1964, grant awards positioned ABCD as a local authority

dispensing knowledge, planning, resources, and legitimacy among its public and private partners. While programmatic results were not yet available from the bevy of experimental programs it launched, early results on
the administrative side were becoming clear: partnering with the Boston
School Department proved time-consuming and unpopular amid civil
rights protests, whereas partnering with neighborhood-based nonprofit
organizations appeared responsive, innovative, and flexible. When the
new Johnson administration in Washington, DC, sought to launch a War
on Poverty larger than what had been inherited from the Kennedy administration, ABCD had few results to show. What it did have, and what won
ABCD's executive director a trip to Washington in 1964, was an administrative structure that became a model of liberal urban governance.

Building the Nonprofit Sector from Washington

Certainly not the only inspiration for the War on Poverty, ABCD nonetheless served as one prominent model from which federal bureaucrats
designed a policy agenda for President Lyndon Johnson's Great Society.
The legislative package encompassed by this vague yet hopeful moniker
identified nonprofit organizations as agents of a federal strategy to reduce
poverty and the expansion of nonprofit capacity and activity as a policy
goal backed with government dollars. Much of this work built, consciously,
on the efforts of the preceding years that had laid useful intellectual and
organizational foundations. With organizations such as ABCD in mind,
bureaucrats and policy makers responsible for the War on Poverty moved
quickly to formalize the kinds of funding relationships and anti-poverty
priorities begun under Kennedy. Through policy and public grantmaking, they built a state apparatus in which private nonprofit entities implemented priorities and competed to win resources. Lower tiers of government had certainly partnered with nonprofit organizations before, but
never had the federal government entered into such close relationships,
with such small organizations, at such a scale as it did during the 1960s.
Rather than sites of experimentation, neighborhood-based nonprofit organizations became an important part of the state's social safety net and a
permanent infrastructure in urban areas.

   The Kennedy administration's juvenile delinquency program provided
an administrative template for the new poverty program that Lyndon
Johnson instructed staff to move "full speed ahead" with when he entered

the White House.[65] David Hackett, the chair of the President's Committee on Juvenile Delinquency and Youth Crime, described the "efficacy" of a single managing unit able to oversee and support action at the neighborhood level. Doing so produced, he found, "new and imaginative administrative and program arrangements" on the ground that blended public and private action.[66] Boston's ABCD was one such example, and representatives from the organization presented their administrative structure to policy makers in Washington on several occasions.[67] White House documents framed it as a model of how "we can win" the war on poverty through public-private partnerships that paired federal resources and reach with local community action.[68] Heeding this advice, the team developing Johnson's poverty program continued the existing grant-based system and again empowered federal agencies with the authority to solicit grant proposals, design a rubric for their evaluation, and issue grants directly to local groups. In such an administrative structure, federal funding existed not as a right but as a privilege to be won. This design worked well enough for the experimental and limited nature of the juvenile delinquency program, but a program pledging to eradicate poverty wherever it existed was another challenge altogether. As War on Poverty observer and scholar Sar Levitan noted at the time, much—perhaps too much—hinged on an applicant's "sophistication in the art of grantsmanship."[69]

Even as the Johnson administration touted the poverty program as something new and different, those involved also deliberately grounded their proposal in familiar ideas of self-help and local charity. It was the asymmetrical pairing of big vision and a limited tool kit that characterized grantmaking specifically, and the liberal response to poverty and Black political activism more generally, and which contrasted with the big vision and expansive dollars allocated to urban renewal, the Cold War, and, in time, the Vietnam War.[70] Private charity and government aid had coexisted in the response to poverty in the United States for centuries, and the White House sought to tap into this history in the political work of selling the new poverty program.[71] The White House pitched the War on Poverty's signature Community Action Program as a means "to seek solutions through the traditional and time-tested American methods of organized local action to help the individual help himself."[72] Though this suggested language never made it into the Economic Opportunity Act, the sentiment remained at its core. Talking points written to win over Republican policy makers—but that likely appealed to wary Democrats as well—noted the program was "not a Federal handout or a national dole" but rather "preserves our basic national principles of equal opportunity, local initiative, voluntary service, Federal-state-local cooperation, and of public and private cooperation."[73] Such lobbying worked. In August 1964, Johnson signed the Economic Opportunity Act as the key enabling legislation for the War on Poverty and his wider Great Society legislative agenda. The legislation announced poverty reduction as a national priority, committed nearly $950 million to the cause, and expanded the federal government's role in offering job training, education, social services, and community mobilization.

Research has since captured the extent to which 1960s-era policy spurred the growth of the nonprofit sector but has not fully recognized that this was a deliberate goal by Washington bureaucrats, and not merely a secondary consequence.[74] With its specific intent to create new nonprofit organizations in urban and rural communities, Title II of the Economic Opportunity Act and the Community Action Program it launched meant that the public-private response to poverty that communities like Boston had begun to test had graduated from the experimental phase to a new degree of permanency. The Title II program sought "to provide stimulation and incentives" for communities to develop local anti-poverty programs "conducted, administered, or coordinated by a public or private nonprofit agency."[75] Title II was hardly the only federal program that used this approach, though it may have been the most prominent example. A range of federal funding pools created under the Economic Opportunity Act specifically, and the Great Society agenda more broadly, positioned the federal government as a funder and nonprofit organizations—including neighborhood groups, hospitals, and universities—as the service providers. Not all Great Society programs operated in this manner; indeed, some of the most prominent legislation provided direct aid to individuals.[76] Still, the War on Poverty and Great Society funneled significant resources in direct and indirect channels to private nonprofit organizations to such a degree that political scientists at the time coined new terms of "private federalism" and "creative federalism" to describe the practice and note the ways these new channels deliberately circumvented the influence of mayors and governors.[77]

The Economic Opportunity Act and the funding initiatives it authorized did more than designate private nonprofits as eligible recipients of funding; it regulated the ways nonprofits could deliver those services and thereby expanded federal power over and oversight into the day-to-day operations of local organizations at both the citywide and neighborhood levels. The nature of federal grantmaking meant that the rules set by Congress and the bureaucrats charged with distributing federal dollars created

national standards to evaluate applications and monitor successful grantees.[78] The most famous rule about grantee organizations mandated the
"maximum feasible participation" of poor people in the poverty program.
Written as a throwaway phrase, the legislative words generated significant
controversy as poor people used it as a justification to demand a seat at the
table, and it became a phrase that federal funders had to define, monitor,
and enforce.[79] Clarifying legislative amendments in 1966 and 1967 then
stipulated that grant recipients on the ground have a board of directors
with no more than fifty-one persons, of whom one-third would be representatives of the poor, one-third public officials, and one-third civic leaders from business, education, religious, or welfare organizations.[80] While
these rules nominally ensured some degree of democratic control over
public resources, they also represented a significant degree of intrusion
into the organizational structure of local nonprofit organizations. Allegations of financial impropriety by grantees—allegations that were almost
always politically motivated and racially biased—prompted a similar set
of mandated standards around payment structures, accounting practices,
auditing practices, and budget allocations.[81] Though grantees resented the
proverbial strings attached to federal grants, those strings served to stan-
dardize organizational practices in communities around the country and
collectively draw neighborhood nonprofits into the state apparatus.

The plan to fight a War on Poverty via publicly funded and privately
delivered social services paired the reach and resources of the US government with the seeming innovation, flexibility, and localness of community
nonprofits. Policy makers recognized grant funding as both a carrot to
draw private entities into the work of national programs and a stick to
discipline how they did so. Through this governing tool of incentive and
enforcement, Washington helped build—and shape in its desired image—
entire networks of community agencies in cities and rural areas around
the country. The War on Poverty reflected the purposeful goal of creating a
modernized system of local charitable action in which the federal government's role was to coordinate via federal agencies and supplement with
federal funds what was being done by private nonprofits on the ground.

Fighting the Private War on Poverty

Just as policy makers hoped, local officials jumped at the chance to win
funds allocated under the War on Poverty and curried favor with those
evaluating proposals. For a public program, merit and need were only

partial factors in distributing federal grants, weighed alongside considerations of reputation, relationships, and political optics. Massachusetts's
governor, Endicott Peabody, wrote to congratulate the president on his
new poverty program, pledging the commonwealth's support. He boasted
of the state's readiness and desire to be "the first in the Nation" to put
forward a "comprehensive program."[82] For his part, Boston's mayor designated ABCD as the city's lead agency tasked to make "the antipoverty
program . . . the number one priority."[83] Such flattery, as well as ABCD's
prominence and experience, tipped the scales in Boston's favor. Officials
in Washington soon rewarded ABCD with funding for a host of social
service programs to be deployed in eleven neighborhoods targeted for
their high rates of poverty. Citywide, 16.7 percent of Boston families lived
in poverty, but that number climbed in certain neighborhoods, hovering
around 20 percent in many of the targeted neighborhoods and reaching
40 percent in the South End.[84] Yet, as those leading and watching ABCD
soon learned, winning funds and implementing the strategies proved two
very different tasks. The gulf between them revealed almost immediately
the benefits and burdens of federal dollars as a funding source, of competitive grantmaking as a means of governing, and of deputizing private
organizations to manage public problems.

The local paper called ABCD an "odds-on favorite" to win funding
under the War on Poverty, correctly citing the value of the organization's
reputation more so than its actual plans for or success in reducing poverty.[85] After several months of planning and negotiation at the end of 1964,
funding awards totaling almost $2 million began to make headlines in Bos-
ton in the first half of 1965. Local news coverage announced with pride
the programs enabled by federal dollars to ABCD, including program
planning at the Boston School Department, day care expansion at the Columbia Point and Orchard Park public housing developments, community
health provision at the Bromley-Heath public housing development, elderly services in Charlestown, and summer camp programs. Each of these
programs represented a different set of partnerships with nonprofit organizations spread across the city, ranging from multiservice centers and tenant groups to the Harvard School of Public Health and Associated Jewish
Community Centers.[86] Staff at ABCD once again found themselves serving a dual purpose of drawing in national resources and redeploying them
locally. By 1967, ABCD managed seventy-seven grants under the Community Action Program and $7 million in federal grants from agencies includ-
ing and beyond the War on Poverty's lead agency, the Office of Economic

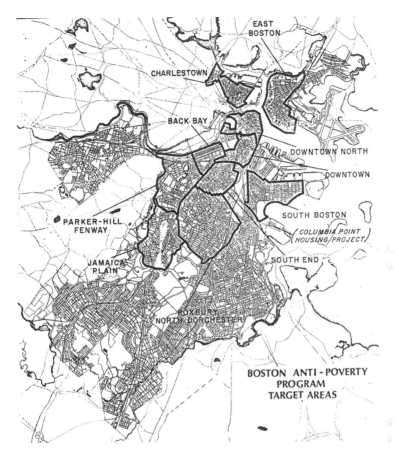

FIGURE 2.2. *Anti-Poverty Target Areas in Boston (1964)*. Following the signing of the Economic Opportunity Act of 1964, Boston submitted an application to the federal Office of Economic Opportunity seeking War on Poverty funding. Building on programs already begun thanks to funding from the Ford Foundation, Boston's Action for Boston Community Development mapped out the high-poverty areas where the city would target its programming. ("Boston Anti-Poverty Program Target Areas," in *Poverty Indices by Boston's GNRPs*, Progress Report 4, box 14, folder "City of Boston, Mass; Programs and Data," OFFB, LBJL. Image courtesy of Lyndon B. Johnson Presidential Library.)

Opportunity.[87] Counted in dollar amounts and number of grants, these achievements were successes for ABCD, but they posed administrative challenges the nonprofit proved ill-equipped to handle.

Not long after award announcements of War on Poverty funds started coming into Boston, it looked as though ABCD would have to permanently shut down.[88] In part, the influx of attention and funding revealed preexisting problems. The successes at winning grants did not necessarily translate into management skills, and, in the words of one observer, ABCD became "much like an overgrown boy whose administrative trousers do not fit," where no "sufficient supervisory and administrative controls exist."[89] Stories of discontent between ABCD's leadership team and Executive Director Joe Slavet had begun to leak in the *Boston Globe*, and reviews by the Ford Foundation revealed poor financial management. The organization appeared to be "walking a financial tightrope," with "no effective reporting or control system" and "cash forecasting . . . a hit or miss affair."[90] After starting 1965 with a surplus of $800,000, accountants projected ABCD would run out of cash by the end of September.[91] At the Ford Foundation's urging, Slavet added twelve new administrative positions to ABCD's staff—including a deputy director, budget director, and internal auditor—that, while costly, would bolster internal operations.[92] Many of organization's shortcomings reflected poor decisions by ABCD's leadership unaccustomed to the scale of grant management and operations of the War on Poverty. They also, however, pointed to the constraints federal grant programs imposed on cities and their leading anti-poverty agencies.

The federal anti-poverty dollars that ABCD and Boston officials so desperately sought turned out to be a double-edged sword, bringing new administrative scrutiny, financial complications, and political pressures as unfamiliar as they were unwelcome. One of these mixed effects was that public dollars carried expectations of transparency that produced reputational consequences as well. The prestige that grants under the president's committee and War on Poverty bestowed on nonprofits like ABCD could just as easily be retracted, undermining whatever confidence such awards had once conveyed. Indeed, allegations of mishandled funds became a favorite way of Southern politicians to undermine the leadership of Black-led community action projects, and even when cleared of wrongdoing, they served to interrupt program delivery.[93] Such a threat put added pressure on staff, above their standard legal obligations, to manage and track every single dollar moving through its coffers. Accusations of fraud in Boston's poverty program triggered an immediate freeze on federal spending; negative press in local and national news soon followed. *Newsweek* ran an article lambasting the poor administration of Boston's anti-poverty program, turning ABCD from national model to cautionary tale.[94] Investigations by a team of four federal observers found the scandals to be isolated incidents, and relatively minor ones at that.[95] One staff member, for example, enrolled 135 teenagers from non-poor families in a youth program; another issued $1,400 in forged checks.[96] Restitution was made and funds released, but the embarrassment remained, raising questions about responsibility in delegated governance that leaders in Boston struggled to answer. Mayor Collins made a public appearance on a local television broadcast to restore confidence in the program, and he helped coordinate the replacement of ABCD's board chairman.[97]

Public grantmaking posed a second challenge in its institutional design, in which the pressure of policy makers to direct as many public resources to program delivery worked at cross-purposes with the need of grantees to cover overhead costs. Initially, federal funders required grantees to charge each grant for the time administrators and accountants spent on each program—as was the practice for program staff—but this proved unrealistic for those whose tasks, such as developing an agency budget, often served multiple programs at once. ABCD proposed and eventually won approval to charge a predictable percentage of each grant for overhead expenditures, extending a practice typical in defense-related federal contracts to the social realm. Negotiations with each federal agency, however, proceeded so slowly that ABCD's executive director reported, "Moving the 'feds' on this has been like moving the Rock of Gibraltar."[98] Eventually the Office of Economic Opportunity (OEO) agreed that 13.2 percent of its grants to ABCD could be allocated to overhead expenditures, whereas the Departments of Labor and of Health, Education, and Welfare settled on 6.5 percent and 10 percent, respectively.[99] ABCD struggled as well under the scrutiny of federal auditors, who examined each cost and identified expenditures they considered improperly charged. In early 1965, for example, one federal agency claimed ABCD had $86,000 worth of such expenses, called disallowances, that it owed back to the government.[100] ABCD negotiated the total down to $35,000, but as a regular part of the grant management process, such negotiations produced a slow and expensive process that left accounts unresolved for years, if not decades.[101]

In the meantime, ABCD delivered its public programs with the private aid of philanthropic funding. After the Ford Foundation coinvested with the federal government under the juvenile delinquency program, this practice continued under the War on Poverty. In particular, the foundation proved willing to cover the overhead expenses federal funders denied and brought a degree of purposeful flexibility to ABCD that enabled it to weather the austerity and strictures of federal funding. Grants from the Ford Foundation soon covered two-thirds of ABCD's overhead

expenditures. Foundation staff initially found this "unreasonable," preferring that their dollars support programs, but recognized that it had become standard "practice to charge the Federal agencies as much as the
traffic will bear and the balance to the Foundation."[102] ABCD used money
from the Ford grant to offset disallowances, sustain programs, and test new
ones. The new team of accountants at ABCD pulled dollars from the Ford
Foundation pot to pay salaries, rent, and bills and then replenish them
when federal reimbursements or checks arrived.[103] At ABCD's request,
the foundation frequently shifted the dates of grant terms, backdating them
earlier, extending the periods longer, and shifting dollars between previously allocated operating or program expenses.[104] This flexibility, in effect, subsidized the federal program and staved off severe interruptions in
programming and staff layoffs in Boston but also hinted at the limitations
of government grantmaking and challenges of building institutional capacity.[105] Philanthropic funding enabled ABCD to stay afloat as an organization and to manage anti-poverty programs across the city, but it also
meant that those government efforts depended on the beneficence of private funders.

Perhaps the most prominent point of tension over the publicness of private organizations surrounded expectations for citizen involvement, captured in the vague policy mandate for "maximum feasible participation."
While policy makers had no idea the phrase would take on such power in
the War on Poverty, they did write it with the expectation that it would
nudge grantees to involve poor people in the planning and implementation
of the poverty program. Such language indicated at least some increased
precision over participation since urban renewal but still left little specificity
around what truly constituted meaningful involvement of poor residents.
At the time of ABCD's initial War on Poverty applications, its board of directors proudly included the most prominent figures in Boston's leadership
class. Handpicked by the mayor, who himself sat on the board, the group
included university presidents, local clergy, high-ranking city officials, and
business leaders. The recalcitrance ABCD officials had to broader resident involvement, particularly from poor and/or Black residents, exposed
their biases and faith in credentialed experts to lead the program. It also
revealed their attempts to predict what funders would want to see. Stock-
ing a board of directors with the city's leading civic, religious, and business
leaders seemed good practice, and running the kind of community elections that Black activists called for risked, it seemed, slowing down the fast-
moving train of Boston's poverty planning and implementation.

Such excuses rang hollow with civil rights leaders in Boston, who called out the hypocrisy of a public program with no public involvement and appealed to both press and funders for support. Local activist Bryant Rollins summed up the concern that "policy is made by professionals who live in the suburbs and commute into the ghettoes to solve the ghettoes' problems."[106] Similar demands for inclusion and decision-making power arose in War on Poverty programs across the country as people weighed the challenge of pursuing public goals in private spaces.[107] The local conversation in Boston gained increased prominence with the spring 1965 visit of Martin Luther King Jr. to Boston, where he made the administration of Boston's War on Poverty a central part of his platform. In a speech on Boston Common, King bellowed, "Now is the time to make real the promise of democracy." In a private session with Mayor Collins, King demanded that the poverty program create a meaningful role for poor people.[108] Amid a litany of demands to right the wrongs of racial segregation and discrimination in the city, perhaps Collins saw tackling ABCD as the easiest path to appeasement. He met King's demands with an immediate promise to reconstruct ABCD's board of directors. At the time, the forty-three-person board had only six African American members but would transition to have twenty-two appointed members and twenty-two elected members from the target neighborhoods. Debates over how the election would be held, the location of polling places, residency requirements, and more dominated the spring and early summer in Boston, until ABCD held an election for twenty-two board seats in July 1965. Federal observers traveled from Washington to witness the election that one observer called an "experiment in grassroots democracy"; they seemed to overlook that the election was not for public office, but rather a private one that simultaneously included residents in the poverty program through privatized channels.[109]

The outcome of the neighborhood elections moved ABCD closer to fulfilling its funding mandate and public role, but private mechanisms of exclusion persisted. The election elevated over two dozen new representatives to the board, including ten residents of public housing and several unemployed persons from across the city. As was becoming a common practice around the United States, the board became more diverse, but the officers of the board—members of the executive committee—remained the stalwart bankers and civic leaders that had controlled the board for years. These were the men who made the majority of decisions for the organization.[110] Community representatives on the board maintained a far more impressive attendance record at meetings and often constituted a majority at meetings but were voted down repeatedly by the smaller executive committee who retained the final say.[111] After a year of getting outvoted and outmaneuvered, only a third of the representatives on ABCD's board and subsidiary organizations sought reelection in 1966. Board member Rita Taylor, who had been one of the public housing residents elected to the board in 1965, reflected, "I'm disgusted and discouraged," and she refused to run again. "So you get elected. You have no power," Taylor lamented.[112] Roxbury resident and cab driver John Davis shared Taylor's sentiment: "They have all those fancy degrees and they can express what they want better than I can, so they get their point across better than me, but I live in the community. I know what we need."[113]

Local activists understood ABCD's reliance on federal funding and from the bottom up triggered top-down federal oversight to censure the Boston program for continued civil rights violations. When two finalists for a new leadership position at ABCD were both Black men, observers noted that the position was downgraded in status and compensation and made only a temporary position. Local activists wrote a telegram to US Representative Adam Clayton Powell (D-NY) in the summer of 1965 alleging discrimination and requesting federal assistance. They claimed "no poverty program would be preferable to one that is to be discriminatorily administered."[114] That fall, ten Bostonians from the Roxbury–North Dorchester neighborhood—the largest of the eleven target neighborhoods, where over a quarter of families lived in poverty, over half of students failed to meet grade-level achievements, nearly 40 percent of adults did not have a high school diploma, and the infant mortality rate was 34 percent—flew to Washington, DC, using funds raised in the community to lodge a complaint with ABCD's primary federal funder, the Office of Economic Opportunity.[115] They delivered a petition with nearly two hundred signatures to the head of the OEO, Sargent Shriver, requesting that he delay funding of $4.2 million to ABCD in Boston for a manpower program "until power for poverty programs be given directly to the elected people."[116] With over a million OEO dollars slated for the Roxbury–North Dorchester area in the coming year, such a request was surprising, bold, and risky but a political position neighborhood residents stood behind.[117]

Even as it survived federal investigation and fund freezes, ABCD bore the imprint of its challenges, and by the start of 1966, the nonprofit hardly resembled its former self. Quiet departures of both ABCD's executive director and board chair ushered in new leadership; new accounting staff and internal procedures governed the relationships between ABCD and its funders and its neighborhood-based grantees; and an expanded board of directors included representatives elected by their neighborhoods. Never one to be silent in his opinions, Logue let his frustrations be known, blaming the War on Poverty's chief general, Shriver, for how unrecognizable ABCD had become to the man who had originally conceived of the organization. Aspersions that "Shriver doesn't know enough about cities" aside, Logue's characterization of ABCD's transformation and identification of funding sources as at the root of that transformation were accurate.[118] The introduction of government funding at the scale ushered in by the War on Poverty infused not just dollars but sets of democratically oriented rules more familiar to public entities into private entities on the ground. Both public and private aspects of ABCD would continue to define the organization, and often do so in tension within the nonprofit and between ABCD and its funders and area residents. Even as ABCD continued to evolve, however, it was clear that grant funding—whether hoped for, awarded, or cut off—would structure Boston's response to poverty.

Conclusion

Near the end of his time in the White House, Lyndon Johnson instructed each federal agency to write a narrative history of its accomplishments. The history for the Office of Economic Opportunity occupies several boxes at Johnson's presidential library in Austin, Texas, and in its writing reveals the outsized role that nonprofit organizations played in the conception, implementation, and aspirations for the poverty program. In "project after project," the document reads, the poverty program "was designed specifically to involve organizations outside the structure of government."[119] The hope, the authoring bureaucrat continued, was that "the next generation would see the need to organize an operational third force—the private one—in American society. Collective organizations, private non-profit institutions would do more and more of the public business." The piece concluded that "OEO was a very, very useful bit of experience in how to get this done."[120] Indeed it was. Changes to the federal grant system were so profound—in amount and form—that research into federal funding initiatives in the 1960s concluded that that the federal government had become "a major philanthropist."[121]

The expansion of the nonprofit sector in American cities and its ties to the state significantly remapped the federalist system used to govern the United States in prior eras and represents one of the most profound legacies of midcentury social policy. That public funds were distributed on the creativity of the proposed solution rather than purely on need mimicked the grantmaking practices of private foundations and the experimental ethos of midcentury social science, in which a solution need only be found and scaled. It also expanded a state apparatus built around what would later be defined as neoliberal tenets of competition, innovation, and scarcity. Over the first half of the 1960s, the federal government created a number of these funding pots and issued grants to public and private entities committed to a wide range of social welfare goals. Though intended as temporary and experimental programs, the collective impact of this profusion of federal funding in fact built the opposite: a permanent infrastructure that positioned the federal government as a source of revenue and local nonprofits at the front lines of welfare provision and anti-poverty efforts. The choice to work with and through nonprofit partners to address urban poverty had been a deliberate choice and, for many, a promising one, though few could have predicted how extensive and how enduring these partnerships would become. The idea of a robust, democratic, associational sector in the United States stretched back to the colonial era and, in the 1960s context of the Cold War, civil rights movement, and postwar liberalism, seemed a quintessentially American solution to one of the biggest challenges facing the country.

ABCD reflects, simultaneously, the triumphs and disappointments of this approach to governing generally, and to poverty reduction specifically. As an entity conceived as a project of urban renewal, born as a program to combat juvenile delinquency, and one that matured under the War on Poverty, ABCD proved adaptable and lasting.[122] The competition-based structure of grantmaking programs, political pressures to take immediate action on the issue of poverty, and fiscal uncertainty of municipal governments created a potent mix of desperation and hubris among officials seeking federal dollars. Just as policy makers and local elites had envisioned, ABCD bridged, sometimes painfully and awkwardly, the public and private realms and democratic and undemocratic impulses. As a nonprofit organization, it proved responsive to funding opportunities, burdened by grant reporting, thin on funding margins, and closely audited; it also became more tied to government processes representing the city in federal meetings, implementing citywide strategies, amassing data from school and police departments, distributing public dollars, monitoring a network of agencies, and holding local elections.

ABCD failed to substantially reform public schools, increase participation, transform city government, or eradicate poverty. That it failed while having prominence and funding speaks to the limitations of expecting private social agencies to solve structural problems. At the same time, that it nibbled at the edges—even at times in meaningful ways—was enough to justify the wisdom of the approaches. As local residents continued to emphasize, this public-private approach left much to be desired as a means of reducing poverty. Too many white elites still controlled the poverty program, and the decentralized nature of service delivery reinforced poverty as a social problem rather than an economic one. Still, the public-private structures cemented under the War on Poverty created some new spaces in urban governance that residents continued to claim, carve, and control.

CHAPTER THREE

The Residents

In the winter of 1967, Mel King received a letter terminating his employ-ment as director of a neighborhood youth program at the United South End Settlements (USES) and giving him two days to vacate his office. During his fifteen years at the agency, King and his bosses had clashed before, and publicly. Though he kept a strict boundary between his profes-sional role and political work, King's reputation as an activist in Boston and his vocal criticism of USES's major funder, Action for Boston Com-munity Development, was well known.[1] When King and USES's execu-tive director, Charles Liddell, found themselves in yet another standoff, Liddell saw an opportunity to finally resolve the problem once and for all.

For Liddell, the choice was a pragmatic one rooted in a financial cal-culation. The funding for the youth program, and King's salary to run it, came locally from ABCD but originated from a federal grant. By 1967, ABCD's position between USES and the federal government was a fa-miliar one, and the once troubled nonprofit had learned to flex its respon-sibility to make grants and monitor the funds it redistributed. To that end, ABCD insisted on controlling one seat on the youth program's advisory board. The ask seemed reasonable enough to Liddell, who saw no need to risk a $100,000 grant over just one seat. King disagreed, and was willing to lose his job over a belief that community members should fill all seats on the advisory board. He saw in ABCD's stipulation an effort to moni-tor a program run by a Black man for a majority Black neighborhood as well as an opportunity to reaffirm the gulf residents increasingly identified between participating in the poverty program and controlling it. To King, administrative details were never just administrative details; it was all, he stated, "a matter of trust."[2] Residents of the South End agreed, recogniz-ing the racial politics at play in the standoff.

News of King's dismissal rallied hundreds in protest. Within a few hours, eighty mothers demanded that USES allow "community control over its programs," and two days later a crowd of eight hundred supporters presented a petition with five thousand signatures.[3] While King met behind closed doors with the predominantly white leadership teams from USES and ABCD, protesters gathered outside, battling the freezing temperatures of Boston's winter by singing civil rights songs. Some carried posters from King's past campaigns for the Boston School Committee and painted "restore" over outdated election details.[4] Eventually the parties reached a compromise. ABCD won its representative on the advisory committee, and USES would rehire King. Yet, instead of returning to his youth program, King would take a new role at USES, organizing South End residents to ensure the growing nonprofit sector remained responsive to community needs. The local Black newspaper called the reinstatement "a major step forward for the concept of community development."[5]

Nonprofit organizations often provide infrastructure for social movements, but in the 1960s, they also became targets of them as the ties between nonprofits and the state presented African Americans both opportunities for inclusion and new spaces for exclusion. Though the use of civil rights vocabulary and strategies to critique King's dismissal might have surprised the white elites in Boston who saw themselves as poverty warriors and good liberal allies, it should not have. Race shaped the political context and policies of the War on Poverty at a national level and at the local level, where nonprofit organizations took on new roles and entered new partnerships.[6] In a segregated urban landscape where neighborhoods carried racial identities, the organizational entities increasingly tasked with delivering programs, liaising with city officials and supposedly solving community problems, carried both spatial and racial identity markers.

Legacies of racial discrimination—and the violent enforcement thereof—had structurally excluded African Americans from fully accessing the public sphere and, in the centuries before the War on Poverty, rendered the nonprofit or charitable realm a central space for service provision, identity formation, community organizing, and advocacy in Black communities. These activities were not unique to Black Americans, but in the postwar period Black-led and Black-serving organizations performed double duty. Not only did they have to supplement the municipal government during a period of declining revenue; they also had to replace it in ways not asked of organizations serving white neighborhoods, where municipal agencies were more likely to perform their duties and where residents were more likely to be represented in government.[7] Lacking such rights and privileges, civil rights activists demanded funding to nonprofits in Black neighborhoods and community control over those resources and the areas they targeted. The administrative work of founding and running nonprofit organizations meant that the nonprofit sector became a battleground for 1960s-era movements for freedom and equality rather than simply their backdrop.

For Black communities, the anti-poverty program and resources it deployed into urban neighborhoods could not be separated from the broader struggle for freedom, equality, and rights. Nor did they want it to. In Boston and around the United States, African Americans and other marginalized groups recognized the simultaneous opportunities and limitations of the War on Poverty and the array of grantmaking programs that accompanied it. Funding programs could deliver important material resources to communities long denied access to public spending, even as they invested in service delivery over the kinds of structural political and economic changes those active in the civil rights movement saw as the route to full equality.[8] The poverty program dictated from above how grantee organizations operated, but room still existed on the ground to give local shape to programs and organizations.[9] By linking social justice movements to the infrastructure of nonprofit organizations, Black and Latinx residents in Boston fused the politics of identity, governing, and change in a variety of combinations and with different models for neighborhood nonprofits. Taken together, these efforts constructed nonprofit neighborhoods as means of governing predominantly Black neighborhoods in a segregated metropolis and of challenging those color lines. They were wrought out of both need and desire, in ways consistent with a longer historical tradition and reflective of the contemporary context of urban crisis.

Civil Society in Black and White

When policy makers connected the War on Poverty to a long tradition of charity and self-help in the United States, they likely were not picturing the Black civil society organizations that, like their white counterparts, traced their origins to the colonial era. Segregation characterized every facet of American life, well into the 1960s, and the nonprofit sector or charitable realm was no exception. Yet, as was the case in so many realms of American life, African Americans built a vibrant associational life of civic and charitable organizations within the confines of segregation.[10] These entities offered culture and comradery, services denied by white governments, entities to pool resources, and platforms to demand freedom. They were spaces for survival and celebration at a time when the public sector legally, systematically, and violently excluded Black men and women from participating as equal citizens. In many ways, this was a familiar role for the nonprofit or charitable organizations, which have always incubated social movements and provided an infrastructure for people to join, fundraise, advocate, and serve.[11] Such has been the case in the push for labor protections, women's rights, child welfare, and religious freedom; it has been especially true in the long fight for Black freedom in the United States.[12] So when the War on Poverty and other policies of the 1960s invited nonprofit organizations to take a more formalized role in urban governance, Black communities stood ready, bolstered by experience and infrastructure stretching from the era of abolition through to the era of civil rights.

In the absence of a public sphere that included them, Black Bostonians built their own alternative from the founding era on and connected the day-to-day activities of their associational and charitable organizations to the long quest for freedom. In 1783, Massachusetts became the first state in the new nation to abolish slavery, and one year later Bostonian Prince Hall received a charter from England recognizing his African Lodge of Masons. Hall, a former slave manumitted before the American Revolution, advocated full citizenship for African Americans, writing several petitions to the Massachusetts legislature on the subject.[13] Despite his local prominence, white Bostonians rebuffed Hall's interest in joining the fraternal order of the Freemasons. In response, Hall founded his own lodge as the first Black secret society in the fledgling United States.[14] It was a moment of simultaneous protest and incorporation that would continue to define Boston and shape Black life more broadly across generations. In the late nineteenth and early twentieth centuries, the settlement house movement responded to the arrival of women into cities with shelter and services. Settlement houses emerged famously from Chicago under the leadership of Jane Addams, who inspired similar efforts in Boston. These entities, however, rarely accepted African American women. In response, a group of six Black women founded their own settlement house in the South End to provide shelter, services, and community.[15] By 1904 these Boston women officially incorporated as the Harriet Tubman House,

taking their name from their personal friend and naming Tubman honor-
ary president of the organization in the years before her death.[16] Tubman
House and the growing cluster of Black settlement houses in the city promoted issues of importance to Black women and lent their facilities as a
meeting place for a variety of Black women's associations, many of which
nurtured the next generation of civil rights activists.[17]

Melnea Cass, known later as the "First Lady of Roxbury," began her
long career in Boston as an advocate for African Americans in a settlement house. At the Robert Gould Shaw House (named for the leader of
the famed Massachusetts Fifty-Fourth Regiment of Black soldiers in the
Civil War), Cass helped found a nursery school for Black children and
later founded and fundraised for a mothers club. For Cass, like so many
African American women, these activities were a tactic of survival and
of building community in a city that was often hostile to their existence.
Through these connections, Cass joined the NAACP and eventually
became president of the Boston branch in the early 1960s. Later, when
asked about her involvement in nonprofits in Boston, Cass responded,
"Oh, I belonged to all, dear."[18] She certainly made her mark. Mayor Collins called on Cass to join the initial board of directors for ABCD. Accepting the request, she served initially as the only woman and only official
representative of Boston residents on the governing body.[19] Cass consistently raised questions to the other ABCD board members about equality,
civil rights, and community leadership, though her lone voice often fell on
deaf ears.

The challenges Cass mounted from within ABCD's board of directors
mirrored a broader movement for racial justice in Boston and other cities
during the postwar period. Like Cass, many of the city's prominent civil
rights leaders held affiliations to local nonprofits. They served as board
members, volunteered their time, paid membership dues, and found employment in these entities—often across a handful of organizations. Consider the following examples: Mel King ran for the Boston School Committee three times—in 1961, 1963, and 1965—while also working at the
United South End Settlements doing youth development work. Ruth Batson also ran for the school committee, also unsuccessfully, starting in the
early 1950s with the slogan "Mother, Educator, Civil Worker," and led the
NAACP branch's education committee to demand recognition of the segregation in the city's schools. When those efforts continued to move too
slowly, Batson joined a group of mothers to create a grassroots organization, Operation Exodus, to bus Black children to empty seats in schools

in white neighborhoods.[20] Noel Day worked with South End youth at the St. Marks Center but spent his free time helping organize a boycott of Wonder Bread until the company agreed to hire Black workers. Day was then instrumental in launching a "Stay Out of School Day" boycott by students to protest education inequality.[21] In 1964, he launched a campaign to unseat US Representative and Speaker of the House John McCormack. Even in brief, these examples reveal the deep linkages between organizations, service provision, and advocacy that civil rights leaders purposefully built long before 1960s-era urban policies began to recognize their utility.

In the early 1980s, Mel King wrote a book on Black activism in Boston. The work, *Chain of Change*, traces the arc of King's life in the South End from the 1950s onward, but the title captures a longer and larger pattern of advocacy, aid, and community organizations in the centuries-spanning Black freedom movement. People and organizations forged the chain that connected campaigns for abolition to women's rights, to civil rights, and, in time, to poor people's rights. People infused resources, ideas, and commitment through nonprofit organizations, generating physical spaces and communities of support that transferred from one generation to the next. The administrative basis of the War on Poverty in the 1960s offered members of Boston's Black community a possibility of adding a new link in the chain, but no guarantee that it would.

Participating in Boston's War on Poverty

The landscape of nonprofit organizations, civil rights organizing, and neighborhood segregation all emerged from the same taproot of racism in America. It therefore stood to reason that existing community entities might benefit from a new policy framework that designated funds for, and encouraged formal governing ties to, nonprofit organizations. The War on Poverty, a policy agenda imbued with requirements for "maximum feasible participation" and a preference for neighborhood delivery, presented an opportunity for Black organizations to gain new resources and authorities for the kinds of activities they were already doing. Black activists in Boston, as elsewhere, knew from experience, however, that legal rights rarely translated into reality without the monitoring, mobilization, and pressure of activism. As such, Black Bostonians met the War on Poverty with excitement and caution, knowing they would have to carve out a space for themselves in the program and new governance regime it inaugurated.

Keenly aware of the power ABCD held in the poverty program, civil rights activists used familiar tactics to assert the presence of Black community members at the decision-making tables. Martin Luther King Jr. made the expansion of ABCD's board of directors a top issue when he led a march in Boston in 1965. Mayor Collins eventually conceded and, in a decision that was only partially his to make, agreed to grow the board's size and have communities elect at least a portion of seats on the board. With calls for "maximum feasible participation" echoing around the country, Collins's approach fit squarely in line with mayors in Philadelphia, Los Angeles, and elsewhere looking to exert control over the War on Poverty but also conceding to the democratic demands of poor constituents.[22] This victory, like many, proved more symbolic than substantive as the white-led board transferred some of its authority to the much smaller executive committee, effectively concentrating power among a majority white group that maintained a regular use of its veto power over the larger, more representative board. This pattern of pressure, concession, and hollowing out of authority continued. Following the resignation of Joseph Slavet as ABCD's executive director, the Boston NAACP demanded and won a meeting with the finalist for the position. George Bennett hailed from New Haven, where it was reported in Roxbury that he had placed little value in community organizing.[23] A meeting between Bennett and local Black leaders occurred, but the hiring went forward without, the NAACP announced, "the support or confidence of the major civil rights groups."[24]

Though resistant to opening its own ranks, ABCD's leaders did see value in creating spaces at the neighborhood level for community, particularly Black, involvement. It was here that white leaders at ABCD saw an appropriate role for Black-led organizations and Black residents to tap into War on Poverty funding given the intersections of race, poverty, and neighborhood. The decentralized structure of ABCD and the implementation of the city's anti-poverty program reflected directives in the Economic Opportunity Act, which "encouraged" grantees "to make use of neighborhood-based organizations," to bring program delivery and, to a degree, program management one step closer to urban residents.[25] It also reflected a calculated response to civil rights activism that devolved some authority to the neighborhood level while still retaining significant power within the centralized citywide agency. The tension between expanded-yet-constricted participation and the choice to funnel it through private neighborhood nonprofits embodied the kind of privatized inclusion that characterized nonprofit neighborhoods during and beyond the War on Poverty.

As part of this effort, staff at ABCD crafted a new management structure that designated an ABCD subsidiary in each of Boston's eleven residential neighborhoods to be overseen by elected Area Planning and Action Councils. These entities, known by their acronym APACs, received a share of the city's annual anti-poverty funding—about $1.4 million in total in 1967—that helped establish these neighborhood nonprofits with physical space, administrative staff, and local organizers. By 1967, these APACs together employed 860 people, involved four hundred people as board members, and attracted more than twenty thousand voters in local elections to determine boards of directors.[26] They became hubs of activity. The Dorchester neighborhood elected Doris Graham to their APAC board. She sometimes devoted sixty hours per week to the role, she explained, "so that we can get what we know our area needs."[27] Black residents under the Roxbury–North Dorchester APAC, in particular, embraced their opportunity to shape the anti-poverty program and better align it with their local civil rights advocacy. They sent a group of residents to Washington, DC, for example, to critique ABCD's leadership and ask federal funders to enforce greater resident control.[28]

The second mechanism by which ABCD decentralized its programs involved subgranting funds it received to neighborhood nonprofits for implementation. ABCD had some experience with this kind of deployment from its earlier efforts related to urban renewal and juvenile delinquency, and in 1967, the organization hit a peak of nearly eighty separate contracts that distributed about $12 million to neighborhood organizations.[29] These dollars, including those that went to the APACs, enabled the expansion of nonprofit organizations as a visible part of the city's built environment, as funds paid for office space in storefronts, public housing apartments, and old houses. Bostonians heard about these neighborhood nonprofits in barbershops, beauty parlors, and local stores as well as from police stations and courts that started referring residents for various programs.[30] The services these organizations provided included federal programs such as legal services, health care, Head Start, and job training, but they also supported grassroots programs designed and launched by community residents. ABCD's funds supported the voluntary busing program Operation Exodus that Ruth Batson helped launch, a Job Wagon in the South End, a Thanksgiving dinner for the Neighborhood Youth Corps, a community playground, and a local credit union.[31] In many ways, these infusions of funding epitomized what social scientists and bureaucrats in Washington had envisioned for the War on Poverty and provided financial and programmatic opportunities to neighborhood nonprofits both old and new.

For communities living with the daily reality of poverty, the growth of neighborhood nonprofits brought valuable opportunities. War on Poverty funds offered the possibility of a job—often one that included training and the chance to contribute to the community. This was particularly the case for women, who found employment as classroom aides, health aides, neighborhood workers, and more.[32] At Boston's Columbia Point public housing development, for example, seven residents worked at the local APAC and twelve found work at the health center attached to the development—the first of its kind in the country and a model for employing so-called nonprofessionals in health care roles.[33] Beyond the individual benefit of a salary, albeit an often low one, the inclusion of local residents in program planning and delivery at the neighborhood level improved the organization and increased community trust. Doris Graham from Dorchester testified before a congressional subcommittee on all the skills and knowledge neighborhood workers brought to nonprofits: "They are community people; they know the feelings; they know the ills; and they know the way of the community. By this they are able to sit down and relate" with those seeking help or struggling.[34] At the same hearing, Betty Meredith from the South End Neighborhood Action Program reiterated the same message: "All the degrees in the world can't help someone who's never been really hungry to know how much an empty stomach hurts, or what it's like to live in a fourth-floor, cold-water walkup flat with no heat, no plumbing, and rats and roaches. Or how it feels to have to tell your kid that no matter how well he's doing in school and how much he'd like to be a teacher, he has to drop out of school now and go to work because he's 16 and the other kids have to eat."[35] In both the material resources and mandates for participation, the War on Poverty helped draw women like Meredith and Graham into the nonprofit sector.[36]

Yet, even as ABCD devolved certain resources and authorities to neighborhood nonprofits, it retained significant power over the community groups it funded and oversaw. The kind of oversight ABCD sought over Mel King's youth development program was not unusual, and it suggested a broader pattern of competition, monitoring, regulation, and control that characterized ABCD's partnerships with neighborhood nonprofits. As one example, ABCD retained the ability to ratify whomever the neighborhood APAC boards selected as their executive director. Many saw this as a ceremonial box to check, until the community board for the

South End Neighborhood Action Program (SNAP) selected Archie Williams for the role. A graduate of Brown University and Boston University Law School, Williams was an attorney practicing in Roxbury and active in the Boston civil rights movement. He had even been a finalist for a job at ABCD's headquarters in downtown Boston. ABCD's executive committee, however, voted down Williams's nomination twice, both times citing his "lack of administrative experience."[37] This move prompted an editorial in the *Bay State Banner*, the city's Black newspaper, and Boston NAACP leader Thomas Atkins called the decision "blatant racism."[38] Many speculated that Williams's involvement in pushing ABCD to diversify its board earlier in 1965 earned the ire of Mayor Collins and influenced the executive committee's vote.

Structural limitations—both of ABCD's design and beyond its control—similarly constrained the growth of the neighborhood-based groups and drained power from these sites of participation. The administrative pressures federal funders placed on ABCD extended to the local subgrantees as well, who soon felt the reach of a growing, decentralizing state. ABCD's inconsistent cash flow from above, for example, resulted in short-term contracts and insufficient overhead below, undercutting the ability of community nonprofits to deliver programs. A February 1965 contract between ABCD and a nonprofit in the South End for family and job development programs covered only eight months. In March of that same year, ABCD subcontracted with the Roxbury Federation of Neighborhood Centers to operate two day care programs and a home management program, but only for a period of four months.[39] These practices resulted in low salaries at the neighborhood level, often causing high rates of staff turnover and inconsistent program offerings. As law required, ABCD's subgrantees had to send updates on their program delivery and financial tracking, but few managed to do so without sufficient accounting staff. Many of the challenges that plagued ABCD became exaggerated in the very places where need was highest.

Consider Boston's Head Start program, which ABCD managed and local nonprofits ran in the summer of 1965. Rheable Edwards directed the program for ABCD. A Black woman born in Arkansas, Edwards received her second master's degree, this one in social work, from Boston University before working at the Boston Housing Authority, leading the local NAACP's housing committee, and joining ABCD first as a researcher and then as the director of the city's Head Start program. From this position, she coordinated the hundred-plus Head Start classrooms managed by over

twenty neighborhood nonprofits.[40] As a federal preschool program, Head
Start operated on dollars carrying a number of regulations and organizational structures, which ABCD passed down the chain.[41] Stipulations
covered the number of students in each class, residency requirements for
participants, job descriptions and corresponding salaries, equipment lists
to be furnished, facility requirements for students and parent groups, and
monthly reporting requirements.[42] Community nonprofits had to hire a
registered public accountant and provide proof of doing so before the
program began.[43] Such formalities reflected good governance procedures
implemented to ensure the proper stewardship of public funds and quality of programming but served just as much to burden community groups
with unfunded mandates.

Freedom House in Roxbury won one of the contracts for a Head Start
program, experiencing firsthand the benefits and burdens. Approval of
Boston's federal grant for Head Start programs happened only a handful
of months before students arrived.[44] Community agencies such as Freedom House were responsible for significant planning and preparation
of the summer program but, due to funding regulations, did not receive
compensation for time spent recruiting staff, screening students, preparing facilities, procuring equipment, and setting up record-keeping proto-
cols. ABCD instructed nonprofits such as Freedom House to "take up the
slack," often doing so even before contracts were signed, and expected
community members interested in employment to volunteer their time in
training programs.[45] By the time ABCD sent out the first round of checks
to its neighborhood partners, ten days of the summer session had passed.[46]
Edwards's team at ABCD assisted where it could in furnishing classrooms
with items such as books and Band-Aids but also encouraged agencies
to solicit donations and "borrow bicycles, wagons, beautiful junk, etc." for
their summer classrooms.[47] Despite every effort, some groups, including
ones as well established as Freedom House, ran deficits on their Head Start
programs of about a hundred dollars, the cost of one teacher's weekly
salary.[48]

When a congressional subcommittee held hearings about the War on
Poverty in Boston, administrative challenges over funding amounts and
structures dominated the testimonies. It was one of the few things on which
ABCD and representatives from neighborhood APACs could agree. Representatives from both the citywide agency and neighborhood entities
called on Congress to extend grant periods for several years, provide
more programmatic flexibility, keep funding levels consistent, implement

FIGURE 3.1. *Head Start sign-ups at Freedom House (1965)*. Freedom House sponsored several Head Start classrooms in Boston as part of the city's War on Poverty. These women, pictured at Freedom House, were either enrolling children in Head Start preschool or applying to work in the classrooms. That they are seated under redevelopment plans for the neighborhood underscores how local nonprofits supported both physical and human renewal. (Del Brook Binns, "Five Women Sit and Write on Paper," A004205, box 71, folder 2813, FH, NU. Image courtesy of Northeastern University Archives and Special Collections.)

community-derived plans, and cover more overhead and neighborhood worker salaries. Short grant periods undermined the ability of groups to hire, and, as one representative from the South End stated, "You can't solve these kinds of problems in a few months."[49] George Bennett, ABCD's latest executive director, blamed the funding strictures for the limited participation in Boston's anti-poverty program. "To talk of *Maximum Participation* and to fund *Minimum Participation* is a paradox," he testified.[50] To Bennett, participatory mechanisms cost time and money, which ABCD felt it could not spare. Neighborhood representatives, in contrast, saw the funding constraints as a symptom of a broader lack of trust in poor people and people of color, and as a means for the federal government and ABCD to undermine their activities. After not getting a chance to testify,

Leroy Boston from the South End interrupted the hearings, demanding his voice be heard. His protest won a few minutes, which he dedicated to the difference between being told to administer a program and the power to plan it for themselves. "We should definitely have more community-controlled programs," he stated before being told to be quiet.[51]

Black-led and Black-serving organizations stood to benefit from the influx of federal dollars into Boston via ABCD, but it took mobilization of both visible protests and quiet grant writing to ensure dollars moved from the central office downtown into the neighborhoods where organizations delivered the programs. For all the rhetoric of participation, Black Bostonians fought an uphill battle that found predominantly white institutions such as ABCD more willing to add a few seats at the table than to turn over actual control. Struggles for power within and beyond the anti-poverty program revealed points of conflict for a public program that flowed through private hands. Still, demands by Black residents for more funds and control endorsed the presence of neighborhood nonprofit organizations in urban governance. The challenge then became finding ways to steer resources in directions supportive of not just programmatic goals but advocacy ones as well.

From Individuals to Community

More financially precarious and without the full autonomy grassroots activists had demanded, neighborhood-based nonprofits preserved some room for staff to shape and deliver their own anti-poverty programs. Staff members, particularly Black staff members, infused an advocacy agenda into their programming and committed organizational support to social movements for racial justice. They tested the bounds set by public and private funders while also devising ways to work within them to support issues such as welfare rights and educational equality. Though it gained prominence in Boston, and at times nationally, for its neighborhood-based approach to reducing poverty, the Roxbury Multi-Service Center (RMSC) mirrored trends playing out in traditionally disenfranchised communities in US cities. The nonprofit relied heavily on public grants, many of which arrived via ABCD. Despite the constraints such dollars imposed, staff brought a racial consciousness to their work that expanded their scope from aiding individuals to strengthening the community. In so doing, the men and women at RMSC redefined the War on Poverty from the ground up and reimagined the role of neighborhood nonprofits in urban affairs.

Much like ABCD, the Roxbury Multi-Service Center existed as a concept long before it filed incorporation papers and, also like ABCD, could trace its conceptual and physical origins to Boston's urban renewal program. Planners behind the Boston Redevelopment Authority and ABCD sought to open multiservice centers in two neighborhoods undergoing renewal to test the efficacy of the comprehensive, community-based response to poverty espoused by liberal politicians and philanthropists. The proposed entities would provide the "visible, concrete, and reality-oriented services" that Logue considered necessary to help poor families but had been sidelined in the hunt for funding to get ABCD off the ground.[52] When momentum picked up again, the choice of Roxbury and Charlestown as the initial targets for multiservice centers purposely included one predominantly Black neighborhood and one predominantly white neighborhood to appear equitable in resource allocation and give the social experiment a veneer of scientific objectivity. In a familiar pattern, a 1964 grant request to the Ford Foundation for these centers netted interest and concern but little, initially, in the way of funding, prompting over a year of anxiety for those in the communities where planning had already begun.[53]

Public and private grants eventually enabled RMSC to rent space, hire staff, and begin supporting the people of Roxbury. When the agency opened its doors in 1965 on Blue Hill Avenue, staff shared four rooms on the third floor of a building above a poultry market.[54] Borrowed card tables and folding chairs furnished the offices, but staff would have to visit the drugstore across the street to use a telephone.[55] Still, in these humble accommodations, staff sought to build something new, oriented toward the people who needed their services most. Notable for the time, though not for the Roxbury neighborhood, both the board and the staff were majority Black, and nearly equally split between men and women.[56] The high number of staff with backgrounds in casework and training as social workers revealed that while RMSC was based in a community, the philosophy behind the organization remained rooted in an understanding that poverty was a problem of individuals or families that typically indicated cultural or social failings. Staff designed programming around child rearing, home management, and case management, working with over five thousand families during the first years of operations in a coordinated family-centric model of service.[57] Federal funders were so pleased with

FIGURE 3.2. *Hubie Jones and Gertrude Cuthbert at the Roxbury Multi-Service Center (1965).*
The Roxbury Multi-Service Center opened in 1965 with funding from the Ford Foundation
and the federal Office of Economic Opportunity as a neighborhood agency to coordinate and
provide services. Gertrude Cuthbert (*seated left*) served as the first executive director, and
Hubie Jones (*standing*) took over that role in 1967. ("Gertrude Cuthbert, Roxbury Multi-
Service Center ED, (seated left); Hubie Jones, Executive Assistant; and Trish Di Virgilio,"
ca. 1965, Image A029499, RMSC, NU. Image courtesy of Northeastern University Archives
and Special Collections.)

RMSC's model that the US State Department brought delegates from
Central and South America as well as Sweden and Taiwan to tour the
facility and meet staff.[58]

One of RMSC's first employees, Hubie Jones, grew frustrated, however, with the limited tools at his disposal to help people experiencing
poverty. Raised in the South Bronx by a father who worked as a Pullman
porter and labor organizer, Hubert "Hubie" Jones settled in Boston after
graduating from Boston University's School of Social Work. Ready to deploy his training as a social worker at RMSC, however, Jones encountered
people requesting help with housing and education, with little interest in
the casework he provided. He later reflected that, as a social worker, he
had been "trained to always look for the 'underlying problem' when a

client comes to you for services," yet he soon realized "that a person's 'underlying problem' might be that they were poor. They, simply, don't have money."[59] It was little more, Jones commented, than a "band-aid on cancer."[60] In a report summarizing the first year of operations, staff reported that Roxbury residents had been coming to RMSC with "evictions, abuses practiced by landlords," requests for "aid in providing a different school for their young children," and pleas for investigation into the "quality, content and methods of public education." The individualized, case-based services RMSC had been funded to provide did not address these structural issues of inadequate housing and education that "cut into the entire fabric of life of the whole family," a staff member noted.[61] Staff began to reframe the organization to better target the discriminatory, punitive, and extractive policies at the root of the problems Roxbury residents were experiencing.

The evolution at RMSC from improving individuals to strengthening communities coincided in the late 1960s with the conclusion of the organization's first major grant cycle as well as with a growing escalation of movement activism and uprising in Boston and elsewhere. This timing brought new possibilities for change but also administrative vulnerabilities. Gertrude Cuthbert, the executive director, decided to step down rather than launch a second strategic plan, and of the organization's forty-nine staff members, thirty-three left the organization in 1967 due to a lack of funding. RMSC might easily have folded. Jones took over, however, and steered the nonprofit in a new direction that recognized, one report recounted, the limitations of "case-by-case intervention . . . in view of the magnitude and the deplorable environmental and institutional problems faced by community residents."[62] Even as Jones stepped in, however, grant funds tied to specific service programs around legal services, job training, housing, health services, and youth development kept RMSC afloat and engaged fifteen hundred Roxbury families every year.[63] The Office of Economic Opportunity remained RMSC's largest single funder well into the 1970s. Strengthening the community as a whole could not replace their existing programmatic offerings due to funding considerations, and instead had to come alongside and through it. The challenge for Jones, as for all nonprofit leaders faced with similar arrangements, centered on how to use RMSC as an advocacy platform to keep building capacity in the communities where need remained high and resources remained scarce.

By the time Jones took over RMSC in 1967, not only had his thinking and the organization's situation changed from when it opened in 1965; the world had changed too, ushering in a new political context where a language of Black power, welfare rights, and anti–Vietnam War sentiment roiled those anxious for change. The first few years of RMSC's operations paralleled a series of civil rights victories that, through legislation and legal victories, began to dismantle Jim Crow barriers to voting, public accommodations, and equal representation. These protections, when combined with the spending of the War on Poverty and Great Society policy agenda, signaled to many white Americans that the era of inequality had passed. For many African Americans, however, lived reality told a different story, in which discrimination and violence persisted in ways that followed old patterns and forged new ones. In Boston, schools remained segregated and unequal despite the historic passage of the statewide Racial Imbalance Act in 1965; housing remained dilapidated and unaffordable despite the expansion of public housing around the city. A language of Black power increasingly animated local politics as residents called for community control over the poverty program. The year 1967 was marked by protest locally and nationally, including mobilizations in the first months of the year surrounding Mel King's dismissal from USES. It was also a year of uprisings against police violence that put the full value of community organizations on display and confirmed their utility in managing Black urban spaces during periods of crisis.

As entities recognized by both city government and Black residents, RMSC and organizations like it in the Black community helped protect residents during a June 1967 uprising in Roxbury. Several nights of unrest, arrests, and violence erupted in Roxbury after police tried to forcibly remove women protesting welfare cuts from the Roxbury welfare office. The women, organized as the Mothers for Adequate Welfare, staged a sit-in before locking themselves to the office doors with bicycle chains. As supporters assembled outside, word that police officers had started beating the demonstrators inside galvanized observers on the street. A report on the incident noted that officers stationed outside began "to hit [those assembled] with their clubs. . . . As people fell they were kicked and beaten." Throughout the night, rumors of the use of tear gas prompted people to scatter and officers in riot gear marched in phalanx formation while shooting carbines in the air. Community nonprofit leaders worked to protect the demonstrators, dispel tensions, and track those taken in police wagons and ambulances. Nonprofit spaces such as Freedom House, Operation Exodus, and RMSC served as meeting places, from which leaders telephoned the mayor and provided shelter and first aid to those who were injured.[64] The Boston uprising in June elevated RMSC to a more visible role and to an organization offering more than social services, during a period that kicked off a "long, hot, summer" of similar events around the country. The agency later updated its crisis manual should things "bust loose" again, which they would during the 1974 busing crisis.[65]

The National Advisory Commission on Civil Disorders, known colloquially as the Kerner Commission, later affirmed this role of community organizations in its 1968 report on the riots of the previous summer. After surveying 24 of the 167 rebellions reported during the first nine months of 1967, including Boston, the commission famously declared the United States as "moving toward two societies, one Black, one white—separate and unequal." The report, "part exposé of the riots, part history of American racism, and part synthesis of postwar social scientific theory," according to historian Elizabeth Hinton, identified the socioeconomic context of American cities as deeply implicated in the urban unrest.[66] Among other proposed remedies, the commission called for the expansion of multiservice centers and what it called Neighborhood Action Task Forces, entities similar to the APACs deployed in Boston.[67] Urban governance, the report warned, had to find ways to include "effective communication between ghetto residents and local government," "increased accountability of public officials," and "expanded opportunities for indigenous leadership to participate in shaping decisions and policies which affect their community."[68] It was time to bring urban governance closer to the "democratic goal of making government closer and more accountable to the citizen."[69] Hubie Jones and the staff at RMSC agreed, and they had their own clear vision of how to achieve it.

Tackling the policies and practices that shaped Roxbury as a place of segregation and poverty meant moving from individual services to those aimed at strengthening the community as a whole. As one tactic, staff at RMSC devoted new energies to bolstering other organizations around the neighborhoods working with the same people and on the same issues as they were. This approach recognized the policy environment in which these organizations functioned as spaces where public funding reached vulnerable communities, but also that they were spaces where grassroots power grew. RMSC helped start a parent council seeking better education for Black children and provided office space for the Massachusetts Welfare Rights Organization. Seeing a need in Boston's Latinx community, RMSC staffer Frieda Garcia started organizing Spanish-speaking residents and replicated RMSC's multiservice center model by starting a new nonprofit, La Alianza Hispana.[70] La Alianza provided services to the Puerto Rican community of Boston and advocated on their behalf with city agencies to ensure Spanish-speaking children, for example, had their needs met in schools not designed for bilingual instruction.[71] When the leader at a local nonprofit resigned, Jones offered his services on a part-time basis to shore up the organization; and when a fair housing nonprofit faced financial insolvency, RMSC absorbed several of its programs to ensure their continuation.[72] In ways that echoed old ideas about civil society as well as the new centrality of organizations such as RMSC to urban governance, staff saw the expanding network of neighborhood nonprofit entities as both a means and an end.

Jones recognized, too, that building the power of the community required defining and knowing it, and he worked closely with residents to do so. It was an approach that demonstrated both his training in social work with his father's involvement in union organizing and a version of researching far different from that at the Boston Redevelopment Authority. RMSC outlined a seventeen-block area of the Sav-More neighborhood of Roxbury and deployed a neighborhood team including three organizers, a housing specialist, a social worker, a youth worker, and several neighborhood aides to survey residents about their needs and organize community-building activities such as a cleanup campaign. The group also founded a youth center that hired twenty-six teens with the aim of involving them in "the action program for their neighborhood."[73] Even as the focus on a bounded neighborhood geography gave RMSC a definable territory and a constituency, the institutions that kept Sav-More and other areas of Roxbury poor lay beyond neighborhood boundaries. As such, RMSC launched a program to investigate structural problems of displacement from urban renewal, inadequate welfare policies, and the exclusion of students from public school, using those findings to push for policy change at municipal and state levels.[74] The Task Force on Out of School Children, for example, gathered community, university, and government officials and identified regulations that disproportionately excluded Black and Latinx students from the Boston Public Schools for lack of English fluency, behavioral problems, and perceptions of mental disability.[75] Jones later recalled: "It wasn't the kids. It was the school system. The problem was systemic, and something had to be done."[76] The report led to legislation in the commonwealth and set a precedent for federal law that guaranteed children's educational needs were met.

At a time of federal budget cuts for social welfare and what RMSC

identified as a clear federal "retreat from . . . our black ghettos" following the election of Richard Nixon in 1968, RMSC inserted itself as the
governing body for the Sav-More area of Roxbury involved in providing
housing, education, law enforcement and support for Black businesses. It
did so on behalf of government and in the absence thereof, increasingly
turning to the language and philosophy of Black power. Jones launched a
strategic plan in 1969 built around a theory of race-conscious community
development in an effort to better align his organization with where the
Black freedom movement stood at the end of the decade.[77] "The mood
and thrust of the community is drastically different than it was in 1965,"
the report explained, as the Black freedom movement shifted "from an
emphasis on civil rights and integration to an emphasis on Black economic and political power." Lest any doubts remain, staff affirmed: "We
believe in the concepts of black power and community control as means
toward achieving substantial changes in institutions that affect the lives
of residents" and considered nonprofit organizations such as theirs as
providing "the organization of residents which is needed to make these
concepts become living realities."[78] The Boston group echoed language of
activists and organizations in cities such as Oakland, Newark, and Brooklyn and infused these values and politics into their emerging nonprofit
neighborhood.[79]

RMSC lived and amplified these politics through events hosted and
holidays celebrated, aligning community, organization, racial, and political identities. On October 15, 1969, the nonprofit shut down to observe
Vietnam Moratorium Day and held an open workshop on "War and the
Black Community."[80] Staff participated in antiwar protests, highlighted
the deaths of Black soldiers, and tied federal cuts in social services funding to the cost of war.[81] As an organization, RMSC joined a movement
of Black community organizations in Boston to celebrate Malcolm X's
birthday, May 19, as an official agency holiday and hosted a series of community events, including workshops on "Race and Repression," "Nation-
alism and Nation Building," and Black economic development.[82] Local community newsletters featured a column on Black history and encouraged
an accurate "Black count" for the 1970 census.[83] The selection of which
days to celebrate as holidays certainly reflected symbolic choices but also
communicated priorities to Roxbury residents and staff members, for
whom the daily operations of the nonprofit were inextricably wrapped up
in the daily struggle for freedom, justice, and safety.

The pivot toward a more full-throated celebration of Black power and, often, a more confrontational stance against city agencies, did carry risks given the uncertainties and politics of grant funding. RMSC staff routinely had to navigate rules that bound the resources at their disposal and had to constantly weigh the reputational and legal risk of pushing those boundaries. These calculations, however, became even more important and difficult as agency staff expressed growing interest in taking a public stand against the increasing police violence and repression against African Americans in Boston and around the country. Staff members had been pushing for action against state violence and "the level of intimidation and harassment of blacks . . . throughout the nation."[84] They proposed issuing a public service announcement or taking out an advertisement in the *Boston Globe* to build awareness among white readers and solidarity among Black ones, and distributing buttons that read "We Are in Danger." Supportive of the idea, Jones circulated a letter to area nonprofits and individuals to rally support. His letter linked local incidents of repression, including the arrest of a community organizer, Ted Parrish, in the South End, to the recent police murder of Fred Hampton in Chicago as "part of a dangerous process to crush the legitimate anger and political activity of Blacks."[85] Jones won endorsements and donations from over two hundred individuals and organizations for the advertisement—including the local Black Panther Party, the Massachusetts Welfare Rights Organization, and Operation Exodus—confirming a groundswell of support.

Perhaps unsurprisingly, RMSC's board of directors had a different reaction to the staff proposal. In a group where 80 percent of board members resided in Roxbury, their response was one of support for the cause—all the more so after a Boston police officer shot and killed a Black patient at Boston City Hospital in 1970. The officer claimed that, despite a dislocated shoulder, the teenager, Frank Lynch, had lunged at him, prompting the officer to repeatedly discharge his weapon. When the department issued no charges against the officer and took no disciplinary action, RMSC board members volunteered to represent Lynch's mother in a civil complaint.[86] Still, the board remained divided around whether agency funds could support the proposed advertisement.[87] Alan Morse Jr. felt "money raised for the Center should be used for services provided to the Community and not for political purposes," whereas Elma Lewis supported Jones's position, arguing, "Black People have never been safe, we have to support our people." Eventually, in a close vote, the board authorized funds for the advertisement, which ran in April 1970.[88] Text enumerated incidents of harassment of African Americans in Boston and listed RMSC's phone number, encouraging readers to call for more information.[89] Columns of individual and organizational sponsors scrolled across the bottom, communicating solidarity and identifying nonprofits as sites of political engagement and advocacy. Whether or not the advertisement caused a backlash, it did not rise to the occasion of debate at the next RMSC board meeting.[90]

As Jones and his colleagues pushed RMSC in new directions, they used their funding, limited as it was, as a platform to pursue a broader agenda that prioritized the safety and well-being of African Americans. Under other circumstances, the state ought to have provided emergency shelter, food, first aid, communication, and peacekeeping in a crisis, but in these scenarios the state was the oppressor. Statements about "we in the black community" and the importance of voting for "OUR community" on internal and external documents gave RMSC a racial identity, as the organization positioned itself as a defender of Black lives through service provision, research and advocacy, publicity campaigns, and legal representation.[91] They connected specific service areas of education, housing, and welfare to the Black freedom movement and carved out spaces within the confines of grantmaking to embrace an ideology of Black power. Board meetings became places where members debated the merits of building new schools in the Black community versus integrating existing ones, and how and when to signal RMSC's stance on the issue.[92] By engaging in policy advocacy and allying their organization to others in the same struggles while still operating on government grants, Hubie Jones and the RMSC staff created nonprofit neighborhoods as spaces of urban governance. It was a model different from ABCD's, but one that nonetheless elevated the role of neighborhood nonprofit organizations. That such a small entity could simultaneously deliver federal welfare programs and work toward structural change revealed the radical possibilities of the War on Poverty, and its greatest limitations.

From Participation to Control

The War on Poverty's framework of participation as a means of political inclusion left much to be desired, especially when it came to urban renewal and the continued physical and economic development of urban neighborhoods. The kind of participatory deliberation modeled at Freedom House in the early 1960s represented a clear step toward capturing the

preferences of residents living in areas, such as Washington Park, slated
for renewal. Still, gallery walks of renewal maps and town hall–style meetings left the bulk of decision-making power and economic profit in the
hands of BRA officials and private developers. By the end of the decade,
Black power's politics of community control and self-determination bolstered resident demands with a vocabulary and ideology through which
to claim a role in urban redevelopment greater than participation. Residents sought to own and fully control the development process for their
neighborhoods and to maintain economic lives in them. They funneled
their action through a relatively novel form of nonprofit organization: a
community development corporation, or CDC.[93] In the second half of the
1960s, African American and Puerto Rican Bostonians founded CDCs and
presented them as legitimate representative, governing, property-holding
bodies.

After the United South End Settlements rehired Mel King in 1967,
he organized a local citizens group, Community Assembly for a United
South End, or CAUSE, and took to the streets protesting urban renewal
plans for the neighborhood. It was exactly the kind of community organizing he was rehired to do and the kind of political brazenness that had
gotten him fired. The complaints against the BRA's plans for the South
End were familiar: not enough community input and not enough affordable housing. In April 1968, King and his allies in CAUSE protested at
the BRA's downtown offices for four consecutive days before taking over
a parking lot in the South End. The demolition of housing had created an
open parcel, which, until the direct action prevented it, had been used for
parking by suburbanites commuting into the city for work. Hundreds of
community members set up tents to occupy the lot, renaming it Tent City.
Celtics star Bill Russell delivered food to protesters from the soul food
restaurant he owned just a few blocks away in the South End.[94] Boston's
Tent City lasted a few days and ended with promises by the city to replace
the affordable housing that had been cleared. Mel King vowed to carry
the movement to the statehouse and soon launched a campaign for state
representative. Other activists started neighborhood organizations committed to housing and economic development in the South End.[95]

When Mel King and his fellow South Enders took over the Fitz-Inn
parking lot in 1968, the idea of community-driven neighborhood development had been percolating in Boston for a couple of years. As early
as 1963, advocates in the South End considered forming a "development
corporation, supported by the community," but these early conversations,

FIGURE 3.3. *Tent City protests (1968)*. After a series of unsuccessful meetings with the Boston Redevelopment Authority in late April 1968, Mel King and members of the Community Assembly for a United South End blocked access to the Fitz-Inn parking lot in the South End. Protestors used cars and their bodies to prevent suburban commuters from parking, while children held posters saying "BRA Go Away" and "We Shall Not Be Moved." The occupation lasted several days and included the arrest of King and others before a bulldozer cleared away the "Tent City" erected by the protestors. Note King holding a paper bag on the left edge of the image. (Ollie Norton Jr., "CAUSE Preventing Cars from Using Parking Lots on Dartmouth St.," for *Boston Globe*, April 26, 1968, BGLC, NU. Image courtesy of Northeastern University Archives and Special Collections and the Boston Globe.)

led predominantly by white men, focused on the relatively narrow goal of housing redevelopment and justified their effort on purely economic grounds.[96] Only through a nonprofit, they argued, could the public and philanthropic financing be made to work to keep the units affordable to current residents. Similar logic emerged in Washington, though it tended to focus on the potential of community development to promote business development over the housing-centric focus in Boston.[97] These arguments formed a template onto which residents layered an agenda of civil rights and Black power, framing housing not just as a material product but a political, social, and economic one for long-marginalized people.

The first instance of community development in Boston began as an effort to participate in neighborhood planning but quickly evolved into an effort to design, construct, and manage development. In an effort to improve school facilities and transportation networks in the city, planners at the BRA identified the residential neighborhood of Madison Park as an ideal locale to site its Campus High renewal project.[98] To the city, Madison Park's proximity to the center of Boston made it desirable and its designation as a predominantly Black neighborhood made it disposable. When the city revealed its plans in May 1966 to replace fifty-seven acres of the residential neighborhood in Lower Roxbury with expanded roadways and a new high school, however, residents mobilized to fight the clearance.[99] They employed tactics of direct action—including a huge bonfire of illegally dumped trash in Madison Park—and community organizing.[100] Backed with technical expertise from Cambridge-based Urban Planning Aid, a group of planners and architects politically committed to combating top-down renewal programs, residents surveyed the neighborhood about priorities and mapped an alternative set of plans for the designated renewal area, including designs for new affordable housing.[101] The community group formally incorporated as the nonprofit Lower Roxbury Community Corporation (LRCC) in early 1967 in order to access philanthropic funding and enable the possibility of contracting with the BRA.[102]

More than bricks and mortar, LRCC's plans raised concerns about process, reflecting the broader politics of community control at stake in Lower Roxbury and other communities like it. LRCC began lengthy negotiations with the BRA to gain community input into the renewal process, or, as one brochure explained, "to get the new housing built . . . the way we want it."[103] Initially this meant ensuring an adequate supply of affordable housing, but a community newsletter gave voice to a growing suspicion that professional developers prioritized "profit not people." To truly develop the neighborhood in the way the community wanted, residents would need more than a voice. LRCC president Ralph Smith urged residents to attend BRA hearings to demonstrate "what the people of this community want—which is to be their own developers."[104] In early 1967, the BRA conceded to the grassroots demands. In a precedent-setting agreement, the BRA designated LRCC a sponsor-developer for a fifteen-acre area designated for four hundred units of low- and moderate-income housing.[105]

Control over the development process gave residents the power to infuse their identities into the plans in a celebration of the neighborhood's people and outward sign of their political achievement. A small loan from a local foundation enabled LRCC to hire an architect, John

Sharratt, whom the board considered unique among the candidates for his "knowledge of the community and its housing desires" and ability to translate that knowledge into renderings.[106] LRCC materials proudly informed residents about the planned mix of multistory apartment buildings and town houses, a community gathering space, and, to honor the social and cultural heritage of residents, the incorporation of "Southern trees and plants" and "bright-colored flower beds and rock gardens for our people who came from the Caribbean."[107] Beyond the physical infrastructure of the community, LRCC planned to coordinate the provision of social services, business development, education, and housing relocation. This was a group whose board meetings balanced planning for an annual fall festival, dealing with the increasing problem of rats as construction began, and voting on design renderings that narrowed buildings by three feet on each side to stay in compliance.[108] Even as the BRA tried for years to claw back power from the nonprofit, this early victory against the BRA provided a political and organizational blueprint for others around the city.[109]

Following the path forged by LRCC, Puerto Rican residents in the South End organized as the Emergency Tenants' Council (ETC) in 1968 in response to BRA plans for demolition in their neighborhood. The city's plans made little effort to accommodate existing residents, particularly the elderly population, and had accelerated blighting conditions causing health and safety hazards such as illegal trash dumps and no code enforcement.[110] Adopting the motto "We shall not be moved" at a community meeting of four hundred people in June 1968, the group officially incorporated later that summer as a nonprofit community development corporation seeking "new housing . . . controlled by the community" and to be "the sponsors, developers, and managers" of the physical renewal, just as had been done in Lower Roxbury.[111] Residents living within ETC's catchment elected the board of directors in annual elections and received regular bilingual newsletters with updates about redevelopment, social and economic support programs, and cultural events.[112] Initial support and funds came from local religious communities and foundations.[113] Recognizing their effort as a political struggle over the future of their neighborhood, ETC registered new voters and organized residents to show up at city council meetings to demonstrate their strength. In 1969, the BRA designated ETC as the redeveloper for the plot of land known as Parcel 19 in the South End, recognizing the nonprofit as the body that "represents" the community in contracting with the city.[114] In the next municipal

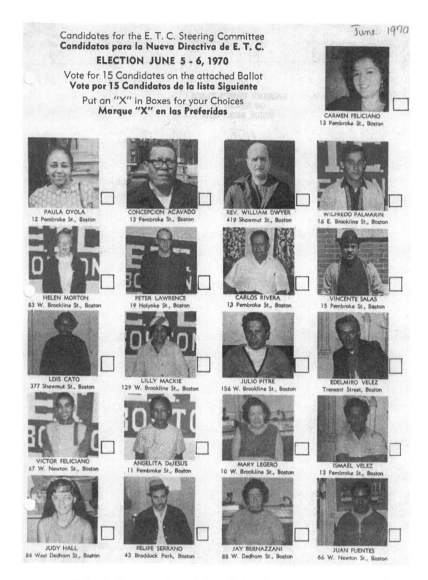

FIGURE 3.4. *Ballot for Emergency Tenants' Council's Board of Directors election (1970).* Organized in 1968 to demand community control over the development of Parcel 19 in the South End, the Emergency Tenants' Council hosted annual elections for its board of directors. This ballot from 1970 is in both English and Spanish given the strong presence of Puerto Rican families in Parcel 19, which the community later named Villa Victoria, or "Victory Village." (ETC Development Corporation, "Candidates for the ETC Steering Committee," June 1970, box 17, folder 72, IBA, NU. Image courtesy of Northeastern University Archives and Special Collections.)

election, poll watchers noticed a 75 percent increase in registered Puerto Rican voters. As architect John Sharratt noted, the mayor "made a smart trade—land for political support."[115]

ETC's redevelopment plans used housing as a canvas to express priorities and identity. Preliminary plans asserted ETC's "right . . . to rebuild their community," "respect for the ethnic character of existing residents," and "meaningfull [sic] participation."[116] The group adopted a five-phase plan for redevelopment that included redirecting traffic to make a more pedestrian-friendly community, a central plaza for gatherings, building of new low-rise town houses for families, and a new nineteen-story building for the elderly. Housing would be for both ownership and rent, at a variety of subsidized and market-rate prices. Leading the charge behind ETC's commitment to rehab roughly 250 units and construct 500 were two brothers, both in their twenties, from Puerto Rico. ETC's executive director, twenty-seven-year-old Israel Feliciano, joined the US Army in 1963 and upon his discharge worked in Chicago before relocating to the South End. His twenty-three-year-old brother, Victor, had moved to the continental United States seven years earlier.[117] The resident-led organization worked with the same architect as LRCC, John Sharratt, who accompanied Israel Feliciano on a visit to his hometown in Puerto Rico and incorporated the design he saw there into the new housing, with traditional Spanish-style slanted tile roofs and pastel colors that mimicked the Victorian homes surrounding Parcel 19. Residents named the development Villa Victoria.[118] Given development rights and having produced architectural plans, the Emergency Tenants' Council now faced the task of financing the construction to fulfill its vision of an improved community. The innovative ways ETC did so set a national example of packaging public and private financing through a community-led organization.

The housing that groups like LRCC and ETC built served, residents hoped, a third purpose beyond the shelter provided and community identity they reinforced. Owning and managing housing meant collecting rents, offering nonprofit organizations a sustainable funding source within their control. Revenue generated through housing redevelopment would, in theory, then underwrite the social services that ETC offered residents. The focus reflected a combination of factors, including the availability of land through ongoing renewal projects, the protest politics through which residents demanded a voice and later control in the redevelopment process, and the seeming predictability of rent as a stable source of income. Housing would serve as a dual social and economic purpose in keeping CDCs afloat and better insulated from the pressures of philanthropic and government funders, even as government programs remained essential to keeping the housing developed subsidized at affordable rates.

This notion that nonprofit community groups might develop revenue streams had attracted Robert Kennedy, then a senator from New York, to the idea of community development corporations. After touring the Bedford-Stuyvesant neighborhood and hearing from resident leaders, he recognized the importance of investment and business in neighborhood-based strategies to reduce poverty. Different proposals emphasized this investment capital as coming from the government or from community residents—often both.[119] The idea won both liberal and conservative support in Washington, DC, for packaging a business sensibility, an exit ramp of government funding, and community empowerment.[120] Kennedy's support led to the inclusion of a rather vague Special Impact Program in the 1966 Economic Opportunity Act as a way to encourage early CDC activities, and mention in the Kerner Commission report, as well as to an ultimately unsuccessful Community Self-Determination Act of 1969.[121] Support came from Black power activists, too, who saw in the fusing of social and economic goals a route to political power and control not yet possible via the War on Poverty. Across the country, CDCs became one vehicle for encouraging what became known as "Black capitalism," as the nonprofit status of these organizations enabled philanthropic and government support to target and reach for-profit minority-owned small businesses.[122] And while housing remained a particularly visible—and particularly complex—focus, it was not the sole focus of CDCs in Boston or elsewhere. Indeed, the first Special Impact grant in Boston went to CIRCLE Associates, formed in 1969 as a nonprofit to support the development of Black business in Boston.[123]

The physical transformation of Parcel 19 into Villa Victoria took nearly a decade, but the social and political work done by establishing ETC and building a nonprofit neighborhood were quickly apparent. Decisions and resources flowed through not just ETC but a growing interlocking network of agencies that shaped the neighborhood. When ETC completed the redevelopment of Parcel 19 nearly ten years later, it existed, according to internal documents, as a "corporate conglomerate" after incorporating for-profit and nonprofit subsidiaries on paper to own, develop, and manage property and to provide social services.[124] The city recognized it as a representative body of the community, and the social cohesion reinforced through design, programming, and linguistic choices marked in multiple ways that this space in the South End was made by and for Puerto Rican residents. ETC, later named Inquilinos Boricuas en Acción, stood at the physical, economic, social, and political center of Villa Victoria, and while it never threw off its financial dependence on government and philanthropic grants, ETC had cemented itself as a private entity with a public governance role.

By the end of the 1960s, mobilization by groups such as the Lower Roxbury Community Corporation and the Emergency Tenants' Council had shifted the political landscape of development in Boston. Demands for community control took new organizational forms in community development corporations. Through these nonprofit vehicles, residents had won development rights to own and manage the physical transformation of their neighborhoods, and they recognized the ability to do so as a step toward claiming more economic and political power in the city. A wave of CDC activities followed in Boston, in which neighborhood groups who had not seen housing and economic development as core to their missions created new nonprofit entities. The Roxbury Multi-Service Center created the Quincy-Geneva Development Corporation to develop housing in the neighborhood; La Alianza Hispana, itself a product of another multiservice agency, created the Nuestra Comunidad CDC; and several neighborhood groups under Action for Boston Community Development created their own development corporations over the next decade.[125] They did so as a response as much to meet the needs of residents for affordable housing as to meet their own organizational pressures of revenue, seeing emancipatory potential in redevelopment.

Conclusion

African Americans in Boston, as elsewhere, had been envisioning a more equal future and had been using nonprofit organizations to help make that vision a reality for centuries by the time the US government sought to more directly engage these entities. For people whose race served as a barrier to access public-sector services and privileges, racial identity also served as a defining characteristic of the alternative private sector. Black men and women invested socially, politically, and economically through gifts of time, talent, and treasure to build their own institutions that could supplement an exclusionary democratic system and thus promote change. These patterns of organization building paralleled the long fight for freedom and nurtured it forward from the eighteenth century into the postwar period of the twentieth. The emphasis on nonprofit involvement in urban governance during the 1960s reflected policies designed to decentralize social welfare goods and services, but it was equally a product of local activism that demanded resources and authority for community organizations.

The War on Poverty's investment in private community organizations came as a welcome opportunity for both recognition and resources, especially to those historically barred from government support. Government grants underwrote service provision at the neighborhood level, engaged residents as board members, and hired others as part- and full-time staff. It was a governance revolution that infused public dollars and the authority to deploy them into private organizations by imposing an organizational framework atop the urban landscape of neighborhoods. Yet, in American cities characterized by segregation, neighborhoods carried not just a spatial designation but a racial one as well. The approach to governing urban areas that emerged over the 1960s thus fused via both policy and local implementation organizational, racial, and neighborhood identities. This pairing—what signaled to everyone in Boston that, for example, the Roxbury Multi-Service Center was a Black organization and the John F. Kennedy Multi-Service Center in Charlestown was a white organization—provided the outlines for nonprofit neighborhoods, which residents in predominantly Black neighborhoods then legitimized through their demands for control and their work in these organizations. Public-private partnerships were not exclusively for Black neighborhoods, as those in charge of Boston's anti-poverty program weighed political calculations to ensure dollars moved to white neighborhoods of Charlestown and South Boston as often as to Roxbury and the South End. Still, the movement of government dollars into organizations embedded in the city's Black communities carried particular resonance in the long fight for freedom, though it held no guarantees of whether this new governance system would reduce or reinforce patterns of exclusion.

The element of choice characteristic of grantmaking meant that Black residents had to mobilize to ensure the organizations they trusted and claimed an ownership of received funding through institutional channels inaugurated under the War on Poverty. This mobilization took visible forms through protests and campaigns as well as more hidden forms such as participation in board meetings and applying for grants—and it produced mixed results. The demand for more meaningful and inclusive participation in ABCD, for example, won a restructured board of directors that added more seats for community representatives yet simultaneously reduced the power of that body in official decision-making. Resident-led governing councils, embodied in Boston by Area Planning and Action Councils, oversaw neighborhood anti-poverty programs, while the decisions they made remained subject to approval from above. Grants enabled neighborhood nonprofits to provide supplemental programs but also limited how, where, and for whom to deliver the programs.

Despite these cyclical waves of expanding and contracting power, residents found ways to harness what resources and authority they did capture in pursuit of broader goals, which remained a contested and evolving target. As the Black freedom movement shifted over the 1960s to increasingly call for not just integration of African Americans into predominantly white institutions and spaces but also Black control over those arenas, so, too, did the momentum of organizational activities shift. Black residents in Boston wanted more than a seat at the table; they wanted to control the table. Hubie Jones and his colleagues at the Roxbury Multi-Service Center found ways to use the organization as a platform to push municipal agencies such as the departments overseeing schools, police, and welfare. In direct and indirect ways that sometimes drew on resources provided by government grants, the organization provided infrastructure for local activism. In doing so, it demonstrated that neighborhood nonprofits were more than service providers; they were sources of leadership, advocacy, and support beyond the narrow programs they were contracted to deliver.

There were critics of Jones's tactics at RMSC and tensions, too, as staff tried to balance personal and professional identities and the pressures of funding and change in a segregated city. People navigated the funding environment that increasingly shaped their urban areas in various ways, and some completely rejected it, launching their own alternative funding structures. Following the assassination of Martin Luther King Jr. in 1968, a group called the Boston Black United Front called for ABCD to be "abolished as an umbrella agency in the Black Community" with full oversight transferred to neighborhood-based, Black-led organizations.[126] With donations from a handful of white suburban donors, the group launched a grassroots foundation to support Black organizations and small businesses, prioritizing groups that did not receive aid through ABCD. Another group sought to challenge the power of the funding group United Community Services, a precursor to the United Way, by launching a United Black Appeal to encourage workplace giving directly to Black organizations.[127] These efforts included men such as Hubie Jones and Mel King, who balanced participation in federal programs with an outright critique of them, and revealed the diversity of politics and approaches to the new landscape of private provision of public services. Despite disagreements about the full emancipatory potential of government grants, a shared commitment to working through nonprofit organizations united these efforts.

With a range of visions of what the system might look like and what kind of future they could deliver, a resounding message emanated from the grassroots that validated the kind of approach policy had outlined and called for more funding, authority, and trust in private nonprofit organizations. Nonprofit neighborhoods required this level of local endorsement as much as they required the policy apparatus to become a politically legitimate means of governing urban areas and responding to crises that arose in a period of municipal austerity, economic precarity, and racial inequality. The radical potential of the War on Poverty lay in its support of private organizations, which residents turned into platforms to critique the social, political, and economic order and connected to local and national movement activism. To varying degrees, nonprofit neighborhoods were Black-controlled spaces when few existed and, even more powerfully, Black governing spaces when even fewer of those existed, if at all. At a time when so many called out for the promises of democracy to be made real, government support of nonprofit organizations seemed one route to achieve this.

CHAPTER FOUR

The Bureaucrats

In November 1967, the *Boston Globe* broke its own rule. Not since 1896, when William Jennings Bryan ran against William McKinley for president, had the *Globe* endorsed a candidate in a local, state, or national election. Boston's mayoral election of 1967, however, seemed too important and unpredictable to sit quiet, so the editorial board endorsed Kevin White over Louise Day Hicks. Before the editorial even described the two candidates, it described the city itself: "The problems of the city are real," it read. "They are the potholes in the street, the smell from the sewer, education for the children so they can have it better than their parents. The problems are the elimination of slums, good rubbish collection, a decent salary for the police officer so that he will not have to work a second job to support his family." The editorial noted "opportunities" and "progress in the last decade," but an uprising in Roxbury just a few months prior suggested "trouble" lay ahead too. It was a local mayoral race that, to many, served as a referendum on civil rights in the North. Coverage of the election reached newspaper readers in Los Angeles, Detroit, New York, and Baltimore, while British viewers followed coverage on the BBC.[1]

Though still a relatively unknown figure when he ran for mayor in 1967, Kevin White seemed destined for political office. His father and grandfather had both served as Boston City Council presidents, and he married the daughter of William Galvin, another former city council president. At the young age of thirty-one, White won a statewide election to be the commonwealth's secretary of state, thanks largely to the support of his father and father-in-law at the 1960 Democratic Party nominating convention. Many speculated—correctly—that White's interest in the mayoralty was strategic, setting him up for higher office down the road.

On the campaign trail, White walked a careful political line, both criticizing the school system and raising concerns about busing as a remedy to its current ills. He seemed a blank slate compared to the hard-line message of his opponent, Louise Day Hicks of South Boston. Her slogan, "You know where I stand," barely veiled her position on race and education and her staunch opposition to busing.[2] As a school committee member in the early 1960s, she became a household name in Boston by refusing to acknowledge any race-based discrepancies in the school system and vocally opposing the statewide Racial Imbalance Act of 1965.[3] Hicks won the open mayoral primary in September, beating second-place finisher White and a wider field that included former Boston Redevelopment Authority chief Ed Logue and other familiar faces from the Massachusetts statehouse. The fear that Hicks, the most divisive candidate in Boston's recent history, might win drove the *Globe*'s endorsement.

As the anti-Hicks choice, White campaigned on a vision for the city that sought to meet the political moment and appeal to a city divided. He pledged to bring municipal government to the people, promising, among other things, to set up "Little City Halls" around the city. Such neighborhood-centric rhetoric certainly echoed that of Mayor Collins in 1960 but reversed the promise Collins had made to bring people into government. White's commitment to decentralize city administration and govern at the neighborhood level responded to the intense parochialism and segregation that still gripped Boston during an era of change. His approach rhetorically and, in time, administratively, was not to break down those rigid boundaries but to empower people within them. This endorsement of neighborhood governance appeared responsive to the demands of majority Black neighborhoods angered at the persistent failures of the government to undo patterns of structural exclusion and energized by calls for community control as well as majority white neighborhoods resistant to policies of integration and protective of the institutions that advantaged them. Talk of government decentralization may not have fired up voters, but the political ideology such campaign rhetoric represented helped assemble a coalition in an uncertain time. On November 7, 1967, a narrow majority of Bostonians elected Kevin White as the city's next mayor.

Once in office, White reinvented the work of municipal government and made good on his promises of decentralization. He did so as a political and pragmatic response to the times when segregation persisted, fiscal crisis threatened, and a rising conservative tide loomed, and with the help of federal policies passed under both Democratic and Republican administrations that translated a preference for localism into policy.[4] Though Nixon became more associated with devolutionary policies that pushed resources and authority down the federalist ladder, it was Johnson who first experimented with such tactics in his Model Cities program and Law Enforcement Assistance Administration. These programs rewarded lower tiers of government testing new approaches to the urban crises of poverty, protest, and crime, simultaneously extending federal support while framing those problems as fundamentally local ones. Johnson's liberal version of devolution and decentralization laid an intellectual and administrative foundation for Nixon to further experiment with Community Development Block Grants, revenue sharing, and other funding mechanisms that solidified the federal government's retreat from American cities. Shifting politics and policies at the federal level left much to be desired by mayors such as White, but they created opportunities too.[5] Federal grant dollars that had once gone directly to neighborhood nonprofits now passed through the hands of state and local governments.

Mayor White's embrace of neighborhoods masked a centralizing trend in his administration that increased the power and reach of city hall. Charged with making funding decisions and monitoring the work of both municipal agencies and neighborhood nonprofit organizations, city hall became a powerful choke point for funding related to urban development, poverty reduction, law enforcement, and employment. It did so amid a changing economic landscape in Boston and nationally, and in a period of intense racial violence in Boston that preceded and followed the desegregation of public housing, schools, and parks. White responded to these circumstances with the new tools at his disposal, doubling down on the involvement of nonprofit organizations and consolidating power over them in municipal government. Doing so allowed Boston to diversify public services without dismantling hierarchies of race, to meet the needs of minority populations without altering the practices of government, and to distribute spoils without ceding power. Nonprofit neighborhoods became useful constructs to city hall. No longer a tool for experimentation or solving the problems facing US cities, public grantmaking became a means for Boston's mayor and municipal government to shore up their own political power and manage the consequences of racial and economic segregation and underinvestment in urban neighborhoods.

Little City Halls, Big City Hall

Bostonians rarely praise New York City, but Mayor White looked to it for policy inspiration. The idea of Little City Halls belonged to John Lindsay, who, as mayor of New York City, launched a program bearing that name in 1966. As did many proposals of that decade, it began as an effort to moderate racial hostilities. After Lindsay and his staff found success brokering an understanding between African American and Italian communities in East Manhattan, he saw the potential of setting up municipal offices around the city as places for residents to air grievances and interact with city officials. Lindsay ended up with a smaller program than many had hoped, but he still used his seat on the national Kerner Commission to promote the reform effort as a way to prevent future urban uprisings.[6] In Boston, Kevin White adopted the idea, hoping his version of Little City Halls might mitigate racial tensions without becoming known as a program for Black neighborhoods. Attempts to decentralize the most basic tasks of municipal government and appear responsive to citizen concerns, however, concealed changes in his administration that pulled in an opposite direction. While White spoke a language of neighborhoods, his actions centralized governing authority within his office as handpicked bureaucrats increasingly oversaw the federal grant programs that kept the city afloat.

In 1967, White campaigned to bring government closer to the people and approached the mayoralty with what one observer called a "deeply personal style of political leadership."[7] He developed a practice of going on "walking tours" of the various neighborhoods and listening to the residents' concerns. The tours made for good optics and good politics, which a writer for the *Boston Globe* likened to a "scene right out of the Enchanted Village, Boston's municipal Santa Claus heard all the good men and women."[8] Only thirty-eight years old at the time of his election, White cut a sleek profile walking through the neighborhoods—an image more recently memorialized in a bronze statue of White at Boston's Faneuil Hall—that intentionally or not, starkly contrasted with his predecessor, John Collins, a wheelchair user. In more substantive ways, too, White differentiated himself from Collins, whose 1960 promise to "plan with the people" seemed by 1967 only partially enacted.

As interested in reducing political alienation as he was in actually improving service delivery, White sought to build government outposts in residential neighborhoods.[9] These visible, accessible municipal offices would provide, he reasoned, "flexibility, coordination, speed, expertise, convenience to citizens, and most important of all, coordination of city services."[10] These Little City Halls in Boston would be information nodes both for residents to gain referrals and basic services and for administrators to investigate needs related to municipal service delivery (street lighting, trash collection, police, traffic lights, playgrounds, social services) and send information back to city hall about problems in the neighborhoods.[11] They were to be offices where citizens could learn about their government, and the government could learn about its citizens. They were not, however, places where decisions were made or even debated. Mayor White even admitted as such, noting, "They don't have any power.... They are dependent on me."[12]

After Louise Day Hicks's supporters dubbed her opponent "Mayor Black" during the election season, White actively worked to ensure this signature program avoided any association with race and adopted the program citywide.[13] He argued that "a pothole is as much a nuisance in East Boston as it is in Roxbury," and in July 1968, he opened the first Little City Halls with four staff people and a mobile trailer in traditionally white ethnic neighborhoods of East Boston and Brighton.[14] This assessment missed the reality that a pothole was likely to get fixed more quickly in East Boston than in Roxbury and departed somewhat from the recommendations of the recently released Kerner Commission report, which urged the establishment of municipal outposts in urban ghettos as a "significant opportunity to accomplish the democratic goal of making government closer and more accountable to the citizen."[15] Still, the ordering of openings made political sense to Mayor White, and in the fall of 1968, Boston's fourth Little City Hall finally opened in a predominantly Black neighborhood of Roxbury, where residents and research had long pointed to the inadequacies of municipal services.

Officially called Neighborhood Service Centers, Boston's Little City Halls made themselves useful to residents. They offered a range of quotidian services and strove to be more than mere complaint centers. In an op-ed to the *Boston Globe*, White's appointee to head the program outlined the range of services residents could expect, including making payments on water and sewer bills, paying municipal taxes and filing for tax abatements, applying for public housing, registering to vote, and getting marriage and death certificates.[16] Bureaucrats in the outposts responded to problems, dispatching inspectors to look at frozen pipes, maintenance workers to clear storm drains, and parks crews to fell downed tree limbs. Nearly all the centers fielded calls about housing issues—about the quality of public housing, absentee landlords, code enforcement, assessment issues—though the Roxbury branch also saw regular calls about police violence and mistreatment. Research at the time noted that Little City Halls tended to benefit those with higher incomes, especially homeowners, whose complaints were more easily remedied than those needing to tackle decades of discrimination and segregation.[17] Nevertheless, the bureaucrats handled a wide range of calls and built up a referral list of neighborhood nonprofits.

Residents also brought concerns that fell outside the jurisdiction of the street-level bureaucrats who staffed the neighborhood offices. In those situations, staff had a ready list of neighborhood nonprofits whose services might match what residents needed and could take the complainant off the city's hands. In Jamaica Plain, for example, a growing drug problem increased the referrals city staff made to youth service providers. The Little City Hall in the South End shared a building with the South End Health Center, and in Chinatown the outpost collaborated with Chinese American organizations.[18] Taken together, these referrals from the government to nonprofit service providers moved one researcher to call the Little City Halls "organizational catalysts" that knit new governing relationships at the neighborhood and city levels. Each referral by Little City Halls staff members defined the boundaries of what did or did not fall within the city's purview, even as it legitimized and noted the citizens' concerns. It was as much in these mobile trailers as it was in the changing funding arrangements that nonprofits began to forge local governing ties with the city government.

Those following the spotlight Mayor White shone on neighborhoods might have missed another set of activities occurring in his administration. Back at city hall, the mayor assembled a team noted for being flush with talented, bright men—and in time, some women—to head municipal agencies. For a city whose politics has been so dominated by the Irish political machine, surprisingly few of White's cabinet members were from Boston. A perfect storm of political winds brought the group together, though the higher than typical municipal salaries that White offered helped, too. Some had joined White's campaign to help defeat Louise Day Hicks; others found themselves as unemployed Democrats given the rising Republican tide nationally; and others were connected to Harvard University, where Samuel Huntington, government department chair, advised White on hiring. A young Barney Frank, who would later become a stalwart of the Democratic Party as a US representative from Massachusetts, for example, took time off from his doctoral studies at Harvard to join the city staff as the mayor's secretary and right-hand man.[19] Few of those hired knew White before 1967, but they functioned as an informal cabinet, gathering on Wednesday mornings to discuss policy before work in a room adjoining White's office. This was no distribution of power to those typically without it, but a consolidation and creation of power among highly educated, professional, politically savvy, predominantly white men.

White deputized each of his cabinet members with new responsibilities and roles that centralized power in his office, particularly as it related to government grantmaking. As head of the Office of Public Service, Daniel Finn oversaw the Little City Hall program and served as a direct conduit of information to and from the mayor. Other cabinet members gained their enhanced roles thanks to federal funds, which under Johnson and then under Nixon increasingly passed through the hands of municipal agencies. Johnson had initially tested decentralizing or devolutionary approaches with Model Cities legislation in 1966 and the Omnibus Crime Control and Safe Streets Act of 1968. These two programs distributed monies to states and cities, giving those governments the responsibility to allocate funds locally, in stark contrast to the majority of urban renewal funds, which went to quasi-public agencies such as the BRA, and the War on Poverty, which went directly to nonprofit community action agencies. Mayors had, to varying degrees, always maintained some influence over those earlier programs, but now they had a recognized key role in not only overseeing local funds but in distributing them. To help him do so, White created several new positions and offices, all of which fell under his mayoral cabinet. There was the Mayor's Office of Criminal Justice to oversee funds from the Law Enforcement Assistance Administration, the Community Development Agency to oversee Model Cities, and, a few years later, offices to manage the Community Development Block Grants and the Comprehensive Employment and Training Agency. It was the men who led these offices that surrounded White each Wednesday morning, debating policy, distributing resources, and running the city.

Little City Halls presented a new face of government at the neighborhood level, helping the mayor seem responsive to the needs of residents during a period of escalating racial and political tension in Boston. Appearances, however, did not tell the full story. Behind the veneer of decentralization, White's time in office was one of considerable, though somewhat hidden, centralization of control. Federal policy increasingly vested grantmaking powers in lower tiers of government that gave mayors like White the ability to grow their governance apparatus without growing the size of government. It was an opportunity White seized, strategically insulating his bureaucratic decision-making in a nearly all-white cabinet and farming out implementation to neighborhood nonprofits as the appropriate spaces of inclusivity, diversity, and problem management.

A Model City

Lyndon Johnson had high hopes for the Demonstration Cities and Metropolitan Development Act of 1966. It was supposed to solve a variety of problems that had become visible in the early stages of the War on Poverty and become a signature program for the newly created cabinet agency for housing and urban development. The legislation, however, got off to a rocky start. Concerns that the word *demonstration* in the legislation's title had become synonymous with the words *protest* and *riot* prompted a quick rebrand into Model Cities. The name change encapsulated a larger uncertainty about the goals and purpose of a program that aimed to improve the grantmaking that increasingly characterized federal policy with yet another experimental grant program. With nearly $1 billion in authorized federal funds, White eagerly sought a share of the pie. Boston officials submitted an application that extended many of the ideas behind the Little City Halls, as well as the tensions encompassed therein. Washington bureaucrats continued to smile favorably on Boston's proposals, supporting the city with planning and general funding to improve city governance. For its Model City, Boston then built a nonprofit neighborhood.

A large percentage of the early War on Poverty funding had gone to cities—as it had under urban renewal and the Juvenile Delinquency and Youth Control Act—but the US federal government lacked both an overt federal urban policy agenda and a means of driving it. With cities increasingly seen as a problem, not to mention a core base of the Democratic Party, Lyndon Johnson created a cabinet-level Department of Housing and Urban Development (HUD) in 1965 and formed a task force to review federal aid to cities and develop a signature program for the new department.[20] Chaired by political scientist Robert Wood, the group found what seemed to be an incongruity between rising expenditures in federal grant programs and worsening conditions in American cities. Such a finding would hardly have surprised grassroots activists and urban mayors, but it came as a shock to technocrats who had optimistically hoped that federal investments in anti-poverty programs would improve urban conditions.

Members of Wood's task force were alone neither in surveying the federal funding landscape nor in their surprise discovering substantial increases in its amount and complexity over the postwar period. One of several commissions on intergovernmental relations in the 1950s and 1960s calculated that federal grants-in-aid had been stable at $2 billion in 1940 and 1950, then rose to $7 billion in 1960 and $11 billion only five years later.[21] Such growth represented increased expenditures on urban renewal as well as War on Poverty and Great Society programs related to education, health, and social security. Moreover, the number of federal grant programs was on the rise, up from 161 in 1962 to 429 seven years later.[22] Taken together, these figures reveal a growing federal government that continued to rely on lower tiers of government and private partners for policy implementation. These findings stunned members of the task force, who, in their final report, expressed as much concern with *how* the federal government operated as on *what* it did.[23] The US government had become, in the words of sociologist Elisabeth Clemens, a cumbersome and inefficient "Rube Goldberg state" that appeared to be failing to solve the crisis of American cities.[24] A loose consensus on the problems did not, however, translate into an obvious policy solution.

The range of metaphors used to describe what cities needed reveals the confusion that permeated the Model Cities program from its conception and implementation through to historical accounts of the initiative.[25] Labor leader and task force member Walter Reuther initially proposed an "urban TVA" modeled on the Depression-era Tennessee Valley Authority to be tested, he proposed, in a single city of Detroit. Staff members in the Johnson White House wrote elsewhere of neighborhood service centers or "one-stop shops" with public and private services akin to Boston's Roxbury Multi-Service Center.[26] Others saw Model Cities entities as newer versions of the urban renewal agencies, with the accompanying power of eminent domain and the ability to issue grants and loans to individuals for housing rehabilitation.[27] Still others pitched Model Cities primarily as an employment program, drawing on the "new careers" theory popular at the time that promoted employment in the fields of health, education, and welfare as an antidote to deindustrialization.[28] Tellingly and characteristic of midcentury liberalism, the task force downplayed the roles of racism and capitalism as linked social and political-economic forces in urban decline. In a classic example of 1960s-era policy making, the final legislation captured this uncertainty.

Enacted in November 1966, the legislation Johnson signed for Model Cities functioned as a flexible pot of dollars that cities could tap with "new and imaginative proposals" blending strategies of physical development from urban renewal with social development from the War on Poverty's community action.[29] Municipalities were to devise new governing systems, test them in a defined area with 10 percent of the city population, and use

Model Cities funding to supplement and better coordinate existing federally sponsored programs. Preliminary research identified at least forty-four federal grant programs cities might streamline under Model Cities.[30] Efforts proven to be effective at the neighborhood level would, in theory, get scaled up to the citywide level under Model Cities, though the funding for that scaling up remained just as elusive as it had been for earlier generations of demonstration programs. To win enough votes to pass the legislation, the policy makers broadened Model Cities substantially from Reuther's initial proposal, spreading the available dollars farther and thinner.[31] The final legislation allowed up to 150 cities or metropolitan areas of differing sizes to participate, immediately creating a climate of scarcity and competition to those eager for funding.[32] The mayors of Newark, Detroit, Chicago, New York, and Cleveland endorsed the legislation and testified in support, hoping to curry favor for their forthcoming requests.[33]

Boston's application for Model Cities exposed the political uncertainty surrounding the 1967 mayoral election and distrust of city government by Black residents following tension over the city's anti-poverty programs. City officials had started planning for Model Cities early in 1967, when the mayoral election was still months away, the field of candidates remained large, and Mayor Collins sat quiet about his intentions to either run again or retire. Collins took what he saw as an obvious step in tapping the heads of the Boston Redevelopment Authority and Action for Boston Community Development as the agencies to lead Boston's Model Cities application.[34] After all, these entities had proven adept at winning federal funds and represented the physical and social renewal programs that Model Cities sought to unite. He did so, however, in the aftermath of protests around Mel King's dismissal from United South End Services and in the months before the June uprising in Roxbury. The choice to exclude resident voices, particularly of Black residents, in the Model Cities application became a willful or ignorant misstep.

As they had numerous times before, African American leaders in the city mobilized residents to claim their federally mandated right to "widespread citizen participation in the [Model Cities] program."[35] Two public meetings in April each drew over five hundred attendees.[36] The question came down, as it always did, to control and whether it would rest in the hands of an appointed board of citizen representatives according to the mayor's proposal or an elected board as demanded by the community. Ultimately, the decision went to the city council, which had to ratify the city's application before submission to Washington. On its third vote, the council passed a resolution put forward on behalf of a community coalition by Tom Atkins, a civil rights activist who that fall would be elected as the first Black member of the city council, to create an eighteen-member body of elected representatives to design and oversee the Model Cities program.[37] In a clear snub to Mayor Collins, the resolution granted the board the "right to approve" Model City proposals by the city.[38] It was a bold move and a huge step toward community control. As a true public-private entity, the Model Neighborhood Board, as the new group was named, existed as a publicly chartered private organization that hired staff with a share of the Model City funds.[39] According to the city, the group embodied "a new concept in community-level government" and was later celebrated as "a radical experiment in community power" as Boston represented one of the few, if not only, programs nationally, that gave both oversight and implementation powers to an elected group of residents.[40] The election of the Model Neighborhood Board later produced one of the most diverse and representative governing bodies in the city.[41]

Boston's application promised to make a designated Model City area an "urban laboratory," testing new approaches to service delivery that emphasized public-private partnerships.[42] It was one of fifteen applications from Massachusetts in a pool of 190 national submissions to make the May 1967 deadline.[43] Boston's Model Neighborhood Area linked Roxbury, North Dorchester, and Jamaica Plain and was divided into six subareas. As a manufactured zone comprised of racially segregated neighborhoods, the area made for good politics and was fittingly artificial for Boston's "laboratory." It was also, one application summarized, an area that had "not aged gracefully" over the years.[44] In the Model Neighborhood, residents had incomes 20 percent below the citywide average and male unemployment hovered 50 percent below citywide averages. Residents were five times more likely to be employed as domestic workers, twice as likely to work in the service industry, and 50 percent more likely to work in unskilled manufacturing than residents in another areas.[45] Unquestionably, poverty physically and socially defined the area as residents struggled to find work and earn wages sufficient to meet the rising costs of housing. This was a problem neither unique to Boston's Model Neighborhood nor one whose causes lay within its boundaries. Even as the strict designation focused resources into high-need areas, it set a specious expectation that these problems might be remedied through local activity.

With Model Cities, Boston tested a new approach to urban governance that simultaneously furthered the city's reliance on local nonprofits and

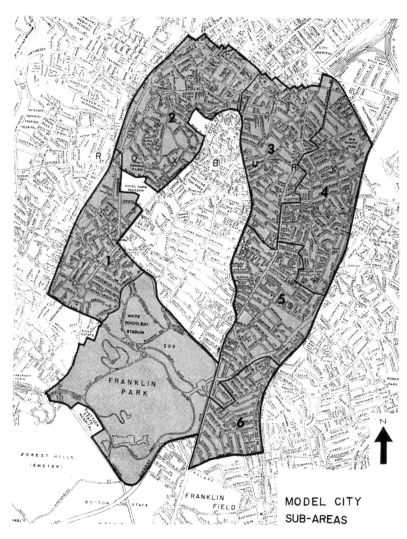

FIGURE 4.1. *Boston's Model City (ca. 1968).* Boston's Model City comprised six subareas and resembled a doughnut. The area in the middle, Washington Park, had received significant federal investment via urban renewal, so Boston used the program of Model Cities to coordinate the physical, economic, and social investments of the surrounding neighborhoods via a new governance model. ("Model City Sub-Areas," Employee Guidebook," box 117A, Model Cities Collection, Boston City Archives. Image courtesy of Boston City Archives.)

enhanced the municipal government's role in coordinating and overseeing those efforts. The application outlined a dual strategy of individual improvement to address "the fundamental problem of dependency, alienation, and inadequate income" and institutional reform to strengthen the "quality of services now delivered to the community."[46] This framework suggested an understanding of poverty that blamed people and governing structures, and responded with a plan to change both through partnerships with neighborhood nonprofits across a range of issues, including housing, public facilities, health, education, crime and delinquency, recreation and culture, social services, jobs and income, relocation, design and planning, and participation. In each of its program areas, the city government planned to outsource many tasks to nonprofits, boasting that this experiment in decentralization and privatization would produce "no loss of efficiency" while appearing responsive and flexible to citizen preferences. The Boston application, over a year in the making, highlighted the existing strength of the nonprofit sector in the target neighborhood that had been bolstered through earlier federal programs, explaining that residents "have channeled their efforts into numerous self-help enterprises, mainly neighborhood action organizations and small social agencies."[47] Such language uplifted the work of grassroots organizations while also naturalizing their presence as a means of governing the resource-deprived Model Neighborhood.

Even as Boston's Model Cities program recognized the contributions of neighborhood nonprofits and even as the Model Neighborhood Board gained unprecedented powers over the demonstration program, the city government held a central role in the program. Both the federal administrative structure of Model Cities and the design of the Boston experiment framed a new role for city government as grant manager that set the stage for a wider shift in the municipality's governance over the long run. When Model Cities funds actually arrived in Boston in 1969, Kevin White ran city hall. He recognized the program as another opportunity to respond to demands for community control and diversity in city government as well as to consolidate his office's reach. White created a new city department, the City Demonstration Agency, to oversee the federal program and appointed Paul Parks, an African American engineer trained at Purdue, as the head of the agency.[48]

Parks brought little policy or bureaucratic experience to the post but was known as a leader in the local civil rights movement. He had grown up in Indiana with a Native American father who was a veteran disabled during World War I and an African American mother who fought for anti-lynching bills for most of her life. She often insisted on keeping the shades drawn to prevent people from shooting into the house. At the prompting of a math teacher, Parks enrolled in the civil engineering program at Purdue University, and when the United States entered World War II, he expected university enrollment would exempt him from the draft. Parks's reputation for trying to desegregate dormitories and local restaurants, however, moved Purdue's dean to actively recommend Parks for service as a punishment to get him off campus. Parks survived both the war and the segregated military and, on returning to Purdue, continued to fight for civil rights. He organized to move Black and Jewish students out of the university's International House and into traditional dormitories, and he was arrested trying to desegregate the local movie theater. Parks later reflected, "It's hard to explain to people . . . what the impact of being discriminated against meant."[49] After working at the state highway commission in Indiana, he took a job at an architecture firm in Boston and then founded his own engineering firm. Volunteer work, however, soon overshadowed Parks's professional identity, as he became involved in the local NAACP's decades-long fight to desegregate the Boston public schools. As the Boston School Committee appeared increasingly intransigent, Mayor White offered Parks an opportunity to shape a different branch of municipal government through the Model Cities experiment. He started by shaping the City Demonstration Agency's full team of 240 municipal workers as the only city department to have majorities of Black and female employees.[50]

Though the Model Neighborhood Board retained the authority to approve contracts, the job of monitoring them fell to bureaucrats in city government, who gained a significant control over nonprofits that worked on behalf of the city. Parks's team became a choke point between HUD and community groups, monitoring contacts, tracking data, evaluating programs, and sending regular progress reports to Washington. While some of Boston's Model Cities contracts went to for-profit corporations and city agencies, most went as grants to neighborhood nonprofits for program activities ranging from recreation and youth services to economic development, adult education, legal services, housing, health care delivery, day care centers, elder services, and ambulance services.[51] These negotiations, Boston staff reported to HUD, moved slowly and "represent a large expenditure of staff time."[52] In its first year, the city managed $4 million in subcontracts for goods, services, and personnel for Model Cities.[53] By the third year, the budget swelled to more than $7.5 million.[54] Such growth indicated not an influx of federal funds but a rerouting of funds already within Boston's city government to administer more resources through the City Demonstration Agency and build up the reach of this department. In many ways, this power replicated in the city government that which ABCD had over its grantees through other War on Poverty programs.

The city's grantmaking authority over the array of neighborhood non-profits in the Model Neighborhood afforded the local government a window into the affairs and information of private organizations, and power over them. Such power manifested in quotidian details, such as stipulations for operating hours at the Federated Dorchester Neighborhood House's teen center and what recreational activities it offered on a city contract.[55] It appeared in the processing of grant contracts, as delays in contract approval, short contract periods, and the slow transfer of funds created interruptions in service delivery and staff turnover for nonprofits. Mothers Tutoring Mothers, for example, struggled to retain staff, and La Alianza Hispana reported "agency cash flow problems . . . as we float around without a contract."[56] The authority the city now held over its nonprofit partners in the Model Neighborhood manifested in more indirect ways as well. To prepare the federal reports, the city built reporting requirements into its grants, proposing a "federated information system" of data sharing between public and private agencies.[57] As is standard in grantmaking arrangements, nonprofits had to submit monthly invoices, narrative reports from each department, and copies of all intake forms with details about individuals seeking assistance.[58] Yet by embedding grantmaking in the city government, these program reports made the Model Neighborhood legible to government bureaucrats in both Boston and Washington, DC. City hall gained unprecedented access to the inner financial, programmatic, and administrative workings of the private organizations across the city.

The city did more than just look; it soon began to shape the internal workings of nonprofits. Though the Model Neighborhood Board remained outside city government, it nonetheless offered technical assistance to over seventy organizations in the designated area on how to write proposals, execute a contract, and organize new programs so as to better comply with city regulations.[59] HUD flooded grantee cities with sample forms, budgets, and manuals that standardized Model Cities agencies across cities as well as further systematized contracting, data collection, and reporting between city governments and nonprofit partners.[60] While still present, the boundaries between public and private were becoming harder to discern, sometimes even raising legal challenges. Labor disputes, it turned out,

became a complicated arena as organizations debated whether city employment regulations around insurance, hiring, and pensions applied to those
paid by Model Cities funds but who worked at contracted nonprofits.[61]

By the time Model Cities wrapped up funding and programming in
Boston in the mid-1970s, it was hard to assess what had changed for the
Model Neighborhood. At an individual level, some changes were meaningful. Small grants and loans for housing rehabilitation improved the financial footing of those able to own their home.[62] Extended programming
for young people provided important opportunities for tutoring, summer
employment, recreation, and cultural awareness. Elders received services
thanks to Model Cities funding, as did children with speech and language
delays.[63] Community organizers made contact with individuals and drummed
up attendance at neighborhood meetings to discuss local priorities.[64] Programs helped patch holes in the city's traditional operations. La Alianza
Hispana used funds to "inform Spanish speaking residents" about city
government and to develop a bilingual curriculum for the Boston Public
Schools.[65] In Roxbury, funds paid for training for residents in park maintenance, who then performed 95 percent of all such services in Roxbury
during the Model Cities program.[66] The larger initiatives planned for in
Boston's Model Neighborhood—such as new family day care centers, neighborhood health clinics, and economic development activities—found less
success, experiencing lengthy delays and receiving insufficient funding. Perhaps tellingly, the city's experiment in governing through grantmaking left
a mixed record.

Though harder to see at the time, the long-term consequences of Boston's Model City program lay in how the city government operated. Boston
closely hewed to the federal framing that the "urban crisis" reflected "governmental fragmentation," and its local initiative became a means to redefine the role of city government locally, not through government reform
but through partnerships with neighborhood nonprofits.[67] Grants helped
compensate for the government's failures to include non-white residents
with better representative systems, but they did so on a temporary basis
dependent on federal aid that sidestepped any deeper reckoning with the
segregation and discriminatory patterns in municipal government. The
Model Neighborhood Board remained, per its name, tied to that one program, and useful programs such as La Alianza Hispana's translation services could not substitute for bilingual competencies in municipal departments. These programs thus not only left the root problems intact, they
helped dismiss those problems as solved by compensatory nonprofit pro-

grams rather than substantive reform and rerouted the funding decisions to do so through city government. Bureaucrats handled the day-to-day management while the mayor stood close by, unafraid to bend the grant-making apparatus to his political ends.[68] Sometimes those political goals diversified and improved urban governance in historically marginalized neighborhoods, as was the case with Model Cities. Other times, as political winds shifted, the newly empowered city hall could steer grantmaking programs in entirely other directions.

Safe Neighborhoods

Boston's Model Cities program unfolded locally and nationally alongside a major federal effort to reduce crime, which, like Model Cities, funneled federal resources to lower tiers of government for a wide array of public and private projects. Legislation passed under the Johnson administration and largely implemented under Nixon's established law enforcement as a federal policy priority. The grantmaking structures under the Law Enforcement Assistance Administration (LEAA) largely mimicked those of Model Cities, enabling Mayor White to continue flexing the city government's growing powers of grantmaking and oversight. The city's LEAA program, however, soon eclipsed the Model Cities' anti-poverty focus in size, scope, and attention to public infrastructure. The city made some grants to neighborhood nonprofits for efforts related to community policing and community-police relationships in predominantly Black neighborhoods but used the vast majority of funds to expand public carceral capacity in the police, courts, and jails. The abundance and permanence that soon characterized Boston's law enforcement grants to municipal departments contrasted, by design, with the austerity and precarity of those to neighborhood nonprofits. It was a contrast that revealed limits to what the city government and its federal funders were willing to outsource as well as how policy arenas of law enforcement and anti-poverty could use similar tools to vastly different ends. White's administration used the LEAA program to both make and deny grants to manage the racial politics of urban governance.

In a policy area more associated with his successor, Lyndon Johnson ushered major law enforcement legislation through Congress in 1968.[69] During the 1964 presidential campaign, Republican Barry Goldwater accused Johnson's expanded welfare state of fueling what Goldwater

considered a "rise in crime and disregard for law and order."[70] Such rhetoric furthered a long-standing and racially biased connection between welfare and crime, politically pushing Johnson to add a war on crime alongside the War on Poverty. He passed legislation to that end in 1965 after
winning reelection.[71] Still, urban unrest and the perceived lack of federal
attention to it so haunted the remainder of Johnson's term that *Time* magazine accurately forecast "law and order" as the prime issue of the 1968
election.[72] Republican Richard Nixon won on a law-and-order platform,
but not before Johnson and the Democrat-controlled Congress passed
the Omnibus Crime Control and Safe Streets Act of 1968, establishing a
national anti-crime strategy and the Law Enforcement Assistance Administration as a management agency for transferring federal funds to state
projects. Even as the Safe Streets Act reinforced the localism of policing,
it created a distinct federal role in funding, regulating, and steering local
law enforcement units. LEAA funds left Washington in block grants to
states, which then redistributed them locally.

Fighting crime became big business for states like Massachusetts, and
a potentially lucrative opportunity for Boston. Over its thirteen-year history from 1968 to 1981, the LEAA spent an estimated $7.5 billion of gov-
ernment funding.[73] As with most federal funding programs, the legislation
made headlines years before Boston saw any funds for planning or programming. Nevertheless, Mayor White readied the city for the opportunity
before the ink dried on the bill. He established the Mayor's Safe Street Act
Advisory Committee to manage the program and apply to the new state
entity, the thirty-member Massachusetts Committee on Criminal Justice,
through which Boston competed against cities including Lowell and Spring-
field for a share of the monies instead of against cities such as Philadelphia, Chicago, and Seattle, as was the case under Model Cities.[74] This shift
to a state-level system of funding allocation put pressure on the state to
include smaller municipalities and towns. White's preparations, however,
were successful. After receiving slightly over $1.3 million in LEAA funds
in 1969, the commonwealth received more than $5 million in 1970, over
$9 million in 1971, and nearly $20 million in 1972.[75]

As was true under Model Cities, the administrative apparatus of the
LEAA program consolidated discretionary funding decisions about law
enforcement and prosecutorial priorities in city hall. Even though it directed just a fraction of the overall funds going to law enforcement departments in Boston, the apparatus gave the mayor's office overhead resources to expand its own grantmaking capacity and authority to monitor

those grants.[76] The Mayor's Safe Street Act Advisory Committee, which counted as many as forty-five full-time employees before settling at around nineteen staff members, spent what the director lamented were "literally hundreds of man hours" on reviewing grants across five areas: community anti-crime, police, courts, corrections, and juvenile delinquency.[77] The office designed its internal processes through trial and error.[78] After all, grantmaking was still a relatively new role for city hall that carried with it new skill requirements and new organizational arrangements for municipal employees. Over time, review procedures were standardized with quarterly and annual reports, fiscal and program monitoring, and higher evaluation standards, and staff time was freed up to conduct regular site visits.[79]

The city recognized the potential value of neighborhood nonprofits and, by making resources available, incentivized community groups to put policing, crime prevention, and criminal justice programs on their dockets.[80] Officials took a particularly heavy hand in working with nonprofit grantees under the LEAA program, framing such involvement as necessary to maintain its compliance with the federal regulations. In practice, this meant recommending budget cuts, revising program narratives, predetermining salary levels during the grant application phase, and more "continual contact" with successful nonprofit grantees in "day-to-day activities of funded projects."[81] Donald Mason, head of the Mayor's Office of Criminal Justice, framed "the intensity of this review process" as indicative of "active, aggressive criminal justice planning" in Boston.[82] His comments also signaled, however, the low regard city bureaucrats had of its community partners. Bureaucrats might have given more of their time to nonprofit grantees, but they gave more of their dollars to public entities such as the police, courts, jails, and correction departments. Upward of 85 percent of Boston's LEAA funds went toward expanding capacity in public agencies, which were also more likely than their nonprofit counterparts to receive grants after applying, and to receive larger allocations.[83] Selectively partnering with nonprofits offered political advantages to the city, where, just as at the national level, the LEAA program could not be disentangled from the long history of racism and policing.

Funding under Boston's Safe Streets program created both threats and opportunities for predominantly Black neighborhoods, which struggled, as so many did, as places systematically and simultaneously ignored and harassed by the police. These practices left African American residents in the seemingly contradictory position of both protesting police abuse and asking for a higher presence when, as the *Bay State Banner* put it, "Living and working without being mugged, molested, or robbed is a matter of vital concern to community residents."[84] A survey of Roxbury residents confirmed this concern as well as the limited trust in the Boston Police Department, where fewer than 2 percent of the officers were African American, to sufficiently respond.[85] Proposals from neighborhood organizations for grassroots programs of community security and deterrence enticed city officials, who funded such programs "as an adjunct to police services in their community."[86] This justification, as it so often did around nonprofit service providers, enabled an appearance of reform and left untouched the discriminatory policies and practices of the Boston Police Department.

Though lopsided, funding programs like the LEAA facilitated points of mutual benefit between the city and, in particular, predominantly Black neighborhoods. Nonprofit grantees knew the value they provided to the city government, what one Roxbury-based group recognized as "put[ing] a bigger feather in the Mayor's cap each day" and "a boon to the Police Commissioner and every Police officer."[87] Community agencies saw little choice but to pursue available dollars that could keep people employed and strengthen neighborhoods through grassroots initiatives. At the Cathedral and Castle Square housing developments, the South End Community Security Program—a spin-off nonprofit from a War on Poverty grantee in the South End—for example, organized elderly escorts and mailbox monitors on the days welfare checks were delivered.[88] The Roxbury Multi-Service Center used funds to build neighbor connections through "house watch contracts" (a promise to look out for a neighbor's house) and recommendations for household security.[89] It also hosted monthly police-community meetings, which routinely drew large crowds—a meeting with the police commissioner attracted over 750 attendees. And in December 1973, it opened a "Mini-Center" at Roxbury's local police station to assert a citizen presence in monitoring and communicating with police officers.[90] By funding such projects, the city recognized the community reputation of neighborhood nonprofits and harnessed that trust for policy and political agendas.

Consider one of the city's most successful community programs: the community patrol at the Bromley-Heath public housing development. By the early 1970s, Bromley-Heath, like many public housing developments, suffered from deferred maintenance and was becoming a dangerous place. LEAA funds supported a grassroots effort by residents to hire fifteen uniformed, unarmed, patrolmen to serve as a "visible deterrent" to crime for up to fifteen hours a day.[91] The resident patrols received training from the police to conduct citizen's arrests, served as a first responders, kept records of incidents, and called for police backup when necessary. Though Congress appropriated LEAA funds to reduce riots, the Bromley-Heath patrols dealt with far more quotidian and quality-of-life concerns of purse snatchings and stolen vehicles.[92] The success of the project gave residents paid employment and meant that elderly residents felt more comfortable going outside. Residents celebrated the program, as did the Boston Housing Authority, whose spokesman noted that the community patrol had a "better record" than the official BHA security. Based on the success of the Bromley-Heath demonstration, the city allocated other LEAA funds to similar projects at the Columbia Point, Commonwealth, Mission Main, and Mission Extension developments in 1974.[93] City officials congratulated themselves on their "sensitivity to local needs."[94]

The involvement of city officials as funders in nonprofit work increased surveillance unwelcome by those doing the work on the ground. "Reams and reams of forms and data have been made out for whose sake?," an organizer for a Roxbury-based community security team asked the mayor's office, describing "the degree of written work" as "hindering."[95] The monitoring of federal funds, while done in the name of compliance, was so precise that a city grant manager noticed "out-of-town calls have increased" at a Mattapan grantee.[96] Such oversight gave the mayor's office extraordinary power over grantees, and it was not shy about invoking this power to discipline community grantees seen as straying from the original grant agreement. As an example, Linda Weiss, a city grant manager, denied the South End Security Program's request for a funding extension based on the use of LEAA-funded community patrols to distribute surplus food items such as dry beans, macaroni, oats, and evaporated milk to the elderly. She cited "extra-programmatic activities which take time away from the primary components of the program" as grounds for dismissal.[97] Whether he agreed with Weiss or not, Walter Jabzanka, the director of the South End nonprofit sponsoring the security program, fired William Shabazz from overseeing the patrol or else "run the risk of the program not being refunded," he noted. The program could only be successful, Jabzanka rationalized, "if there is a co-operative effort on the part of the director, staff, funding source, and community resident."[98] Fair or not, the director's justification highlighted the pressures facing neighborhood nonprofits.

Though a single set of grantmaking guidelines governed LEAA monies, they heavily favored the large, public grantees over the smaller nonprofit ones in design and implementation. Budget cuts from year to year
were more difficult to absorb on grassroots budgets, and rules about funding limits were more difficult to circumvent. Some of the city's more prominent and successful programs simply disappeared when LEAA funding
ran out. The Bromley-Heath patrol, for example, received national attention from LEAA as a successful model but had little recourse when the
nonprofit ran out the clock on its eligibility for LEAA funds.[99] The residents won a temporary grant from HUD and cobbled together grant funds
for a while before eventually shutting down.[100] After several years of budget cuts, the director of RMSC's security program wrote to the mayor's
committee, pleading, "We've used ingenuity up. What's desperately needed
is more money."[101] The practice in Boston of denying grant extensions
aligned with a clear directive from the Massachusetts statehouse to deny
any and all requests for more funding.[102]

The vulnerability of neighborhood nonprofit grantees contrasted with
the larger, public grantees that found ways to navigate the strictures of
government grantmaking. Large entities, such as the Boston Police Department, could overcome limits to the number of phases of funding a
grantee could reapply for by having enough internal departments to create new projects or initiatives over the course of the decade. They also
were more likely to receive grant funds for equipment that would persist
beyond a grant cycle. Purchasing new weapons, reorganizing departments
and units, providing training, and enhancing data-processing capabilities
differed from paying the salaries of community security workers.[103] Guns
represented a one-time cost; salaries carried on year after year. It was also
politically and administratively easier to permanently absorb an experimental program already within the government, such as through the county's court system or the city's police department, as part of the annual
operating budget than it was for an external, community group to make
that leap onto the books. These grant preferences and design choices exacerbated the discrepancies in funding amounts between municipal and
neighborhood nonprofit grantees.

Boston's LEAA program produced an uneven carceral apparatus that
heavily favored the public sector but still involved the nonprofit one, revealing three critical lessons. First, government grantmaking could directly build up public infrastructure, but only under certain political and
policy conditions. Congressional authorization, local ambitions, and a po-

litical culture that celebrated law enforcement combined to produce the funding patterns on display in Boston's LEAA program. Framing the urban crisis as a problem of law enforcement enabled a funding climate both nationally and locally that earlier lenses of poverty or discrimination alone did not. Second, funding community organizations proved useful politically, because their participation in the city's law enforcement strategy took pressure off the city or city agencies to reform their practices. Third, and finally, the persistent vulnerability of community organizations, the austerity imposed on them, and the surveillance done to them by city grant managers reflected administrative choices that reinforced the city government's control over private nonprofit organizations. Even as LEAA appeared to occupy a very different policy domain than Model Cities, both programs operated on a shared internal logic and set of administrative processes that drew in formerly excluded residents through private means. Over the late 1960s and early 1970s, city officials honed their skills at grantmaking in ways that would prove useful as the city soon faced its biggest crisis to date.

Crisis in the City

Nothing tested Mayor White's administration like busing, and no other event better cemented nonprofit neighborhoods as a governing apparatus in Boston. The issue of segregation in the Boston Public Schools haunted White's campaign and mayoralty as legal challenges made their way through courts, as students staged walkouts, and as racial violence loomed. By the early 1970s, many already considered White's leadership a "great disappointment," because he often deferred to the courts as the final arbiter and to community organizations as the local responders.[104] Black leaders called White "weak" and said he was "hiding behind a liberal façade," criticizing him for taking the Black vote for granted and extending only tokenized support.[105] White might not have visibly or vocally led on the issue of desegregation, but he did strategically manage the city during a period of turmoil and violence with the tools at his disposal. Beginning in 1973, his office steered the city's grantmaking apparatus under Model Cities, LEAA, and other funding programs toward mitigating the violence and uncertainty of desegregation. The city's management of the busing crisis demonstrated the flexibility of these funding programs and reinforced their ability to draw private entities into governing, but it also focused attention on the symptomatic problem of violence rather than the underlying problem of discrimination while simultaneously shifting responsibility for a public failure to those most harmed and with the least power.

Tensions had been roiling—and sometimes erupting—in the years before Judge Arthur Garrity found the Boston School Committee complicit in upholding a system of racial segregation in the Boston schools and designed a new system of school assignment that meant cross-city busing in the fall of 1974. That legal case, *Morgan v. Hennigan*, was the direct result of a 1972 filing by the Boston NAACP that charged the Boston School Committee with violating the rights of African American students guaranteed by the Thirteenth and Fourteenth Amendments and the Civil Rights Act of 1964. The case was also the culmination of over a decade of organizing and mobilization: Black parents launched community schools and independent busing programs that brought African American students to open seats in better-resourced schools; legal advocates won the passage of the Racial Imbalance Act in 1965 in the commonwealth; and students participated in Stay-Out-of-School protest days in June 1963 and 1964, before in 1971 coordinating a citywide Black student strike.[106] Even before Garrity's 1974 ruling, it appeared likely the city would undergo a court-mandated desegregation plan as federal agencies and the commonwealth began withholding funds from Boston's schools due to civil rights violations.[107] Waves of retaliatory violence accompanied these legal challenges both at the schools and beyond them, leaving the mayor and others waiting for a spark that would set the city afire.[108]

Admittedly, Mayor White had limited tools at his disposal, because the legal authority for overseeing the city's education system rested with the intransigent Boston School Committee. What he did have were dollars—specifically grant dollars—and the power to distribute them. As early as 1971, city hall started directing federal grant dollars to help manage what was openly being called a school crisis. Following the 1971 strike by Black students, the city allocated funds to the Task Force on Out of School Children—the group started several years earlier by Hubie Jones and RMSC—to launch a Boston High Crisis Response Program focused on "prevention of future disorder."[109] Student demands emphasized the recruitment and retention of Black teachers, but the demands were interpreted by the city as "threats to public safety."[110] City hall also sought supplementary funds from the federal LEAA office to enable the city to "survive the opening of school" in 1974.[111] African American senator Ed

Brooke (R-MA) issued a telegram to the LEAA office in Washington endorsing the city's application. "Goodwill and determination are not enough," he wrote, where "Expertise and Funds are needed" instead.[112] Notably, White did not steer the apparatus of government grantmaking toward building more just or equitable public institutions, instead tapping neighborhood nonprofits to manage the very real but also symptomatic issue of school violence. These choices revealed the realities of discretionary grantmaking—where the city had to frame the problem in a way likely to win favor from funders—and reinforced the policy shift ongoing in the United States that framed social policy through a carceral, law-and-order lens.

The existing network of local LEAA grantees also steered their attention to the escalating school crisis out of necessity, concern, and a lack of faith in public institutions. As an organizer for the Roxbury Security Program noted, "Although we are not required (by contract) to intervene in these situations, we have an obligation to the community to 'get involved.'"[113] After all, neighborhood nonprofits in predominantly Black areas had a track record of stepping in during times of violence, having helped keep the peace, liaise with the mayor's office, protect legal rights, and ensure care during the 1967 uprising. Many of the same groups repeated these activities in the early 1970s, often at the invitation of school administrators in an indication of how fluid the boundaries between public and private, social welfare and carceral state had become on the ground. During the 1972–73 school year, members of the Sav-More Community Security Program at RMSC helped manage the school dismissal process at the nearby King School to decrease schoolyard tensions. They kept calm better than police officers, who tended to escalate the situation with their shotguns and dogs, which were brought in on more than one occasion.[114] Additionally, the team worked with teenagers, parents, and teachers to provide security for a school dance at the Jeremiah Burke High School for six hundred teens.[115] Following a particularly tense episode, the RMSC team established systems of community monitors, escorts, emergency transportation, and an experimental rumor control center between community groups and the local police station that later became permanent.[116] These were all activities beyond the stated intent on their LEAA grant applications to the city, but they sufficiently aligned with the city's overall goal of preventing another uprising.

The absence of visible leadership from the mayor during this period of turmoil shifted authority to neighborhood entities, framing the violence surrounding desegregation as a local, individual problem rather than a pervasive citywide one. This tactic sought to appeal to both white resistors demanding neighborhood schools and Black activists; both groups, while at different ends of the spectrum, had similarly lost faith in the ability of city hall to protect their interests. As a result, Little City Halls became targets of protests against busing, repositories of information about school assignment, spaces for presentations about school safety, and partners to police and community agencies to promote a peaceful start to the school year.[117] Nonprofit leaders from the Roxbury Multi-Service Center and Freedom House and Paul Parks from Model Cities coordinated their efforts to support students and their families.[118] The newly formed City-Wide Educational Coalition used LEAA funds to hire parent organizers and neighborhood safety teams in subdistricts that it mapped across the city. On behalf of the city and in the absence of other municipal action, the coalition also released a newsletter, established a rumor control network, hosted parent meetings, and coordinated a team of four hundred volunteers "stationed at bus stops and schools where confrontations were likely to occur" in the summer before busing began.[119] To the extent that city departments engaged in this work, they did so as detached funders or via the police department, whose new Tactical Patrol Unit patrolled schools in riot gear. The unit's efforts were uneven, reinforcing a reputation for racism and failing to protect Black students, requiring, by extension, the necessity of nonprofits to compensate.[120]

After the school year, and thus busing, began on September 12, 1974, the mayor started receiving daily logs of the violence and rumors in the city and continued to do so over years of protests and resistance. Released in June 1974, only a few months before the start of school, Judge Garrity's busing plan called for Black students from Roxbury to attend the nearly all-white South Boston High School, and vice versa, pairing two of the most politically active neighborhoods. The daily logs attest to the mayor's success in building a decentralized network of public and private entities around the city as well as to the city's reliance on them. Little City Halls as well as nonprofit groups such as Freedom House reported rumors to city hall—everything from planned boycotts to rumors of fights and sexual assault—and actual incidents of stones thrown at buses, mass gatherings in the streets, fire alarms pulled, and students needing medical attention.[121] Representatives of those agencies stood on the front lines to protect students when reports about buses wired with bombs, protesters with two-by-fours, and large crowds poured in from all over the city.[122] City-based

FIGURE 4.2. *Busing information phone bank at City Hall (1974)*. During the 1974 busing crisis in Boston, the city made grants to parent groups and local nonprofits and also operated a crisis hotline at city hall, staffed, it appears, with municipal workers and volunteers. Calls reported rumors of violence or disruption and also checked on the veracity thereof. In the image, note the referral number to the nonprofit METCO on the window, the designation of a rumor about closing South Boston High as false, and the maps of Boston public schools in the adjoining room. (Mayor Kevin White photographs, Collection 0245.002, Chronological file, 1974 Busing Information Phone Bank, BCA. Boston City Archives Digital Photograph Collection.)

youth workers and nonprofit-based security teams helped load students onto and off of buses and got called into area schools.[123] The daily logs embody as much the tension and violence of the period—with days of more than eighty false fire alarm pulls and multiple students requiring hospitalization—as they do to the relationships that developed between city hall and neighborhoods.

Grants had bestowed on nonprofits semiofficial status such that they operated alongside the Little City Halls with little differentiation on the daily log between the actual public authority and the private one. The work and limitations of the D-Street Community Security Program, a resident patrol of the D-Street public housing development managed by the South Boston APAC, offer a notable example. When members of the Ku Klux Klan began recruiting at a park in South Boston, the LEAA-funded D-Street patrol reached out to the thirty-six Black families in the majority white housing development and inquired about their needs. Most expressed concern for their safety, particularly after a seventeen-year-old resident, George Pratt, had been killed a year earlier outside his family's apartment by a sniper, later found to be a local teenager.[124] The patrolmen then connected seven Black families with the area's Little City Hall and housing authority to apply for transfers to another area; this action solved the immediate issue without addressing the underlying racism and helped resegregate the city's public housing.[125] The group also mapped the physical layout around the remaining Black families' units for threats of fire bombs, rocks, and shootings and helped install screens after rocks targeted their windows.[126] While these were useful activities that, as one grant report boasted, "assisted in the prevention of a full scale racial crisis from erupting," D-Street's efforts still fell short of ensuring racial equality or of dismantling the threats to it.[127]

The ability of neighborhood nonprofits to mobilize quickly in response to busing and direct longer-term capacities toward the crisis carried a flip side—one that similarly held advantages for the city. Things quickly built could be quickly disassembled. Its heavy reliance on existing grant relationships and organizations enabled the mayor's office to deescalate once the immediate crisis had passed. By the third year of busing, when violence and protest continued to characterize the start of the school year but the biggest tests of the city's school system had passed, the widely celebrated City-Wide Educational Coalition lost its LEAA funds.[128] The city's decision to defund the groups that had been deemed so essential at the start of busing was justified, in part, by the group's successes. The public safety threat had abated. When the nonprofit sought to address "some of the *real* issues of educational reform," city grant managers encouraged them to seek private funding on their own.[129] Support to build a "city-wide, multiethnic parent constituency dedicated to bringing about quality integrated education for all Boston children" simply was not a priority for the city.[130] Neighborhood groups whose funding was not directly tied to busing—such as the D-Street housing patrol and Roxbury community patrol—returned to their regular dockets, seeking to demonstrate to the city a reduction in crime to justify future funding.

Busing strained the city of Boston nearly to the breaking point. The violence of its early years gave the city a national reputation and made clear that racism structured not just the American South but the North as well. Children lost time in school, students and parents landed in jails and hospitals, and Kevin White barely won reelection in 1975. Still, the city survived. The moment revealed how crucial nonprofits had become to the city and yet how inconsequential. Neighborhood nonprofits managed day-to-day policy implementation and played a clear governmental role, ensuring the safety of Black families in majority white public housing developments, reducing the risk of riots in schoolyards, and riding buses with kindergarteners while adults and teenagers pelted them with stones. Public agencies might have performed such activities but, either for lack of ability or will, did not. Yet the limits of such activities were also starkly on display. The most significant institutional reform in Boston—the desegregation of the city's schools—came not from a neighborhood group but from the courts. Mobilization laid groundwork for the *Morgan v. Hennigan* decision, but the lasting, substantive, equalizing change came via the public sector. Busing belied the inability of nonprofits to create structural change even as it relied so heavily on them.

Conclusion

For a politician whose mood swings could get the best of him and who took a deeply personal approach to governing, Mayor White's narrow victory for a third term in 1975 proved particularly painful. Such a slim margin felt like a betrayal, and one account called him a "ravaged and listless victor."[131] Busing and a corruption scandal erased the favorability he had accumulated through the years. Any hope of national office went out the window as well, though perhaps that ship had already sailed. White had lost a gubernatorial race in 1970 and then saw his invitation to serve as George McGovern's running mate in 1972 rescinded only two hours after receiving it. Over his first two terms, White had built his administration as a central hub of decision-making with decentralized implementation. The tactic—part his own design and part a reflection of the tools he'd been given by federal policy—had been successful enough to hold the city together, but Bostonians held little love for their mayor. He had overseen the desegregation of the city's schools and the redevelopment of Boston's famed Quincy Market but recognized "it's the pothole, the shade tree, the little amenity that wins votes."[132] After the 1975 election, White built a political machine to further insulate himself and consolidate political power. A former aide recounted White's new obsession, noting nothing was done in the city "unless there was a demonstrable political payoff."[133] Luckily for White, Washington had given him one more tool for achieving that payoff.

142

CHAPTER FOUR

Model Cities experimented with devolved forms of governance and grantmaking, but Nixon disliked the program that he inherited from Johnson and considered it "plagued by delay and duplication, by waste and rigidity, by inconsistency and irrationality."[134] Once in office, Nixon advanced a policy package that Gerald Ford, as president, signed into law as the Housing and Community Development Act of 1974. The legislation consolidated funding for several signature programs under HUD's jurisdiction—including urban renewal, Model Cities, water and sewer grants, historic preservation, and rehabilitation loans—into a single block grant, which Congress distributed based on a set formula that further devolved grantmaking authority to lower tiers of government.[135] Ford considered it the most important piece of housing legislation since the creation of the federal public housing program in 1934.[136] The Community Development Block Grants—known often by their acronym, CDBGs—capped off the era of experimentation and discretionary grantmaking in the long 1960s and increasingly became the vehicle by which city government funded both its public and private partnerships in an age of urban fiscal austerity.

Even as CDBGs combined the most prominent urban policies of the previous decades, they broke new ground in several ways that simultaneously contracted and expanded the power mayors had over federal funds. With CDBGs, local governments such as Boston's gained more control over federal aid, but they frequently saw less of it. Replacing the competitive programs of the War on Poverty and Model Cities, which encouraged service and governance experimentation, with a set formula for revenue sharing appeared to equalize the distribution of funding between states and thereby reduce the grantsmanship or favoritism of earlier grantmaking programs. The design of CDBGs, however, structurally favored the southwest or Sun Belt region friendly to Nixon over the northeast or Frost Belt, and similarly directed resources more to smaller towns and suburbs than to larger cities, including Boston. As one research report noted, "Formulas are political decisions, and altering them requires changes in the distribution of political influence." Although the researchers were referring to federal allocations, the finding applied at the local level too.[137] The shift to block grants also promised to eliminate what one Nixon task force called the "thousand strings" attached to "almost every federal dollar" to free localities to spend resources as they wished.[138] Here, too, reality proved more complicated. Certainly, nonprofits and lower tiers of government griped about the strictures government grants often carried, but many of the eliminated regulations had served to focus funding on the issue of poverty, protect the interest of minority residents, ensure a participatory process of decision-making, and provide recourse to those discriminated against. The elimination of such requirements and federal monitoring under the CDBG program, one Boston consultant testified before Congress, "lends itself to administrative elimination of basic civil rights concerns and protections."[139]

The transition to block grants as a means of federal aid validated and emboldened the changes under way in Boston's municipal government. In 1974, Kevin White created the Mayor's Office of Community Development, whose sole purpose was to manage the grant process for the CDBGs, including assessing applications, managing local contracts, monitoring for HUD compliance, and conducting local program evaluation.[140] This office had greater latitude on where in the city to direct funds—a total over $32 million in the first year—and what constituted urban improvement; it hosted hearings to solicit input from citizens but held no legal obligation to include residents in actual funding decisions.[141] The bureaucrats identified the five priority arenas of housing, neighborhood business districts, human services, capital improvements, and urban renewal and set a loose formula that factored population as well as poverty rates and quality of housing in distributing the funding around the city and in using federal dollars to keep the municipal bureaucracy afloat.[142] After all, the power of grantmaking was the ability to set priorities, demand information, assess budgets, and define time horizons for change. That such power to govern rested in city hall was not the surprise; that this power was reinforced not outright by law but indirectly by resources, that the city extended it into and over private nonprofit organizations, and that it did so as the official response to the problems of economic and racial segregation revealed a profoundly new system of urban governance at work.

The federal program empowered city bureaucrats to make decisions based on local circumstances but also left room for favoritism and prejudice to steer public resources into some neighborhoods over others. For the beleaguered and downtrodden mayor, the timing could not have been better. Though Black voters had secured his reelection bid, White used CDBGs to reward both white violence and Black organizing, unevenly sprinkling dollars around the city to appease dissatisfied customers.[143] These funds became a partisan and political tool. In Boston, CDBG funds disproportionately benefited moderate- and higher-income groups of homeowners and reached predominantly white neighborhoods.[144] After residents in Hyde Park committed twenty-five incidents of racial violence against Black homes and families in a single month, the share of CDBG funds to Hyde Park increased and those for Roxbury decreased.[145] CDBG funds also supported large-scale development projects for hospitals, universities, hotels, and shopping malls that appealed to city developers and investors. Scholar James Jennings later called White's approach "political managerialism."[146]

CDBG funds also supported neighborhood nonprofit organizations and, through such funding, solidified them as a permanent fixture of urban governance as cities barely remained afloat amid a national recession in the 1970s.[147] These funds, however, rarely provided residents and neighborhoods with new programs or services, instead helping the city and its partners manage budget shortfalls in an age of increasing austerity. This was as true of programs already outsourced to nonprofit organizations, such as around human services, as it was of standard municipal functions such as code enforcement, demolition, and boarding up of abandoned property—activities that nonprofit staff started to provide in areas long neglected by the city. Though the amounts ebbed and flowed over the remainder of the decade, the presence of CDBG funds on neighborhood nonprofit annual budgets became standard, including well-established groups such as the Roxbury Multi-Service Center, where over three-quarters of the budget came from government contracts. The city used CDBG funds to structure contracts with nonprofits to reach elderly populations and non-English language speakers and immigrant groups, including La Alianza Hispana, the Cape Verdean Center, and the Chinese American Civic Association, just as it had under Model Cities.[148] These arrangements reflected the needs of particular populations and the trust these nonprofits had built with their communities, but the continued servicing of groups traditionally problematic for municipalities—immigrants, seniors, children, unemployed persons—by private nonprofit organizations reified the status of these groups as outside the traditional channels of government though still beholden to it.

At a time when politicians, including Mayor White, spoke of decentralizing government and empowering lower tiers of government, White's actions moved Boston in the opposite direction. The rhetorical emphasis on localism and neighborhoods enabled the city to justify its hands-off approach and promotion of nonprofit activities, even as the resources for them increasingly came from beyond the city limits and as municipal bureaucrats had more tools at their disposal to monitor, oversee, and steer their distribution.[149] White's administration gained the political benefit

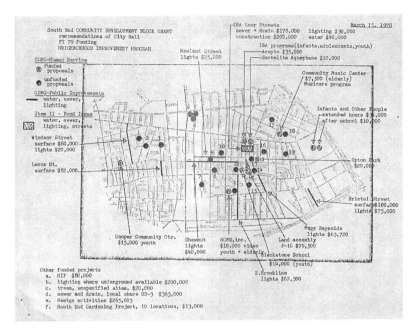

FIGURE 4.3. *Map of Community Development Block Grants in the South End (1978).* Staff at the South End Project Area Committee mapped out all the Community Development Block Grant funds coming into the area. The flexibility of these funds proved quite useful to the mayor, because they could support physical infrastructure improvements and nonprofit-provided services. (South End Project Area Committee, "Task Force on Community Development Block Grant Priorities, Report," March 15, 1978, box 1, folder: CDBG, SEPAC (Collection 60), UMass. Image courtesy of University Archives and Special Collections in the Joseph P. Healey Library at the University of Massachusetts Boston.)

of appearing as the epitome of liberal politics — flexible, responsive, and community-oriented in its support of nonprofit activities — while retaining control of the CDBG funds and deploying them in ways meant to limit Black political power.[150] The local approach of Little City Halls, the broad questions that Model Cities sought to address in urban governance, and the grant management expertise of LEAA all paved the way for the local implementation of the Community Development Block Grant program, which gave funding without expectation of innovation, experimentation, or inclusion.

Community Development Block Grants might have been passed under Republican leadership, but they became a policy that many Democrats, including Mayor White and, soon, President Carter, learned to embrace.[151]

CDBG funds became a tool for White's administration to reward, punish, invest, incentivize, and steer the institutions in the neighborhoods doing the work of governing and provided a way to expand and contract government on demand. They enabled a veneer of inclusion that only reinforced the precarity of traditionally disenfranchised urban residents and their reliance on private entities to fulfill democratic rights of participation, deliberation, representation, and equality. Though the continued funding for neighborhood nonprofits solidified some of the gains of the 1960s, their continued presence in city governance largely stood as a policy failure: the failure to create a more inclusive and responsive government, failure to adequately meet the needs of low-income residents, and failure to dismantle the racism of the city's and nation's political-economic structures.

CHAPTER FIVE

The Lenders

A tour of seventy-one recently rehabilitated apartment units in the South End's Villa Victoria development impressed Robert Schrank. The Ford Foundation had made some grants to help the rehabilitation project, and as a program officer there, it was Schrank's job to visit Boston and assess the grants. In his file on the August 1971 visit, Schrank noted the "immaculate" third-floor apartment he visited and gave the entire project "high marks for construction and management."[1] Credit for such success might well have gone to the Emergency Tenants' Council, the Puerto Rican nonprofit that fought for the project, designed the architecture to reflect residents' cultural heritage, and oversaw its completion. Instead, Schrank highlighted the work of Bob Whittlesey and his nonprofit organization, Greater Boston Community Development, that had helped package the financing behind the deal. "Whittlesey knows housing development, he knows Boston and he has boundless energy," the Ford Foundation officer recorded. Such praise foreshadowed how the presence of consulting entities, even nonprofit ones committed to expanding affordable housing, steadily eroded the role of residents in community development in the quest to secure the loans, investors, and the necessary financing.[2]

A suburban resident with experience in rehabbing housing in the South End, Whittlesey brought useful experience and a slate of Ivy League credentials to his work with the Emergency Tenants' Council.[3] After working in Washington, DC, on the federal renewal program, he had moved to the Boston area in the early 1960s to experiment with nonprofit housing redevelopment. He soon founded South End Community Development to rehabilitate dilapidated housing with the few housing policy tools available for such activity and converted eighty-three units across twenty-three buildings into rentable units.[4] Despite these achievements, Whittlesey became increasingly aware of activism in the South End among residents, particularly African American and Puerto Rican residents, who saw housing not as an end, as he often did, but as a means for economic power and community control. In a choice to address "political needs," Whittlesey pivoted from doing to consulting in 1967, and in 1970 renamed his nonprofit as Greater Boston Community Development (GBCD) to indicate that shift in activity.[5] Instead of purchasing and rehabbing housing, he would aid the growing array of nonprofit community development corporations looking to take on renewal activities themselves.

The idea of technical assistance for nonprofit organizations was not itself new, but the shift embodied in Whittlesey's rebranding of GBCD at the end of the 1960s spoke to the particularities of housing redevelopment, in which the financing proved more complex and bureaucratically challenging than it was for many of the social service-oriented efforts of the decade. Whittlesey recognized the necessity of early capital for CDCs to win long-term financing from banks, federal mortgages, and private individuals and envisioned a consolidated, flexible seed fund built from philanthropic grants, donations, and lines of credit.[6] The seventy-one-unit project Schrank toured seemed to prove that social and economic goals could be met together through well-structured community development projects. The optimism surrounding the Ford Foundation's initial grant to GBCD, which one program officer noted as having the potential "to be one of the most successful approaches the Foundation has funded," appeared to have been well placed.[7] Program offices at the foundation valued Whittlesey's credentials and in his pragmatism found an insurance policy of sorts against the potentially more radical politics motivating community control.[8] More funding soon followed from the Ford Foundation and, in time, from corporations, both to GBCD in Boston and to similar efforts aimed at increasing the flow of capital to CDCs.

At a time when both the public and for-profit sectors failed to supply affordable housing, the Boston experiment suggested a third way forward— one that wound through the nonprofit sector, attracted new investors, structured aid as loans, and framed social goals in economic terms. Such attitudes, common among funders, policy makers, and consultants, reflected the times, when growing fatigue with the civil rights movement, government retreat from its involvement in urban areas, and an economic recession that shrank the endowments of major foundations began to reshape liberal politics and reveal anew its limitations. Many began to argue the state's best tactic to improve urban areas was to encourage and underwrite public-private financing arrangements that would make affordable housing attractive to private investors and create on-ramps for CDCs to not only participate in the economic engines of finance, real estate, and business development but also contribute to them by improving the housing stock and visual appeal of seemingly undesirable neighborhoods.

Boston emerged as an early site of such arrangements, and Massachusetts soon gained national recognition for its policy innovations and financing mechanisms as well as the resultant robustness of its nonprofit community development sector. Later known as *intermediaries*, a middle tier of nonprofits such as GBCD emerged during the 1970s to broker deals between grassroots groups on the ground and institutional lenders to help community entities such as ETC win necessary financing from banks, federal lenders, and private investors and keep the pipeline of affordable housing moving. Serving as a political and economic bridge between the grassroots and treetops, Whittlesey spent the next decades of his career helping design a variety of instruments that converted philanthropic and government dollars into financialized tools.[9] He was not alone in doing so. Mel King, who, by the early 1970s, served as a representative in the Massachusetts statehouse, authored and passed legislation encouraging the flow of capital into CDCs and community development projects in Boston and around the state. These public and philanthropic subsidies from the commonwealth, the Ford Foundation, and others frequently came as low-interest loans and other financialized forms of aid, which intermediaries then packaged to entice market-rate lenders into the previously risky or unprofitable activities of community development. Over the 1970s and into the 1980s, nonprofit intermediaries increased the productive capacity of CDCs and therefore the availability of housing for those who needed it at rates they could afford.

There was a cost to this bargain, however, that traded the radical political possibilities of community development for the financing necessary to make the physical development possible. Intermediaries tried to help CDCs bridge the seemingly impossible position of contributing to urban growth and preventing it from getting too far out of residents' reach by privatizing, financializing, and abstracting urban redevelopment. The shift built on the state apparatus of government grantmaking from the 1960s, but in its increasing embrace of the market as a site of resources and organizational models in the 1970s, accelerated a neoliberal governing regime in American cities. Through those efforts, CDCs and the historically marginalized communities they represented gained a foothold in urban governance and redevelopment, emerging as central economic actors in nonprofit neighborhoods and participants in what sociologists Harvey Molotch and John Logan called "the growth machine."[10] Even subsidized loans needed repaying, however, and as neighborhoods gained housing, the lenders gained profits. A well-balanced portfolio, productive cycling of funds, and the push to grow the value of urban land became priorities on par with—and for some CDCs and intermediaries, over—considerations of community need or power. Proponents of these new tools deliberately traded the unpredictability of philanthropic and government grants for the unpredictability of the market, steering CDCs toward commercial organizational forms and activities. Rather than help CDCs escape the limitations and dependencies of government and philanthropic grants, the financialized forms of aid that intermediaries peddled merely reproduced and intensified these dynamics.

Capital and the Commonwealth

After Boston's Puerto Rican community won the right to develop Parcel 19 in the South End in 1968, GBCD and ETC harnessed the limited policy levers available to them to turn the community vision into realities of new housing, local businesses, and cultural pride. Success in Villa Victoria, however, largely occurred in spite of the federal and state mechanisms available at the time, which remained difficult to access, because they had been designed for for-profit investors operating with different time horizons, motivations, capital, and capacity than a nonprofit community developer.[11] Eventually, Whittlesey worked with ETC to produce a precedent-setting financial arrangement that used specialized tax syndication rules to form a limited partnership that balanced the community's interest in control with the financing requirements of actually purchasing, developing, and owning real estate.[12] It worked to finance redevelopment of one building in Villa Victoria, but it had been time-consuming and expensive and was unlikely to be replicated. Those committed to affordable housing specifically, and urban areas more broadly, needed a different strategy that exceeded the spending levels of the grants-based funding mechanisms of the 1960s. To dismantle the economic, political, and social inequality of urban neighborhoods, nonprofits needed access to capital at a scale and in a form not previously extended to nonprofit organizations. They needed lenders.

The increasingly visible failures of public housing in the United States motivated both public and philanthropic entities to take seriously the interest community groups such as ETC demonstrated and to rethink the policy tools that might encourage such activity. Nixon's election in 1968 and again in 1972 ushered in a range of federal policies designed to reduce the federal government's size and role, particularly in the realm of social welfare programs. In housing, Nixon helped dismantle the federal public housing program, most famously captured on the evening news with the demolition of the Pruit Igoe public housing development in St. Louis in early 1972. Boston had its own share of local uncertainties over the future of public housing too, with high-profile legal battles between tenants and the Boston Housing Authority during the 1960s. Years of neglect, disrepair, and maintenance problems on the part of municipal authorities had eroded the once sterling reputation of public housing, taking with it confidence in the government to provide decent, safe, and sanitary shelter.[13] The private housing market fared no better at meeting the growing need for affordable shelter, which decades of urban renewal only expanded. With a moratorium on housing subsidies in January 1973, Nixon fully removed the federal government from new housing production and eliminated one of the few tools for community developers. The retreat of the federal government and for-profit developers from housing in particular, and urban areas more generally, created an opening for nonprofit entities and an opportunity for local experimentation.

One area of activity emerged via the Massachusetts statehouse. After over a decade of organizing and failed campaigns for the Boston School Committee, Mel King won his first political campaign in 1972. The Ninth Suffolk District in Boston elected King to represent it in the state legislature on his pledge to support community development and create new vehicles to financially empower the nonprofit organizations that had become key participants in urban governance during the 1960s. It was a strategy that shared with Whittlesey's an interest in strengthening the capacity of CDCs and accelerating the flow of capital to them for housing redevelopment, but it was also rooted in a political and ideological commitment to community control. The gains of the previous decade, King knew, were hard-fought but easy to undo, and for all the achievements of community organizing, those wins rarely came with the economic power to turn vision into reality. New state programs were necessary, King argued, to help CDCs secure the commercial financing required to graduate from participating in urban redevelopment to owning and controlling the products of that development. He used his new seat to advance a policy agenda that put the resources and faith of the state behind CDCs.

Consistent with his activism of the 1960s, King pushed a broad progressive legislative agenda in the statehouse. It linked social issues such as housing, education, and prisoner rights to political and economic power, and often funneled public resources through community institutions, particularly nonprofit CDCs.[14] King adopted a capacious definition of community development, seeing it as "a product of both capitalist oppression and organizing attempts against that oppression."[15] CDCs were nonprofit vehicles, he felt, of political and economic empowerment, where those traditionally excluded from government and banking could begin to build collective strength. To that end, King's policy proposals designed a means of channeling capital and capacity building to communities and community organizations long excluded from those public or private resources. The benefits of these investments and the housing and businesses they supported would accrue to the community, to be shared and held in common through a community development corporation. His was a vision at once radical in steering the state toward the economic empowerment of disadvantaged communities, and neoliberal in charting a path through increased participation in the market. He proposed a housing fund, a certification process for CDCs, a CDC-backed cable news channel, and an expansion of the Massachusetts Housing and Finance Agency to support the construction of day care and community facilities. Few of these bills moved forward, but those that did emphasized housing and urban space, tapping into some surprising points of political convergence.

The commonwealth became abuzz with interest in reshaping the role of state government in not only endorsing community development but directly supporting those activities with new funding mechanisms. An empty swath of land known as the Southwest Corridor created one immediate impetus after mobilization by a coalition of residents and planners defeated plans for highway expansion in Cambridge and Boston.[16] King and others wanted to ensure the right of the communities surrounding the cleared land to decide its future. GBCD's profile continued to rise, as Ford Foundation staff and federal HUD bureaucrats praised the Boston group's laser focus on housing and its ability to "insure completion of a project."[17] Whittlesey's reputation won him a seat at state-level policy tables, where he helped reorganize the commonwealth's Department of Community Affairs and rewrite state regulations to institutionalize the role of intermediary nonprofits such as his GBCD.[18] These developments occurred, moreover, against the backdrop of a state and national economic recession in the mid-1970s, giving new urgency to the commonwealth's need to spur economic development. Facing insolvency, rising unemployment, and contracting federal spending, "conditions were ripe," observers argued, "for a new conception of state government's role in the Massachusetts economy."[19] Governor Michael Dukakis believed the state government could act as "a *catalyst* to development," and he courted policy proposals aimed at attracting capital investment to the commonwealth.[20] Though Dukakis had in mind the technology and industry sectors, Representative King saw an opportunity to support community development.[21]

In the mid-1970s, thanks to King's policy leadership, Massachusetts created several intermediary organizations that channeled public capital structured as loans and equity to nonprofit community developers as part of a broader reconfiguration of state economic policy designed to spur development across the state.[22] First, the Massachusetts Community Development Finance Corporation (CDFC) supported CDCs through loans and investments in debt and equity securities, symbolically validating the role of community groups in development. The legislation acknowledged the problems of blight and neighborhood decline as ones unaddressed "by the ordinary operations of private enterprise" and justified state financing for community development as "public uses and purposes for which public money may be expended."[23] A $10 million state bond seeded the public finance corporation.[24] To ensure urban CDCs won a fair share of the loans, King led the legislature to establish the Community Economic Development Assistance Corporation (CEDAC) in 1978 to provided technical assistance to CDCs in conducting feasibility studies, covering preacquisition costs, and packaging financing. Finally, Community Enterprise Economic Development (CEED) operated as a grant program to support organizational capacity building in CDCs through board training, staff assistance, and the formulation of development goals and pipeline.[25] Taken together, these state entities sought to boost the visibility, stability, and suitability of CDCs to access capital from traditional bank lenders. Though radical politics had inspired King's policy agenda, it gained traction in Massachusetts and beyond for encouraging behaviors characteristic of the business world and for promoting a market-oriented approach to urban improvement.

The new policy mechanisms both followed grassroots demand and created it, gaining attention nationally. Though fewer than ten CDCs existed in the commonwealth at the time the new financing entities were created, by 1985 that number had grown to fifty chartered CDCs. It was a response reminiscent to that following the federal War on Poverty, when that grant-making program prompted a wave of nonprofit incorporations around the country among those eager for a share of the funds. Over their first decade, the commonwealth's financing mechanisms poured $21 million into CDC projects around Massachusetts, leveraging an additional $20 million in private funding and $10 million in federal funding.[26] Minnesota, Wisconsin, Florida, New Hampshire, and Ohio also developed programs, though many saw Massachusetts as launching the most comprehensive effort to support community development.[27] At the federal level, policies such as the Community Reinvestment Act of 1977 and the establishment of the Neighborhood Reinvestment Corporation in 1978 used the weight of the federal government to help CDCs strengthen urban neighborhoods physically, economically, and socially. It was, historian Rebecca Marchiel notes, part of a "financial turn in national urban policy," wherein the federal government placed its "faith in financial institutions to do right by low- and moderate-income urbanities."[28] Structuring government aid as loans instead of grants enticed not only those in government, however; it intrigued philanthropists who saw similar promise in shifting CDCs from being outside the market to active cultivators of it.

Field Building in Philanthropy

The enthusiasm program officers at the Ford Foundation had for Whittlesey and the "new organizational forms" he envisioned for GBCD indicated an eagerness to depart from the politics and strategies of the 1960s.[29] By the start of the new decade, liberal funders such as the Ford Foundation maintained their commitment to community action and the provision of social welfare, but increasingly deemed those goals best achieved through the marketplace rather than through expanded state provision or direct support of neighborhood nonprofits. Boston's GBCD provided some evidence of this possibility but pointed equally to the need for more predictable access to the resources necessary for the capitally intensive processes of housing and economic development. While Massachusetts developed the CDFC, CEDAC, and CEED, the Ford Foundation took a similar path. It structured a portion of its funding as working capital via loans, loan guarantees, and other financing vehicles and incubated a new intermediary, the Local Initiatives Support Corporation (LISC), which launched as an independent nonprofit in 1979.[30] The foundation went one step further too, using its visibility and connections to promote this neoliberal vision of urban development that latched CDCs to the economic mainstream.

In the early 1970s, major foundations, including the Ford Foundation, began to see promise in this idea of community development, but they held a technocratic interpretation of it, eliding concerns about power and politics that motivated activities in the neighborhoods themselves. The Twentieth Century Fund, for example, commissioned research on the subject, resulting in the aptly titled book *CDCs: New Hope for the Inner City*. The volume called for the federal government to create "a national system of support" for CDCs comprised of both financing incentives and technical assistance.[31] These arguments narrowly diagnosed a lack of expertise and financing as holding CDCs back, ignoring how categories of race or ethnicity had excluded groups that were now organized and incorporated as CDCs from investment—and how they continued to do so. Program officers at the Ford Foundation embraced the analysis put forward by other funders. In launching LISC, Ford put resources into nonprofit neighborhoods and helped make them profitable, without necessarily making them equitable.

Looking to fix what it diagnosed as a bug rather than a feature of US political economy, the Ford Foundation "adopted a new strategy of heavy concentration upon CDCs" in 1971.[32] This move first included a pool of funds available for technical assistance for "minority and economic development grants and investments" by CDCs. The effort recognized the need for capital and the growing desire, particularly among Black leaders calling for Black capitalism, to achieve social and economic benefits through business development.[33] The issue of housing, however, remained vexing for Ford staff, who grew frustrated with what they saw as the "unresponsiveness" of the state and market to adequately house low-income Americans.[34] They viewed CDCs as able to occupy "that middle area between the private housing market and the public housing authority" and focused their energies on growing a range of intermediaries calculated to draw capital and respect to CDCs.[35] Philanthropists often call these coordinated activities "field building" to generate knowledge, resources, institutions, and attention to popularize an idea.[36] The Ford Foundation's field building around community development marked a retreat from supporting individual CDCs such as ETC in Boston. Instead, the foundation supported revolving loan funds, training programs, research, and technical assistance programs such as GBCD in Boston and others in Detroit,

Philadelphia, New York, and Los Angeles as well as in rural areas in California, West Virginia, and North Carolina.[37]

LISC might have been pitched as a help to CDCs, but its design reflected a keen desire to gain favor with corporate America, both for its own sake and for the CDCs that, even with the aid of philanthropic and government below-market loans, still depended on commercial lenders. In part, the decision to launch LISC and the shape it took echoed a political and economic context that had knocked the Ford Foundation from its lofty heights at the end of the 1960s. A series of events fueled critiques of the foundation's role in American society and what many on the right saw as an anti-capitalist agenda. Ford's involvement in the controversial Ocean Hill–Brownsville community control experiment in 1968, congressional hearings in 1969 about philanthropic support of civil rights, and the public resignation of board chairman Henry Ford II had damaged the foundation's standing.[38] By the mid-1970s, moreover, the national economic recession had shrunk the endowments of major institutions, Ford's included, and further reduced the availability of federal dollars.[39] With its tarnished reputation and resources shrinking, The Ford Foundation's— and, by extension, LISC's—talk of "entrepreneurial efforts" and embrace of the logics, approaches, and resources of corporate America made both political and economic strategic sense.[40]

In 1979, staff at the Ford Foundation launched LISC, what had been an internal program, as an independent, nationally focused, nonprofit intermediary, offering CDCs financial support and technical assistance for local housing and economic development projects. An initial $10 million capitalization for LISC drew on both philanthropic and corporate donations, including from insurers Aetna and Prudential, who were intrigued by the Ford Foundation's latest project and enamored with promises that their "efforts to revitalize deteriorated communities can reach well beyond charity and into the realm of investment."[41] LISC managed four principal "vehicles of assistance" (loans, loan guarantees, grants, and technical assistance) that staff deployed to support CDC-initiated projects with flexible philanthropic capital—though it did so only if the projects carried the possibility of financial return from rents or other revenue.[42] Those fortunate CDCs able to pass LISC's standards often received a combination of both grants and loans, but LISC strategists preferred using loans and loan guarantees because they could "serve to leverage a much larger pool of funds from private lenders."[43] From LISC's perspective, instead of a one-way grant to support services, loans even at lower interest rates eventually returned to LISC and could be used again to enable other community development projects. Loans, unlike grants, also had the benefit of helping prove to skeptical lenders the creditworthiness of individual CDCs and the ability of community development projects to return modest revenue through rents or sales.

Rather than working to address the political-economic structures that had failed to reward the activities CDCs pursued or the processes that had produced the problems these grassroots nonprofits sought to address, intermediaries such as LISC worked to alter the systems of funding that satisfied the desires of corporate actors. The availability of funding from LISC—and the growing curiosity of the corporate partners—created incentives for CDCs. Rhetorically in its brochures and materially through its giving, LISC steered CDCs to pursue individual development projects "that produce equity and revenue" and to focus on the "asset side of the balance sheet." That LISC would support these "revenue-generating projects" through financing and the strategic use of capital put pressure on CDCs to prioritize economic goals either at the expense of or without regard to political goals.[44] By this logic, LISC staff saw it necessary to instill "business discipline" in CDCs, arguing that communities benefited most from organizational growth, stability in local markets, and secure financing.[45]

One year into operations, LISC created local capital pools in cities and rural areas around the country, extending its model and its lending "to improve the physical and economic conditions of depressed, chiefly urban areas by means of projects to develop business, housing, commerce and industry."[46] Boston had quickly become a favored target of LISC's national office and soon won its own local branch thanks to the track record of local CDCs, support in the statehouse, and availability of private capital. LISC helped seed a loan pool in Boston with its own funds but also fundraised more than $800,000 from local sources by 1981.[47] While banks and corporations contributed funds, the largest gift by far came from the Permanent Charity Fund of Boston to help establish an ongoing, renewable resource for community development in the city. The local funder's contribution of $500,000 far outpaced the more typical $25,000 from Shawmut Bank of Boston and John Hancock Mutual Life Insurance. At this stage, the corporate dollars remained charitable gifts—tax-deductible gifts—but if LISC's model worked as planned, groups like Shawmut Bank would get new lending opportunities subsidized by LISC and others when CDCs went looking for loans.[48] Executives from the banking and real estate industries joined the advisory board of Boston's LISC

chapter and within a few years had overseen the investment of over
$2.5 million in local community development projects, nearly 75 percent
of which went out the door as loans or loan guarantees.[49] Whether they
agreed with the strategy LISC promoted or the market-centric language
it used, community groups in Boston responded to the changing funding
landscape.[50] Thanks to the possibility of loans from LISC and from King's
state programs, by the early 1980s, nearly every neighborhood in the city
had one such entity to attract resources for urban development.

Profits, Portfolios, and the Public Good

By the close of the 1970s, the incorporation of state intermediaries such
as CDFC, CEDAC, and CEED and philanthropic ones such as LISC signaled a new day in community development and in the revitalization of urban neighborhoods. Using public and philanthropic capital to help CDCs
purchase property, rehabilitate housing units, and start small businesses
existed as one of those rare policy proposals that Black power advocate
Mel King, elite liberals at the Ford Foundation, and corporate investors
could, at least on the surface, agree on. New pots of money at the local,
state, and national levels sat ready to make loans and extend other forms
of assistance to CDCs that brought deals forward. LISC's "most important
role," one staff member explained, was to broker deals between neighborhood nonprofits and corporate partners, helping package financing in ways
that made social and economic goals compatible.[51] Yet in boosting CDCs
into the marketplace, the new intermediaries still operated under traditional markers of success, measuring value in monetary terms and with an
expectation of profitability, even when dealing with (and as) nonprofit organizations. Pressures to maintain profitable lending portfolios and prove
the financial viability of CDCs steadily steered staff at intermediaries and
CDCs to prioritize the bottom line. Loans, it turned out, came with their
own sets of constraints and powers, not unlike grants.

   The need for affordable housing in Boston pushed CDCs, such as the
Emergency Tenants' Council, in one direction, but initial lending from the
state agencies pulled in another. Early loans from the commonwealth's
Community Development Finance Corporation and other entities focused
on business development, with a heavy emphasis on job creation. Staff at
the CDFC rationalized, inaccurately, that nonprofit intermediaries like
Greater Boston Community Development had the housing arena suffi-

ciently covered and, following this logic, prioritized goals "to stabilize and expand employment opportunities" amid areas in "greatest need of economic revitalization."[52] Looking to fill a market gap, the agency then made venture capital funds—structured as debt or equity—available for "three-way partnerships" between the state, a business, and a community development corporation, which would represent the community's interest and either own the business in whole or in part to "ensure that public benefit and public purposes are maintained."[53] This structure of funding thus charged the CDC with a linked set of social and economic goals. Under this rubric, the CDFC bought securities to support a grocery store in Dorchester; a weatherization firm in Jamaica Plain; a microfilm business servicing local businesses, government, and educational institutions; and one of the state's largest minority contracting firms.[54] Many of these entities, all sponsored by Boston CDCs, also received financial and technical assistance from CEED and CEDAC as well as from the City of Boston via block grant funds and training allocations from the Comprehensive Employment and Training Act.[55] Within three years, the CDFC built a statewide portfolio of fourteen partnerships with $2.6 million invested, which, staff proudly reported, leveraged an estimated $3.7 million in private capital and supported four hundred new jobs.[56]

Investing in business, however, proved a risky undertaking if measured in financial terms. After all, there were reasons beyond access to capital that made starting a small enterprise in high-poverty areas challenging. The highly publicized failure of Our Market in Dorchester demonstrated the fragility of launching community economic enterprises. In 1979, when the First National Supermarkets decided to close its store in Codman Square, the local CDC tried to attract a buyer to keep the business in operation, because area residents depended on it for food. When no buyer appeared, the staff at the Codman Square CDC decided to buy the property and business for $50,000 with a mortgage from the First American Bank, a loan from the First National Bank of Boston, and equity and a loan from the CDFC. Keeping with the vision of community development, the grocery employed thirty residents and had an eighteen-member board of directors elected from over five hundred residents who purchased memberships to the new market.[57] Mayor White cut the ribbon on opening day in 1979, celebrating the possibilities of urban revitalization. One year later, despite significant changes in management, layout, and merchandising policies, Our Market closed after losing an estimated $1 million. An article in the *Boston Globe* likened the rapid collapse to "Codman Square's version of the Charge of the Light Brigade—a naïve and gallant ride into the valley of debt."[58] As a rather public embarrassment for the CDFC and community, Our Market highlighted both the ability of a state intermediary to package deals and the challenge of doing so in a financially profitable way.

What had begun as a citywide success story of the kind of community investment King had envisioned quickly became a justification to constrict citywide financing and loan opportunities for CDCs.[59] An Our Market board member later explained that the market "was horribly underfinanced" with a debt burden far exceeding the actual equity in the business.[60] It was doomed to fail from the start for reasons far beyond Codman Square; one-off deals, even subsidized ones, could not balance decades of divestment and poverty. CDFC staff defended their choices, noting that their failure rate in lending was close to the 55 percent failure rate of the Small Business Administration and understandable in the context of a down economy and distressed economic markets.[61] Such an explanation mattered little. Local banks that were already skittish about lending to CDCs became even more so. As the CDFC prioritized coinvesting with other public and private lenders to "maximize . . . limited resources," the retreat of private lenders willing to support projects such as Our Market caused a deep conservatism at the CDFC as well.

The frustrations the commonwealth's CDFC experienced in lending for business development contrasted with LISC's strategy and experience with property development. The broader market dynamics of the urban growth machine that conspired to squeeze more and more value out of urban land made physical development a safer investment for both CDCs and their investors. The challenge here was the reverse of that for business development; the economic goals were easier to meet than the social ones of keeping residential and commercial property affordable. An early LISC loan of $250,000 to the Emergency Tenants' Council (which had by that point renamed itself Inquilinos Boricuas en Acción, or IBA) contributed to the $12 million cost of constructing 190 units of affordable housing at Villa Victoria. Consistent with LISC's strategy, Boston CDCs received a combination of grants and loans that, by design, connected public and private sources of investment across the stages of a single project. Several grants between 1981 and 1983 accompanied the loan, helping IBA strengthen its management practices and develop a business plan for real estate development. By 1983, IBA completed construction, rented out all units, and used that rental income to repay the loan in full with 8 percent interest.[62] It was one of the first CDCs in the country to successfully repay a LISC loan. Across town, in 1983, LISC issued a bridge loan for construction costs and a grant to cover the project manager's salary to enable the Dorchester Bay Economic Development Corporation to rehabilitate a four-story 20,000-square-foot commercial property. Within a year, a commercial tenant moved into the new facility, enabling the CDC to repay its full loan by 1985. The Boston projects provided proof, LISC boasted, "that when social investments are properly structured and secured they can return in full principal and interest to the lender for reuse in future projects."[63] An outside evaluator agreed, writing, "The original surprise in LISC is that the business works at all. The biggest surprise is that it works so often."[64]

LISC's continued success depended on cycling the repaid funds in a carefully structured loan portfolio. In a deliberate effort to increase the number of loans issued relative to that of grants, LISC staff based in New York shifted the ratio of loans to grants from two-to-one in 1980 to five-to-one by 1982. By 1983, of the $18 million the intermediary and its local affiliates spent supporting community development projects, $12 million had been in loans.[65] The interest rates on the loans ranged from 3 percent to 11 percent, with most at 8 percent—less than half of market-rate loans at the time. LISC's broad purpose centered on the social value of community development, but loan analysts put aside the content to ensure a productive loan portfolio diversified across several measures—geographic location, risk level, project type, interest rate, and loan period—and responsive to changes in the marketplace and federal policies.[66] A cut in federal long-term financing meant, according to LISC analysts, that starting in 1982, their "best lending opportunities over time will be in the longer-term categories" and presented a strategic "lending opportunity."[67] The portfolio also favored housing development over business development given what the analysts considered "the comparative ease of making housing-related investments through nonprofit institutions."[68] Such a highly structured loan portfolio seemed to be working from LISC's point of view. By 1985, only thirteen of LISC's 197 loans across the country were in default, translating to a loss of only $410,852 on more than $27 million loaned out.[69] The paper infrastructure of LISC's activities—applications, correspondence, reports—came to expose the cold calculations of its portfolio approach. Reports on LISC's activities boiled down to a few lines on each deal, with financial terms cleanly laid out and little mention of the human impact the funding might achieve.

Structuring funding as loans altered the criteria by which analysts at LISC distributed aid and, by extension, the kinds of projects CDCs would be more likely to finance. Under a grant system, staff typically looked for

FIGURE 5.1. *Villa Victoria housing.* After the Emergency Tenants' Council (ETC) won the right to develop Parcel 19 in the South End, it faced the challenge of securing financing. With the assistance of Greater Boston Community Development, ETC emerged as an early example of how affordable housing could be possible and profitable for both the sponsoring nonprofits and the lenders that underwrote them. ETC, which later changed its name to Inquilinos Boricuas en Acción, developed both high-rise towers and low-rise town houses surrounding a community plaza. ("Villa Victoria Housing," ca. 1980–95, A008835, IBA, NU. Image courtesy of Northeastern University Archives and Special Collections.)

social and programmatic returns: how many people would be served, the ability to complete the project, and the community-level impact. Under LISC's loan system, however, return on investment moved from a qualitative assessment to a quantitative metric of financial profitability. The evaluation metrics by which LISC directed loans prioritized portfolio composition, markets, and technical expertise over concerns of justice or the needs of any individual neighborhood. To understand LISC's impact, the Ford Foundation hired an independent evaluator, who found that the foundation had produced an intermediary with "an undeviating commitment to the most impoverished communities in America, but is not interested in giving money away."[70] This was not a group compelled by being equitable with its resources but instead by strategy, results, and organizational strength. Continuing, the evaluator labeled LISC as a group that "unabashedly 'creams'" and "takes the best deals," not a group interested in "spread[ing] the wealth around" with "no obligation to be 'fair.'"[71]

As LISC's investments started to steer CDCs in Boston and cities around the country toward profit-oriented projects, the intermediary shaped the national conversation around community development in that direction as well. Those involved with LISC tended to speak with a vocabulary borrowed from free-market economics even as they pursued liberal goals of reducing poverty and improving urban neighborhoods. Staff repeatedly noted the advantages of private funding such as LISC's, which offered "the freedom to select projects," unlike public funding that was seemingly bound by idealism, favoritism, and bureaucracy. They also noted that the "commitment to safeguard the political consensus" reduced considerations of power or equality to the seemingly neutral logics of a balance sheet.[72] Writing for the Center for the Corporate Public Investment's newsletter, LISC chairman Robert Lilley boasted that LISC's investments put "capital to work" and had found an interest among corporate partners "in funding [charity] in a business like way."[73] Such celebratory accounts made little mention of the central role of philanthropic and public capital in subsidizing private investors and enabling them to reap a full market-rate return on community development projects. Neighborhoods and their residents reaped the use value of affordable housing produced by CDCs and financed with subsidies and the help of intermediaries, but investors continued to reap the exchange value.[74]

Just as in grantmaking, the choices about lending shaped urban neighborhoods. The turn toward market-oriented funding structures over the 1970s narrowed the practice of community development even as it increased opportunities for CDCs.[75] By providing capital at strategic moments in the development process, LISC succeeded in enabling CDCs to compete for traditional bank loans.[76] The need to prove profitability, however, incentivized CDCs to pursue projects most likely to win favor with LISC and the CDFC as well as with traditional lenders, and found them increasingly in housing and commercial development. Some, such as IBA, succeeded in this environment. The favor that the Ford Foundation officer gave in 1971 continued, and a variety of innovative, public-private financing arrangements underwrote the transformation of a decrepit Parcel 19 into the community of Villa Victoria, where affordable housing for elders and families surrounded a community plaza and small businesses. Intermediaries helped legitimate CDCs as managing the physical and economic development of nonprofit neighborhoods, but CDCs continued to face a structural disadvantage in the market. Pressures to subvert, or at least align, social goals with economic ones became increasingly common in cities such as Boston, where policies later labeled as neoliberal became governing realities.[77]

"From the Ground Up"

The financing pressure on CDCs to pursue real estate development aligned with priorities in Boston. A growing Massachusetts economy and an aging housing stock meant that residents in Boston's low-income, predominantly Black and Latinx neighborhoods were neither well nor affordably housed; it also meant that housing development made a more stable, predictable, safe, and profitable investment for both CDCs and their backers. CDCs around Boston were eager to jump into the fray, seeing an opportunity for their neighborhoods and their organizations. Yet both before and after Representative King passed legislation and the Ford Foundation designed LISC in the second half of the 1970s, neighborhood nonprofits in Boston struggled to hold back the decrepitude and displacement around them. At the end of the decade, when a community group in Dorchester sought to redevelop three buildings in Dudley Square, it encountered firsthand the array of public and private intermediaries eager to assist as well as the pains of pursuing urban redevelopment from the ground up.

As mayor, Kevin White agreed on the existence of a housing problem and on the wisdom of positioning CDCs as the ones to fix it. His embrace of these neighborhood nonprofits reflected their increasing acceptance as stewards of public resources aimed to simultaneously meet economic, social, and political goals. The growing enthusiasm for CDCs, however, often preceded the actual availability of dollars from either the commonwealth or LISC during the 1970s. In the meantime, Community Development Block Grant funds remained the most productive tool in the city's kit to steer urban revitalization and the most predictable funding source for CDCs to maintain cash flows for organizational expenses such as salaries, office rent, services, and development projects. White's administration deployed the grantmaking tools it had come to know well and distributed CDBGs to strategically help CDCs acquire and dispose of tax-delinquent properties at low cost to developers, quiet community protest with promised attention to residential neighborhoods, and speak a contagious language of economic growth and stability. In 1975, the city contributed $1.1 million of CDBG funding to the Roxbury Action Program for the rehabilitation and construction of 120 housing units and $1.5 million to the Emergency Tenants' Council for the rehabilitation of 150 units of low- and middle-income housing.[78] A few years later, the city allocated funds to CDCs in Roxbury and the South End as well as in Chinatown, Hyde Park, Jamaica Plain, Dorchester, and more. Though relatively modest given the full cost of housing redevelopment, these municipal allocations helped move CDC projects forward in pragmatic as well as symbolic ways.[79]

Beyond the political win White achieved in supporting community organizations looking to improve their neighborhoods, his strategic deployment of CDBG funds for housing development helped meet his goals of growing the tax base in Boston and squeezing more revenue out of the land in the city. In an era of municipal austerity, the continued reliance on the property tax as the primary source of revenue steered his administration to focus on housing rehabilitation and construction as part of its broader urban revitalization strategy. The mayor's plan for CDBG funds centered on a premise increasingly popular among Democrats that government's role "is not to compete with or attempt to replace private investment," nor for that matter to change the policies that regulated it, "but rather . . . to provide a setting and incentives to encourage this private investment."[80] In this framework, attention to the housing market highlighted the desire for building "stability" and "confidence" in the local housing market over the provision of shelter.[81] The economic returns city officials and CDC directors expected to see through housing development and the social need for it reflected a surging housing market in the Boston metro region.

Governor Dukakis's programs to support business development in the commonwealth might have foundered in low-income areas—as the case of Our Market made clear—but elsewhere helped jump-start the state's high-tech economy with direct consequences for the regional housing market.[82] Emerging from the 1970s recession, real estate speculators recognized the rising importance of professional services to the city and purchased downtown real estate before successfully convincing Mayor White to undo the program of rent control he had initiated during his first term.[83] Pressures in the housing market soon followed: the price of a single-family home tripled between 1975 and 1984, and rental prices increased 48 percent.[84] As in other cities, Boston's housing market got pulled in two directions by condominium conversions in desirable neighborhoods and cycles of speculation and abandonment in impoverished ones, which together reduced the availability of housing and drove up rates at both high and low ends.[85] By 1980, 54 percent of families in Boston qualified for subsidized housing, while an astonishing twenty-three thousand housing units sat vacant due not to weak demand but to an aging housing stock that landlords could either not afford to repair or simply chose not to. Unevenly distributed around the city, vacancies were highest in predominantly Black neighborhoods, with rates as high as 17.2 percent vacant in North Dorchester, 15.4 percent in Jamaica Plain, 13.8 percent in Roxbury, and 12.7 percent in the South End.[86]

A surplus of vacant housing, however, did not directly translate into market opportunities for Boston's growing number of CDCs, nor was it certain that these neighborhood-based nonprofits were the proper entities to manage growth in the citywide housing market. The advent and availability of public and private funding sources by the end of the 1970s had supported the emergence of a local CDC sector increasingly positioned to make socially productive affordable housing deals economically productive for investors. Nevertheless, changes in federal urban policy and the local housing market made redevelopment increasingly expensive for local groups. Further from the days of the federal bulldozer and top-down planning that had cleared vast swaths of land over which activists demanded control—as had been the case in Lower Roxbury and the South End—CDCs in the late 1970s and early 1980s had to acquire abandoned properties or vacant lots on a piecemeal basis and bring the individual buildings to intermediaries such as GBCD, LISC, and the commonwealth's CDFC and CEDAC for financing, because even small parcels could cost a substantial sum.[87] Scouting individual buildings in this way—often triple-deckers or small apartment buildings—made producing affordable housing a more time-consuming, complex, and expensive endeavor and less likely to create political and economic empowerment at the scale that marginalized communities sought.

One mile south of the Villa Victoria, Dudley Square sits on the border between Roxbury and North Dorchester. The intersection of several major streets—Blue Hill Avenue, Magazine Street, Hampden Street, and Dudley Street—had once been home to a thriving business area with a market, barbershop, publishing house, fur shop, coffee shop, and drugstore known for its milk shakes.[88] The Dudley Town Common and St. Patrick's Catholic Church anchored the neighborhood both physically and socially. Once a predominantly Irish and Italian parish in the first half of the twentieth century, St. Patrick's had become home to increasing numbers of Black, Latinx, and Cape Verdean congregants in the 1970s in a pattern that mimicked the broader demographic changes as migrants from the islands of Puerto Rico and Cape Verde moved to the area, as did African American and Latinx families displaced from elsewhere in the city by rising costs and urban renewal. These new Dudley residents found what organizers and authors Peter Medoff and Holly Sklar described as an "unnatural earthquake" of racism and divestment that shook the neighborhood slowly and violently in the 1970s and 1980s to render it one of the poorest and most abandoned areas in the city.[89]

Dudley Square exemplified the selective policy enforcement and neglect that characterized so many urban neighborhoods at the time and contributed further to its decline. By 1981, a third of the area in the neighborhood lay vacant, fueling a cycle of arson, abandonment, and illegal trash dumping that was becoming increasingly common in cities around the United States.[90] Ché Madyun, who with her family moved to the area in 1976, later recalled a neighborhood where "fire engines used to run up and down the street every night" and where "you could always smell smoke."[91] One of those fires caused significant damage to the basement and first floor of 391-397 Dudley Street, one of the anchor commercial buildings in the neighborhood, rendering it uninhabitable.[92] Such issues both reflected and exacerbated plummeting real estate values and an escalating list of necessary repairs to merely keep buildings at code. Renters often faced horrid conditions but, out of lack of alternatives and fear of eviction, tolerated them. The Bermudes family, for example, moved into a four-bedroom unit at 308 Hampden Street with no hot water, no electricity, and damaged walls, joining neighbors dealing with rodents and insects, broken locks, no lights, and falling-in ceilings.[93] In the winter of 1981, when a nun from St. Patrick's found an eighty-six-year-old woman in her apartment with frostbite, residents took the landlord to court and reached out to local nonprofit La Alianza Hispana for assistance.[94]

Though special to Dudley residents, La Alianza was a typical neighborhood nonprofit. It had been born in the expanding nonprofit sector of the War on Poverty when Frieda Garcia, then working at the Roxbury Multi-Service Center, observed a dearth of services for the city's growing Spanish-speaking population. With the help of federal funding via the Model Cities program, Garcia and a small team incorporated La Alianza Hispana as an independent nonprofit organization in 1971 and began offering a range of social services in education, employment, health, housing, recreation, and youth development out of their office in Dudley Square.[95] By the early 1980s, La Alianza depended nearly entirely on government contracts to cover its range of services, and when federal and state cuts prompted a wave of layoffs, those remaining began to rethink its funding strategy.[96] The agency's director at the time, Nelson Merced, held the organization together through a patchwork of philanthropic grants and public contracts, including from the Massachusetts Department of Public Health for a drug and alcohol prevention program, from the Massachusetts Department of Social Services for a youth advocacy and counseling program, and from the Massachusetts Department of Education for a supplemental education program. Even with those contracts, however, La Alianza frequently ran deficits and used emergency short-term loans to make payroll.[97]

Expanding from social services to housing intrigued Merced, seeing in that pivot an opportunity to stabilize both the organization's bottom line and support the neighborhood. La Alianza, like RMSC in Roxbury, had long been involved in assisting residents with housing and taking on negligent landlords, but in 1980, the organization explored a housing revitalization program for the first time. "The housing needs in the area are totally overwhelming," Merced reported to the board.[98] As Dudley residents took the property owner to court for code violations and the handful of buildings involved went into receivership, La Alianza started to calculate what it would take to purchase, rehab, and keep affordable the anchor buildings of Dudley Square. Soon thereafter, the board voted to incorporate a separate nonprofit, founding Nuestra Comunidad ("Our Community") Development Corporation, and applied for grant assistance from one of the commonwealth's programs to get it up and running.[99] The new CDC differed from the Emergency Tenants' Council and the Lower Roxbury

FIGURE 5.2. *Opening La Alianza Hispana's new offices (1974).* Frieda Garcia (*right*) founded
La Alianza Hispana in 1971 as a multiservice center for Boston's growing Spanish-speaking
population. Three years later, Mayor Kevin White (*second from right*) attended the opening
of the neighborhood nonprofit's new offices in Dudley Square. La Alianza then helped start a
community development corporation, Nuestra Comunidad, to help revitalize Dudley Square.
(Mayor's Office of Public Service Photo Service, "Boston Mayor, Kevin White, Holds a Small
Garden Spade at the Groundbreaking Ceremony for La Alianza Hispana's Community Center," October 23, 1974, A005401, LAH, NU. Image courtesy of Northeastern University Archives and Special Collections.)

Community Corporation in that Dudley Square had not received the same
shock and threat of urban renewal that had prompted the organization in
those other neighborhoods. Instead, Nuestra Comunidad represented a
new wave of CDCs that emerged to tap into funding opportunities offered
by state and philanthropic programs.[100]

The decay and unsafe conditions that prompted the receivership of
several Dudley buildings exposed negligence on the part of the owner but
also the wider real estate and labor market conditions that had depressed
rents below what owners needed for upkeep and above what families
could afford to pay. This presented a problem for La Alianza Hispana and

Nuestra Comunidad, just as it did for the property owners. Funds from the state, through CEDAC, paid for consultants to conduct a feasibility study of the buildings in question, which were found to be barely habitable and prohibitively expensive to repair. Back taxes, liens on municipal water and sewer bills, and mortgage debts totaled near $150,000 for just one building—a sum unattainable from possible rental income alone.[101] At the Hampden Street building, for example, rents could support only 11 percent of the necessary repair list, which included issues with the roof, plumbing and electrical systems, and heating. The prospects looked worse for the Dudley Street building, where rental income of $7,500 was a small fraction of the $200,000 needed to rebuild after the fire damage. These numbers were even the optimistic estimates that assumed the city would forgo liens on the properties, the bank would lend more capital than the buildings had in equity, and tenants would pay the rents necessary to make the venture just break even.[102]

Little market incentive existed to purchase and rehabilitate the buildings, but La Alianza and city and state governments saw social and economic reason, broadly defined, to take action. After all, that was precisely the problem CDCs aimed to solve. Doing so would assure the tenants a level of decent, sanitary housing and also add to the city's tax base, stabilize a declining real estate market, and bolster confidence in the neighborhood among residents and onlookers. One observer thought that it would also produce some "political mileage for the Mayor in making this 'contribution'" of city resources and public endorsement for the project.[103] The Dudley buildings, on the one hand, represented so much more than the twenty-six apartment units they held; on the other hand, the number paled in comparison to the neighborhood's housing needs. It was, one funding application described, "a modest but symbolically important first project."[104] Public and philanthropic programs existed to help CDCs like Nuestra, but tapping into those wells proved difficult and uncertain, requiring a good dose of politicking and relationship management with city officials, local bankers, politicians, and LISC staff.[105]

Meetings and negotiations went on for years, even after Nuestra gained the investment—of resources and attention—from prominent intermediaries. Bob Whittlesey's Greater Boston Community Development managed the syndication process to raise capital for the project from investors interested in supporting a nonprofit project in exchange for a reduction in their taxes, but he delivered only sixteen of the twenty-four anticipated investors. This shortfall then triggered problems for Massachusetts Hous-

ing and Finance Agency, CDFC, and LISC, all of which had promised
to issue loans on the expectation of larger equity produced in the syndication proceeds.[106] Consultants from GBCD helped Nuestra qualify for
public housing subsidies via the Boston Housing Authority. Those subsidies, however, only covered the Hampden Street buildings, because the
fire damage to the Dudley Street ones proved too extensive to qualify for
the "moderate rehabilitation" program.[107] Finally, in the fall of 1984, the
fledgling Nuestra Comunidad CDC closed on the properties. Their pro
bono lawyer, an associate from Goulston & Storrs, sarcastically offered to
send the full binder of closing documents to the intermediaries involved
in the deal "as shining proof of why these projects so rarely occur."[108] The
system of loans and financing assembled by the commonwealth and private funders had come to resemble the patchwork quilt of grant funding that characterized the social service side of neighborhood nonprofit
organizations.

The Hampden and Dudley projects signified the move by neighborhood CDCs to engage more directly in housing rehabilitation and rely on
financing and consulting intermediaries to help them do so. By the early
1980s, the state financial agencies focused increasing attention on the
housing arena, touting the economic benefits with comments that housing
efforts "were particularly fruitful" and "return[ed] property to the tax
rolls."[109] The high capitalization costs of housing financing, as opposed to
business development, also improved the leverage ratios that state intermediaries claimed credit for unlocking and tracked as evidence of impact.
An obsession with growing value and an expectation that a few new units
of housing would reverse market declines fueled the interest in housing
from intermediaries like LISC as well as by nonprofit CDCs, which, in
addition to envisioning a social benefit for their communities, saw an economic benefit for their organizational bottom lines through the prospect
of rents.

A shared logic and financial pressures inserted nonprofit CDCs and
the low-income neighborhoods they served into the broader political-
economy of real estate and finance that transformed urban areas during
this period.[110] The quickening pace of community development failed to
dent the local housing market, which continued to entice young professionals intrigued by city living and line the pockets of developers and their
investors.[111] Even as the creation of new intermediaries and funding instruments helped CDCs pursue more housing projects, the full benefits of those
projects increasingly accrued to those outside the community: investors

seeing returns, intermediaries proving their model, governments collecting property taxes, and property owners seeing rising market values.

Community Development as Mainstream

In a surprising matchup of two familiar Boston politicians, the 1983 mayoral election represented a contest between two different visions of community development and the utility of CDCs to urban governance. It was the first election since 1968 in which Kevin White would not be a candidate and the first since the budget cuts from the Reagan administration and statewide referendum on real estate taxes, Proposition 2½, dramatically reduced the city's revenue. Out of a crowded primary, the general election pitted two Democrats—state representative Mel King, the first Black candidate to advance out of a primary, against city councilor Ray Flynn, famous for staunchly opposing busing in the 1970s—in a race that embodied the broader tensions and transformations of the Democratic Party.[112] Both candidates ran on platforms that critiqued downtown interests in a contest that became yet another "year of the neighborhoods." Their respective celebrations of community control could not be disentangled, however, from the still-salient racial politics surrounding school desegregation. Despite divergent ideas about what community control could (or should) achieve and what it might look like, both candidates pointed, astonishingly, to the work of community development corporations and the intermediaries that had sprouted around them as models. This alignment of politics and a particular vision of governance demonstrated a growing acceptance not only of community development corporations in American cities but also of tying CDCs to the housing and financial markets.

King's campaign built on his decades of political activism and coalesced around a diverse "Rainbow Coalition" of voters from across the city. As a Black candidate with a progressive track record, it had taken two mayoral campaigns to make it past the primary stage. He had run against Kevin White in the 1979 election and after that defeat, published a book on Black community organizing in Boston. Equal parts history, political theory, and mobilizing tool, *Chain of Change* laid out a progressive agenda for Boston that, consistent with King's legislative record in the statehouse, envisioned neighborhood nonprofits as governing units for communities to voice opinions and hold the political and economic power with which to enact them.[113] To mount his 1983 campaign, King reached out to pro-

FIGURE 5.3. *Mayoral candidates Mel King and Ray Flynn debate (1983).* The 1983 mayoral race in Boston between Mel King and Ray Flynn represented two different versions of what community development would look like in Boston. King was the first non-white candidate to make it out of the primary election and ran on a progressive platform called the "Rainbow Coalition." ("Mayoral Candidates Mel King and Ray Flynn in Debate at Old South Church," November 1983, Boston Globe Photographs. Image courtesy of Northeastern University Archives and Special Collections and the *Boston Globe*.)

gressive voters across the city, often via the nonprofits that represented various neighborhood and demographic identities. Into the Rainbow Coalition he welcomed gay and lesbian voters, elite progressives, and immigrant communities of Caribbean, African, and Asian residents.[114] Each of these populations had its own coalitions of nonprofit organizations, in which King recognized political, social, and economic power.

In contrast to King's progressive vision of community development, Flynn's was a pragmatic politics that circumscribed the activities of neighborhood groups even as he welcomed them into city governance. He ran a relatively traditional Boston campaign for mayor. An Irish Catholic from South Boston, Flynn had been an All-American basketball player at Providence College and had a brief professional career before being cut by the Boston Celtics in 1964. In the early 1970s, he launched a political career

first in the statehouse and then as a city councilor, where he built a reputation for defending the interests of white, blue-collar Bostonians. The tactic worked, and despite massive drives to register new voters by the Rainbow Coalition, Flynn won 55 percent of the vote. Following his victory
over King and coached by political analysts looking to pacify King's voters,
Flynn put his support behind the CDCs, which had, many noted, proven in
the previous decade to both generate local support and get housing built.[115]

After the Boston Redevelopment Authority spent the late 1960s and
early 1970s undercutting community development, under Mayor Flynn it
endorsed the concept as part of a broader strategic recognition of how
CDCs could help address city needs. By the early 1980s, the agency had
softened its staunch opposition to the decentralized neighborhood development activities and instead came to see the practical benefit of having CDCs work in residential neighborhoods while the BRA maintained
an active renewal agenda focused on large-scale projects—including the
Charlestown Navy Yard, Copley Place, and North and South Stations—
that aimed, as always, to "generate considerable growth" and "increased
tax revenues."[116] Support for CDCs also came from the city's new Neighborhood Development and Employment Agency, headed in the early
1980s by an alumnus from Kevin White's administration, Paul Grogan. The
agency functioned as a neighborhood-focused analogue to the downtown-
focused BRA and became the municipal hub for distributing CDBG
funds. The agency celebrated a "sprawling network of nonprofit organizations" in the city and sought ways to draw corporate and philanthropic resources "to significantly increase the effectiveness" of the public sector.[117]
Brokering partnerships between the public, private, and nonprofit sectors
became the primary goal for the city agency in its housing development
strategies.

Local foundations in Boston continued to champion not only community development but the increasingly financialized forms of social assistance that incentivized a particular version of it. The city's community
foundation, known first as the Permanent Charity Fund and later as the
Boston Foundation, had been one of the initial backers of both early CDCs
and the intermediary organizations that arose to assist them.[118] Then in
1985, the Godfrey M. Hyams Charitable Trust went a step further and
used its endowment to create a secondary market for social investments
by purchasing debt from Boston LISC. As productive as LISC's loan pools
had proved for local CDCs, once capital was loaned out, LISC had to wait
years for repayment, particularly with a shift to longer-term debt financ-

ing that, in the meantime, shrank its capacity to loan. To accelerate the
lending cycling, the Hyams Trust reduced its grant budget for housing to
purchase $1 million of Boston LISC's debt, incorporating it into the foun-
dation's $45 million endowment portfolio. This purchase accounted for
about half of Boston LISC's outstanding obligations, most of which would
not see complete repayment for four years, which served to rapidly rein-
fuse capital back into the loan pool to be used for new loans. In a joint press
release, the executive director of the Hyams Trust explained that the decision simultaneously "achieve[d] both the foundation's social objectives
and its investment objectives."[119] This justification would later be known
as a "double bottom line" of meeting both social and economic goals.

Funding channels available to community development corporations
continued to evolve throughout the 1980s, as government agencies and intermediaries fine-tuned the subsidies that incentivized private investment
in community development. By 1986, even the US Congress adopted the
market-oriented and financialized strategies tested by intermediaries such
as Greater Boston Community Development, the Massachusetts Statehouse, LISC, the Hyams Trust, and the corporate-led Boston Housing
Partnership. The Tax Reform Act of 1986 created the Low-Income Housing Tax Credit (LIHTC) as the latest step in a long history of using tax
policy—via tax syndication, tax shelters, and now tax credits—to draw
private capital into the construction and maintenance of affordable housing.[120] In particular, the LIHTC appealed to corporations looking to reduce their tax burden, as opposed to earlier syndication processes that targeted individual investors.

The legislation was a signal achievement for LISC and others who backed
the measure and later helped create a market for the new tax credits.[121] In
1988 alone, LISC raised $52 million from forty corporations using the tax
credit. These funds supported thirty-three CDCs in fourteen cities and
helped those groups finance two thousand units of housing.[122] In Boston,
intermediaries hosted a conference with a technical overview of the new
legislation and recommendations of how investors and developers might
benefit from financing combinations offered by LIHTCs.[123] Soon a secondary market emerged for LITHCs as developers—for-profit and nonprofit—sold their credits to those who had nothing to do with housing.
The physical and economic development of urban neighborhoods became
fully tethered to the choices of private investors as policies increasingly
steered public resources through intermediaries to accommodate the demands of financial investors seeking profit.

Boston continued to emerge as a national leader in the broadening field of community development, and many local advocates found a national audience. Greater Boston Community Development rebranded in 1989 as the Community Builders to begin work at a national scale.[124] National LISC hired Boston's director of the Neighborhood Development and Employment Agency, Paul Grogan, as its new president in the mid-1980s. Despite no experience working in a CDC, Grogan had made a name for himself earlier in the decade forging partnerships in education, job training, and housing with Boston's business community.[125] Grogan replicated the example of the Hyams Trust and led LISC to create its own secondary market, the Local Initiatives Managed Assets Corporation, capitalized with $10 million in 1988.[126] This continued the pattern of structuring money as loans instead of as grants, which had previously covered expenditures such as salaries and office space, pressured CDCs to seek revenue-producing projects to keep their organizations afloat.

As a candidate for president in 1988, Governor Michael Dukakis further elevated the community development efforts from Massachusetts and cemented the kinds of financing arrangements that fueled such activities as emblematic of a new Democratic Party. His version of community development owed much to the legislation written by Mel King but had long departed from King's initial vision. Dukakis purposely sought to distance himself from Lyndon Johnson's version of liberalism and King's of Black power, and proudly celebrated a role for finance and markets in social welfare activities. Previewing the "third-way" politics that Bill Clinton would espouse in the 1990s, Dukakis dismissed government's role as one of *doing* through "overly centralized state bureaucracy" and instead celebrated one of *brokering* through "local partnerships" enabled by "the state's technical assistance and financial support."[127]

Conclusion

The year before Michael Dukakis ran for president, a reporter for the *Boston Globe* interviewed Mel King upon the opening of a new, mixed-income housing development in the South End located across the street from his own house. King reflected, "I walk out of my house every day and look at the building and remember what it took for us to get this far."[128] A sense of fatigue and accomplishment must have tinged his words. Nearly twenty years had passed since King and his allies took over the parking lot where the housing complex now stood and reclaimed the land as Tent City. Despite promises from the Boston Redevelopment Authority, the parking lot stood empty for over a decade while federal and city subsides supported developers building luxury condominiums, a high-end shopping mall, and professional office space in the neighboring Copley Place development.[129] Neighborhood protests called out the years of broken promises and hypocrisy as the Copley Place development further displaced residents and squeezed the housing market.

Protests helped sustain attention to the need for affordable housing in the South End, but it took a CDC and several intermediaries to get some built. Incorporated in the early 1980s, the Tent City Corporation negotiated for the rights to build mixed-income housing on that formerly occupied parking lot as part of the broader Copley Square–South End redevelopment plans. It did so with the technical assistance of GBCD and from the commonwealth's CEDAC program as well as a $32 million financing agreement drawing on a familiar list of government programs and intermediaries. The final tally of 271 new housing units represented less than half of what the Tent City Corporation had hoped for but was still larger than most projects in the decades after large-scale urban clearance had slowed. Even if it stood out for its size, Tent City's financing, institutional relationships, and emphasis on economic value captured the new era of community development that had emerged from the 1970s. Materials described the Tent City development as a model of "balanced growth" in the city, but the Copley development loomed literally and figuratively. The city justified its support for the Copley project by promising proceeds from a repaid loan for Copley's construction to help foot the bill for Tent City; the land Tent City occupied had initially been cleared for the Copley development; and Tent City existed atop a seven-hundred-space parking garage built by the Copley developers to accommodate mall patrons and suburban commuters.[130] Those involved hoped the public-private partnerships assembled might "become a positive symbol of Boston's ability to solve such difficult urban dilemmas."[131]

Despite such optimism, the existence of a public-private partnership and eventual delivery of a needed 271 units of housing could not solve the problems in Boston, which, on balance, developments such as the one at Copley Place exacerbated even as they created modest gains in affordable housing. At best, arrangements such as those behind the Tent City development put a minor dent in a problem greater in scale, scope, and structure than a single CDC could hope to tackle. As the project neared completion, the Tent City Corporation anticipated between ten thousand and fifteen thousand applicants for the 203 subsidized units, only a portion of which had been set aside for those with the lowest incomes.[132] On the first day of enrollment, two thousand people waited in line three or four abreast for a chance to apply. A mother of two, Angela Lyes, showed up four hours before the doors opened to get her application in, hoping to escape her current housing situation in Roxbury, where rats and roaches infested her unit and broken lights left the hallways dark. As if that was not enough motivation to seek new accommodations, Lyes's building was slated for conversion to condominiums. Each applicant had a similar story, including Glynis and Darryl White of Mattapan, who were sharing a bedroom with their two children in a three-bedroom unit they split with two other families.[133] Community developers had built a tent city out of bricks and mortar that still left many out in the cold.

Boston provided evidence that CDCs could produce affordable housing and repay the loans that enabled them to do so, and sometimes at a profit to the lenders. Neighborhood nonprofits had already established themselves as conduits of social and political power over the previous decades, and with the financing arrangements of intermediaries, they added economic power to that array by the 1980s. CDCs such as the Emergency Tenants' Council, Nuestra Comunidad, and Tent City rehabilitated housing, responded to abandonment, repurposed vacant lots, attracted subsidies and investment, strengthened local housing markets, and protected the interests of residents. Through both the physical changes they delivered to urban neighborhoods and the processes by which they did so, CDCs reinforced nonprofit neighborhoods as spaces where decision-making and resources flowed through nonprofit entities. The model on display in Boston, however, only loosely resembled what community activists had promoted in the late 1960s, when demands for community control linked the physical redevelopment to economic and political power for those long denied it. By the 1980s, the horizons had significantly narrowed to a near exclusive focus on housing and included active participation in financialized means of operating. The shift reflected a response to broader economic currents and the kinds of public and private funding available; nonetheless, it replicated inequalities based on race and income rather than reducing them.[134]

Even as nonprofit CDCs operated on the front lines of affordable housing production, the policies and landscape of intermediaries that helped them do so had transformed a once radical idea about Black and Latinx economic and political power into an engine of neighborhood revitalization that returned profit not to low-income residents but to investors. By the mid-1980s, Boston had gained national recognition for its infrastructure of nonprofit intermediaries. These groups—far more likely to be founded and led by credentialed white men, such as Bob Whittlesley, than the CDCs with which they partnered—had politically and economically mitigated the risk in community development.[135] Their involvement soothed investors still hesitant to lend to community nonprofits and spread potential losses among philanthropic and government intermediaries to assure corporate lenders a competitive return. Intermediaries encouraged community development but soon became ends unto themselves with their own organizational processes, budgetary pressures, networking opportunities, political access, public visibility, and priorities that just as often clashed as aligned with the goals residents espoused for their neighborhoods. These pressures flowed downstream to CDCs, evident in the promotion of housing over business incubation, in the selection of projects based on possible revenue, and in the professionalization of CDC staff as everything hinged on financial bottom lines over social or political ones.[136] A profound change in the system of affordable housing production had not produced a structural change to an unequal and widening housing market. Staff at nonprofit intermediaries recognized the inadequacy of their piecemeal approach but accepted limited achievements over none and saw value in keeping the growth machine churning for the city as a whole.[137] They accepted a privatized and financialized inclusion over continued exclusion.

Housing intermediaries and the financial products they promoted by the mid-1980s accelerated a neoliberal politics that prioritized profit and embraced public-private partnerships to achieve a narrowly defined set of social goals. Though few involved would have seen themselves as champions of a neoliberal agenda, the promotion of community development through financialized nonprofit intermediaries bore many of the hallmarks of neoliberalism. The pursuit of social goals by market means, the abstraction of people and places in investment portfolios, the celebration of "partnership" and downplaying of power differentials, the creation of a competitive marketplace for loans, the promotion of individual or on-off solutions, and the concentration of power defined American neoliberalism and, it turns out, flowed through the nonprofit sector. That community development helped justify such logic revealed how vulnerable marginalized communities remained despite the acceptance of CDCs by those in government, banks, and foundations. It also foreshadowed the central role of nonprofit organizations more generally in neoliberal policies during the later 1980s and 1990s as vehicles expected to make social goals compatible with economic ones. Community development activities helped pave the way for these expectations to take hold not just in housing but in a variety of policy arenas.

CHAPTER SIX

The Partners

On the heels of a recession in the 1970s and renewed attention to housing in Boston, the commonwealth experienced a period of sustained economic growth during the 1980s. It became known as the "Massachusetts Miracle" in a clever, if misleading, bit of political speech. The public incentives Governor Dukakis created to lure the high-tech and biotech industries seemed to have worked, which in turn helped keep a new generation of knowledge workers employed, housing prices high, and professional and financial services firms busy. Boston's metro region appeared to have not only emerged from deindustrialization but begun to thrive as a hub of a new economy. These achievements, and the credit he took for them, became a signature talking point on Dukakis's presidential campaign trail in 1988. The golden road of Route 128 continued to hum with activity, and even downtown Boston saw a resurgence with demand for luxury condominiums, office space, and consumer goods.

Yet at the end of the decade, a report by the Boston Foundation dared ask the question on the lips of many in the 1980s: "Some say that a rising tide of prosperity lifts all boats, but whose boats are those we see, broken on the shore?"[1] In a clear rebuttal to Reagan's oft-quoted economic rationale, the authors of *In the Midst of Plenty* noted that, although poverty rates were down since 1980, one in six Bostonians still lived below the poverty line at the end of the decade.[2] Poverty rates were also, frustratingly, higher in Boston than they were at the start of the War on Poverty in 1960, erasing the modest gains achieved by 1970. Boston, like so many urban centers in the United States, experienced the 1980s as a cascade of urban crises.[3] Issues such as budget austerity, unemployment, school dropout rates, homelessness, crack cocaine, and displacement were all manifestations of a widening of economic inequality triggered, in part, by the state's boom and compounded by unresolved legacies of racial inequality. Even as people disagreed on why certain boats failed to rise, it was clear at least whose foundered on the shore: single mothers and children and people of color.

The intensification of poverty in Boston occurred, moreover, at a time of retreating federal aid and declining state and local revenue. In November 1980, Massachusetts voters sent a message that they wanted—or rather, demanded—reductions in public spending and tax cuts at every level of government. By a slim margin, Massachusetts voters supported Ronald Reagan for president, and by a wider one approved a ballot measure to reduce the property tax across the state.[4] Known as Proposition 2½, the referendum capped local property taxes at 2.5 percent, limited annual tax increases, and required cities and towns to aggressively reduce taxes annually until the 2.5 percent threshold had been reached. Following California's tax revolt in 1978, Massachusetts's Proposition 2½ dramatically altered the tax formulas on which towns and cities based their annual spending, causing what economists called a "sudden quantum lurch to the public economy of Massachusetts."[5] Reductions in revenue sharing, social welfare spending, and direct aid to individuals from the Reagan administration then compounded these local cuts, bringing new levels of austerity to Boston and its residents. The fates of neighborhood nonprofits and the city of Boston had become so intertwined over the previous decades that the dramatic cuts to government spending threatened to pull both asunder. Despite Reagan's faith in private charity to compensate for a retreating state, the American nonprofit sector had expanded dramatically over the postwar period not in spite of government spending but because of it.[6]

With limited prospects from the federal government, state and local officials actively drew corporate leaders into the work of solving the city's problems, celebrating with new vigor the idea of public-private partnerships that included corporations and business leaders into the work of urban governance. As governor, Michael Dukakis pledged to make Massachusetts a national model for "genuine public-private partnership," and, in the final years of his mayoralty, Kevin White proclaimed in 1983 such arrangements "an urban improvement whose time has come."[7] Coming from proud Democrats, such rhetoric demonstrated how far the party and its ideological position had already retreated from the commitments of the New Deal and Great Society and how proactive liberal leaders were in encouraging neoliberal governance practices.[8] At the same time, the embrace of private corporations and community organizations in moments of fiscal and political uncertainty had been a winning formula for urban renewal and the crisis of the 1960s, and it might just work in a new era. Government publications, political rhetoric, and administrative allocations catered to a surprisingly receptive audience of urban elites, who worried that the visible manifestations of poverty threatened Boston's improving reputation and, by extension, their personal and professional investments in the city. Courting projects based on their revenue potential and tapping the resources of business executives, however, meant accepting the terms of their involvement, which often centered on a critique of government action and a desire to relocate responsibility for public activities to the private sphere.

The rhetoric of public-private partnerships, however, obscured the range of governing arrangements brokered in Boston during the 1980s and flattened the tensions in such arrangements.[9] Who or what constituted the private and the public, and the terms of the partnership ranged widely, reflecting the ongoing negotiations between those with resources and those needing them, and those committed to democratic processes and those looking to skirt them. The binary of public-private left nonprofit organizations in an ambiguous role given their legal status as private corporations but ones chartered for a public purpose and often operating with public funding. In time, both economic elites and grassroots groups found ways to exploit that ambiguity to their advantage. Boston's most prominent public-private partnerships incorporated new nonprofits to manage or embody the partnership, seeing tax-exempt status as financially advantageous and politically appealing. New organizations such as the Boston Compact and the Boston Housing Partnership coordinated responses to crises of too many school dropouts and too little affordable housing, while the Dudley Street Neighborhood Initiative joined local funders and residents to build a new Dudley Square.[10] Even with such diversity of arrangements, clear consistencies anchored these approaches, which were often initiated and conceived by economic elites, encouraged and underwritten by government agencies, and designed to meet the perceived specialized needs of minority populations while leaving the broad political, economic, and social structures in place.

Only some of these efforts included neighborhood nonprofits as partners, revealing, simultaneously, their utility, malleability, and expendability. Neighborhood nonprofits, particularly from predominantly Black and Latinx areas, had spent the previous decades claiming both public and private roles, positioning themselves as more rooted in disenfranchised communities than the government and more attentive to social welfare needs than corporations. This groundwork made neighborhood non-profits valuable partners for the 1980s, able to legitimize and diversify partnerships often brokered by white men. The authority neighborhood nonprofits derived came from their ties to the bounded geography of a particular nonprofit neighborhood in ways that, it turned out, carried both benefits and limitations. Groups such as the Dudley Street Neighborhood Initiative represented residents in partnerships for Dudley Square, but those same neighborhood ties became a justification to belittlingly ex-clude neighborhood nonprofits from municipal policy or urban reform, spaces reserved for those with, supposedly, a citywide view.[11] Much of the popularity of public-private partnerships among business types and the politicians catering to them stemmed from their ability to simultaneously include and exclude neighborhood nonprofits and the urban populations they represented.

Goals for Boston

The City of Boston's reliance on the property tax as its primary source of revenue made the November 1980 passage of Proposition 2½ particularly painful. Projected deficits triggered an immediate reduction in public em-ployment and services across the commonwealth, and in Boston, the city government eliminated 21 percent of its workforce to chip away at a $75 million shortfall.[12] Included in that cut were 351 staff members in the mayor's office, which consolidated several departments before dipping into Community Development Block Grants to make payroll.[13] In the twilight of his sixteen years as mayor, Kevin White did what he could to keep the city afloat. After all, that kind of crisis management had characterized most of his time in office, as had his engagement with nonprofit organiza-tions as a means of doing so. This time, however, Proposition 2½ and cuts from the Reagan administration meant the city had even fewer options to structure partnerships. As a result, the city government under White and then his successor, Ray Flynn, embraced the involvement of corpo-rate elites, who expressed concern about Boston and a desire to shape its future. During an era of cuts, an initiative on private-sector partnerships became the sole addition to the city's otherwise shrinking agenda.

Even the traditional remedies for budgetary woes were unavailable to Boston in 1981. The municipal bond market, to which local governments often turned for capital improvement projects such as repairs to schools, hospitals, and streets became prohibitively expensive as cities and towns already held debt and watched their credit ratings fall and interest rates rise.[14] Federal revenue-sharing formulas implemented under Nixon became steadily unfavorable to Boston over the 1970s, and Reagan's elimination of the program and subsequent cuts to urban aid worsened the budgetary problems.[15] At the state level, the governor displayed some willingness to help municipalities, but only after public pressure mounted.[16] Even then, the commonwealth faced its own budgetary challenges and made cuts to human services and welfare provision that further compounded municipal reductions. The situation became so bad that cities and towns raised library fees and rentals for softball fields in a futile effort to fill the gaps.[17]

Concern soon mounted among corporate executives, who worried that the economic pressures facing the city would reignite social problems of the 1960s, risking the city's reputation and their bottom lines. Their fears carried a kernel of truth, even if they were rooted in racist assumptions about Black criminality and pathology. Boosters celebrated Boston as a livable city, and Mayor White claimed that the allegations of Boston as a racist city were "blown out of proportion." But racism and racial violence—perpetrated often by white Bostonians even as Black Bostonians got framed as the problem—continued to tarnish the city's reputation.[18] Busing in the mid-1970s raised the city's profile on the national stage, as did the Pulitzer Prize–winning photograph of a white teenager spearing a Black civil rights attorney, Ted Landsmark, with an American flag in 1976. In 1979, the shooting of a fifteen-year-old Black student at football practice by three white Charlestown teenagers reignited conversations about race in the city and the day-to-day violence enacted on Black residents.[19] Alarm, however, quickly shifted to the city's reputation, as corporate elites read about the "hidden tax" of racial unrest. It was a tax, newspaper coverage argued, levied "most heavily on the business community" and the real estate and banking industries.[20] Racism, it seemed, risked profits.

Corporate leaders saw a connection between race, unemployment, and poverty but ignored how their own hiring practices or the unequal investments in housing and schools accelerated those patterns. They might have pointed to the destruction of single-room occupant housing in the 1960s under urban renewal, the recession of the 1970s, and the loss of rental housing to abandonment, arson, and condominiums as triggering both a wave of gentrification and price escalation. Or they might have pointed to how substantial cuts in direct aid to families under the Reagan administration cost families, on average, $1,555 per year in benefits.[21] Instead, corporate elites pointed to a cycle of Black unemployment and limited opportunities, blaming schools for failing to prepare students for work and Black individuals for resisting employment. This cultural and behavioral explanation for the formation of a new ghettoized urban underclass set up the business class in Boston as heroes rather than villains.[22] White urban elites expressed a concern for social welfare, though they tended to promote individual uplift and targeted African Americans with assistance without acknowledging the persistence of ongoing structural impediments. They framed their motivations as compassion, not self-interest, and they downplayed redistributive policies in favor of those based on market-based competition.

Federal labor legislation reinforced this narrative. Passed originally in 1973, the Comprehensive Employment and Training Act (CETA) created various incentives for private corporations to help address problems of job training and employment. Several years into the program, however, reports indicated that few corporations knew of or were moved by the government's CETA incentives. To further entice this crowd, Jimmy Carter's administration updated the legislation to more directly cater to corporate needs and encourage job creation and on-the-job training programs. To anchor this new CETA program, a Title VII program prompted the creation of local Private Industry Councils (or PICs).[23] Department of Labor guidelines outlined a range of forms PICs could take, and in 1979 Boston formed one and incorporated it as a nonprofit organization. Mayor White commended the effort as "represent[ing] a tradition of which Boston is proud—a tradition of business leaders concerned enough about the future of Boston and her residents to invest their time and effort."[24]

Consistent with the federal guidelines, the Boston PIC framed its work as connecting job seekers with job providers. In congressional testimony on the program, the executive director of the Boston program, Catherine Stratton, later explained the organization as an "intermediary" serving "as a coordinative, catalytic organization focusing on systemic problems."[25] The Boston PIC's board of directors included sixteen executives from area companies representing the banking, insurance, and manufacturing industries as well as leaders from local labor unions, city government, ABCD, and the Urban League. As president and chairman of State Street Bank, William "Bill" Edgerly chaired the Boston PIC's board and described it in terms familiar to his peers: involvement in the effort made "good business sense," he argued, with its "catalytic" activities and "profession-ally managed" operations.[26] Initial ad hoc efforts focused on preparing unemployed workers for the growing electronics manufacturing indus-try, with sponsors such as Honeywell providing training to electronics assemblers.[27]

The Boston PIC's first major effort focused on the problem of youth unemployment. Without openly targeting Black teenagers, the Boston PIC's strategic focus on urban teens nonetheless was consistent with long-standing and racist assumptions about young African Americans as a prob-lematic population. This logic overlooked continued underfunding of the school system, discrimination in the labor market, and insufficient wages of service employment to arrive at a hypothesis that keeping teenagers occu-pied would reduce violence and crime, solve a culture of bias by improving the image of teenagers, and compensate for structures of discrimination.[28] By such logic, corporate executives involved in the PIC leaned on their peers to create two thousand summer jobs in 1980, primarily in professional office settings. As the intermediary holding the public-private partnership together, the PIC tasked ABCD with identifying eligible youth, networked with the National Alliance of Business and the Boston Chamber of Com-merce to create jobs, and packaged federal CETA funds to cover intern-ship stipends and two-thirds of the cost of running the program.[29]

Soliciting job promises, however, proved easier than actually filling jobs, and praise exceeded results.[30] Many of the private-sector jobs of-fered through the PIC required skills beyond those of high school stu-dents or were located in transportation deserts. Only 129 PIC jobs out of the two thousand promised were filled in the first year.[31] Results were bet-ter the next year, with an estimated five hundred placements for students around the city, but this number of placements was still lower than the levels that had been achieved by summer employment programs through ABCD and other public works programs. When Reagan's federal bud-get cuts reduced those programs, the PIC failed to compensate despite its promises to do so.[32] Still, the PIC earned praise for the leadership, vision, and generosity of corporate involvement; the press noted the PIC as a "bright spot" that "deserves praise" and "deserves credit" for getting in-volved in urban issues.[33] The National Alliance of Business bestowed the PIC with awards. The glowing accounts of the council encouraged similar partnerships across a broader policy terrain.

When the *Boston Globe* profiled him as the "professorial banker," Bill Edgerly almost canceled the interview.[34] It was the kind of attention he

hated, seeing no need to celebrate what he saw as a standard role for a
bank president. He had considered becoming a French teacher but, at his
parents' urging, studied math and engineering at MIT before pursuing
graduate work at Harvard Business School. He climbed the professional
ladder in the financial department of a local manufacturing firm before
taking a job as the head of the city's prominent State Street Bank, then
struggling in the recession of the mid-1970s. Under Edgerly's stewardship,
the bank pivoted toward financial services, becoming a national leader in
asset management with, by the time of his retirement in 1992, $1 trillion
of assets in custody.[35] He fostered a reputation as quiet, sharp, and tough
and with an old-fashioned view of corporate citizenship. These characteristics earned Edgerly a spot on many public commissions and task forces,
including Mayor White's Committee on Violence and the Massachusetts
Capital Formation Task Force, through which he gained a sterling reputation among city leaders.

Building on the PIC's visibility in the for-profit and nonprofit sectors, Edgerly began to promote public-private partnerships as a model
for dealing with a host of urban issues.[36] His reputation landed him on
national commissions too, which placed him in a wider network of public-
private partnership advocates. One such group, the national business
group Committee for Economic Development, published a report titled
Public-Private Partnerships: An Opportunity for Urban Communities that
framed such arrangements as "a source of energy and vitality" for American cities.[37] It was a message Edgerly evangelized in Boston, starting with
a conference he helped organize in 1982. The PIC and the Committee
on Economic Development invited real estate developer James Rouse,
known locally for his work redeveloping Quincy Market and nationally
for starting a housing intermediary similar to LISC, to keynote the gathering. Rouse urged government and business leaders to work together
on issues of housing, unemployment, and schools, painting a grim and
racially charged image: "The jungle at the heart of American cities is getting worse," he noted.[38] The conference energized the 150 government,
university, corporate, and civic leaders in attendance, who, at a follow-up
meeting a month later, formed a group called Goals for Boston. With the
slogan "Progress through Partnerships," the group promised to expand
the kind of public-private partnership inaugurated by the Boston PIC.[39]

Goals for Boston framed social welfare priorities as good for economic
growth, showing a concern about Boston and its residents as well as a
keen desire to protect its members' investments and the city's competitive

edge. In effect, it was a rebooted version of the city's urban renewal–era pro-business cabinet known as The Vault, revived for a new generation of executives who once again sought to steer the city's agenda to accommodate the corporate class.[40] The group's schemes targeted not just the Boston Redevelopment Authority but a broader array of public institutions. In meetings and in print, Edgerly appealed to executives to seize the mantle of local leadership, announcing in the *Boston Globe* that the "responsibility is shared, and so are the benefits." He echoed the report from the Committee on Economic Development, arguing that businesses ought to consider the social improvement of their communities as "tied so closely to their bottom-line interests that it requires direct and effective action."[41] The transition to an economy centered on technology and professional services buoyed salaries and real estate prices for those at the top of the income ladder, as did the "discovery" of city living by young white professionals.[42] Yet even with these draws, corporate recruiters admitted that the highest barriers to luring professionals to Boston remained the poor quality of housing and schools.[43] Goals for Boston's efforts to upgrade those public institutions reflected its own interests as much as the interests of those most in need.

Appealing to business interests this way exonerated the organization from any role member firms had played (and continued to play) in creating the uneven development of the city and enabled business leaders to be the champions for problems that they had facilitated. Boston banks had a history of discriminatory lending that first denied Black families access to capital and then, when such practices became illegal, created racially targeted lending programs. The infamous Boston Banks Urban Renewal Group had been largely responsible for the increased racial segregation of the 1960s and early 1970s that prompted the 1977 federal Community Reinvestment Act.[44] As a result, many of the institutions involved in Goals for Boston held mortgages in the very neighborhoods they now sought to save while seeking praise and profit for doing so.[45] The offering of resources from corporations required the recipients, Edgerly argued, drop the "adversarial style of the past" and accept the terms extended.[46] Such language made clear that these would be partnerships not of equals but of control, in which corporations traded a slice of resources for the conciliation of community groups and subservience of city government. The city government willingly, if not happily, agreed.

In a period of declining resources, the interest of corporate leaders whetted the mayor's appetite. What had started as a pragmatic strategy to address urban poverty during an era of municipal austerity carried ideological consequences into the next decade, shaping a new Democratic Party, locally and nationally, confident in the promotion of social welfare through the private sector. The Committee for Economic Development encouraged local governments to "adopt an entrepreneurial approach," and Mayor White followed suit.[47] In one of the last publications of his administration, White released a short pamphlet on "solving" the "challenge of the 1980s" through public-private partnerships. The language and logics of the 1983 pamphlet previewed the neoliberalism that would later come to dominate the Democratic Party as it tried to win back power from a rising conservative tide. It critiqued government spending rather than the austerity of budget cuts and called for "more effective strategies" and partnerships between the public and the private sectors guided by innovation, efficacy, and proof. In a move as desperate as it was innovative, White's administration promoted departments related to schools, public housing, libraries, the elderly, fair housing, neighborhood development, parks, and veterans services as "prospective public partner[s]." Each of these, he claimed, had "the capacity to be a successful partner in a public-private partnership."[48]

A Compact for Education

Goals for Boston picked up two of those municipal departments at White's fire sale, viewing the partnerships as particularly valuable to their own interests in economic competitiveness and social stability. The poor performance of the city's schools and the increasing visibility of homelessness and decrepitude were particular embarrassments—if not liabilities—to those looking to lure professionals to the city. To corporate executives, these issues spoke to the failures of the local government. Scandals, court cases, and turnover had rocked the school department over the preceding decade, undermining confidence among residents who agreed on little else and fueling disdain for the government's failures to manage escalating urban crises. It was a local version of a national conversation about the poor state of American education.[49] Local elites in Goals for Boston seized this moment in US political culture, forming the Boston Compact and the Boston Housing Partnership to coordinate activity and deploy public and philanthropic resources. Though differing in structural details, the two initiatives shared ties to the business community and an insistence on detaching democratic processes from the provision of basic public goods. Even as confidence in such approaches outpaced the reality of their results, these partnerships demonstrated the applicability, adaptability, and, to many, the superiority of such arrangements in urban governance.

The Boston Compact emerged from frustrations with the employment-focused programs under the Boston Private Industry Council as well as a mounting concern with the dropout rates in the Boston public schools. Several years into the Boston PIC's summer jobs program, local employers blamed the public schools for inadequately preparing high school students with the cultural orientation and basic skills necessary in a labor market characterized less by manufacturing and more by a knowledge economy. Jobs in data processing, technology, professional offices, and hospitals required basic literacy and numeracy that graduates of Boston public schools lacked. Placing blame on the schools conveniently absolved area businesses for their failures to hire Boston residents but still exposed a grim reality, made more visible in a report by the *Boston Globe*'s investigative Spotlight Team in the summer of 1982.[50]

Investigation into the schools found a staggering 45 percent of students who entered ninth grade dropped out before graduation, two-thirds of sixth-graders tested at least two years behind in reading, and one-third of graduates tested as functionally illiterate.[51] In a school district where 70 percent of the students identified as ethno-racial minorities, such statistics revealed the disproportionate failures of the school system to support non-white students. Latinx students, particularly those who spoke Spanish at home, routinely got held back before eventually dropping out at even higher rates. Though their arguments gained little traction with those in positions to take action, youth and labor advocates tied the sizable portion of Boston's young adults without a high school degree to the comparably low wages paid by service work and the discrimination minority workers faced in the labor market. These patterns were not unique to Boston, but they became particularly acute in a metro region still characterized by segregation and an economy increasingly dominated by knowledge workers.[52]

Ongoing disruption in the school department created an opening for corporate leaders to step in with their dollars and ideas. By 1982, Boston was on its ninth superintendent in eleven years—a period when Judge Arthur Garrity effectively ran the school department following his desegregation decision in 1974. After issuing more than four hundred legal decisions, Garrity began to phase out his role, a decision he justified, in part, on the growing involvement of business leaders, seeing them as "contribut[ing] substantially to fashioning a school system in which excellent education is provided in a racially nondiscriminatory fashion."[53] The newest superintendent, Robert Spillane, came to Boston from New York state government. Among Spillane's first actions was the laying off of seven hundred teachers to trim a budget that had nearly tripled under Garrity.[54]

As Spillane read reports about the school system, he also read the political context. School enrollment had fallen substantially and steadily since the implementation of busing, highlighting both a long-term exodus to the suburbs by those who could afford it and an accelerated withdrawal from the public school system with the start of busing in favor of parochial and private education. Enrollment fell by nearly a third over a decade, with estimates that it would shrink another third by the mid-1990s. The traditionally vocal political constituencies of Boston—working- and middle-class Irish and Italian families—were no longer public school consumers, while those who were both public school defenders and consumers—ethnic and racial minorities—remained sidelined from political power. Spillane considered the school system "abandoned" and deliberately sought the political and economic buy-in of the business community.[55] He found a ready-made coalition in the Boston PIC, Goals for Boston, and the Tri-Lateral Council for Quality Education. The Tri-Lateral Council was a nonprofit headquartered at the Federal Reserve Bank of Boston and founded in 1974 to connect the Boston public schools, the city's chamber of commerce, and the National Alliance of Business.[56]

In September 1982, Spillane helped announce a new Boston Compact, which one reporter likened in importance to a twentieth-century version of the Mayflower Compact. As the name was designed to suggest, the Boston Compact was a public agreement binding the schools, the school department, city government, the business community, and local universities in a commitment to improve the quality of education in Boston and ensure that such improvements translated into jobs for graduates. The elite group diagnosed the school dropout rates as a malady of individuals, responding with a behavioral course of treatment that placed job coaches in public schools. The compact became a joint effort, in the words of one local sponsor, to turn students into "future employees."[57] The one hundred business signatories to the compact pledged four hundred jobs and a verbal commitment to hire Boston public school graduates. In exchange, the school system promised increases of 5 percent per year in graduation rates and job placement and that, by 1986, all graduating seniors would meet a minimum standard of achievement in reading and math.[58] The terms of the compact emphasized accountability, metrics, and incentives, which placed most of the burden of action on the school system.

Despite its language of partnership, the compact reflected the closed-door process of its creation. Planning happened by invitation only, in meetings that included a handful of business leaders and one school department representative—the only African American in a room planning for a school system where more than two-thirds of students were racial minorities.[59] Community groups and the teachers' union were sidelined for fear that a more democratic and participatory process might scare the business money away.[60] When John O'Bryant and Jean McGuire, the two Black members of the school committee, finally saw the strategy, they could only amend it at the edges to ensure a proportional number of Black students were involved in the program.[61] O'Bryant begrudgingly endorsed the Boston Compact, commenting later, "It's like apple pie and motherhood: any committee would have voted for it."[62] His comment indicates the narrow political ground from which Black leaders could critique partnerships that targeted areas of shared concern but did so through strategies that centralized governing power away from neighborhood nonprofits. Even Mel King, then a candidate for mayor, spoke with praise, albeit tepid praise, about the compact and only urged that community groups had more say in its formation.[63]

Despite the involvement of some of Boston's most prominent corporations—ranging from Filene's and Houghton Mifflin to State Street Bank and John Hancock Insurance—few financial resources arrived from them. Their contributions came in the form of jobs, a thinly veiled charitable offer that benefited the companies' workforces and reputations. Compact documents emphasized that "whenever possible" the partnership would function "by reallocating *existing* school resources," and, if necessary, the school department would fundraise. Accordingly, the school department rerouted $10 million of its budget over three years to support the Boston Compact. The reallocated dollars hired attendance clerks and "career specialists," many of whom, in a bid to please the unions, were recently terminated teachers. Rather than taxes or cash donations, corporations pledged jobs for successful students and contributed in-kind services, such as sponsoring a school and guiding the headmaster, many of whom were replaced under the compact, in a "detailed planning process."[64] Brighton High gained resources for building repairs and training programs from its sponsor, Honeywell, while English High gained a corps of tutors and cast-off office furniture from its sponsor, John Hancock Insurance. Other schools were less fortunate; by the very nature of being donated goods and services, the benefits fell unevenly.

Corporations resisted taxes or other means of footing the bill for the compact but soon provided some philanthropic gifts consistent with the desire to circumvent government bureaucracy and reward individual initiative. As an ardent supporter of the Boston PIC and the Boston Compact, Bill Edgerly helped make urban education a popular cause of corporate largesse; supporting the issue nearly guaranteed flattering portraits of those so clearly benefiting from the Massachusetts Miracle.[65] As corporate profits mounted, gifts for urban education became a way to soften their image, downplay the visible inequality, and soothe the guilt of economic elites. In the months after the compact's announcement, the Bank of New England pledged $300,000 to sponsor a teacher award program that would make monetary gifts of $6,500 to a handful of "Teachers of the Year."[66] A cascade of similar gifts followed, supporting a $10 million fund known as the Boston Plan for Excellence. A local foundation, the Permanent Fund for Boston (known now as the Boston Foundation) managed the pot, which the Bank of Boston seeded with $1.5 million to mark its two hundredth anniversary in 1984.[67] Other area giants, including John Hancock Financial Services, New England Mutual Life Insurance Company, and the Goodwin, Proctor & Hoar law firm made similar gifts to grow the fund's endowment, enabling annual grants for teacher innovation and scholarships at the elementary, middle, and high school levels.[68] Most prominently, the ACCESS program (short for Action Center for Educational Services and Scholarships) all but guaranteed graduates from Boston public schools sufficient aid to pay for college. The program's launch in 1986 made national headlines and the nightly news.[69] These initiatives responded to the austerity facing Boston schools but ensured the power of distribution and choice remained in private hands able to foster competition among teachers, reward some schools over others, and bestow gifts on students deemed deserving. These supplementary sources of funding and decision-making drained authority from the school department and city government, doing little to remedy the infrastructure problems in aging school buildings or tackle the issues of equity for students with specialized language or learning needs.

Without using the term *neoliberalism* to describe the Boston Compact, many saw the document as embodying a new liberalism that maintained a commitment to goals of quality education for all but achieved those goals via private implementation and market principles. *Rolling Stone* and *Time* both profiled the Boston Compact within its first year, highlighting the performance standards, results-oriented focus, and accountability of the schools.[70] Such characteristics were framed as a hard-nosed improvement on the supposedly loose, disorganized efforts of the Great Society and aligned with how compact advocates pitched their work.[71] The compact earned Boston a reputation for innovation in governance that those involved in the partnership hoped might "presage similar partnerships around other issues of public concern."[72] By the mid-1980s, representatives traveled from across the country and across the globe to learn from the Boston experiments. A federally funded partnership program with the National Alliance of Business worked to replicate the Boston Compact in Albuquerque, Cincinnati, Louisville, Memphis, Indianapolis, San Diego, and Seattle.[73] With endorsement from Prince Charles and city corporate executives, London launched the Docklands Compact, modeled on the Boston effort, in what scholars have since identified as a ground zero of neoliberal urban policies in the United Kingdom.[74]

Results, however, from the experiment's first five years frustrated corporate backers, who threatened to end their commitment because of the schools' supposed failure to fulfill theirs. The dropout rate actually grew over the course of the Boston Compact, and students who did graduate were often deemed unfit for work by hiring managers.[75] Those employed as a result of the compact were likely headed that way already and often found themselves in low-wage clerical jobs with limited potential for promotion.[76] Students most at risk of dropping out or of unemployment, many noted, were not captured by the compact's insistence on targeting "job ready" students in an effort to inspire others to follow suit.[77] Teachers reported a general lack of enthusiasm for the compact's job placement strategy, while local advocates emphasized the continued failures of the program to reach those truly in need.[78]

By threatening to exit the partnership, business leaders won even more power over the Boston School Department in a renegotiated "Compact 2" in 1988.[79] New policies based on corporate leaders' preferences for competition, choice, and discipline in governing increased choice in student assignment plans, decentralized authority to individual schools, and limited the Boston Teachers Union's bargaining power.[80] These changes extended the earlier performance standards, standardized the curriculum, increased testing, and revised promotion policies consistent with a neoliberal policy agenda. In the early 1990s, with the free time and resources afforded by his retirement, Edgerly became a vociferous supporter of charter schools and school choice. Using his experiences with the Boston Compact as a platform to lobby the state legislature and his ties to business leaders, he founded an updated version of Goals for Boston called CEOs for Fundamental Change in Education.[81] Though public resources contributed to the compact, the public goods they paid for increasingly were framed as a privilege to be won rather than a right to be guaranteed.

A Partnership for Housing

Established around the same time as the Boston Compact, the Boston Housing Partnership joined city government, banks, and community development corporations in 1983 to increase the stock of affordable housing by financing it at scale. The interest in CDCs among Boston's business elite demonstrated how much these entities had evolved from their 1960s origins in Black power and community control and how successful housing intermediaries had been in positioning these neighborhood developers as productive and revenue-producing entities during the 1970s and early 1980s. Local intermediaries such as Greater Boston Community Development and national ones such as the Local Initiatives Support Corporation helped CDCs finance housing projects, but the efforts remained atomized. As CDCs sought more stability for their organizations and neighborhoods, and as intermediary organizations courted corporate investors for their loan pools, they attracted the attention of Goals for Boston—in particular, Bill Edgerly. He became a leading force in the Boston Housing Partnership and its experiment to finance five hundred units of affordable housing in one packaged deal. Operating at such scale, the logic went, would address the problems that plagued individual CDCs but also spur market confidence and jump-start growth in depressed areas.

The products of urban renewal were finally coming to market, bifurcating the housing market and leaving those with low incomes few options for either private or public housing. The conversion of single-occupancy units into expensive condominiums dramatically condensed the housing market as Boston had lost an estimated ten thousand licensed lodging rooms—typically a source of affordable shelter—since 1970, leaving barely two hundred in place by 1985.[82] Conditions in public housing deteriorated too, but desperate families still added their names to the growing

five-year waiting list at the Boston Housing Authority, which in the early
1980s doubled to top 12,500 names.[83] Those who could find housing ended
up paying an increasingly high percentage of their incomes for shelter despite efforts by nonprofit community developers to keep neighborhoods
affordable.[84] A dramatic increase in homelessness—including among women
and families—followed in Boston as well as in other major US cities undergoing similar changes. If elite Bostonians did not see evidence of growing poverty with their own eyes, they certainly read about it in the *Boston
Globe*.[85] Conditions became bad enough to worry those at the top of the
wealth ladder whose investments depended on continuous growth in urban real estate.

The Boston Housing Partnership began as Edgerly's vision to fill a gap
between what he saw as the government's inability to solve the problem
of affordable housing and the business sector's lack of incentives to do
so. He convinced many Goals for Boston members to join this new effort,
including John Hancock Insurance and Bank of Boston. Edgerly also won
over several developers and law firms that shared his interest in scaling
up affordable housing production and had the means to do so. The commitment of both resources and attention from prominent corporations
attracted funds from local and national foundations, investments from
LISC, and Community Development Block Grants from the city.[86] Once
incorporated as a nonprofit organization, the partnership would package
these philanthropic and public funds with commercial rate loans on behalf
of a group of CDCs, sparing them the burden of seeking loans individually.
The Boston Housing Partnership hired local housing finance expert Bob
Whittlesley as the executive director, and Whittlesley contracted with his
former organization, Greater Boston Community Development, to assist
the CDCs actually doing the work.[87] Initial materials for the partnership
described how "the economics of [housing development] made it virtually
impossible for the private sector to meet this challenge alone," dismissing
any kind of policy-based approach given members' views of the housing
market as sound and their investment in its continued growth.[88] The analysis revealed the neoliberal frameworks that had come to underpin many
of the city's partnerships and reflected views increasingly held in the housing field for pragmatic, if not ideological, reasons.

By the 1980s, CDCs had tied their own bottom lines to the growth
machine of real estate, retaining their skepticism of city redevelopment
plans even as they sought to slow it by keeping a few units and buildings
affordable. Unlike the Boston PIC and Boston Compact, which remained

firmly in the hands of Boston's elite, the Boston Housing Partnership's board contained more diversity. Chaired by Edgerly, the board of directors represented a veritable who's who of housing in Boston. In addition to bank and city government representatives, it included several CDC directors and prominent Black leaders such as Doris Bunte from the Boston Housing Authority and Hubie Jones, formerly of RMSC and at the time dean of social work at Boston University.[89] The presence of people such as Jorge Hernandez from Inquilinos Boricuas en Acción and William Jones from Codman Square Housing Development Corporation signaled both the acceptance of CDCs in affordable housing production and their political utility in "represent[ing] a minority constituency," according to partnership materials.[90] The presence of minority board members, however, did not ensure the partnership's strategy would seriously examine the intersections of race, policy, and housing finance that neighborhood-based meetings often highlighted.

Whether CDCs agreed with the partnership's technocratic faith in streamlining a complex legal and financial process, they knew how to recognize a funding opportunity. The Boston Housing Partnership's initial request for proposals garnered responses from fourteen CDCs in Boston, which collectively identified 1,061 housing units for possible rehabilitation and subsidy. It was nearly double the amount for which the partnership had planned. Negotiations ensued, producing a deal in which the partnership agreed to package financing for seven hundred units rehabilitated by ten CDCs across the city. As a group, the CDCs included both older entities tracing their roots to community action programs of the 1960s as well as more recently formed groups looking to take advantage of funding for neighborhood residential improvements. They brought different levels of experience in real estate and different levels of connection to their communities, but all saw the power of housing and economic development for neighborhoods long characterized by divestment.[91]

Edgerly's strategy of scaling up financing for CDC projects added to rather than reduced the process's complexity. It took two years and fifteen municipal agencies for the partnership to reduce the cost of acquiring the properties for the seven hundred units promised. The consolidated tax syndication pool from which Whittlesey raised equity for the purchases produced less than expected. Four Boston banks agreed to provide construction loans, but only once the Federal National Mortgage Association agreed to purchase the loans. The Massachusetts Housing and Finance Agency committed to purchase the mortgage-backed securities sold by the federal agency provided it raised sufficient funds from the issue and sale of a tax-exempt bond.[92] Grants from foundations and CDBG funds would cover development fees and project management costs for each of the ten nonprofit developers. Short-term loans of working capital came via the state's Community Development Finance Corporation and Boston's LISC chapter.[93] Finally, to cover shortfalls between development costs and market-rate rental or sale income at moderate and low-income levels, the commonwealth pledged rental assistance certificates that, when paired with HUD Section 8 certificates, kept 70 percent of the units at affordable rates. The chain of financing proved so complicated that even those involved wondered whether there existed even "one individual who understands how this works."[94]

True to its name, the Boston Housing Partnership wrestled local, state, and federal governments, public agencies, private banks, foundations, and business leaders into a single financing chain, but it did so at great cost to neighborhood community developers. Many of the lending and funding partners had signed on to the project reluctantly, only after lengthy negotiations and pricey delays. Even the federal lender resisted from the start, and nearly abandoned the deal after a tour of the targeted properties in Boston.[95] Negotiations added time and expense as each partner in the financing chain required a new legal opinion and renegotiated financing agreements for every adjustment to the seven-hundred-unit deal. A consultant to the Quincy-Geneva CDC called the legal fees "astronomical," and another adviser grumbled that the deal involved seventeen different law firms.[96] While understandable from the perspective of lenders looking to protect their assets, the additional opinions and the delays they caused put unanticipated burdens on the CDCs, which had to purchase buildings before having secured construction financing to avoid losing the development opportunity altogether. The executive director of the Fields Corner CDC expressed a "real fear that if the Partnership failed to deliver, we'd be stuck and perceived as another slumlord."[97]

For all its uncertainties, the Boston Housing Partnership successfully rehabilitated 710 units of housing in Boston's low-income neighborhoods at a scale not thought possible. Praise for the partnership emphasized outcome over process and celebrated the ability of this public-private partnership to deliver results that government, nonprofit, and corporate entities had seemingly failed to do alone.[98] LISC's president, Mitchell Sviridoff, praised the partnership as "the best in the country, the most original, the most competently managed."[99] Soon, the Boston effort became a model

for other partnerships, including the statewide Massachusetts Housing
Partnership. Representatives visited from Chicago, Cleveland, Dallas, and
London to inquire about the Boston program, as did federal agencies and
corporate groups, including the US Chamber of Commerce and the National Alliance of Business.[100] In the Boston Housing Partnership, these
visitors saw a way to overcome the limitations of government activity by
entrusting public-private partnerships to distribute public resources and
positioning CDCs as neighborhood representatives in citywide partnerships,
vehicles of public resources, and planners of neighborhood development.

Focused as it was on improving housing financing rather than on shaping housing policy, the partnership's very visible success distracted from
subtle changes to Boston's housing market. A $1 billion building boom had
immense consequences for the availability and prices of housing in Boston.[101] New luxury condominiums, high-end hotel chains, downtown office
towers, expensive consumer stores, and parking garages pushed rents and
home prices up and returned profits to lenders and firms involved in the
Boston Housing Partnership. Boston banks—even those involved in the
partnership, continued to lend in predatory and discriminatory patterns.[102]
The overall decrease in affordable housing in the city increased rates of
homelessness, especially among families. In response, local corporations
made public gifts to another philanthropic pot at the Boston Foundation,
the Fund for Homelessness, which became a popular target of charity ga-
las and yuppie fundraisers.[103] These donations helped Boston's traditional
homeless shelters and neighborhood nonprofits open transitional spaces
for families, but, like the education-oriented Boston Plan for Excellence,
attention was fixed on the raising of funds and mechanisms of their distribution to avoid discussion of housing or tax policy.

With decidedly mixed results, Goals for Boston nonetheless dubbed
the Boston Housing Partnership a success based on its ability to produce
units of affordable housing and its mere existence as a partnership linking
so many public, private, and nonprofit entities. Desperate for resources
and tied in their own ways to the growth machine, city government and
neighborhood nonprofits had few tools at their disposal to challenge such
assertions, if they had even wanted to. Their presence added authority
and authenticity to the partnerships, but their role was to follow, not lead,
and to implement, not strategize. In a decade defined by Reagan's line
that "government is not the solution to our problem, government is the
problem," corporate elites in Boston seized the mantle of public leadership and reduced government, Goals for Boston materials declared, to
merely asking "how can we help."[104]

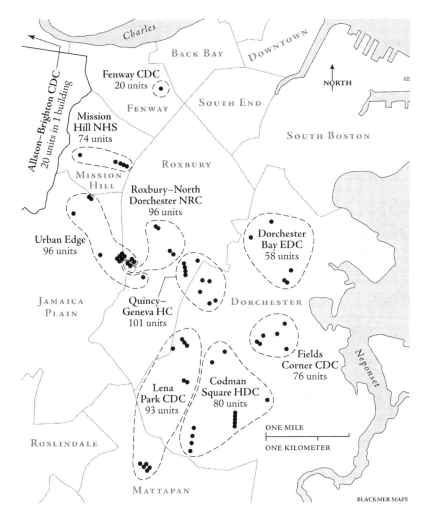

FIGURE 6.1. *Map of housing nonprofit developers financed through the Boston Housing Partnership (ca. 1983).* The Boston Housing Partnership designed a new way to scale the production of affordable housing by community development corporations by packaging the financing. Its first project financed ten local nonprofits to renovate seven hundred units of housing and later became a statewide and national model. (Data from Thomas F. McCormack, "The Implementation of the Boston Housing Partnership," master's thesis, Department of Urban Studies and Planning, Massachusetts Institute of Technology, 1985.)

An Initiative for Dudley Square

With all the talk of public-private partnership, it remained an elastic concept during the 1980s. It captured business-led efforts such as the Boston
Compact and Boston Housing Partnership as well as a foundation-led effort
in the Dudley Square neighborhood that, between 1984 and 1988, evolved
into one of the nation's most visible examples of grassroots neighborhood
redevelopment. Though the Dudley Street Neighborhood Initiative (or
DSNI, as the group became known) rejected the centrality of elites in the
revitalization of the neighborhood, it embraced some of the core tenets of
public-private partnerships—notably, a desire to sideline city government
and place many of the core aspects of municipal governance in a nonprofit
organization. In a neighborhood characterized by divestment and neglect,
residents saw this as a more effective way to reduce poverty and as a more
democratic and just process to ensure that improvements aided neighborhood residents. With a very different configuration of a public-private partnership and with a more contested creation, DSNI emerged as a surprising bridge from the era of community control in the 1960s and 1970s to an
era of privatization in the 1980s and 1990s. Along the way, the continuous
making and remaking of public-private partnerships in Dudley Square
produced one of Boston's truest nonprofit neighborhoods.

Stories say the Dudley Street Neighborhood Initiative began in a car,
on a drive between downtown Boston and one of the city's poorest neighborhoods.[105] It was a journey short in distance but worlds apart for the lawyers and banker visiting the neighborhood nonprofit La Alianza Hispana
as part of their charitable work as trustees for the Mabel Louise Riley
Foundation. The foundation's nearly $20 million endowment had been a
bequest from Riley on her death in 1971. She had inherited the fortune
from her father, an English immigrant who designed textile machines for
the ever-spinning mills of New England and the Deep South. Mabel Riley
never married, and, without heirs to run the foundation, a small team of
three Boston lawyers and one banker administered the Riley Trust, which
philanthropic professional Newell Flather staffed part-time. In its first
decade, the Riley team made standard gifts to promote the arts and provide for poor children, but a 1984 grant request from La Alianza Hispana
pulled at a growing interest in funding local community development groups.
Flather arranged for a site visit and drove two trustees to Dudley Square.

There to inspect the poor quality of the carpet in La Alianza's office
space and assess the request to fund new floor coverings, the trustees

were shocked at the trash, abandonment, and depression of the surrounding Dudley neighborhood. It was, trustee Robert W. Holmes Jr. later recounted, "a place defined by neglect."[106] Viewing a map in La Alianza's office, the trustees assumed the shaded parcels depicted new housing before a staff member corrected them that it detailed a street-by-street accounting of abandoned lots and buildings. A daily reality for residents of the area, the emptiness came as a shock to those more familiar with the skyscrapers and cranes of downtown. In Dudley Square, the Massachusetts Miracle had exacerbated cycles of speculation, abandonment, and arson characteristic of urban neighborhoods in the 1980s. While La Alianza and its affiliated CDC, Nuestra Comunidad, had begun to expand their work from social to physical development, their efforts remained piecemeal despite eventual inclusion as one of the ten CDCs in the Boston Housing Partnership. In what became a much retold story that privileged the perspective of those footing the bill, the Riley trustees hatched a plan on the drive back downtown to concentrate the foundation's philanthropic investments in Dudley and do a lot more than replace the carpet.

For both political and legal reasons, the Mabel Louise Riley Foundation needed community partners in its new Dudley Initiative, and so Flather spent the summer of 1984 surveying the landscape of nonprofit organizations. After all, as an impersonal exercise rooted in analysis, grantmaking contained the power to adopt certain neighborhoods and select the partners to work with. Much of what Flather learned "pleased and . . . surprised" him, despite having made grants to area organizations for some time.[107] Still, Flather expressed to the trustees his reservations about the choice of Dudley and noted the number of comments he received from other philanthropists that the foundation's strategy was "bold, if not brave."[108] With a professional obligation to protect the Riley Foundation's financial resources and reputation, Flather pondered whether it would be wiser, "from the perspective of effective grantmaking," to seek out another neighborhood in which to experiment. While the high poverty rates of Dudley Square made it an attractive target, its racial and ethnic diversity had the potential, it seemed, for political gridlock between strong constituents of white, Black, Latinx, and Cape Verdean residents that might scuttle the foundation's effort. Ultimately, however, this "entirely new approach to grantmaking" seemed sufficiently "challenging and stimulating" to Flather and the trustees, who vowed to press forward and channel the foundation's resources in a single geographic area.

The Riley Foundation's entrance both hastened the activity in Dudley and demonstrated the foundation's power to curate its list of partners.

Others had their eyes on Dudley Square too. A team from MIT's Department of Urban Studies and Planning was working with La Alianza Hispana to survey the neighborhood and plan for its future, and the Boston Redevelopment Authority drafted a redevelopment plan for two million square feet of high-rise office space, a galleria mall, five hundred hotel rooms, and fifteen hundred units of moderate-income housing in Dudley Square.[109] Flather skirted both of these efforts, instead assembling a team of consultants to the Dudley Initiative with prominent figures from the nonprofit world—such as Michael Rubinger at LISC, Paul Grogan from city government, Bob Whittlesley at the Boston Housing Partnership, and Pat Clancy at GBCD—as well as local nonprofit executives— such as Nelson Merced of La Alianza Hispana, Melvyn Colon of Nuestra Comunidad, and Richard Millet of the Roxbury Multi-Service Center. The neighborhood-based nonprofit leaders brought racial diversity to the group, though also privileged an organizational perspective removed from the grassroots. In closed sessions over several months into the winter of 1985, fewer than ten people designed the Dudley Initiative for the Riley Foundation to fund, selecting a geographic boundary, a structure for the board of directors, and an initial plan for neighborhood development. It was the same desire for speed and efficiency that shaped the Boston Compact, and it was the same prioritization of action over process. Yet a neighborhood-based revitalization plan gave a spatial grounding and defined constituency to the Dudley Initiative that differed from the city-wide Boston Partnership and Boston Compact.

Expecting gratitude and support, Flather and the Dudley Initiative advisory group encountered resistance when they presented their plans at two community meetings in February and March 1985.[110] The Mabel Louise Riley Foundation had put considerable thought into the community meeting: selecting a central location, rehearsing presentations, planning on-site day care, ordering a banner, printing name tags, and arranging simultaneous translation services for Spanish and Cape Verdean Creole speakers. Advertisements in several languages and local media outlets alerted residents to the gatherings as well as the two potential snow dates.[111] Nearly two hundred Dudley residents showed up to hear about the plans others had made for them. When it was time for questions, Ché Madyun scanned the presenters on the dais, stood up, and asked how many of them actually lived in Dudley Square. Maybe one hand went up.[112] Trained as a dancer, Madyun moved, like so many had, to Dudley out of necessity and learned to soothe her kids at night when fire engine sirens blared. In the silence that followed her question, another attendee,

Earl Coleman, asked, "Who the hell is Riley?" Fadilah Muhammad added, "I don't see a place here for any of us."[113] Tellingly, only four seats on the proposed twenty-three-member Dudley Initiative board were reserved for residents. The moderator quickly regained control of the meeting and agreed on the spot to restructure the governing board with a majority of seats reserved for residents.[114] It infused more democracy into what remained a private initiative. Flather and the Riley trustees watched from the sidelines as a board of directors elected by residents met twice a month to begin building DSNI in 1985. By demanding control over DSNI and validating it as a governing body, community residents began to reshape and redefine the partnership that would make DSNI famous.

Grassroots leadership and participatory processes for decision-making separated DSNI from the business-led partnerships of the decade, but even in its reconstituted form, DSNI still pointed to the failures of local government and the necessity of private action against public problems. It was an old strategy that DSNI leaders updated for the times, pairing protest tactics with formal partnership agreements. Funds from a more hands-off Riley Foundation paid the salary of a community organizer for DSNI, who mobilized residents and led a demonstration against the illegal trash dumping that posed a health risk and stood as a painful metaphor for the value of the neighborhood.[115] DSNI also began to work closely with city government, which, by the mid-1980s, had become one of the largest landowners in Dudley after vacant lots fell to public ownership due to tax delinquency. The city had a financial interest in selling the lots to deep-pocketed speculators eyeing the redevelopment possibilities given the BRA's plans and then DSNI's efforts at revitalization. Dudley residents, on the other hand, sought to develop a land use and acquisition strategy before, as they explained in a grant request to the Riley Foundation, "market pressures" produced "an irreversible trend of displacement."[116] DSNI's collaboration with the director of the city's public facilities department, Lisa Chapnick, to identify and clean up city-owned lots soon led to the formation of a public-private committee to review the lots and plan for their disposition.[117] It was a partnership of sorts that included a private entity in public decisions, but it also was one that DSNI saw as insufficient for its goals. More than participation, DSNI wanted control and governmental power in its slice of Boston. It wanted the power of eminent domain.

Few words elicited more hatred or fear in urban planning than *eminent domain*. The Boston Redevelopment Authority, like its counterparts in cities across the United States, had wielded such legal power in urban renewal projects of the 1950s to clear the West End and New York Streets neighborhoods, transforming eminent domain into the symbol of displacement and overreach.[118] Even considering to vest the authority in DSNI to seize privately held land distressed community members and bureaucrats alike. This was not, however, the 1950s. The political and organizational landscape had shifted, as community developers gained a larger role in shaping the built and economic environments of their neighborhoods and intermediary organizations and financing programs made such activities possible and productive. DSNI's leadership saw eminent domain as the next logical step in that evolution, and they had the aid of loans from the Ford Foundation, pro bono legal counsel arranged by Riley trustees, and consulting services from Greater Boston Community Development to take that step.[119] At a practical level, exercising eminent domain would enable DSNI to package the vacant lots that dotted an area dubbed the Dudley Triangle into a thirty-acre community land trust, and to then coordinate new housing and economic development for an "urban village." Still, empowering a neighborhood nonprofit in such a way represented a bold, if not radical, step. Chapnick recognized what was being asked: for the "city to delegate its role . . . its financial role, its property role, its legal role." She also knew, however, that this was a place where "government had failed" and so took seriously DSNI's arguments that, somewhat paradoxically, outsourcing responsibility represented a more democratic and responsive form of governance in Dudley.[120]

During an era when city government had limited resources and little popularity, the Dudley Street Neighborhood Initiative offered the city a compelling administrative and political opportunity. The director of the BRA, Stephen Coyle, endorsed the strategy early on, seeing in the partnership an easy win for him to dispose of city-owned property and support a community effort.[121] Clearing the agency's docket of a poor neighborhood helped Coyle at a time when his office was overseeing $3 billion of downtown building and on the verge of launching a new master plan for the city.[122] Mayor Flynn became an eager supporter too, recognizing an occasion for city government, in general, and for him, as mayor, to be on the side of residents, particularly residents of color. Flynn had long styled himself a champion of neighborhoods — as did every local politician in the city known for its parochialism — but his version sprung from the white enclaves of South Boston and Charlestown and staunch opposition to busing during the previous decade. DSNI's request offered the mayor a chance to support a neighborhood that had overwhelmingly voted for

FIGURE 6.2. *Dudley Street Neighborhood Initiative's Ché Madyun and Peter Medoff (1987).*
After raising concerns about the lack of resident representation in the Dudley Street Neighborhood Initiative (DSNI), Ché Madyun (*seated*) was elected to chair the organization's new
resident-led board. The group then hired Peter Medoff (*standing*) to serve as the executive
director. Medoff coauthored a book on Dudley called *Streets of Hope.* The map behind them
shows vacant land in Dudley that DSNI sought to target and redevelop with eminent domain. (Stephen Rose, "Ché Madyun and Peter Medoff, President and Executive Director, Respectively, of the Dudley Street Neighborhood Initiative, Pose in Front of Map of Roxbury,"
December 18, 1987, Boston Globe Photographs. Image courtesy of Northeastern University
Archives and Special Collections and the *Boston Globe*.)

his opponent, Mel King, in 1983. In a well-orchestrated photo op, Flynn stood surrounded by Dudley residents holding signs reading "Take a Stand, Own the Land" and made clear his message that "city government ought to be the best friend of neighborhoods."[123] The eminent domain request, the mayor rationalized, gave DSNI "the power so they could do something for themselves."[124] With a rhetoric of self-help, divestment of government authority, and faith in the private sector, Flynn helped DSNI become the first community group in the country to gain the power of eminent domain.[125]

Flynn called the partnership with DSNI a "win-win" for the city and the neighborhood, using language increasingly popular during the 1990s but that masked, as catchphrases often do, a more complex array of outcomes.[126] DSNI gained a power awesome in its symbolism and legal authority but constrained in its application. The power to control the future of Dudley Square enabled the construction of new housing, resident organizing against drug dealing, the painting of a community mural by local teenagers, and investments in local businesses—all activities that distributed millions of public dollars through DSNI. The fullest expression of a nonprofit neighborhood to date in Boston inspired visits from the West Coast in the aftermath of the 1992 rebellions in Los Angeles, won financial support from the Ford Foundation for a book on the Dudley Initiative titled *Streets of Hope*, and launched the local political careers of Dudley residents.[127] Yet DSNI's governmental role could not stem the tide of condominium conversion that drove up rental rates or the escalation of credentials necessary for steady employment in Boston's knowledge economy. That the neighborhood entered the twenty-first century as still one of the city's poorest suggested, perhaps, that the neighborhood had not won in the mayor's win-win language but rather only lost by a smaller margin than before. It was no accident that such groundbreaking grassroots empowerment occurred within precisely drawn neighborhood boundaries. DSNI's partnerships—with the Mable Louise Riley Foundation, the municipal government, and the lenders that later financed the construction of new housing in the Dudley Triangle—simultaneously elevated and constricted the status of nonprofit entities in urban governance.

Conclusion

"In the nineties, collaboration may take the place of confrontation."[128] Coming from William Edgerly, who had recently retired from State Street

Bank a very wealthy man and converted some of his assets into a philanthropic vehicle, Foundation for Partnerships, such a statement seemed
less of a prognostication than a proclamation. Edgerly's initial shunning of
policy change had evolved over the 1980s, such that he became an ardent
supporter of charter schools and school choice, successfully lobbying the
state legislature in 1993 to expand such policies as part of a broad education reform agenda. His support of charter schools specifically and of collaboration more generally stemmed from his view that the partnerships of
the 1980s had worked and provided a blueprint for the next decade.

By the end of the 1980s, Bostonians took the existence of their public-
private partnerships as evidence of the superiority of this mode of governance. Such rhetoric overlooked that the governing arrangements of the
1980s had both elevated a corporate class into policy making to promote
a neoliberal agenda and produced a nonprofit neighborhood where all
decisions, resources, priorities, and programs flowed through a nonprofit
organization. These seemingly contradictory results, however, shared a
critique of government and faith in the ability of nongovernmental entities to perform governing roles. Neighborhood nonprofits, most vocally in
minority neighborhoods, had been leveling such criticism against governments for decades and found new, if surprising, alignment with corporate
leaders.

Though not initially promoted as part of a named neoliberal agenda,
over time, these partnerships and others like them formed the basis of
such a policy framework among those committed to social welfare goals
and critical of government's handling of such issues in the past. Public-
private partnerships increasingly became a target of policy and a platform for it during the 1990s, somewhat ironically for a governing strategy
that sought to solve public problems by avoiding public policy. In their
widely read treatise, *Reinventing Government: How the Entrepreneurial
Spirit Is Transforming the Public Sector*, authors David Osborne and Ted
Gaebler pulled several examples from Boston and Massachusetts to make
their point that the best form of government was that which harnessed
the best of state and market provision. They also quoted a member of
Governor Dukakis's cabinet on the benefits of partnership arrangements
as "cheaper, more efficient, more authentic, more flexible, more adaptive"
than governing by government alone.[129] These characteristics neatly captured the application of a business logic to government operations and are
what made partnerships "not only great policy, [but] also great politics,"
according to Mayor Flynn.[130] Though the Dudley Square effort prompted

the mayor's comment, he could easily have been talking about the Boston PIC, the Boston Compact, the Boston Housing Partnership, or any number of partnerships forged to address crises in the city such as homelessness, AIDS, and gang violence. His comment, moreover, could also have easily come from Governor Dukakis during his 1988 presidential campaign or from President Clinton in 1992. Such was the popularity and perceived utility of partnerships at the time as they increasingly became a political project of the Democratic Party.

Partnership, however, often proved a misnomer for arrangements that kept the balance of power with economic elites. Public-private partnerships emerged primarily where private dollars existed, leaving an uneven landscape of attention and investment. Few in Boston had the privilege of seeing through the long-term consequences of responding to diminished state capacity by further removing authority from the public sector and reducing government to a "catalyst," not a leader.[131] Much of the day-to-day work of creating local partnerships came from people—former teachers rehired as career coaches, project managers at CDCs, parents worried about their kids playing in rat-infested empty lots—responding to the circumstances around them with what they considered the only tools at their disposal. As a result, CDCs gained new resources for and from housing development, and some, like DSNI, gained quasi-governmental authority in their neighborhoods. But these victories ultimately did little to slow the widening economic and racial inequality in Boston. The seeming acceptance of neighborhood nonprofits came at a price—namely, an inability to escape the geographic confines of their creation and shape the landscape of policy and economic transformations happening at a scale far beyond the few square miles of a nonprofit neighborhood.

CHAPTER SEVEN

The Coalitions

Mayor Flynn had a lot to celebrate when American voters elected Arkansas's governor, William Jefferson Clinton, as president of the United States in 1992. During the campaign, Flynn had served as a national cochair for the campaign, stumping for the ticket across the country. He also served as president of the US Conference of Mayors, a position that, coupled with his high favorability in Boston, gave Flynn a national reputation and a platform to shape urban policy for the new administration. In a series of policy proposals for president-elect Clinton, Flynn presented "America Ready to Go" as a gift from the city of Boston to the nation. Cities were, he argued, so much more than "providers for the sick, the homeless, and the needy"; with the right policies, cities could become the "economic engines that can drive America forward."[1] As evidence for his recommendations, Flynn used examples from Boston, "the best laboratory I know," to advance a clear and consistent message about the future of urban America: "The key to revitalization is a new partnership."[2] With the popular but ambiguous language of "partnership," he touted alliances between the public and private sectors as well as between the federal government and municipalities as the key to finally address the persistent problems of urban poverty that, despite renewed interest in urban life among the professional class, still characterized the lives of so many in cities like Boston and, in Flynn's view, held back urban areas from their true potential.

The message reinforced Clinton's campaign promise to chart a new course in US politics that rejected, Flynn recapped, both the "big-money policies of the 1960s" and "the trickle-down policies of the 1980s."[3] A desire for a so-called third way untethered from these anchors of American political memory had already shaped politics at the local and state levels in Massachusetts during the Reagan era, giving Flynn a suite of policy options that paired a 1960s-era commitment to social welfare with a 1980s-era attention to markets. He affirmed a clear role for federal aid to cities but advocated an approach to urban governance that channeled that aid with a businessperson's eye toward efficiency, accountability, and results. These were "strategic investment ideas, not government hand-outs," he wrote, that were "fiscally prudent," in which "minimal dollars must be leveraged for maximum results."[4] It was a policy agenda for a new Democratic Party and a neoliberal era.

More specifically, Flynn advocated in "America Ready to Go" two linked policy routes that were consistent in concept and contradictory in results. Even as he used a language of partnerships, Flynn knew the limits of what they could do and the vagaries of what the term actually meant. In Boston he had already started to move toward a new, expanded concept of "coalitions" that were larger than one-off partnerships and anchored more deliberately in urban space. To that end, his first proposal for Clinton drew on the successes of the Massachusetts Miracle. Flynn touted tax credits and other government investment programs to lure business to cities and grow urban economies around technology, knowledge workers, and professional services. He cited the recent work of a Harvard Business School professor, Michael Porter, on competition, which would soon lead to an article "The Competitive Advantage of the Inner City," to encourage policies that harnessed regional advantages and supported start-up enterprises.[5] Flynn recommended the president expand the economy and US workforce by pairing these efforts with investments in public infrastructure such as high-speed rail and use the tax code to encourage investments in housing, commercial space, and entrepreneurship in designated Urban Enterprise Zones.

The encouragement of business, particularly knowledge-based businesses with professionalized workforces, stood somewhat in tension with Flynn's other identified policy opportunity: neighborhood nonprofit organizations. The inclusion of community groups helped distinguish the Democratic approach to urban revitalization from the Republican one, and it reassured minority voters of the party's commitment to principles of diversity and inclusion. "I have seen, in a number of cities, how grassroots programs can work," Flynn stated, arguing that "the optimum service delivery is neighborhood-based."[6] He recalled efforts related to housing, economic development, youth violence, health, and social services and promoted a new program known as Healthy Boston barely off the ground by the time of the report's release in 1992. He proposed national networks of multiservice centers and community health centers to provide coordinated services, capitalization of community banks to issue microloans for individuals and seed capital for community development corporations, and a national street-worker initiative to work with and monitor urban youth. Many of these built on examples already under way in Boston over the past decades and represented a final push by the mayor to make good on those federal promises to scale what worked. In both his pro-enterprise and pro-neighborhood proposals, Flynn positioned the federal government as pulling strings and private entities doing the visible work of expanding urban economies and managing the unevenness of late capitalism. Emphasizing the political popularity of this two-pronged approach to urban revitalization, Flynn left unstated, however, the clear lesson from Boston. This two-pronged strategy reinforced a two-tier city.

Talk of "empowerment" proved politically prudent to insinuate both a responsiveness to minority voices and a willingness to outsource responsibility. This approach required an administrative structure, which neighborhood nonprofits were able and eager to provide. As private, identity-inflected entities, neighborhood nonprofits provided a convenient proxy for targeting those whom the Boston bureaucrats labeled as "hard to serve . . . populations."[7] Over the 1990s, Boston's city government increasingly targeted neighborhood nonprofits and encouraged the formation of nonprofit coalitions to serve the same communities. It was a nod to efficiency and to grassroots empowerment that furthered the creation of nonprofit neighborhoods as spatial and organizational units of governing tied in formal and informal ways to the state as well as economic units with tax incentives designed to lure investment and pull poverty-stricken areas into the commercial marketplace. Tempted by the potential of grant dollars, coalitions emerged from predictable places such as the South End and Roxbury, where nonprofit organizations had long served as liaisons and advocates at city hall for Black and Latinx Bostonians, but also from groups of immigrants, gays and lesbians, and teenagers who had, by the 1990s, learned the full value of a community organization and established their own nonprofit entities. The whir of local activity to form coalitions based on the possibility of funding, however, exposed again the desperation among nonprofits, the power of grantmaking to elicit a response, and the wide acceptance of privatized inclusion as a response to public problems.

As a policy document, "America Ready to Go" likely made few waves. More than anything else, it was a promotional move by Flynn, who had his eye on an appointment in the new administration. Yet, even in that self-serving manner, the document embodied the neoliberalization of the Democratic urban agenda and the value of neighborhood nonprofit organizations to it. As they had for decades by then, neighborhood nonprofits used government resources to serve on the front lines of a state response to poverty, managing the individual and community burdens of poverty, segregation, and divestment while also trying to fight them. Beyond those services, however, neighborhood nonprofits had gained identity markers of ethnicity and race and of place in the urban landscape; their leaders were spokespeople of neighborhoods and groups in ways that both set the expectation of diversity in urban governance and helped meet that standard. The celebration of these community- or neighborhood-based organizations and their inclusion in political and governing coalitions offered elected officials, particularly white elected officials ranging from Mayor Flynn to President Clinton, a means of realizing goals for diversity, pluralism, and empowerment without a road map for actual inclusivity or equity.

Persistent Poverty

Though Flynn's "America Ready to Go" sought to portray Boston once again as a shining city upon the hill with expertise in forging partnerships and getting results, the reality looked far grimmer. The boom of the Massachusetts Miracle had given way to a bust—a recession that caught Boston by surprise in the late 1980s and early 1990s, spelling more trouble for Boston's neighborhoods. Quantitative and qualitative research confirmed how unevenly the prosperity had been shared and how even those with expanded employment and income during the height of the miracle in the 1980s saw losses that set them back even further during the recession that followed. For some, these findings came as a shock; for others, they validated an existence that, although improving, remained precarious. The Boston Foundation had taken a leading role in the city's conversations about poverty starting in the 1980s and, as local conditions continued to deteriorate, pivoted from researching poverty to more actively strategizing for its remedies. In both phases, the foundation emphasized that categories of race and ethnicity, gender, and age structured the experience of poverty, which validated local poverty knowledge rooted in identity and leadership from the city's nonprofit sector.

As the newly appointed head of the Boston Foundation in 1985, Anna Faith Jones posed questions about the landscape of poverty in a city that many at the time claimed was on the rebound. Jones had worked as a program officer at the foundation for ten years and, with her appointment as president and CEO, became the first Black woman to head a major foundation in the country. Jones had graduated from Wellesley College and her father, Mordecai Johnson, had been the first Black president of Howard University and was credited by Martin Luther King Jr. for introducing him to Mahatma Gandhi's work.[8] Though Jones herself had not experienced poverty, she recognized its grip on the city. Once at the helm of the Boston Foundation, she launched a $10 million, five-year research and grantmaking initiative to examine the issue of poverty in Boston during the otherwise flush mid-1980s.[9]

The Boston Foundation's initial survey of seventeen thousand Boston residents about poverty produced a sobering assessment of the coexistence of increased prosperity and persistent poverty. The 1989 report from this survey, provocatively titled *In the Midst of Plenty*, revealed that, although rates of poverty had declined since 1980, one in six Bostonians still lived below the poverty line. Contrary to popular myths about welfare queens and the long-standing association of Blackness and poverty, the numbers of people experiencing poverty in Boston had fallen consistently across different racial and ethnic groups.[10] It was a point the report made forcefully, as was the finding that Black and Hispanic Bostonians were disproportionately represented among the poor, with 23 percent of Black and 46 percent of Hispanic residents living under the poverty line compared to only 8 percent of white residents. Gender mattered too, with women three times more likely to be poor than men.[11] The report's authors highlighted that nearly half of those in poverty were already working, and 95 percent of the people surveyed said they were looking for work. Perhaps the problem was not with the people or their education, as those involved in the Boston Compact had tried to argue earlier in the 1980s, but rather with the changing nature of work and the wages it paid. These findings only became more pertinent and Jones's vision more trenchant moving into the 1990s, as whatever gains achieved during the Massachusetts Miracle began to erode.[12]

For all the insight gained from the survey research, it also introduced new questions about diversity among those living in poverty and prompted an effort to better understand these dynamics. A grant from the Rockefeller Foundation, which had launched a national, multicity anti-poverty program, helped expand this initial work at the Boston Foundation in 1988 as part of a national conversation about a ghettoized urban "underclass."[13]

Boston's new Persistent Poverty Project existed as a research and action initiative "to explore the stubborn and deeply disturbing problem of urban poverty."[14] Three components anchored the approach: a seminar series of prominent academics, including economists and historian Michael Katz; focus groups to explore diversity of experiences among Boston's poor residents; and the formation of a forty-member Strategy Development Group to assess the findings and chart what became known as a "new social contract" to "eradicate chronic, intergenerational poverty in the Boston community."[15] In structure and results, this qualitative research reinforced the importance of identities or demographics in shaping poverty and the mechanisms to cope with it, laying intellectual and administrative groundwork for citywide conversations about governance and inequality.

The prominence neighborhood nonprofits had achieved over the preceding decades as brokers between residents and major institutions in Boston was captured in the Persistent Poverty Project's second and third activities: focus groups and the advisory Strategy Development Group. First, the foundation contracted with neighborhood nonprofits to host and facilitate conversations, recognizing them as trusted community entities, able to draw a crowd, and having the physical space to host. A total of twenty-eight groups met, representing intersections of Boston's linguistic, immigrant, racial, gender, age, and neighborhood populations in groups such as Latino men or Black girls.[16] Separate reports highlighted white, Black, Latino, and Asian American poverty in Boston, reinforcing the diversity that now characterized the city. A new wave of immigration made Boston a far more racially and ethnically diverse city, with immigrant and refugee populations from Cambodia, Vietnam, Korea, Laos, El Salvador, Mexico, Nicaragua, Brazil, Haiti, the Dominican Republic, and the Caribbean as well as Cape Verde, Ireland, and Russia arriving after federal immigration policies changed in 1965.[17] As a research initiative, it was a far cry methodologically from the studies that informed the Boston Redevelopment Authority and Action for Boston Community Development in the 1960s.

Researchers traced themes across the different focus groups as well, often reinforcing the importance of neighborhood nonprofits even as participants explained their poverty as a product of something larger. Several focus groups highlighted the "importance of cultural, social and religious organizations and institutions" to meeting the specific needs of different Boston communities. The final report highlighted, for example, how Chinese American participants turned to local nonprofit agencies for translation assistance, such as when letters arrived in the mail or as points of contact for government services, and as spaces to sustain their cultural identity in a diaspora.[18] Such findings pointed to the value of nonprofit organizations in reducing at least the symptoms of poverty, but other comments hinted at the need for something larger too: a policy response. Several groups described the persistence of discrimination in employment, their disappointment in public institutions, and the pain of negative stereotyping of people and neighborhoods in the media.[19] Participants also spoke to the contradictions of social welfare policies that, at best, failed to enable advancement and, at worst, undermined it. Personalized accounts populated the final foundation reports, recounting the pains of having to choose between welfare benefits for housing or food and securing a new job, having to forgo an interview because of inadequate public transit and an inability to purchase a car, and having to risk unsafe childcare to pursue education or training.

While the staff at neighborhood nonprofits convened residents, many of their executive directors joined the Persistent Poverty Project's Strategy Development Group as experts and representatives charged with translating poverty research into poverty action. The forty members of the group, hand-selected by the foundation in 1991, told a history of Boston and attested to the priorities of the moment. It was one of the most diverse teams assembled in Boston. For most, sitting on this foundation-selected board stood as a profound achievement after working for decades to gain recognition and resources for their communities. Directors from Freedom House, La Alianza Hispana, the Hispanic Office of Planning and Evaluation, and the Chinese Progressive Association populated the group, as did representatives from a local union, the Jewish Community Relations Council, and researchers from the University of Massachusetts at Boston, Boston University, and Simmons College. By the early 1990s, several members—including Hubie Jones, Frieda Garcia, Nelson Merced, and Gus Newport—had moved on from their origins in neighborhood groups, having attained eminence as race leaders. Others had gained prominence as the first to hold various positions, including Right Reverend Barbara Harris of the Episcopal Church, the first woman and first Black woman ordained as bishop in the Anglican communion, and the Honorable Julian Houston, the first African American appointed to the Massachusetts Superior Court. For balance, the foundation tapped leaders from more grassroots entities too, including Reverend Eugene Rivers of the Ella J. Baker House. A former gang member and graduate of Harvard College with strong Black nationalist roots, Rivers made his ministry out of working with gang-involved youth in Dorchester. A summary publication celebrated the Strategy Development Group for its majorities of women, people of color, and people who had experienced poverty firsthand, though it made little mention of how their personal biographies inadvertently endorsed theories of individual uplift.[20] They could not have been more different from the Goals for Boston crowd of the 1980s, but they nonetheless represented a body of distinguished, if not elite, leaders.

There were several directions that the data from the survey, findings from the focus groups, and conversations in the Strategy Development Group might have pointed to, and, given the prominence of the leadership group and dollars invested, many were eager for the recommendations. The final report of the Persistent Poverty Project, *To Make Our City Whole*, put in writing many of the recommendations those involved had been advocating for a long time, including a focus on the root causes of poverty and the failures of governments to meet the needs of all Bostonians. Yet, alongside these critiques, which to some might have suggested the need for a broad policy agenda of antidiscrimination and structural changes to political and economic institutions, the document depoliticized questions of power into ones of process and steered clear of proposing actual policy-based solutions.[21] To combat racial-ethnic and economic exclusion, the Persistent Poverty Project's final recommendations centered on "a new social contract" between engaged citizenry and a "respectful, responsive" government. Values of inclusion, diversity, dialogue, and empowerment would anchor this new contract and serve as the yardstick by which to measure success. Preferences for individual action, community engagement, shared governance, and decentralized action repeated themes familiar under neoliberal frameworks, even as those involved would have balked at such an association.[22] While not rooted in the business-centric logic of efficiency, the new social contract nonetheless legitimized the idea that goals of democracy and racial-ethnic representation could be best pursued by drawing private entities into the work of public government.

The Strategy Development Group's diversity gave political weight to its recommendations that would shape an understanding of poverty that simultaneously acknowledged and erased the intersections of identity and poverty. An open letter in *To Make Our City Whole* from Thomas Menino, who had become mayor in 1993, captured the tension at the heart of the report's findings: "Poverty knows no geographic boundary. It does not discriminate on the basis of age, race, sex, or ethnicity."[23] His words

CHAPTER 1

The Findings of the Strategy Development Group

FIGURE 7.1. *Strategy Development Group (1994)*. As part of its Persistent Poverty Project, the Boston Foundation convened a group of Boston leaders to form the Strategy Development Group. Members of the forty-person body came from the city's most prominent neighborhood nonprofits and was hailed for its racial and gender diversity. (Members of the Strategy Development Group, in *To Make Our City Whole*, 1994, box 15, folder 29, PPP, NU. Image courtesy of Northeastern University Archives and Special Collections.)

disabusing stereotypes about poor people, as well as the report's broader assertions to that end, stood out in a national poverty discourse still shaped by Reagan's welfare queen and further influenced by Clinton's vow to "end welfare as we know it." Yet Menino's color- and gender-blind sentiments also obscured the central finding of the Persistent Poverty Project that discrimination did make some people more likely to be poor, allowing a hesitancy to dismantle the structures of that discrimination to persist into yet another decade. Attention to community building, social capital formation, and self-actualized empowerment through neighborhood nonprofits, and the challenge of simultaneously recognizing identity categories and moving beyond them, produced a poverty program in Boston rife with contradictions. Not the least of which was a more coordinated effort by the city government to empower coalitions of neighborhood groups while extending few of the material or administrative tools to actually do so.

Governing by Coalition

The Healthy Boston program developed alongside the Strategy Development Group's new social contract in the early 1990s and represented, internal updates suggested, "a laboratory for the concepts generated by the Persistent Poverty Project."[24] Healthy Boston's focus on health specifically, and the existence of the program more generally, owed to a relatively small federal funding opportunity in 1991 that brought resources to Boston and elicited a large response from hopeful neighborhood applicants looking for a share. Mayor Flynn already pitched the program to the incoming Clinton administration as "on the cutting edge of public policy," but, like most programs driven by grant opportunities, Healthy Boston overpromised, underdelivered, and spurred a whirlwind of activity.[25] It also had little to do with actual policy beyond the administrative move to formalize nonprofit neighborhoods as the governing infrastructure in Boston. Healthy Boston, like so many grantmaking programs, reorganized the existing efforts of neighborhood nonprofits that were unenthused about another initiative but unable to sit out the latest round of the grantmaking game.[26] This version pushed neighborhood nonprofits into newfangled organizational "coalitions" as coordinated bodies for empowerment, poverty reduction, and an improved means of governing a multicultural and multiracial city.

Healthy Boston sprang from a funding opportunity and political expediency. Going into the 1990s, Flynn held high favorability ratings despite

declining city coffers and what the largest foundation in his city was calling a problem of persistent poverty. He was nearing the end of two terms
in office and, though he had promised to retire, announced in the summer
of 1991 that he would indeed pursue a third term as mayor.[27] A candidate
in search of a new signature initiative, Flynn saw in a federal Medicaid program the hook he was looking for and, following the delivery of $5 million
to the city's Department of Health and Hospitals, an excuse for a celebratory press announcement. The dollars were minimal, but after nearly a
decade of Republican administrations in Washington, DC, any federal aid
to cities came as a welcome boost to resources and momentum. Flanked
with representatives from across his administration—including the public schools, public housing, and community centers—and from prominent
neighborhood nonprofits, Flynn announced Healthy Boston as a program
to "improve health status in the broadest sense of the word."[28] The program promised to distribute grants to coalitions based in neighborhoods
around the city instead of to individual organizations, and it would "decentralize health and human services from distant institutions to the neighborhoods where people live."[29] For Flynn's campaign, Healthy Boston
played the political hits from his eight years in office and pitched "coalitions" as the new "partnerships."

As grant applications often did, the city grafted Healthy Boston onto
ideas about urban improvement already percolating in Flynn's administration and used the resultant federal dollars to unite them moving forward. One thread came from the mayor's vocal support of the Dudley
Street Neighborhood Initiative, which had proved politically and administratively prudent for the mayor. That partnership offered a road map to
respond to the demands of a multiracial neighborhood as well as evidence
that entities like DSNI served as useful governing entities to liaise with the
city and represent the interests of neighborhood residents. What made
DSNI particularly useful, many gleaned, was its structure as a coalition
that brought together in a formal process residents and the various organizations serving them. At a time when many in Boston felt the city's nonprofit landscape was characterized by "disorganization," DSNI offered a
model of coordinated, comprehensive action at the neighborhood level.[30]
Following this successful example, Healthy Boston dangled federal dollars to prompt the formation of coalitions across the city. The goal was to
link organizations large and small serving the same neighborhood populations to break down the silos of housing and health, for example, and
thereby improve health and socioeconomic outcomes.

Flynn may have claimed public credit for Healthy Boston, but everyone in town knew it was Judith Kurland's idea. Flynn had appointed Kurland commissioner of the Boston Department of Health and Hospitals in 1988—the first woman to hold the role. She brought experience from the health realm, having previously held a leadership position at the New England Medical Center, as well as from the political realm, having worked in DC congressional offices. Kurland designed Healthy Boston according to the latest thinking in global health about "healthy cities/healthy communities." In 1986, the World Health Organization adopted a broad understanding of health based on its intersection with a range of environmental factors, calling for comprehensive planning around health akin to the kinds of planning done for urban renewal. The conversation about healthy communities in the United States was still small in the early 1990s, particularly compared with progress in Europe, but thanks to Kurland, Boston was among the first US cities to put these ideas into practice, joining statewide movements in California, and later Colorado and South Carolina.[31] Consistent with the ethos of healthy communities and the notion of participatory planning, Kurland's Boston Department of Health and Hospitals partnered with the nonprofit United South End Settlements, then under the leadership of Frieda Garcia, to host an April 1991 conference on "Building Health Through Communities" to introduce what the keynote speech billed as "a frontal attack on poverty."[32] Garcia then joined Flynn when he publicly launched Healthy Boston later that year, adding her endorsement of the program and, by extension, he hoped, of his campaign.

From the start, Healthy Boston embodied many of the tensions underlying both the liberal and neoliberal approaches to social welfare and advanced many of the approaches outlined in the Persistent Poverty Project. Even as it bore many of the hallmarks of 1960s-era poverty programs with its rhetorical emphasis on comprehensive and coordinated action as well as its reliance on neighborhood nonprofits for service delivery, Healthy Boston was very much a product of the 1990s, when values of private-sector leadership, austerity, and multiculturalism reigned and metrics and measurement shaped decisions. Kurland and her team framed health broadly—as reliant on "good jobs, decent housing, enough food to eat, recreational facilities, and safe neighborhoods"—but expected improved coordination of services at the neighborhood level to compensate for the broader uneven economic development of the city.[33] Indeed, no new services or programs would be offered through Healthy Boston, which encouraged residents "to work together to solve problems instead of looking to government." The plan was to make government and nonprofit services more "user-friendly" by "improving the efficiency and cost effectiveness."[34] Boston identified "community pride [and] racial harmony" as key indicators—albeit subjective ones difficult to quantify—of healthy communities but made little direct effort to undo patterns of discrimination.[35] Officials might have dubbed Healthy Boston a "public policy approach for the urban agenda of the 1990s," but the city continued to eschew policy changes for administrative ones, and political changes for technocratic ones.[36]

Though government brochures touted Healthy Boston as a "bold new initiative," many in neighborhood nonprofits worried this would be yet another unfunded mandate. After years of scrambling for government grant opportunities, neighborhood nonprofits had developed a deep skepticism of programs one nonprofit staffer described as "promising a new model that would change the world," and many were reluctant to rely on these programs.[37] They knew from experience that the city government's dual role as grant seeker to the federal government and grant maker to neighborhood nonprofits would merely replicate at the local level the same wringer of competition, austerity, and negotiation. Nonetheless, Kurland presented the details of Healthy Boston to a packed auditorium of prospective applicants on a cold Saturday morning in November. Most admitted they were there for the money, even though the amounts were small.[38] Coalitions could apply for between $30,000 and $60,000 in planning funds to support the hiring of a coalition coordinator, and later compete to receive one of only five implementation grants of $250,000 to $350,000.[39]

The city justified its decision to allocate more in planning funds than in implementation by arguing that it would stretch the government's endorsement and create "a major fundraising opportunity" for both funded and unfunded coalitions to attract private resources from foundations to advance plan into action.[40] Such logic captured the social capital bestowed by even a small grant but also conveniently masked a strategic decision by the city to manage what some anticipated as "potential for political backlash" if only a handful of neighborhoods received initial support.[41] Within a year of launching Healthy Boston, the city approved twenty planning grants to community coalitions in various stages of formation and in nearly every neighborhood of the city. The funds typically enabled coalitions to hire a coordinator but little else. Such wide dispersal of the already limited funds solidified coalitions across the city, reinforcing, yet again, the

UPHAM'S CORNER COALITION

Community Coalition Profile, December 1993

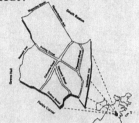

HEALTHY BOSTON

COMMUNITY DESCRIPTION

Upham's Corner is located in the Northern Section of Dorchester, sharing boundaries with Roxbury, from Grove Hall to the Newmarket business district. Its main characteristic is the diversity of residents, businesses and institutions, and the effort to improve the relationship amongst them in a community that has undergone tremendous change in the past twenty years. From an almost homogeneous neighborhood in the early 70's, Upham's Corner has seen the exodus of thousands of white middle class families who have been replaced by a population of newcomers from Latin America, Southeast Asia, West Africa, and the Caribbean.

COALITION HISTORY & MEMBERSHIP

Upham's Corner has a long history of collaboration among its organizations and institutions. This collaboration has responded directly to some of the problems that have affected the community, for example: a Neighborhood Housing Service to address the issues of home ownership and maintenance of existing housing stock; a Drug Task Force to deal with the increase in drug trafficking, gang activities, and violent crime; and a Mobile Methadone Program to reduce the spread of AIDS. The current coalition membership of 17 includes the local health center, the Bird Street Community Center, Dorchester Bay CDC, civic associations and crime watch groups, two public schools, ethnic, religious, and cultural organizations, and the Board of Trade.

COALITION ACCOMPLISHMENTS

From its inception in 1990, the coalition has taken the lead in dealing with crime and the fear of crime. A candlelight vigil attracting more than 500 residents was organized in 1991, following a tragic murder at a local restaurant. In the summer of 1992 a crime summit took place at a local theatre. The coalition co-sponsored a day long street fair and community festival with the participation of more than 2,000 people in the summer of 1993, and in the fall participated in a gun buy-back amnesty program. The coalition helped form a neighborhood association and a leadership youth committee.

COMMUNITY ASSESSMENT RESULTS

A two part survey was conducted in 1992, using a racially, ethnically, and linguistically diverse team of outreach workers and teens to interview more than 1,300 residents. For 32% of them, English was a second language. Focus groups were conducted of people in civic associations, crime-watch groups and agencies. Among the significant findings of the assessment were: 51% of the respondents selected public safety and 40% selected youth/youth services as their first or second priority. 56% selected AIDS as their top health issue.

STATUS OF ACTION PLAN

Submitted its Action Plan on August 30, 1993, proposing the creation of a "Family Advocacy and Support Center" as its highest priority. The center, to be run by the coalition, will have three components: Youth Counsel Advocacy, Community Family Advocacy, and Community Linkage Advocacy, to connect socially endangered youth and their families to the services and support they need . The proposal is currently under review.

For More Information, Please Call:

Upham's Corner Healthy Boston Coalition
500 Columbia Road
Dorchester, MA 02125
Tel (617) 282-6330 Fax (617) 282-2507

For More Information about Healthy Boston, please contact:

Healthy Boston
City Hall, Room 603
Boston, MA 02201
Tel: (617) 635-3140 FAX: (617) 635-3496

- **Population (1990 census)** 23,163

- **Ethnic Diversity (1990 census)**
  35% White (including Polish and Irish), 28% Black (including Haitian), 12% Cape Verdean 20% Hispanic (mostly Puerto Rican and Dominican), 4% Asian (mostly Vietnamese)

- **Key Community Resources**
  Racial and ethnic diversity, strong resident leadership, and commitment to collaboration by the membership.

- **Community Traditions/Pride**
  75 years old Strand Theatre, a centre for the Performing Arts, with a wide range of cultural and educational programs and a special commitment to youth and ethnicity.
  The Bird Street Community Center, with a unique program in Martial Arts, has produced several national champions in the past four years.

- **Major Public/Private Investments**
  Adjacent to new $60 million South Bay shopping plaza.

Community Indicators	Uphams Corner	Boston
% Under 18	30.3 %	19.1 %
% 65 +	10.3 %	11.5 %
% Single Parent Families	49.4 %	43.7 %
% Long Term Residents (5+ years)	50.7 %	47.8 %
% Linguistically Isolated	17.4 %	8.8 %
% Adults with H.S. Degree	62.2 %	77.8 %
% Adults with College Degrees	15.5 %	33.0 %
Unemployment rate (1990)	11.8 %	8.3 %
Median Family Income	$27,515	$34,377
% Below Poverty	24.7 %	18.7 %
% Children Below Poverty	37.3 %	26.3 %
% Homeowners	29.3 %	30.9 %
* Infant Mortality Rate (per 1000 live births)	12.0	11.5
* % Lack of Prenatal Care	11.1 %	7.9 %

* Data comes from area larger than neighborhood

Source: Census 1990 - Birth Records 1988-1990

FIGURE 7.2. *Healthy Boston profiles of Upham's Corner and Egleston Square (1993).* The Healthy Boston program invited nonprofit organizations to form coalitions based on shared geographies or identities and then funded the coalitions in an effort to improve coordination among nonprofits and between the nonprofit sector and the city government. The Upham's Corner and Egleston Square coalitions, like several in the program, focused on violence among gang-involved youth, helping elevate this issue as a citywide priority. (Healthy Boston, "Healthy Boston Community Coalition Profiles," December 1993, box 16, folder 77, PPP, NU. Image courtesy of Northeastern University Archives and Special Collections.)

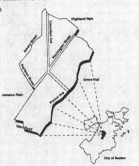

EGLESTON SQUARE COALITION

Community Coalition Profile, December 1993

HEALTHY BOSTON

COMMUNITY DESCRIPTION

Egleston Square is at the intersection of two major city neighborhoods—Roxbury and Jamaica Plain—and borders a third, North Dorchester. It is characterized by diversity and fragmentation related to the presence of many cultures and languages, reinforced by the geography of major streets which literally divide the Square. A predominantly low income area with many undocumented people exacerbates problems of unemployment, illiteracy, and lack of access to health and human services. After years of neglect and disinvestment, Egleston Square is now engaged in revitalization efforts to redevelop the commercial area, create and rehabilitate low and moderate income housing, and improve access to health and human services.

COALITION HISTORY & MEMBERSHIP

In the early 1980s, several resident groups and agencies worked to form the Egleston Square Neighborhood Association and re-open the library. In 1986, seven neighborhood organizations incorporated the Jackson Square Development Collaborative which then entered into a joint agreement with the City for development of light manufacturing. Subsequently, a Master Plan for Egleston Square was developed to serve as a blueprint for economic development, replenishment of the housing stock, creation of green space, and the development of youth services. With the advent of the Healthy Boston movement, the Egleston Square Coalition formalized its structure and now includes 24 resident groups and agencies, such as tenant organizations and the neighborhood association; the merchant's association; several health and human service agencies; a CDC, churches, and area schools.

COALITION ACCOMPLISHMENTS

With the support of the Coalition, Urban Edge, the CDC, has been designated to develop Egleston Center, a mixed retail-office complex. Urban Edge also developed an unused warehouse into a youth services building which currently houses an alternative high school and the YMCA. These projects were facilitated by a Partnership Agreement with the City of Boston, resulting in Egleston Square being designated an Enterprise Zone. The Coalition has also been instrumental in fostering the development of several new programs and services for residents including establishment of an alternative high school, recreational programs for youth, the Take-Back-The-Streets drug elimination program, and the Family Van—a mobile health care unit.

COMMUNITY ASSESSMENT RESULTS

The Coalition conducted a community assessment through agency inventories, community meetings, focus groups, and issue-identified work groups. The resource assessment identified many more resources in the community than members realized, with no glaring gaps in service, but limited capacity throughout. The following needs emerged from the assessment: strengthen the network of youth providers in the Egleston area; involve more residents with area providers; share information among residents and providers; and develop stronger community bonds through shared celebrations and events.

STATUS OF ACTION PLAN

The Coalition is developing its Action Plan with a focus on collaborative programming for families and children, building upon the Master Plan's blueprint to develop more programs for youth. Components include parent support and education programs, direct services for youth, and support and education for youth workers. Peer leadership programs have been established in several Coalition member organizations and hopefully will be expanded and provide additional support to the Coalition.

For More Information, Please Call:

Egleston Square Coalition
c/o Mirna Rodriguez, ESNA
3134 Washington Street
Roxbury, MA 02119
Tel : (617) 524-5052   Fax - not available

For More Information about Healthy Boston, please contact:

Healthy Boston
City Hall, Room 603
Boston, MA 02201
Tel: (617) 635-3140   FAX: (617) 635-3496

- **Population (1990 census)** 9,570

- **Ethnic Diversity (1990 census)**
  50% Black (mostly African-American), 34% Hispanic (mostly Puerto Rican and Dominican), 15% White, and 1% Asian.

- **Key Community Resources**
  Ethnically diverse community, strong resident and merchants associations, commitment to "doing business differently together," adjacent to Franklin Park, new partnership agreement with Public Facilities Department.

- **Community Traditions/Pride**
  Celebration of cultural diversity; "Hands Around Egleston", an annual street fair (3 years).

- **New Projects/Development**
  On-going rehab of Washington St. business district, including planned Egleston Center, a mixed office/retail complex, and storefronts and apartment building.

Community Indicators	Egleston Square	Boston
% Under 16	30.7 %	19.1 %
% 65 +	10.5 %	11.5 %
% Single Parent Families	62.5 %	43.7 %
% Long Term Residents (5+ years)	53.0 %	47.8 %
% Linguistically Isolated	13.0 %	8.8 %
% Adults with H.S. Degree	56.9 %	77.6 %
% Adults with College Degrees	17.9 %	33.0 %
Unemployment rate (1990)	13.5 %	8.3 %
Median Family Income	$23,737	$34,377
% Below Poverty	23.0 %	18.7 %
% Children Below Poverty	47.7 %	28.3 %
% Homeowners	17.9 %	30.9 %
* Infant Mortality Rate (per 1000 live births)	24.9	11.5
* % Lack of Prenatal Care	9.7 %	7.9 %

* Data comes from area larger than neighborhood

Source: Census 1990 · Birth Records 1988 -1990

FIGURE 7.2. (*Continued*)

power of public grantmaking over private entities and its ability to shape the city's associational infrastructure. Healthy Boston continued and accelerated this government embrace of nonprofit neighborhoods.

Healthy Boston's request for proposals enabled neighborhoods and communities to define themselves in ways that sometimes reflected traditional governmental or bureaucratic boundaries and other times came as a surprise to Kurland's team. The South End coalition, for example, followed the original urban renewal boundaries, pointing to the permanence of ties between physical change, political construction, and community formation.[42] Others applied as dispersed communities with both a geographic anchor and a wider catchment of Bostonians across the city. Healthy Boston also included grants to coalitions representing the city's gay and lesbian community, the Haitian community, Chinatown and the wider Asian American communities, and Spanish-speaking communities. The power to self-determine a coalition included the power to name one's community, and the coalition for Lower Roxbury named itself the "I Have a Dream" coalition in a clear signal of racial politics and activism.[43] In a fulfillment of Flynn's hope to appear inclusive, these groups represented the organized interests of those whom his administration identified as problematic or hard-to-reach populations. Grant funding connected these people to city government, creating visibility for marginalized groups and enabling the city to claim support of them.

Just as the city government grafted Healthy Boston as a framework onto existing trends, so, too, did community coalitions use the grant program as a way to formalize existing relationships between organizations and insert their communities into the city's governing apparatus. Healthy Boston presented a particular opportunity for GLBT organizations in Boston, who had, by the early 1990s, experience discussing health in both its narrow and broad definitions after framing AIDS as both a health crisis and a human one about rights, services, and respect. Funding from Healthy Boston enabled the coalition to extend this work to the needs of queer youth, who, the coalition noted, faced higher rates of "school failure, running away, substance abuse, violence and suicide."[44] The immediate conversations centered on safety and well-being, but the larger aim as a coalition sought nothing less than "to secure the rights and support the empowerment of GLBT youth."[45] Funding via Healthy Boston and the visibility it brought helped the coalition members secure internships for queer youth, provide training for local service providers, launch a foster parent program for queer youth unwelcome or unsafe in their birth homes, and host dances and Pride Day activities.[46] Inclusion in the city's program bestowed new recognition on the GLBT community and paved the way for new political visibility in the city. Public statements and private grant materials from the coalition often "applaud[ed] the City of Boston" and reported "secure relationships" with city agencies, including the mayor's office, police department, and school department, whose track records with queer youth seemed to favor punishment over support.[47] The coalition's public display of gratitude, whether genuine or put-on, was all part of the transactional nature of government grantmaking.

The Grove Hall coalition's application likely came as another surprise to Kurland's office, with its claim of representing a neighborhood ill-defined and largely invisible to municipal bureaucrats. Situated between the Washington Park and Dudley Square areas of Roxbury, organizations in Grove Hall submitted a Healthy Boston application as an act of placemaking and self-determination. Funds from the Hyams Trust had helped launch Project RIGHT, an acronym for Rebuilding Grove Hall Together, as a coalition of resident organizations pledging to do the kinds of things DSNI had done elsewhere in the city: remove abandoned cars, clean up vacant lots, and deal with code enforcement issues around lead paint and other symptoms of absentee landlords.[48] Project RIGHT's effort in Grove Hall spilled over into the Healthy Boston application, uniting grassroots organizations such as block associations, churches, and youth violence agencies with more established ones, including the Roxbury Multi-Service Center.[49] Though the name Grove Hall held physical and social meaning for those working, serving, and living in the area, it did not appear in municipal materials. Nor did it map onto predesignated geographic areas—consisting instead of portions of several urban renewal districts, six census tracts and two zip codes, and Roxbury and North Dorchester—which rendered data collection about the area difficult.[50] To complete its Healthy Boston application, which emphasized metrics, Grove Hall organizations collected their own data through interviews with local residents, focus groups, and quantitative measures.[51] The City of Boston could now see Grove Hall in its late twentieth-century form, as a majority Black neighborhood, ethnically diverse with Caribbean, Central American, and African immigrant communities, and high rates of infant mortality and child poverty.[52]

As a citywide program built on a municipal apparatus, Healthy Boston facilitated connections across coalitions and set policy priorities from the ground up. The issue of youth violence, particularly among gang-involved youth, had been on the rise by the early 1990s and emerged as a shared concern among coalitions.[53] In 1990, seventy-three of the 152 homicides in the city had been victims under age twenty-four.[54] The stabbing of a young Black man in the center aisle of the Morningstar Baptist Church during a funeral for a victim of gun violence in May 1992 shocked Boston but also highlighted the pervasiveness of violence in the lives of many young

Bostonians. One line of response came from Black clergy, who adopted the coalition structure to form the Ten Point Coalition and became a national model for community-police partnerships to reduce youth violence.[55] Another came from within Healthy Boston to, meeting minutes noted, "put pressure on the city as a whole" and "have a larger impact on policy" in what became the Healthy Boston Violence Prevention Initiative.[56] Teen Empowerment, a member of the South End coalition with experience organizing peace conferences for young people, began convening weekly meetings of at least ten Healthy Boston coalitions with shared concerns in the fall of 1994.[57] The group discussed the connections between violence and economic opportunity and devised strategies to coordinate activities through a community bulletin board and ways to distribute flyers for events.[58] Many saw their coalitions as "peace initiatives" of their own variety, uniting neighborhood nonprofits that often competed for resources, territory, and social capital.[59] This collaboration within and between Healthy Boston coalitions epitomized what Kurland and the mayor had wanted for the program.

The entrepreneurialism demonstrated by Boston's new coalitions, however, encountered several roadblocks. Even if shaped by skepticism and need, neighborhood nonprofits responded strongly to the Healthy Boston initiative, forging new communities rooted in identity and locality, lifting up new policy priorities, and collaborating within and across neighborhoods. Yet the support of twenty-one coalitions had been costly, dramatically reducing the availability of funds to actually implement any programs. In its second stage of grantmaking, the city funded only five implementation projects, and limited ones at that: a leadership development program for sixty nonnative English speakers in Allston-Brighton, a job apprenticeship program for eighteen youth in Codman Square, an asthma reduction program in Egleston Square, the foster program for GLBT youth, and increased services for Chinatown residents.[60] By the time the Violence Prevention Initiative emerged, few dollars were left at Healthy Boston.

The majority of coalitions that did not make the first round of implementation opted to split whatever funds remained to keep their coalition coordinators employed, indicating their fatigue with the process as much as the opportunity they found in the coalition model.[61] Some looked elsewhere in the city for funding, hoping to shift their work toward some of the newer municipal programs that had sprung up over the intervening years and followed the Healthy Boston model of funding coalitions of neighborhood nonprofit entities. Efforts such as the Boston Healthy Start Initiative, the public facilities department's Green on Blue program to improve empty lots along Blue Hill Avenue, and law enforcement–based Boston Against Drugs and Boston Safe Neighborhoods as well as newly authorized charter schools all came from different municipal departments.[62] The ability of some Healthy Boston coalitions to roll from one grant program to the next spoke to their durability and utility as governing apparatuses as well as to their inability to break free of the structures of their funding.

Early on in the Healthy Boston program, the city set aside funds for an extensive evaluation, whose findings reinforced what many in the coalitions and at city hall already knew. The evaluators chronicled the slippage from a goal to improve residents' health and their neighborhoods to an abstract goal of a "system change" in how neighborhood nonprofits related to one another and to the city.[63] Meetings between bureaucrats and coalition members opened new lines of communication and working relationships, but relationships and process only went so far.[64] When dollars did not flow as promised, many coalitions dissipated or shrank in their rosters from what were once thirty or even fifty members to a dedicated ten at best. Others became disillusioned when their hopes to "establish a new and equal partnership with the city" produced yet another unequal relationship, or when they clashed with city hall over political or advocacy goals.[65] The assessment could well have been written about any number of government grantmaking programs as Healthy Boston wholly embodied the powers and limitations of this policy-making tool. The program served as a perhaps uncomfortable affirmation of the power of promises amid scarcity and competition to produce innovation and spur activity on the ground.

Though his was not a formal evaluation of the program he inherited and led in its final years, Ted Landsmark's reflection on Healthy Boston captured the tragedy of it all. When Ray Flynn left Boston in 1993 shortly after winning a third term as the city's mayor to take his appointment as ambassador to the Holy See for the Clinton administration, Thomas Menino stepped into the mayoralty and stayed there for an unprecedented twenty-one years. Menino put his own spin on Healthy Boston—grant programs had a way of being malleable for politicians when they needed it—and placed it in a new Office for Community Partnership under the stewardship of Landsmark. A veteran of the civil rights movement, and famous for being the subject of the Pulitzer Prize–winning photograph *The Soiling of Old Glory*, Landsmark had moved from outside government to inside it, working to make the city bureaucracy responsive to residents' needs. To him, Healthy Boston provided one such mechanism. "The city," he wrote five years into the program, "has the perennial challenge of being responsible to the voice of the citizens. The question for government in a multi-cultural and diverse city is always 'what' citizen and 'in whose interest.' Being able to have a vehicle to get input and disseminate information is extremely valuable for the everyday functioning of the city."[66] For a time, and a short time only, Healthy Boston had done just that: the infrastructure of nonprofit neighborhoods made urban governance a wider endeavor with more diverse participants but amounted to little more than yet another program that moved around the pieces on an unequal chessboard.

From Healthy to Empowered

As Healthy Boston spent down its resources, a new federal grant opportunity caught the attention of both city officials and the nonprofit coalitions that pledged in new language a solution to the old problem of urban poverty. It was time for another round of the grantmaking game. As his signature urban policy, President Clinton announced a new Empowerment Zone program in 1993 that targeted high-poverty neighborhoods with coordinated services, connections, and investments in what became known as a place-based strategy. That it included many of the core elements Mayor Flynn had advocated infused optimism into Boston's scramble to put together an application. Perhaps this would be the fundraising opportunity the city had hoped for, given the potential of $100 million in federal prize money. The city relied, as it so often did, on its existing governing infrastructure and drew Healthy Boston's coalitions and their ties between city, neighborhoods, nonprofits, and residents into this next program. The approach was certainly opportunistic in that the involvement of the coalitions bolstered Boston's claims of "empowering" residents, but it also gave neighborhood nonprofits a clear opportunity to shape the city's application and reflected a local political scene that would not have tolerated the total exclusion of community groups.

Flynn's recommendations in "America Ready to Go" shared with the eventual policies support for nonprofits as the organizational embodiment of a new Democratic agenda. Clinton's rise to the presidency owed much to his time leading the Democratic Leadership Council and its promotion of a Democratic Party that departed from its supposed big government roots of earlier decades to forge a "third way" that promoted social welfare but rejected redistribution and promoted entrepreneurialism but softened the edges of American capitalism.[67] Many of the public-private partnerships tested in Boston during the 1980s aligned with this philosophy, which Flynn had sought to highlight in his policy proposal whenever possible. Yet beyond the specifics of partnerships as a means of distributing goods or solving public problems, nonprofit organizations offered more basic advantages to the Clinton agenda. They became political and policy shorthand for private solutions that maintained ties to the grassroots. Drawing these entities into policy not just as service providers but as representatives of marginalized populations made more real the talk of empowerment and multiculturalism core to the Democratic base. Clinton's "third way" between liberal and conservative or between socialism and capitalism also shared a moniker with the "third sector," an increasingly common nickname for the nonprofit sector meant to signal its theorized position between government and corporations or between state and market. Of course, all this remained ambiguous in practice, but talk about nonprofit organizations had done good political work for President Bush, whose celebration of a "thousand points of light" evoked a vision of charitable compassion, and would do similar good for Clinton, whose interest in microcredit, community development financial institutions, and "ending welfare as we know it" as anti-poverty measures embraced capitalist tools wielded through nonprofit organizations.

Once in office, Clinton charged Vice President Al Gore with spearheading a new effort named Empowerment Zone/Enterprise Communities. The program extended a combination of flexible grants, loans, and tax credits to high-poverty, distressed neighborhoods, or "zones," with ready-to-go revitalization plans. The approach tacitly acknowledged legacies of racial discrimination—histories of capital divestment, municipal underinvestment, and segregated neighborhoods—but spoke about poverty in a color-blind language. Empowerment Zones framed the traditional signs of urban blight, such as abandoned housing and manufacturing facilities and high rates of unemployment, as opportunities for the shrewd investor. These untapped markets of potential consumers, workers, and homeowners, the logic went, just required special incentives to lure corporate interest and connect ghettoized areas and their residents to the economic mainstream.

The idea to flood a designated area with assistance and to stimulate economic activity in it predated the Clinton administration by over a decade, tracing its roots to the Republican Party and, before that, to the

United Kingdom. In 1980, representative and later HUD secretary Jack Kemp promoted the idea of enterprise zones to both the Reagan and Bush administrations, borrowing the idea from Margaret Thatcher's government. Though he found limited interest from his own party, several self-styled "New Democrats" embraced the idea toward the end of the Bush administration, after the 1992 Rodney King rebellion in Los Angeles put urban America front and center in national discourse. The momentum from Democrats, however, effectively extinguished whatever interest President Bush had in the idea, because he had little interest in supporting a measure backed by his opponents during a campaign season. When passed under President Clinton as part of the Omnibus Budget and Reconciliation Act of 1993, the rebranded Empowerment Zone program carried a new emphasis on community-based nonprofits. The administration moved quickly. At a strategically scheduled January 1994 celebration of Martin Luther King Day, Clinton and Gore launched their signature urban program, selecting a day that tied the program to continuing racial and economic inequalities in the United States without having to directly discuss race.[68] Gore called it an effort to "ultimately uplift our distressed urban and rural communities," while Clinton framed Empowerment Zones as marking a "new partnership" between government, business, and neighborhoods.[69]

Even as policy watchers anticipated the Empowerment Zone program, the six-month window cities had to pull together applications felt rushed and steered those in Boston to rely on their existing governing networks and ongoing programs. The Boston Redevelopment Authority took the initial lead on Boston's application, outlining a proposed Empowerment Zone covering 5.8 square miles and nearly 10 percent of the city's population. This artificially drawn area traced a strange shape running north to south, capturing many of the city's highest-poverty census tracts through much of Roxbury, the South End, and Mattapan as well as a few industrial areas toward which the city hoped to direct investment. Collectively, the area had a poverty rate of 36 percent compared to 19 percent citywide, and an unemployment rate of 16 percent compared to 8 percent for the city. Perhaps most concerning, however, was the realization that poverty had increased in the zone by 2.1 percent in the previous decade, while it had dropped 1.5 percent across the city as a whole.[70] As for what to do within the boundary, Mayor Menino appointed a steering committee, chaired, strategically, by Black lawyer and businessman Joseph Feaster and featuring many of the same faces as the Strategy Development Group, then wrapping up its work at the Boston Foundation. Beneath the ceremonial working group's veneer, much of the actual work happened in thematic task forces, where the city turned to Healthy Boston coalitions in a validation of their status as valuable community representatives in areas of planning, policy, and program design. In a series of weekly meetings beginning in March 1994, the pertinent coalitions involved presented their communities' most pressing needs, the existing landscape of services, and the efforts by the coalitions that might bolster the Empowerment Zone application. For their input, the BRA promised to "keep everyone happy" and reward coalition members should funds come in.[71]

Not all the coalitions, however, took the BRA's promises at face value; some engaged in direct advocacy campaigns to ensure the spoils made it to the neighborhood entities. This was particularly the case for Chinatown's coalition, which sat precariously on the edge of Boston's Empowerment Zone. The Chinatown Coalition was one that had a geographic basis, but it also served as a hub for the city's broader Asian American community, which, while still small in absolute size, had grown almost 90 percent during the 1980s and remained an underresourced and poor neighborhood.[72] Participating in the BRA's planning process presented the Chinatown Coalition an opportunity to help meet the needs of the community and enhance its visibility. Coalition members, including David Moy of the Quincy Community School and Beverly Wing as the coalition coordinator, wrote a letter to the mayor expressing concern and lobbying for their coalition's full inclusion in the proposed Empowerment Zone application.[73] This effort built on and paved the way for more protests and petitions from the group, which became one of the most politically active of the Healthy Boston coalitions.[74] For them, the Empowerment Zone application represented one of several openings for presenting a united front of Chinatown organizations and gaining entry into city politics and governing.[75]

Boston's application for Empowerment Zone funding celebrated the involvement of nonprofit organizations, such as those in Chinatown, in both the planning and hoped-for implementation as evidence of the city's diversity, responsiveness, and modernity. It was an optimistic and rosy document, like most grant applications, that depicted a city brimming with promise and progress. In a cover letter with the application, Mayor Menino noted the "real heroes" of the application as the "people of diverse backgrounds" and an "infrastructure of community-based organizations second to none in this country."[76] Looking to distance Boston from its reputation for racial violence after busing in the 1970s, the application presented a city that had modernized and now celebrated its diversity

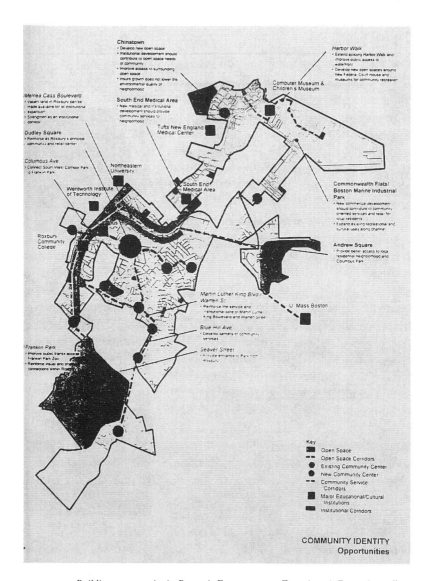

FIGURE 7.3. *Building opportunity in Boston's Empowerment Zone (1994).* Boston's application for the federal Empowerment Zone program framed its proposal around the two goals of expanding neighborhood business centers to areas seen as outside existing commercial and financial opportunities and expanding nonprofit infrastructure for community building and poverty reduction. Local nonprofits participated in the city's application and eventual implementation, including through the development or cosponsorship of new commercial spaces. (City of Boston, "Community Identity Opportunities," in "Boston Works: Partnerships for a Sustainable Community," June 1994, BRA 2630, BPL. Image available via Boston Public Library online collections.)

and strove for inclusion as a sign of its new era. The proposed Empowerment Zone was framed as a multicultural melting pot that was "racially and ethnically diverse by . . . choice," though a more accurate description might have acknowledged an amalgamation of ethnic enclaves of still-segregated communities.[77] The application was pitched as "not from the desks of 'experts' or the halls of academia, but rather from the community itself," thanks to neighborhood nonprofit staff serving as "trusted representatives" and a "deep-rooted neighborhood structure."[78] Even if exaggerated, Boston boasted of its process and goals in a way that revealed how far the city had come since the days of urban renewal and how politically useful the involvement of nonprofit entities continued to be.

From the city government's perspective, part of the reason to include nonprofit entities lay in their ability to mask policies and programs that often undermined the goals of equity that nonprofits advocated and that their presence suggested. Such was the case with Boston's Empowerment Zone plans, which represented a hodgepodge of strategies held together by the vague goal of economic inclusion. Traditional allocations for job training and other social welfare services sat alongside more progressive goals of full-day kindergarten and support for tenant organizing. The application also, however, included plans to court business investment in an effort to expand the city's knowledge economy, particularly in the health care, higher education, and technology sectors, which were just as likely to displace Empowerment Zone residents as they were to improve their economic lot. The plans displayed a neoliberal logic that downplayed the role of government and emphasized personal uplift and measurable results, embodying the metaphor Vice President Gore used to describe government: "more like hardware stores than master builders. . . . We simply give people the tools to do it themselves."[79] To that end, while Boston's application materials spoke openly about the uneven effects of the Massachusetts Miracle just as the Persistent Poverty Project had documented, it avoided talk of any redistributive policies. The rejection of Boston's Empowerment Zone application by federal grant makers turned out to be the most surprising thing about it.

From Empowerment to Enterprise

The existence of a federal program, even without Boston in it, still set the political and policy agendas in which the city operated.[80] In an unusual sign of restraint, the federal Empowerment Zone program decided to invest in only six cities initially. Boston lost out to Atlanta, Baltimore, Camden, Chicago, Detroit, and New York, each of which gained about $100 million in federal aid—with the exception of New York, which received $300 million.[81] Boston did, however, win designation as an Enhanced Enterprise Community. It was a consolation prize named for another tenet of neoliberalism that linguistically suggested a substantive change in what the federal government offered US cities and the goals it designated for them. A heavy emphasis on extending credit to individuals, neighborhood nonprofits, and small and large businesses and the use of tax credits and loans to do so forced the drafters of Boston's Empowerment Zone plans to rethink their strategy in terms of the new tools at hand.

Boston's application won attention for its promise of empowerment but gained resources for extending market activity into the city's poorest neighborhoods—the "enterprise" in Enhanced Enterprise Community. Accordingly, Boston won the bulk of its funds, $44 million, as loans and tax credits, and only $2.95 million as a block grant, which the city could convert into loans at its discretion or use as grants for nonprofit-provided services.[82] In his letter announcing Boston's designation, HUD secretary Henry Cisneros praised the city, writing, "This vision, realized with the public-private partnerships you have forged and the grassroots community support you have built, will empower residents to successfully build a viable community and create new economic opportunities."[83] His language affirmed the utility of neighborhood nonprofits to the city's successful application but said little about their role moving forward. The allocation of dollars, though, revealed the federal priority for nonprofit involvement in poverty reduction.

The structure of funds for the Enhanced Enterprise Community did as much to determine the local program as the participatory process that had shaped the application. With fewer dollars than hoped for, the city scaled back plans substantially and focused by necessity on the loans and tax credits it did win to physically and economically transform pockets of the predetermined zone. The pace decelerated as well, as Menino was slow to appoint a new advisory committee, which Feaster chaired again, and organize community elections for the governing board. Tellingly, many of the neighborhood coalitions that had shaped the application and given it credibility saw their positions diminished in the implementation, even as some individual entities gained substantial funds for construction projects. The Chinatown Coalition, for example, pressed, unsuccessfully, to ensure that the loans were truly accessible to small businesses run by nonnative English speakers.[84] The emphasis on loans and working capital, however, instead favored community development corporations, which, by the 1990s, after the examples of the Boston Housing Partnership and DSNI, had honed reputations as able to manage the physical and financing aspects of projects, and whose organizational model aligned with the enterprise zone's focus on entrepreneurship, business development, and physical revitalization. The clear alignment between CDCs and the new federal program led to the hiring of Reginald Nunnally, executive director of the Grove Hall Neighborhood Development Corporation, to head the nonprofit Boston Empowerment Center, newly established in 1996 to oversee the city's federal program.[85]

Under Nunnally's leadership, Boston's "one-stop capital shop" used the federal subsidies to help several businesses expand manufacturing and processing facilities in the Crosstown Industrial Park, and nonprofits engaged in bricks-and-mortar projects. The South End Community Health Center and the Dudley Street Neighborhood Initiative, for examples, built new facilities and housing that stood as placemaking projects many hoped would anchor neighborhood revitalization beyond their immediate use for medical provision or housing. The involvement of these nonprofits in major construction and placemaking projects extended into concurrent federal policies and signaled the confidence of city agents in these community entities and the value they saw in their services. Elsewhere in Boston, though still within the bounds of the designated zone, federal loans via the HOPE VI housing program underwrote the redevelopment of the public housing complex Orchard Park under the leadership of a local CDC and tenant organization.[86] It reopened as Orchard Gardens in 1999, the same year Boston finally won an Empowerment Zone designation under an expanded version of the program that carried into the twenty-first century new rounds of grants, loans, and tax credits.

The renewal of the federal Empowerment Zone program and Boston's eventual inclusion in it gave the city an opportunity to expand what many saw as an uneven program. As both developers and service providers, nonprofit organizations continued to exert a strong presence in the second phase of the city's program. They benefited from the $10 million spent on human services, including adult basic education and job training, and $3.5 million on youth employment; from loans to support six hundred units of affordable housing and expanded commercial spaces; and from capacity-building efforts to strengthen individual nonprofits and encourage their collaboration. They led redevelopment projects in Dudley Square and Grove Hall, including the opening of the Grove Hall Mecca mall complex, which mimicked the kind of activities Empowerment Zone loans enabled in other cities around the country, where nonprofits worked hard to expand markets in previously ghettoized areas.[87] A joint initiative of a local mosque and CDC, the Grove Hall Mecca opened in 2001 with a CVS Pharmacy, Hollywood Video, Dunkin Donuts, and a Stop and Shop grocery store, the first in the neighborhood in over two decades. These projects stood as signal achievements for neighborhood leaders and residents, particularly given that, despite authorizations of up to $100 million in aid for Boston, the city saw only a quarter of the resources it was once promised.

The arrival of national chains in Roxbury, however, failed to address many of the concerns raised by the Persistent Poverty Project and other groups in the city, even as it was an effort spearheaded by neighborhood nonprofits. New jobs at the hotels, malls, and health care facilities supported by federal loans left untouched the problem of wages even as they expanded employment; training for residents with criminal records helped people reenter the workforce but did little to slow down accelerating mass incarceration; expanding homeownership in the years before a massive foreclosure crisis failed to build wealth in families generationally deprived it; and coordination among nonprofit organizations generated no new resources. Indeed, the transformation of ideas about poverty reduction and the tools available to do so over the previous decades had aligned neighborhood nonprofits, particularly CDCs, with a pro-growth and pro-market agenda. The accessibility of financialized forms of aid and confidence in their ability to transform poor people and places by increasing access to credit and capital positioned many nonprofits as beneficiaries and drivers of the broader financialization of the US economy.[88]

Research on the second stage of Boston's Empowerment Zone program, between 2000 and 2009, found that, though the numbers were slight, poverty decreased in the city as a whole but increased in the zone.[89] Neighborhood nonprofits remained imperfect representatives and inadequate substitutes for a robust welfare state, revealing a structural inadequacy that even their coordination could not overcome. Further research by political scientist James Jennings found that the census tracts with the richest nonprofit infrastructure, largely within the Empowerment Zone, were also those he called the most "distressed." It was a new metric of structural oppression that he devised to capture in one number the social, economic, and environmental factors that kept certain neighborhoods in perpetual struggle.[90] Jennings presented these findings to local nonprofit leaders and veterans of the city's struggles for racial and economic equality, including Hubie Jones and Mel King, and to local foundations, including the Boston Foundation. It was a sobering, if not entirely shocking, finding after so many decades of work.

Conclusion

The Clinton administration launched an era of federal grantmaking at a scale not seen since the 1960s. Even as Clinton sought to distance his policies—and his politics—from the supposed largesse of Johnson and cruelty of Reagan, urban policies of the 1990s borrowed heavily from earlier eras. Vocabularies of comprehensive and coordinated action at the grass-roots echoed the War on Poverty. The emphasis on a bounded urban geography bore resemblance to Model Cities. Involvement of municipal governments followed LEAA and Community Development Block Grants. Aid structured as grants and loans came from housing intermediaries of the 1970s. An emphasis on partnership, competition, and private leadership borrowed from the 1980s. Clinton's Empowerment Zone program put a new spin on things—most prominently his use of the tax code to encourage investment in designated areas and faith in the marketplace to address poverty, particularly among racial and ethnic minorities—but still operated through the nonprofit sector and with community agencies as partners, sponsors, and coalition members. Following Clinton's two terms in the White House, his policies matured from cutting-edge to precedent, and Presidents Bush, Obama, and Trump each embraced aspects of the Empowerment Zone model for their own urban improvement schemes. In their own ways, these administrations launched new rounds of the grant-making game.

The distribution of grants and loans to lower tiers of government and neighborhood nonprofits via competitive processes had proven an incredibly powerful tool, if not for actually solving the problems of urban America than for shaping the activities therein. Grantmaking administratively, materially, and discursively translated political ideologies into reality, and it served as the conduit by which governing systems extended from Washington, DC, to the grassroots. These grantmaking programs tied neighborhood nonprofits to the state and largely defined the terrain on which they operated. Local politics, alternative funding sources, organizational capacity, and existing arrangements mattered, and they variously resisted and accelerated liberal, conservative, and neoliberal agendas. The cumulative product of these policies in all their liberal, conservative, and neoliberal variations, as well as the local translation of them, has been the creation of nonprofit neighborhoods where public resources and representation flowed through nongovernmental entities.

Both the local Healthy Boston initiative and the federal Empowerment Zone program produced nonprofit neighborhoods, though of slightly different varieties. Under Healthy Boston, the city extended agenda-setting, self-determination, and representative authority to coalitions of nonprofits often cutting across traditional city boundaries. Yet, without substantive resources behind such powers, the initiative did more to alter the governance infrastructure than to improve the lives of those living in poverty. In contrast, the Empowerment Zone efforts in Boston extended significant resources through nonprofits but limited the application of those resources to projects and services that aligned with the goal of expanding market access and the improvement of individuals. In each case, the local project reacted to decisions made elsewhere and suffered for lack of either resources or power. The persistence of these absences, counterintuitively, empowered neighborhood nonprofits to find niches for themselves in neighborhoods and, ultimately, obstructed them from meaningfully addressing the issues of racial and economic inequality in Boston.

Perhaps it is telling that the nation's first African American president, Barrack Obama, began his career at a neighborhood nonprofit before rising to the highest office in the world in 2008. Throughout his campaign and presidency, Obama was committed to the principles that the United States remained unequal and that working within institutions and with nonprofit organizations could create change. His faith in nonprofit involvement as either a route to or substitute for political and economic power shaped his policy agenda as much as that of his predecessors. Obama's administration built on the Empowerment Zone model of targeting resources to defined geographic areas and encouraging coordination among public and private entities in a high-need neighborhood, drawing inspiration as well from the celebrated Harlem Children's Zone. Founder Geoffrey Canada built the Harlem Children's Zone as a nonprofit neighborhood of sorts in New York City during the early 2000s to interrupt cycles of intergenerational poverty by serving neighborhood children from "cradle to career" with the colocation and coordination of services such as health and dental screenings, food provision, education and recreation, and parent engagement in a defined zone. Obama, among others, became fascinated with Canada's successes and vowed to encourage this vertically integrated approach elsewhere.

During Obama's presidency, multiple cabinet agencies launched competitive, place-based, grantmaking initiatives that invited joint applications from municipalities and community nonprofits. These included the Department of Housing and Urban Development's Choice Neighborhoods and the Strong Cities, Strong Communities program, the Department of Education's Promise Neighborhoods, the White House's Neighborhood Revitalization Initiative, the Department of Justice's Byrne Criminal Justice Innovation Program, and the Environmental Protection Agency's Sustainable Communities, among others. Each with its own signature focus and zippy name, these programs together signified the administration's guiding principle that "change comes from the community level and often through partnership" and that place-based efforts "leverage investments by compounding resources in targeted places" and "streamline otherwise redundant and disconnected programs."[91] Faced with an intransigent Congress, place-based efforts enabled progress on the Obama administration's priorities without substantial spending and pushed a focus on capacity building of neighborhood nonprofits and their coalitions while still advancing the broader antigovernment narrative of neoliberalism, now decades old. The enthusiasm for place-based efforts extended to the private philanthropic realm too, with national competitions including Living Cities' Integration Initiative and the Rockefeller Foundation's Resilient Cities alongside local ones such as Boston Rising and the Boston Opportunity Agenda.[92]

With efforts emerging from within the city government, the local philanthropic network, and neighborhood nonprofit organizations, Boston's leaders worked in the twenty-first century to bolster its reputation as a hub of social innovation. Many recognized the limitations of these funding initiatives but played along anyway to win a share of the pie and hopefully improve the lives of some. Boston netted a mixed record in these competitions, winning resources in some and missing on others. An application from DSNI, the City of Boston, and twenty-two other partners won Promise Neighborhood funding in 2010 to strengthen life chances for students attending two public schools in the Dudley neighborhood.[93] A partnership between the Dorchester Bay Economic Development Corporation, the City of Boston, and several other nonprofits won Choice Neighborhood designation in 2011 to redevelop several buildings of subsidized housing and transform a former meat factory into a small business kitchen incubator.[94] The Fairmont Collaborative, a coalition of four CDCs and other area neighborhood nonprofits, was named a federal Sustainable Community to help open four new stations on the Fairmont commuter rail line and encourage "transit-oriented development" along the corridor.[95] In addition to the new housing, transit stations, after-school programs, and community planning documents these funds enabled, they achieved the goal of tightening the networks of neighborhood nonprofits and their bonds to the state.

Each of these major federal awards infused millions in grants and loans into Boston nonprofits, and each built on existing efforts that predated the announcement of those awards. They spoke a language of partnership, coalition, and leverage, and of the persistence of poverty. Most overlapped geographically, at least in part, in the same neighborhoods that the Empowerment Zone had targeted a decade before, and that encompassed the Model Neighborhood several decades before that. The concentration of federal aid and local attention within a relatively similar zone successfully directed resources to those most in need but left untouched all that occurred outside it as the city became more expensive and unequal by the day. Rather than remedies for racial and economic inequality, these federal grantmaking programs enabled segregation, poverty, and exclusion to persist in new forms, as marginalized populations continued to disproportionately live in nonprofit neighborhoods and rely on neighborhood nonprofits for public resources, representation, and rights. This was the practice of democracy at its fullest and hollowest. Neighborhood nonprofits had carved out a role in policy and politics managing the cacophony of American cities and compensating for the shortcomings of public institutions, but the social, political, and financial capital they accrued in the postwar years remained precarious—dependent on political goodwill, subject to competition in the marketplace of grantmaking, and constrained by choices made elsewhere.

Conclusion

Nonprofit Neighborhoods

Boston entered the new millennium on an upswing, having finally rebounded from the twentieth century's suburban age. Urban living was no longer an option of last resort but instead a preferred home for those with the ability to choose. Neighborhoods such as the South End offered trendy dining options, renovated brownstones, and boutique exercise studios. The city had been at the forefront of the transition from manufacturing to services, and by the twenty-first century, Boston's economy based on knowledge workers and technology had become the envy of mayors nationwide. A self-congratulatory liberalism fawned over those vowing to do good and do well and cheered as the commonwealth elected a Black governor whose personal narrative spoke to the virtues of nonprofit, corporate, and government work. Massachusetts broke new ground in the movements for marriage equality and universal health care as well as in research on stem cells, genomics, and robotics. The infamous "Big Dig" tunnel project finally buried the elevated highway that had bisected the city, transforming the former eyesore into a park with splash pools, food trucks, and open-air concerts that catered to the professional class working and living along the new greenway. This was a new Boston that boasted livability and forward thinking, and once again stood as a shining city upon the hill.

Such momentum carried Boston to the number one spot in a ranking by the Brookings Institution in 2016, but it was a chart that no city wanted to top. The city, Brookings analysts concluded, ranked as the most unequal in America and its metro region in the top ten.[1] While the extremes of such inequality may have caught observers by surprise, the problem was well documented in the city. Just the year before, researchers at the Federal

Reserve Bank of Boston had released a report on wealth inequality that found "vastly unequal" assets among white and non-white families in Boston, highlighting an inequality that was generations in the making and continuing to widen.[2] Researchers affiliated with the Boston Foundation had repeatedly expressed concern about the unevenness of the city's economic prosperity. Plenty more Bostonians did not need a glossy report to tell them about the inequality they lived every day. Just a few miles from the Rose Kennedy Greenway, residential neighborhoods remained isolated from public transit, underserved by the public school system, underpaid by the service industry, burdened by housing costs, and segregated by race and ethnicity. Perhaps no statistic captures the extremes of privilege and poverty better than life expectancy. In a city with world-renowned hospitals, residents of the Egleston Square neighborhood have in the twenty-first century a life expectancy of less than fifty-nine years, while those living less than half a mile away—two subway stops—in the Back Bay can expect to see their early nineties.[3]

Although extreme, Boston's inequality was not unique in the twenty-first century. The city shared with five others the unfortunate status of landing in the top ten for both unequal city and region in the United States. Political, economic, and social trends beyond the cities themselves had restructured the urban landscape over the preceding decades. At the same time, cities were not passive entities adrift in broader currents; wide swaths of urban residents had contributed in direct and indirect, deliberate and unintended ways to the city's transformation. Mayors, bureaucrats, and city councilors; corporate executives, real estate developers, and civic boosters; activists, executive directors, and board members; residents, voters, and protesters all played a part in moving Boston and cities like it from the age of suburbia to an age of urban renaissance. As so many crowed, it was a public and a private effort that involved nonprofit organizations as simultaneously central and marginal actors.

The pivot to engage neighborhood nonprofits in the work of urban governance appeared at first to be a rare win-win for government and activists. Neighborhood nonprofits became the spaces where residents gathered, accessed public and private services, and exerted political influence; these spaces were also targeted in political rhetoric, policy, and philanthropy through the granting of resources and governing authority. They mediated between citizens and the state, and between consumers and the market. They epitomized democracy at the local level. A concession of certain authority to design, approve, or implement plans for their neighborhoods empowered community entities to hold elections and spend tax-funded resources in ways responsive to local needs and employing local residents.

Yet, in ways evident at the time and from the vantage of history, the construction of nonprofit neighborhoods reinforced the long-standing precarity and marginalization many involved fought so hard to address. Nonprofit neighborhoods became spaces where the seemingly oppositional processes of inclusion and exclusion became two sides of the same coin and where even publicly funded and subsidized private spaces could not fully deliver public democratic rights to those long denied an equal voice, standing, and representation based on their race, ethnicity, or income. The successes and disappointments of community organizations and their layering in nonprofit neighborhoods reflected local politics and processes. They were also, however, products of several tiers of policy at the federal, state, and local levels, funded by public and private dollars, steered by elected and unelected government officials, supplemented with corporate and philanthropic resources, and implemented by local activists and social welfare professionals with a diverse range of identities. Nonprofit neighborhoods were political and policy projects of those looking to manage various manifestations of urban crisis, and they were built within the bounds of a political, economic, social, and spatial inequality visible within these new spaces of urban governance and structured far beyond them. That was true in the 1950s, and it still was in the new millennium, even as the justifications for, and tools of, nonprofit neighborhoods had changed over the intervening decades.

Another way to think through this mixture of continuity and change borrows a vocabulary of *systems* and *structures* from discussions about social innovation, itself an outgrowth of the trends described in this book. The semantics are slight, but essential to recognize contemporary urban problems as rooted in politics and policy and not in practice. In 2006, management guru and Harvard professor Clayton Christenson extended his famous theory of disruptive innovation to the social sector in a piece for the *Harvard Business Review*. In the article, Christenson gave voice to what many leading lights in the nonprofit sector had already been discussing for some time. He argued that true innovation, and therefore true progress on social goals, would only come from "scalable, sustainable, systems-changing solutions."[4] The idea was that a substantive—"disruptive"— change in the delivery, financing, strategy, or organizational models of social welfare provision would accelerate progress toward social goals. It was an alluring idea that gave voice in the twenty-first century to what so many grantmaking programs of the twentieth had claimed to seek: new ways of funding, new ways of tracking results, new ways of incentivizing and rewarding, new ways of collaborating, and new ways of running organizations. Yet, for such talk of interrupting the status quo, conversations around social innovation tend to glide over discussions of power, policy, and politics and overlook the structural basis of the status quo the disrupters have sought to overturn.

Nonprofit Neighborhoods, however, gives evidence for why a structural change has not yet followed a systems change, and why it likely will not.[5] For one, the desire to create new systems has been at the center of policy making, political promises, and private philanthropy since at least the mid-twentieth century. The quest is not new. The perennial goal of a coordinated, comprehensive system of aiding and improving the unfortunate urban masses existed as a stated goal under urban renewal, the Ford Foundation's Gray Areas program, and the War on Poverty. It was the driving impetus for the devolutionary programs of Model Cities and block grants for community development, law enforcement, and general revenue. The promise of public-private partnerships rested on the expectation that the efficiencies of business would tame the seeming chaos of neighborhood nonprofits to produce measurable, replicable results. Demonstration grants have flowed from the top down to discover and then scale bottom-up approaches to old problems. Reams of paper in grant applications, reports, and audits have set and tracked benchmarks, and programs have been evaluated on the expectation that data would either confirm success or inspire a redesign. The rhetoric and details of redesigned systems have varied over time, but the general goal has remained. So, too, has the ideological basis behind these efforts, insisting that US political economy is basically sound and that opportunity need only be extended to those at the bottom of the ladder. The call for better or improved systems of social welfare and urban governance has been one of the most consistent themes of political and urban history.

The second lesson from history is that this insatiable search has, in a way, produced results. The United States has undergone a profound systems change in how cities are governed, how social welfare goods and services are distributed, and in who participates in these processes. The once isolated, independent, and ad hoc neighborhood nonprofit organizations of the mid-twentieth century built entire nonprofit neighborhoods in which these private agencies held the primary responsibility for delivering services, facilitating participation, and representing interests across a wide swath of issue areas, including health, housing, economic development, education, youth services, elderly care, policing, and more. These responsibilities were validated through grants and contracts as well as through new political expectations for participation and partnership. In the 1950s and early 1960s, the federal government positioned neighborhood nonprofit organizations as valuable entities in the work of urban renewal and funded nonprofit agencies for a slew of social goals—what Boston's redevelopment director called "human renewal." As public dollars flowed from Washington to some of the nation's poorest areas, policy makers included a statutory requirement for the "maximum feasible participation" of local residents, who then demanded these promises be kept. Protests and legal challenges then codified who sat on the decision-making bodies of privately incorporated organizations and the routes by which they occupied those seats.

What had started as relationships between the federal government and nonprofits got rerouted as cities then inserted themselves in government grantmaking and clawed back authority from their neighborhood nonprofits and from Washington. The power to distribute funds transformed city hall from a place of doing to one of allocating, monitoring, and evaluating. Calls by residents for control over land and economic development launched policies, programs, and financial packages that drew corporate lenders and capital markets into the development of affordable housing. An entire field of intermediaries, technical assistance providers, and consultants now exists under the realm of community development. The language of partnership and a vocabulary of business pervade the social sector, and the presence of elite donors, civic leaders, and volunteers keeps emergency services afloat. Neighborhood coalitions and zones have redrawn the political and economic geography of the city as well as the ways that resources and representatives connect citizens and city hall. As executive directors, board members, and staff at nonprofit agencies, men and women from marginalized communities now sit at policy-making and philanthropic tables. They have used those platforms as springboards into elected and appointed roles in government. Large-scale urban projects are legitimated by the presence of nonprofit leaders, who serve as proxies for community input. These are all system-level changes of one form or another that have come from disruptive ideas and actions by those seeking change. Urban governance has become a project of building, managing, and maintaining nonprofit neighborhoods.

Third, however, is that a better delivery system, even a more inclusive one, did not and could not substitute for the power to design, control, or shape the system itself. Governing by grantmaking and partnership had seemed responsive to the particular needs of residents by acknowledging that race, ethnicity, gender, sexual orientation, or age mattered and by granting a degree of autonomy to groups previously denied such power. This was, nevertheless, a partial victory. It segmented the polity, creating competition among groups and reinforcing their otherness through a position not in direct relationship with a responsive government but one mediated by private organizations. Neither did acknowledging the role of identity markers repair the damage hierarchies of difference had created, nor dismantle the broader patterns of exclusion that had defined and continue to define some urban neighborhoods and not others. The extension of grants and contracts to neighborhood entities has not protected them against broader forces of capitalism, gentrification, globalization, and deindustrialization and has, at times, accelerated those extractive processes. Ten new affordable housing units could hardly prevent gentrification and displacement, even as they housed ten families in need; just as an after-school program could not reduce school violence or compensate for underfunding, even as it boosted math scores among young people.

The kind of political advocacy and protest often required to move a structural agenda was precisely the kind of activity discouraged, if not outright prohibited, under government grantmaking. Even as it delegated certain powers to private entities, public grantmaking reinforced traditional governmental authority in other ways. Government bureaucrats gained new control over and access to the finances, staffing patterns, program offerings, and client data of neighborhood groups. Political figures—elected or appointed—retained the power to make, pause, or renew grants. While nonprofit leaders gained more contact with government figures, they also had more reason to maintain a conciliatory relationship. The financial precarity of neighborhood nonprofits undermined whatever governing power they gained, constraining organizations and, by extension, limiting the political power of residents to make the kinds of structural, policy-based changes necessary to win full rights of citizenship.

Fourth, that these system changes failed to produce structural change was neither a failure nor a surprise. Nonprofit neighborhoods were not designed as vectors for redistribution. These were governing spaces of discipline, selective uplift, growth, and stability—not economic restructuring or political empowerment—and they were contested at every turn. Activists, residents, and nonprofit workers called out the shortsightedness of these public and private efforts throughout the twentieth century. They did so in public protests and private meetings, in letters and newspapers and books, in campaigns and social service programming, in Boston and Washington, DC, with anger and pleas, with supporting numbers and stories, with urgency and with alternative proposals. They called out nonprofit neighborhoods as political projects and policy products meant to, if not reinforce the status quo, at least not threaten it. These critiques often came as a surprise—if not an insult—to those who considered themselves good liberal allies but nonetheless stood in the way of more progressive change. Nonprofit leaders such as Mel King and Hubie Jones knew the inadequacy of their efforts and continued the work anyway, keeping up the drumbeat for justice and structural, substantive equality whenever and wherever they could. So, too, did those with even less standing: the people whose interests were being represented—well or not—by private organizations and whose day-to-day existence involved them. The willingness of nonprofit leaders to accept public grants from governments and foundations that continued to exclude did not make them sellouts. Instead, it reveals the limitations of their position, recognizes the maneuverability they attained, and recalls the alternate routes proposed and denied.

Fifth, and finally, the lack of structural change should neither disparage the past half century of work by neighborhood nonprofits nor discourage their ongoing work. To the contrary. These community organizations have, with public and private underwriting, improved the lives of countless urban residents. Through their direct activities, neighborhood nonprofits have sheltered and fed the homeless, provided emergency and routine health care, cared for babies and the elderly, tutored students and provided creative and athletic opportunities, built housing and playgrounds, tended gardens, patrolled streets, and represented interests. Indirectly, neighborhood nonprofits have contributed in myriad ways not easily captured in grant reports: economically through the payment of salaries, rents, and mortgages; socially through block parties, waiting rooms, and coalition meetings; and politically through organizing, candidate forums, and board elections. Nonprofits have helped launch political careers and advanced conversations on rights, justice, and equality. That does not make the work of neighborhood nonprofits unimportant; it makes it inadequate. And it sets a goal higher than improving odds of surviving while also recognizing that even survival cannot be guaranteed.

This historical narrative does not carry up to the present day, but it could have. *Nonprofit Neighborhoods* describes a trajectory that the opening decades of the twenty-first century certainly follow. Readers active in the nonprofit sector or in the field of social innovation will no doubt note the plethora of organizations—or, as some would say, enterprises and ventures—that profess new solutions for the very old problems of poverty and inequality. Fine-tuning program delivery, sharpening accounting practices, coordinating across agencies, or increasing offerings, however, has not sufficiently moved the needle in the past, and it will not sufficiently do so in the future. Systems changes have, historically, not produced structural ones.

Neighborhood nonprofits can and should play a role in creating a more just and equal society. Local power and local control are essential elements to moving toward a more equitable future, but they are not, as those with power have sought to convince those without it, an end unto themselves. Instead, the slow work of building social movements and growing political power has been the most productive path to structural change; it is no accident that those activities have been the hardest to measure or track, and the hardest to get funded. The uncomfortable fact remains that inequality and the role of neighborhood nonprofits in urban governance have grown together, not apart. In Boston, the city's most economically and socially distressed neighborhoods in the twenty-first century are also those with the most neighborhood nonprofits.[6] Recognizing this complicated history ought to prompt concern about the systems and structures of the American state as well as reflection on why we have so consistently turned to neighborhood nonprofits to solve some of the most persistent and complex problems.

Acknowledgments

Acknowledgments are often the first thing I read in a book, and I've been writing mine in my head since I started this project. Doing so has been a way for me to mark the various stages of producing a first book and, in moments of loneliness and frustration, recognize the communities of support that have helped me along the way. It is both an honor and a daunting task to commit to paper the words I have kept in my head for so long.

Many of the questions this book engages predate both my entry into graduate school and initial research for this book. As a college student, Annelise Orleck encouraged my ideas and my writing, introducing to me to the power not only of the past but of its study. Her support of my senior thesis and other work at Dartmouth College and her continual support in each stage of my career since then have been central to my survival and success. Annelise was the first person to nudge me toward a PhD, telling me over lunch that teaching could be a revolutionary activity if you choose to make it one. She made that choice, and I have strived ever since to do the same. After college, I worked for two years at the Boston Foundation, where I was introduced to the world of philanthropy, the nonprofit sector, and the work neighborhood organizations do despite odds stacked against them. It was there that I began to see the power and limitations of pursuing public action through private means, and where the persistence of problems I had studied historically remained most visible. Some of my greatest teachers (and greatest cheerleaders) were colleagues at the foundation, especially Geeta Pradhan, Robert Lewis Jr., Marta Rivera, Andrea Martinez, Natanja Craig Oquendo, Lauren Baker, and Jessica Mendes. At one of the final meetings I attended before leaving for graduate school, Professor James Jennings of Tufts University presented the maps of distressed neighborhoods that inspired this historical study and feature in its final chapter.

At Harvard University I found an incredibly supportive community of faculty and peers. Lizabeth Cohen's workshop on twentieth-century US history fostered a scholarly community where I learned to both give and receive feedback that was affirming and critical at the same time. That community buoyed me in the lonely stages of dissertating and cemented friendships that have extended past then. My thanks especially to Casey Bohlen, Shaun Nichols, Andrew Pope, Brian Goldstein, and Theresa McCulla as well as to friends outside the workshop, including Eva Payne, Sandy Placido, and Elizabeth Jemison. I proudly defended my dissertation to a committee of four women, all experts in political history: Liz Cohen, Lisa McGirr, Nancy Cott, and Elizabeth Hinton. To this day I still don't know how Liz served as dean at the Radcliffe Institute for Advanced Study and managed to support her graduate students with such depth of engagement and precision of editing. Both my historical research and writing are all the better for her, as she pushed my work forward in firm and caring ways. Lisa McGirr encouraged me to see the political side of the story I was telling and asked the right question at the right time. Nancy Cott emphasized the role of the state in both the public and the private long before I realized its centrality to my project. They generously read drafts, scheduled meetings, and demanded high quality. In the final stages of my dissertation, Elizabeth Hinton engaged my discussion of government grants and helped me look across different funding programs for shared logics or practices. Beyond my committee, Jim Bildner, Evelyn Higginbotham, Jill Lepore, Christine Letts, Andrew Jewett, Alex Von Hoffman, and Samuel Zipp (visiting at Harvard for a year) helped me grow as a scholar, colleague, and teacher, reminding me why the study of history is important to our present.

As someone who studies institutional funding and often critiques the strings funders attach to their gifts, I have been fortunate to be the beneficiary of some remarkably flexible and hands-off funding. As a graduate student, grants from the Harvard History Department, Rockefeller Archive Center, Foundation for the National Archives, Center for American Political Studies, and LBJ Library Foundation enabled research trips, while fellowship support from the Taubman Center for State and Local Government and Ash Center for Democratic Governance and Innovation at the Harvard Kennedy School as well as the Graduate School of Arts and Sciences at Harvard University provided the time and space to analyze and write up my findings. A postdoctoral fellowship from the Stanford Center on Philanthropy and Civil Society (PACS) enabled two years of unencumbered writing in a beautiful location and a rich intellectual and social life that changed the course of my career and research. A grant from the University of Maryland's School of Public Policy enabled the custom maps by Kate Blackmer, who in her creative design visually communicated the geography of nonprofit neighborhoods.

Archivists, of course, make the work of historians possible. This was true when we could travel to archives and now even more so as I finish this project during a global pandemic where digitization has proven essential to plugging lingering gaps. I want to especially thank the archivists at the Northeastern University Archive and Special Collections, particularly Michelle Romero and Molly Brown, for collecting the papers of community nonprofits and valuing the stories they could tell. I also thank Bethany Antos at the Rockefeller Archive Center; Kristen Swett and Marta Crilly at the Boston City Archives; Dale Freeman at the University of Massachusetts Boston Archive and Special Collections; Autumn Haag at the Roxbury Community College Archive; Allen Fisher at the Lyndon B. Johnson Presidential Library; and staff at the Boston Public Library, John F. Kennedy Presidential Library, and National Archives and Record Administration in Waltham, Massachusetts. Thank you, too, to the interlibrary loan staff at Harvard University, Stanford University, and the University of Maryland.

Interdisciplinary work is more challenging than I anticipated and more rewarding than I could have imagined. The Graduate Forum on Democracy and Markets at the Tobin Project first introduced me to what conversations across disciplines could look like, which my year at the Harvard Kennedy School's Ash Center reinforced. Weekly lunches with people who thought about democracy from theoretical, quantitative, qualitative, historical, and legal approaches opened my eyes to how researchers could speak different languages to talk about the same thing. Many of the questions that Archon Fung, the center's faculty director, posed at those lunches have stayed with me and are ones I continue to grapple with. I hope he sees some of that influence in these pages. Liz Cohen invited me to attend a two-day workshop at Radcliffe on governance and politics in the changing American city, which, in a short time, significantly shifted my thinking. I still return to the notes I took at that conference and am grateful for the connections to Nicole Marwell, Michael McQuarrie, and Jeremy Levine the event facilitated.

I was incredibly fortunate to continue and deepen many of these conversations during my time at Stanford University as a postdoctoral fellow at the Center on Philanthropy and Civil Society. Not only did I get to live in California for two years, but driving cross-country each way became an education in US history that rivaled all the books I'd read in graduate school. It was also wonderful to live temporarily near West Coast family and friends, especially the Mobilio-Pinas, Lyons, and Ali Horowitz. Rob Reich, Woody Powell, and Paul Brest welcomed me to the PACS community and provided one of the richest intellectual spaces I have had the privilege of being a part of. So many of the questions and literatures this book engages reflect my time at PACS and the patience the community had for someone relatively new to the field. They also made sure we had a good dose of fun too. Lucy Bernholz and Johanna Mair modeled what engaging, challenging, and applied research looks like, and as a faculty mentor, Rob Reich created space for me to think and write while also providing counsel along the way. Participants in the PACS workshop—especially Aaron Horvath and Christof Brandtner—became good friends and, in Christof's case, a coauthor. The community of fellow postdocs—Ted Lechterman, Jean Lin, Ling Han, Emily Clough, Morgan Currie, Jessica Feldman—supported me and my research as we all worked to define ourselves as scholars and navigate interdisciplinary waters. One of the strengths of PACS as an intellectual hub was its ability (and resources) to convene various constellations of junior and senior scholars in workshops and conferences where I steadily built my network of scholars similarly interested in nonprofit organizations and philanthropy. My thanks to Kim Meredith, Priya Shanker, Valerie Dao, and the whole team for all their work running PACS so smoothly and for making sure we were well wined and dined while we wrote and discussed.

The highlight of my time at Stanford was, undoubtedly, a book manuscript conference in my second year hosted by the Center on Philanthropy and Civil Society. I invited a dream team of interlocutors who read the manuscript and buoyed me with enthusiasm, new ideas, and new questions at a critical point in revisions. A profound thank you to Alice O'Connor, Lily Geismer, Jonathan Levy, Karen Tani, Lucy Bernholz, Maribel Morey, and Michelle Anderson for their generous engagement with my work. Rob Reich and Woody Powell engaged in work methodologically distant from their own and set a new standard for academic generosity. Woody asked what a nonprofit neighborhood even was and pushed me to bring new analytical clarity to what was then just an alliterative title. Aaron

Horvath both commented on the manuscript and took notes at the workshop so I could just listen.

Without the boot camp that was Stanford PACS, I doubt I would have had the fortune to land at a policy school. Hiring a historian may have been a surprise at the University of Maryland's School of Public Policy, but my colleagues have been welcoming and enthusiastic about my work from the start. Peter Reuter has shared his love of history with me on numerous occasions and in his scholarly capacity pushed me to be more methodologically conscious about what historians actually do. Angela Bies and Bob Grimm invited me warmly into the school's nonprofit scholarly community and passionately supported my work from the very start. Toby Egan has shepherded me through the pre-tenure process as a mentor and advocate, while Rob Sprinkle, Betty Duke, Chris Foreman, Nancy Gallagher, and Susan Parker, among others, have expressed interest in the work of their junior colleague. In Phil Joyce I learned what an associate dean actually does and discovered that having one on your side can be a powerful asset. My thanks to Dean Robert Orr for his commitment to research excellence and his enthusiasm for strengthening our school every year. Committee work is often a frustration for academics, but for me has provided surprising spaces of relationship building, reflection, and learning. I am particularly grateful for my work with Patricia Bory, Nathan Dietz, Alana Hackshaw, Jen Littlefield, and David Mussington, and I am forever grateful for the fierce support and counsel of Nina Harris. My fellow junior colleagues—Apolonia Calderon, Joannie Trembley-Boire, Juan-Pablo Martinez, Lucy Qiu, Luke Spreen, Alec Worsnop, and Cat Worsnop—have provided consistent moral, social, and intellectual support. Thanks to Kati Zang and Sarah Gallagher, in particular, and all the staff who support both faculty and students every day. I feel lucky every semester to teach students who are motivated to tackle some of our nation's and world's greatest challenges and for thinking critically with me about why those challenges exist in the first place. Colleagues at the University of Maryland's Department of History have welcomed me and supported me from across campus, especially Robyn Muncy, David Freund, and Quincy Mills.

Several research assistants helped with this work in direct and indirect ways. Thank you to Sungmoon Lim, Christophe Beaumier, Sophie Siebach-Glover, and Caitlin Sullivan for your careful, thoughtful work. Parts of this book have been shared at conferences, where I have benefited from conversations with co-panelists and commenters. I am grateful to audiences at the annual conferences for the Urban History Association, Organization of American Historians, American Historical Association, Business History Association, Policy History Association, Labor and Working Class History Association, and the Association for Research on Nonprofit and Voluntary Action as well as Cornell University's Histories of American Capitalism Conference. These conferences and others provided opportunities to engage senior colleagues in my work, and while they might not remember our conversations, I do. Thank you to Marissa Chappell, Elisabeth Clemens, Margaret O'Mara, Andrew Morris, Robert Self, Tom Sugrue, Lawrence Vale, and Samuel Zipp. I also want to thank Ben Holtzman and Jeremy Levine for their friendship and for their scholarship, which has deepened my thinking about my own.

Amanda Seligman introduced herself to me at my very first conference while I was sitting by myself. It was a model of scholarly inclusiveness that she has repeatedly demonstrated as my series editor in the Historical Studies of Urban America series at the University of Chicago Press. Her patience is matched by her scholarly insight, both of which I am grateful for. At the press, Tim Mennel has been an ideal steward for this project, leading and listening to move it forward stronger at each stage. I'm grateful, too, to Susannah Engstrom and the whole University of Chicago Press team for making sure this book makes it into the world. Tim could not have found two better reviewers for this manuscript than Brian Balogh and Lily Geismer. Their incisive reviews affirmed key aspects of this project and pushed my thinking on others. Of course, all errors that remain are my own. Outside the formal peer review process, Lily has been a mentor to me and this project at every stage. She has read drafts, shared her work, made introductions, shown up, and offered advice as I've navigated academia. In the final stages of revision, Liz Cohen, David Freund, Brian Goldstein, and Quincy Mills read the introduction and, with their recommendations, made it better.

For all the richness of my academic life, it has been my relationships outside academia that have kept me going and kept me fed, housed, and loved. My grandparents, though they did not live to see this book published, instilled in me a love of history and storytelling. My parents supported my choices unconditionally, reveling in my achievements and commiserating in the challenges at every step. Two weeks before I started my first tenure-track job, my father died unexpectedly. In a deeply unsettling and dislocating time, family and friends threw their arms around us in ways I cannot ever repay and know I won't have to. His death was sudden, but the challenges that preceded it marked many stages of my life and academic pursuits. He would have loved this book simply because I wrote it but also because his interest in history, politics, and social justice inspired parts of it. My mother's strength, commitment to community, and insistence on living a full life inspire me, and her network of friends brings joy and love into my life as much as hers. In what felt like a season of loss, my mother-in-law died as I was completing this manuscript. In both her health and sickness, she provided me loving support and is dearly missed. I feel so fortunate to have an extended family of Dunnings, Dorners, Feduses, Follansbees, Mobilios, and Nicitas that has enthusiastically asked about my work while also reminding me to step away from it. The same must be said of friends, especially Ali Perse and the Perse family.

There are not enough words of gratitude or appreciation to capture what my partner, Zachary, has done for and with me. He has lived with every stage of this project, knowing better than anyone what it has taken to bring it into the world and believing in me when I did not. Though he is a brilliant scholar and keen editor whose insights have unquestionably strengthened this book, what I am most thankful for is the life we are building together. His love, support, and effort make it all possible, and the joy he brings to my life is unmatched. Here's to everything that comes next.

Abbreviations Found in Notes

Action for Boston Community Development	ABCD
Boston Alliance of Gay and Lesbian Youth Records	BAGLY
Boston City Archives	BCA
Boston Housing Authority	BHA
Boston Persistent Poverty Project	BPPP
Boston Public Library	BPL
Boston Redevelopment Authority	BRA
Carmen A. Pola papers	CAP
Chinese Progressive Association records	CPA
Citywide Educational Coalition records	CEC
Community Development Finance Corporation	CDFC
Dudley Street Neighborhood Initiative	DSNI
Emergency Tenants' Council	ETC
Ford Foundation Records	FF
Freedom House Inc. Records	FH
Government Documents	GD
Graduate School of Design	GSD
Grants Management Associates Records	GMA
Greater Boston Community Development	GBCD
Hispanic Office of Planning and Evaluation	HOPE
Housing and Home Finance Authority	HHFA
Housing and Urban Development	HUD
Inquilinos Boricuas en Acción Records	IBA

John F. Kennedy Presidential Library	JFKL
La Alianza Hispana Papers	LAH
Library at the University of Massachusetts at Amherst	UMA
Local Initiatives Support Corporation	LISC
Lower Roxbury Community Corporation Records	LRCC
Lyndon B. Johnson Presidential Library	LBJL
Mayor's Office of Criminal Justice Records	MOCJ
Metropolitan Council for Educational Opportunity, Inc. Records	METCO
Model Cities Administration Papers	MCA
Northeastern University Archives and Special Collections	NU
Persistent Poverty Project Records	PPP
Private Industry Council	PIC
Rockefeller Archive Center	RAC
Roots of the Rainbow Exhibit Collection	RR
Roxbury Multi-Service Center Records	RMSC
University of Massachusetts at Boston Archive & Special Collections	UMass
Vertical File	VF

Notes

Introduction

1. Paul Grogan, "New Challenges for Comeback Cities: Boston Case Study," *Brink*, May 2, 2017, accessed March 2021, http://www.brinknews.com/new-challenges-for-comeback-cities-boston-case-study/.

2. Jitinder Kohli and Douglas J. Besharov, "'Pay-for-Success' Bonds Gain Adherents: Innovative Social Service Financing to Be Put to the Test," Center for American Progress, February 2, 2012, accessed March 2021, https://www.americanprogress.org/issues/general/news/2012/02/02/11055/pay-for-success-bonds-gain-adherents-innovative-social-service-financing-to-be-put-to-the-test/.

3. As quoted in Commonwealth of Massachusetts, Executive Department, "Massachusetts Launches Landmark Initiative to Reduce Recidivism among At-Risk Youth," press release, January 29, 2014.

4. As quoted in Commonwealth of Massachusetts.

5. Massachusetts Juvenile Justice Pay for Success Initiative, "Frequently Asked Questions," revised December 16, 2014, https://www.thirdsectorcap.org/wp-content/uploads/2015/03/MA-JJ-PFS-Frequently-Asked-Questions-Revised-Final.pdf; Liz Farmer, "The Hidden Cost to 'Pay for Success,'" *Governing*, November 12, 2015, https://www.governing.com/archive/gov-cost-pay-for-success-social-impact-bonds.html.

6. The Harvard Kennedy School launched the Government Performance Lab in 2011 to provide technical assistance on pay-for-success projects. Harvard Kennedy School, Government Performance Lab, "Our Story," accessed March 2021, https://govlab.hks.harvard.edu/about-us. As examples of coverage, see Anne Field, "Biggest 'Social Impact Bond' in the U.S. Targets Recidivism," *Forbes*, February 7, 2014; Dax-Devlon Ross, "Tackling Mass Incarceration," Opinionator, *New York Times*, April 2, 2014; Deirdre Fernandes, "Goldman Sachs Buys 'Social Impact Bonds,'" *Boston Globe*, January 29, 2014; Joe Kennedy III, "Social Impact Bonds: Getting Better at Doing Good," *Boston Globe*, October 5, 2014. For an overview

of these arrangements and a guide on designing them, see Suzanne Adatto and Paul Brest, *Pay for Success Handbook*, Stanford Digital Repository, 2020, https:// purl.stanford.edu/jz224zp1899.

7. Massachusetts Juvenile Justice Pay for Success Initiative, "Frequently Asked Questions."

8. Elisabeth Clemens, *Civic Gifts: Voluntarism and the Making of the Nation-State* (Chicago: University of Chicago Press, 2020), 5.

9. Michael Katz, *The Price of Citizenship: Redefining the American Welfare State* (New York: Metropolitan Books, 2001), 143–55. Smith and Lipsky note that government funding mechanisms are characterized by uneven distribution across subsectors and organizational size. Steven Rathgeb Smith and Michael Lipsky, *Nonprofits for Hire: The Welfare State in the Age of Contracting* (Cambridge, MA: Harvard University Press, 1993), 56. Scholarly interest in government contracting grew in the 1980s amid changing social welfare practices. As examples, see Lester M. Salamon and Alan J. Abramson, *The Federal Budget and the Nonprofit Sector* (Washington, DC: Urban Institute, 1982); Lester M. Salamon, "Of Market Failure, Voluntary Failure, and Third-Party Government: Toward a Theory of Government-Nonprofit Relations in the Modern Welfare State," *Nonprofit and Voluntary Sector Quarterly* 16, no. 1–2 (January–April 1987): 29–49.

10. My language of invisibility builds from analyses of other policy instruments. See Christopher Howard, *The Hidden Welfare State: Tax Expenditures and Social Policy in the United States* (Princeton, NJ: Princeton University Press, 1997); Jacob S. Hacker, *The Divided Welfare State: The Battle over Public and Private Social Benefits in the United States* (New York: Cambridge University Press, 2002); Kimberly J. Morgan and Andrea Louise Campbell, *The Delegated Welfare State: Medicare, Markets, and the Governance of Social Policy* (New York: Oxford University Press, 2011); Suzanne Mettler, *The Submerged State: How Invisible Government Policies Undermine American Democracy* (Chicago: University of Chicago Press, 2011). Also, Clemens, *Civic Gifts*, 6.

11. Sarah L. Pettijohn and Elizabeth T. Boris, *Nonprofit-Government Contracts and Grants: Findings from the 2013 National Survey* (Washington, DC: Urban Institute, 2013), 1, 4.

12. Sociologists and political scientists have productively explored the role of nonprofits in urban governance. See Michael Q. McQuarrie, "Nonprofits and the Reconstruction of Urban Governance: Housing Production and Community Development in Cleveland, 1975–2005," in *Politics and Partnerships*, ed. Elisabeth S. Clemens and Doug Guthrie (Chicago: University of Chicago Press, 2010), 237–68; Sarah Reckhow, Davia Downey, and Josh Sapotichne, "Governing without Government: Nonprofit Governance in Detroit and Flint," *Urban Affairs Review* 56, no. 5 (2019): 1472–502; Nicole P. Marwell and Maoz Brown, "Toward a Governance Framework for Government-Nonprofit Relations," in *The Nonprofit Sector: A Research Handbook*, 3rd ed., ed. Walter W. Powell and Patricia Bromley

(Stanford, CA: Stanford University Press, 2020); Jeremy Levine, *Constructing Community: Urban Governance, Community Development, and Neighborhood Inequality in Boston* (Princeton, NJ: Princeton University Press, 2021). Largely absent from these treatments, however, is attention to the historical origins of these arrangements and the reasons for their persistence.

13. Michael Katz, *In the Shadow of the Poorhouse: A Social History of Welfare in America* (New York: Basic Books, 1986), x.

14. Kenneth Jackson, *Crabgrass Frontier: The Suburbanization of the United States* (New York: Oxford University Press, 1985); Kevin Kruse and Thomas J. Sugrue, eds., *The New Suburban History* (Chicago: University of Chicago Press, 2006). On the suburbanization of Boston, see Lily Geismer, *Don't Blame Us: Suburban Liberals and the Transformation of the Democratic Party* (Princeton, NJ: Princeton University Press, 2015).

15. Boston Redevelopment Authority, Research Division, "Boston's Shifting Demographics," July 2015, accessed March 2021, http://www.bostonplans.org/get attachment/5b407528-bf69-4c01-83b9-d2b757178e47/.

16. Mel King, *Chain of Change: Struggles for Black Community Development* (Boston: South End, 1981).

17. Jane Jacobs, *Death and Life of Great American Cities* (New York: Vintage Books, 1961); James Baldwin, interview with Kenneth Clark, reprinted in *Conversations with James Baldwin*, ed. Fred L. Standley and Louis H. Pratt (Jackson: University Press of Mississippi, 1989), 42.

18. Lizabeth Cohen emphasizes changes to renewal and the shift, in her words, from "pluralist democracy" to "participatory democracy." My account frames nonprofit organizations as central sites and mediators of this pivot. Lizabeth Cohen, *Saving America's Cities: Ed Logue and the Struggle to Renew Urban America in the Suburban Age* (New York: Farrar, Straus and Giroux, 2019), 9–12.

19. On localism in twentieth-century policy, see Thomas J. Sugrue, "All Politics Is Local: The Persistence of Localism in Twentieth-Century America," in *The Democratic Experiment: New Directions in American Political History*, ed. Meg Jacobs, William J. Novak, and Julian E. Zelizer (Princeton, NJ: Princeton University Press, 2003). On the rise of neighborhoods and the idea that "small is good," see Suleiman Osman, "The Decade of the Neighborhood," in *Rightward Bound*, ed. Bruce Schulman and Julian Zelizer (Cambridge, MA: Harvard University Press, 2008), 106–47; and Benjamin Looker, *A Nation of Neighborhoods: Imagining Cities, Communities, and Democracy in Postwar America* (Chicago: University of Chicago Press, 2015). Daniel Immerwahr offers a particularly useful study of how preferences for localism began in international policy and translated into the domestic sphere in *Thinking Small: The United States and the Lure of Community Development* (Cambridge, MA: Harvard University Press, 2015).

20. Lester M. Salamon, "Government and the Voluntary Sector in an Era of Retrenchment: The American Experience," *Journal of Public Policy* 6, no. 1

(January–March 1986): 3. This periodization contrasts with David Harvey's, which characterizes nongovernmental organizations in the 1980s and 1990s as the "Trojan horses for global neoliberalism" and frames their ascent as filling a vacuum of a retreating state that then justified further retreat. David Harvey, *A Brief History of Neoliberalism* (New York: Oxford University Press, 2005), 117.

21. Scholars note the concept of urban crisis as fraught and often misleading. I use the term here both in its specific reference to the upheaval of 1960s-era uprisings and in the sense of the longer historical processes historians have attributed to producing the postwar city. Thomas J. Sugrue, *Origins of the Urban Crisis: Race and Inequality in Postwar Detroit* (Princeton, NJ: Princeton University Press, 1996, 2005), xxxvi. Also, Arnold Hirsch, *Making the Second Ghetto: Race and Housing in Chicago, 1940–1960* (New York: Cambridge University Press, 1983); Heather Ann Thompson, "Why Mass Incarceration Matters: Rethinking Crisis, Decline, and the Transformation in Postwar American History," *Journal of American History* 97, no. 3 (December 2010): 703–34; Benjamin Holtzman, *The Long Crisis: New York City and the Path to Neoliberalism* (New York: Oxford University Press, 2021).

22. Katz, *In the Shadow of the Poorhouse*, x.

23. Clemens, *Civic Gifts*, 19.

24. Sarah Deutsch, *Women and the City: Gender, Space, and Power in Boston, 1870–1940* (New York: Oxford University Press, 2000), 167; Katz, *In the Shadow of the Poorhouse*, 163–68; Dennis R. Judd, *The Politics of American Cities: Private Power and Public Policy*, 3rd ed. (New York: HarperCollins, 1988), 3.

25. Andrew J. F. Morris, *The Limits of Voluntarism: Charity and Welfare from the New Deal through the Great Society* (New York: Cambridge University Press, 2009); Brent Cebul and Mason B. Williams, "Really and Truly a Partnership," in *Shaped by the State: Toward a New Political History of the Twentieth Century*, ed. Brent Cebul, Lily Geismer, and Mason B. Williams (Chicago: University of Chicago Press, 2019), 96–123.

26. On the War on Poverty as a political tool, see Frances Fox Piven and Richard A. Cloward, *Regulating the Poor: The Functions of Public Welfare* (New York: Random House, 1971).

27. Salamon notes that, "measured in economic terms, the nonprofit sector equals or surpasses the role played by local government." Lester Salamon, *Partners in Public Service: Government-Nonprofit Relations in the Modern Welfare State* (Baltimore: Johns Hopkins University Press, 1995), 60–61. Scholars of civil society–state relationships consistently note the unevenness of the federalist system as one of its defining features. Salamon, *Partners in Public Service*, 76; James T. Sparrow, William J. Novak, and Stephen W. Sawyer, *Boundaries of the State in US History* (Chicago: University of Chicago Press, 2015), 10, 14.

28. My use of the term *privatized inclusion* draws from Keeanga-Yamahtta Taylor's concept of predatory inclusion into homeownership. Keeanga-Yamahtta

Taylor, *Race for Profit: How Banks and the Real Estate Industry Undermined Black Homeownership* (Chapel Hill: University of North Carolina Press, 2019), 5.

29. Grogan, "New Challenges for Comeback Cities."

30. Ana Patricia Muñoz et al., *The Color of Wealth in Boston* (Boston: Federal Reserve Bank of Boston, 2015).

31. Though not focused on grants, see Gail Radford, *The Rise of the Public Authority: Statebuilding and Economic Development in Twentieth-Century America* (Chicago: University of Chicago Press, 2013) for a somewhat parallel account of experimentation, state power, and local governance.

32. Matthew Lassiter describes the neutrality of modes of governance, but his point holds for tools of governance as well. Matthew D. Lassiter, "Ten Propositions for the New Political History," in Cebul, Geismer, and Williams, *Shaped by the State*, 370. The politics of grantmaking and the push to appear politically neutral became particularly acute surrounding hearings and the 1969 Tax Reform Act, which increased regulations on private foundations. Karen Ferguson, *Top Down: The Ford Foundation, Black Power, and the Reinvention of Racial Liberalism* (Philadelphia: University of Pennsylvania Press, 2013), 235–36; Olivier Zunz, *Philanthropy in America: A History* (Princeton, NJ: Princeton University Press, 2012), 223–30.

33. Even though foundations are legally private, some political theorists argue that as tax exempt entities they ought to be more responsive to the public. Rob Reich, "On the Role of Foundations in Democracies," and Chiara Cordelli, "Reparative Justice and the Moral Limits of Discretionary Philanthropy," both in *Philanthropy in Democratic Societies: History, Institutions, Values*, ed. Rob Reich, Chiara Cordelli, and Lucy Bernholz (Chicago: University of Chicago Press, 2016).

34. For examples of government contracting with for-profit entities that are nonetheless applicable to those with nonprofit entities, see Jody Freeman and Martha Minow, eds., *Government by Contract: Outsourcing and American Democracy* (Cambridge, MA: Harvard University Press, 2009), and Gerald E. Frug, "The City: Private or Public," LSE Cities Working Papers, March 2017, https://lsecities.net/wp-content/uploads/2017/03/FrugGE-2017-The-city-private-or-public-2.pdf.

35. On race and philanthropy, see Noliwe M. Rooks, *White Money/Black Power: The Surprising History of African American Studies and the Crisis of Race in Higher Education* (Boston: Beacon, 2007); Erica Kohl-Arenas, *The Self-Help Myth: How Philanthropy Fails to Alleviate Poverty* (Berkeley: University of California Press, 2015); Megan Ming Francis, "The Price of Civil Rights: Black Lives, White Funding, and Movement Capture," *Law and Society Review* 53, no. 1 (January 2019); Alice O'Connor, *Poverty Knowledge: Social Science, Social Policy, and the Poor in Twentieth Century U.S. History* (Princeton, NJ: Princeton University Press, 2001); and Ferguson, *Top Down*. For a popular account of these dynamics, see Edgar Villanueva, *Decolonizing Wealth: Indigenous Wisdom to Heal Divides and Restore Balance* (San Francisco: Berrett-Koehler, 2018), and Vanessa Daniel, "Philanthropists

Bench Women of Color, the M.V.P.s of Social Change," *New York Times*, November 19, 2019.

36. This complicates Gary Gerstle's depiction of an "enduringly large and powerful central state" (10) of the post–World War II period, though it aligns with his analysis of privatization as a means of growth (6). I emphasize the selective deployment of state capacity and the building of grantmaking and monitoring capacity, particularly at the local level. Gary Gerstle, *Liberty and Coercion: The Paradox of American Government from the Founding to the Present* (Princeton, NJ: Princeton University Press, 2015). Lila Corwin Berman ties the growth of the "American Jewish philanthropic complex" to "the American state's expansion . . . over the course of the twentieth century." Lila Corwin Berman, *The American Jewish Philanthropic Complex: The History of a Multibillion-Dollar Institution* (Princeton, NJ: Princeton University Press, 2020), 5.

37. Recent contributions include Gerstle, *Liberty and Coercion*; Sparrow, Novak, and Sawyer, *Boundaries of the State in US History*; and Cebul, Geismer, and Williams, *Shaped by the State*. Slightly older works on these questions include Jacobs, Novak, and Zelizer, *The Democratic Experiment*; Brian Balogh, "The State of the State among Historians," *Social Science History* 27, no. 3 (Fall 2003); and William J. Novak, "The Myth of the 'Weak' American State," *American Historical Review* 113, no. 3 (June 2008): 752–72. On balance, scholars emphasize the unevenness of the American state but tend not to consider how the state exists at the local, urban level. In contrast, urban histories tend to emphasize policy over the state apparatus. Robert O. Self and Thomas Sugrue, "The Power of Place: Race, Political Economy, and Identity in the Postwar Metropolis," in *Blackwell Companions to American History: A Companion to Post-1945 America*, ed. Jean-Christophe Agnew and Roy Rosenzweig (Malden, MA: Blackwell, 2002), 20–43.

38. Freeman and Minow, *Government by Contract*, 7.

39. This emphasis on continuity follows Matthew Lassiter's call for a push beyond the "red-blue" divide that has characterized postwar political historiography. Matthew D. Lassiter, "Political History beyond the Red-Blue Divide," *Journal of American History* 98, no. 3 (December 2011), 762. See also Cebul, Geismer, and Williams, *Shaped by the State*.

40. The term *associational state* comes from Brian Balogh's work by that name, in which he advances an "associational synthesis" with essays that attend "to the ways in which Americans have braided public and private actions, state and voluntary-sector institutions, to achieve collective goals" (3–4). See the introduction to *The Associational State* for an excellent review of the American Political Development literature on the state, particularly its ties to civil society. Brian Balogh, *The Associational State: American Governance in the Twentieth Century* (Philadelphia: University of Pennsylvania Press, 2015). Ellis Hawley gave historical attention to associations in "Herbert Hoover, the Commerce Secretariat, and the Vision of an 'Associative State,' 1921–1928," *Journal of American History* 61,

no. 1 (June 1974): 116–40. Since then, most work on the state–civil society relationship in the United States comes from American Political Development scholars, including Elisabeth Clemens, *The People's Lobby: Organizational Innovation and the Rise of Interest Group Politics in the United States, 1890–1925* (Chicago: University of Chicago Press, 1997); William J. Novak, "The American Law of Association: The Legal-Political Construction of Civil Society," *Studies in American Political Development* 15 (Fall 2001): 163–99; Theda Skocpol, *Diminished Democracy: From Membership to Management in American Civic Life* (Norman: University of Oklahoma Press, 2003); Sparrow, Novak, and Sawyer, *Boundaries of the State in US History*; Clemens, *Civic Gifts*. See also Morris, *The Limits of Voluntarism*; Jonathan Levy, "From Fiscal Triangle to Passing Through: Rise of the Nonprofit Corporation," in *Corporations and American Democracy*, ed. Naomi R. Lamoreaux and William J. Novak (Cambridge, MA: Harvard University Press, 2017); Cebul and Williams, "Really and Truly a Partnership"; and Berman, *The American Jewish Philanthropic Complex*. Several journals have published special issues on the carceral state, including "Historians and the Carceral State," *Journal of American History* (2015); "Urban America and the Carceral State," *Journal of Urban History* (2015); and "Gendering the Carceral State: African American Women, History, and the Criminal Justice System," *Journal of African American History* (2015). See also Thompson, "Why Mass Incarceration Matters." On the administrative state, see Karen Tani, *States of Dependency: Welfare, Rights and American Governance, 1935–1972* (New York: Cambridge University Press, 2016).

41. Elizabeth Hinton, *From the War on Poverty to the War on Crime: The Making of Mass Incarceration in America* (Cambridge, MA: Harvard University Press, 2016); Julilly Kohler-Hausmann, *Getting Tough: Welfare and Imprisonment in 1970s America* (Princeton, NJ: Princeton University Press, 2017); Marisa Chappell, *The War on Welfare: Family, Poverty, and Politics in Modern America* (Philadelphia: University of Pennsylvania Press, 2011); Premilla Nadasen, *Welfare Warriors: The Welfare Rights Movement in the United States* (New York: Routledge, 2004). See also Annelise Orleck, *Storming Caesars Palace: How Black Mothers Fought Their Own War on Poverty* (Boston: Beacon, 2005); Felicia Kornbluh, *The Battle for Welfare Rights: Politics and Poverty in Modern America* (Philadelphia: University of Pennsylvania Press, 2007).

42. Katz, *In the Shadow of the Poorhouse*, ix–x, xiv–xv. Katz adds a third dimension to the public side—taxation—in *The Price of Citizenship*, 4–9, 361n7.

43. Theda Skocpol, *Protecting Soldiers and Mothers: The Political Origins of Social Policy in the United States* (Cambridge, MA: Harvard University Press, 1992); Seth Koven and Sonya Michel, eds., *Mothers of a New World: Maternalist Politics and the Origins of Welfare States* (New York: Routledge, 1993); Jill Quadagno, *The Color of Welfare: How Racism Undermined the War on Poverty* (New York: Oxford University Press, 1994); Linda Gordon, *Pitied but Not Entitled: Single Mothers and the History of Welfare* (New York: Free Press, 1994); Molly Ladd-Taylor,

Mother-Work: Women, Child Welfare, and the State, 1890–1930 (Urbana: University of Illinois Press, 1994); Gwendolyn Mink, *The Wages of Motherhood: Inequality and the Welfare State, 1917–1942* (Ithaca, NY: Cornell University Press, 1995); Alice Kessler-Harris, *In Pursuit of Equity: Women, Men and the Quest for Economic Citizenship in 20th-Century America* (New York: Oxford University Press, 2001); Rhonda Williams, *The Politics of Public Housing: Black Women's Struggles against Urban Inequality* (New York: Oxford University Press, 2004). Categories of sexual orientation also map onto the "good" and "bad" sides of public welfare. Margot Canaday, *The Straight State: Sexuality and Citizenship in Twentieth-Century America* (Princeton, NJ: Princeton University Press, 2009).

44. On workplace benefits, Marie Gottschalk, *The Shadow Welfare State: Labor, Business, and the Politics of Health Care in the United States* (Ithaca, NY: Cornell University Press, 2003); Colin Gordon, *Dead on Arrival: The Politics of Health Care in Twentieth-Century America* (Princeton, NJ: Princeton University Press, 2003); Jennifer Klein, *For All These Rights: Business, Labor, and the Shaping of the American Welfare State* (Princeton, NJ: Princeton University Press, 2006); Jennifer Mittelstadt, *From Welfare to Workfare: The Unintended Consequences of Liberal Reform, 1945–1965* (Chapel Hill: University of North Carolina Press, 2005).

45. Salamon, "Of Market Failure"; Smith and Lipsky, *Nonprofits for Hire*; Salamon, *Partners in Public Service*; Nicole P. Marwell, "Privatizing the State: Nonprofit Community-Based Organizations as Political Actors," *American Sociological Review* 69, no. 2 (2004): 265–91; Clemens, *Civic Gifts*. For an exception that considers the local level, Nicole P. Marwell, *Bargaining for Brooklyn: Community Organizations in the Entrepreneurial City* (Chicago: University of Chicago Press, 2007); also Scott W. Allard, *Out of Reach: Place, Poverty, and the New American Welfare State* (New Haven, CT: Yale University Press, 2009). For exceptions from historians, Katz, *The Price of Citizenship*, chap. 6; Morris, *The Limits of Voluntarism*.

46. Nicole Marwell and Thad Calabrese frame the organizational financial precarity of nonprofits working on government grants through a "deficit model of collaborative governance." Nicole P. Marwell and Thad Calabrese, "A Deficit Model of Collaborative Governance: Government-Nonprofit Fiscal Relations in the Provision of Child Welfare Services," *Journal of Public Administration Research and Theory* 25, no. 4 (2015): 1031–58. I situate their model in the history of racialized urban development, drawing on N.D.B. Connolly's discussion of how the twentieth-century liberal state solidified and "standardized" Black dependence on "white favor." Connolly, "Strange Career of American Liberalism," in Cebul, Geismer, and Williams, *Shaped by the State*, 86–87.

47. Looking at the New Deal era, Cebul and Williams similarly argue for a decoupling of progressive policy and centralized authority in "Really and Truly a Partnership," 97.

48. Economic and political theories of the nonprofit sector argue that nonprofit organizations exist where states and markets fail to meet consumer or voter

demand. Burton Weisbrod, *The Nonprofit Economy* (Cambridge, MA: Harvard University Press, 1988); Henry Hansmann, "The Role of Nonprofit Enterprise," *Yale Law Journal* 89, no. 5 (1981): 1–15; Salamon, "Of Market Failure." Recent trends, however, have complicated these theories. See Powell and Bromley, *The Nonprofit Sector*, particularly the introduction. Scholars of urban America note, too, that poor areas and ghettos are not the product of an absent state or market but of predatory and exclusionary ones. As examples, Hirsch, *Making the Second Ghetto*; Taylor, *Race for Profit*; Connolly, "The Strange Career of American Liberalism."

49. INCITE!, *The Revolution Will Not Be Funded: Beyond the Non-Profit Industrial Complex* (Durham, NC: Duke University Press, 2017).

50. This framework draws from questions posed by Wendy Brown in *Undoing the Demos: Neoliberalism's Stealth Revolution* (New York: Zone Books, 2015), 10.

51. Urban historians tend to treat nonprofit organizations as empty vessels, and scholars of nonprofits tend to overlook the importance of place. For a review, Christof Brandtner and Claire Dunning, "Nonprofits as Urban Infrastructure," in Powell and Bromley, *The Nonprofit Sector*. For exceptions, see Alice O'Connor, "Community Action, Urban Reform, and the Fight against Poverty: The Ford Foundation's Gray Areas Program," *Journal of Urban History* 22, no. 5 (July 1996): 586–625; Marwell, *Bargaining for Brooklyn*; Julia Rabig, *The Fixers: Devolution, Development, and Civil Society in Newark, 1960–1990* (Chicago: University of Chicago Press, 2016); Levine, *Constructing Community*.

52. Cebul and Williams trace "the pragmatic and political" utility of public-private partnerships to the New Deal. Cebul and Williams, "Really and Truly a Partnership," 97.

53. Works that center the role of philanthropy in (de)funding civil rights activism include O'Connor, *Poverty Knowledge*; Zunz, *Philanthropy in America*, chap. 7; Ferguson, *Top Down*; Francis, "The Price of Civil Rights;" Evan Faulkenbury, *Poll Power: The Voter Education Project and the Movement for the Ballot in the American South* (Chapel Hill: University of North Carolina Press, 2019); and Maribel Morey, *White Philanthropy: Making of a White World Order* (Chapel Hill: University of North Carolina Press, 2021).

54. This has been especially visible in literature on the War on Poverty. For a particularly clear example, see Orleck, *Storming Caesars Palace*.

55. Salamon refers to a "crazy-quilt pattern of different welfare 'regimes'" and frames contracting with nonprofits as a "pragmatic" response. I argue it was also shaped by racial politics and ideology. Salamon, *Partners in Public Service*; Clemens, *Civic Gifts*, 193.

56. Classic texts include Edmund S. Morgan, *American Slavery, American Freedom: The Ordeal of Colonial Virginia* (New York: Norton, 1975), and C. Vann Woodward, *The Strange Career of Jim Crow*, 3rd rev. ed. (New York: Oxford University Press, 1974). For the twentieth century, scholars centering African American and ethnic history frame new forms of inequality as both backlash and directly

tied to liberalism's achievements in the first place. See, as examples, Ansley T. Erickson, *Making the Unequal Metropolis School Desegregation and Its Limits* (Chicago: University of Chicago Press, 2016); Hinton, *From the War on Poverty*; Carol Anderson, *One Person, One Vote: How Voter Suppression Is Destroying Our Democracy* (New York: Bloomsbury, 2018); Taylor, *Race for Profit*.

57. In many ways, the use of nonprofit organizations to amplify the voices of a minority constituency is precisely the purpose these private entities were meant to achieve. Reich, "On the Role of Foundations in Democracies."

58. David Harvey wrote what is often considered the first historical treatment of neoliberalism. Harvey, *A Brief History of Neoliberalism*. Several historiographic reviews since then explore the expansion of, and tensions within, the term. See Kim Phillips-Fein, "The History of Neoliberalism," in Cebul, Geismer, and Williams, *Shaped by the State*, 347–62, and the volume's introduction; as well as the forum responses in *Dissent* by Julia Ott, Mike Konczal, N.D.B. Connolly, and Timothy Shenk to Daniel Rodger's argument against using the term in "Uses and Abuses of 'Neoliberalism,'" *Dissent*, January 22, 2018. By non-historians, see, in particular, Loïc Wacquant, *Punishing the Poor: The Neoliberal Government of Social Insecurity* (Durham, NC: Duke University Press, 2009); Greta R. Krippner, *Capitalizing on Crisis: The Political Origins of the Rise of Finance* (Cambridge, MA: Harvard University Press, 2011); Joe Soss, Richard C. Fording, and Sanford F. Schram, *Disciplining the Poor: Neoliberal Paternalism and the Persistent Power of Place* (Chicago: University of Chicago Press, 2011); and Brown, *Undoing the Demos*.

59. On urban neoliberalism as an uneven phenomenon, see especially Andrew J. Diamond and Thomas J. Sugrue, *Neoliberal Cities: The Remaking of Postwar Urban America* (New York: New York University Press, 2020); Richardson Dilworth, "Neoliberalism, Neoliberal Cities, and the Search for Urban Political Development," *Journal of Urban History* (2021). See also Arlene Dávila, *Barrio Dreams: Puerto Ricans, Latinos, and the Neoliberal City* (Berkeley: University of California Press, 2004); Jason Hackworth, *The Neoliberal City: Governance, Ideology, and Development in American Urbanism* (Ithaca, NY: Cornell University Press, 2007); Timothy P. R. Weaver, *Blazing the Neoliberal Trail: Urban Political Development in the United States and the United Kingdom* (Philadelphia: University of Pennsylvania Press, 2016); Holtzman, *The Long Crisis*.

60. Weaver contrasts "neoliberalization by default" with "neoliberalization by design" in *Blazing the Neoliberal Trail*, 18.

61. This is consistent with treatments that root certain neoliberal governing structures in earlier eras while still allowing for the acceleration of neoliberalism as a governing ideology in later decades. Cebul, Geismer, and Williams, *Shaped by the State*, 8; Diamond and Sugrue, *Neoliberal Cities*, 4–5.

62. Hinton, *From the War on Poverty*; Kohler-Hausmann, *Getting Tough*.

63. This is consistent with N.D.B. Connolly's argument that "the job of political liberalism was to facilitate capitalism" and that Black communities had, long

before the 1980s, lived under a neoliberal regime. "Strange Career of American Liberalism," 70, 86. See also Hackworth, *The Neoliberal City*, on the dual pressures in cities to "facilitate growth with the need to facilitate social reproduction" (26).

Chapter 1

1. Thomas H. O'Connor, *Building a New Boston: Politics and Urban Renewal 1950 to 1970* (Boston: Northeastern University Press, 1993), 147.

2. The business orientation of Boston's renewal program is exemplified by the construction of the Prudential Center. See Elihu Rubin, *Insuring the City: The Prudential Center and the Postwar Urban Landscape* (New Haven, CT: Yale University Press, 2012). See also Cohen, *Saving America's Cities*, 23, 161.

3. John Lane, "All-American City Award (1962) Ceremony in Front of Boston City Hall," A004224, Freedom House Photographs, Northeastern University Archives and Special Collections (hereafter NU).

4. Wilfrid Rogers, "NEW Boston Wows Them: 22 Cities Compared in U.S. Contest," *Boston Globe*, November 17, 1962.

5. James Baldwin, interview with Kenneth Clark, reprinted in Fred L. Standley and Louis H. Pratt, *Conversations with James Baldwin* (Jackson: University Press of Mississippi, 1989), 42.

6. Boston's renewal program attracted early scholarly interest—and offered a convenient study for area academics affiliated with Harvard University's and MIT's Joint Center for Urban Studies—that helped elevate the city's visibility in national renewal knowledge. See Herbert J. Gans, *The Urban Villagers: Group and Class in the Life of Italian-Americans* (New York: Free Press of Glencoe, 1962); chapters by Marc Fried, Chester Hartman, Walter McQuade, and James Q. Wilson, in James Q. Wilson, ed., *Urban Renewal: The Record and the Controversy* (Cambridge, MA: MIT Press, 1966); Langley Carleton Keyes Jr., *The Rehabilitation Planning Game: A Study in the Diversity of Neighborhood* (Cambridge, MA: MIT Press, 1969). Martin Anderson draws heavily on Boston examples in *The Federal Bulldozer: A Critical Analysis of Urban Renewal, 1949–1962* (Cambridge, MA: MIT Press, 1964). On the Joint Center's intellectual legacy, see Christopher Klemek, *The Transatlantic Collapse of Urban Renewal: Postwar Urbanism from New York to Berlin* (Chicago: University of Chicago Press, 2011), 57–59. More recently, Lizabeth Cohen's biography of Ed Logue, *Saving America's Cities*, tells the history of renewal, focusing heavily on Boston.

7. Samuel Zipp, "The Roots and Routes of Urban Renewal," 366–91, and Samuel Zipp and Michael Carriere, "Introduction: Thinking through Urban Renewal," 359–65, both in *Journal of Urban History* 39, no. 3 (2012).

8. Brian Goldstein argues that conflicts over urban design shaped the built and political environment in the decades after renewal as well in *The Roots of Urban*

Renaissance: Gentrification and the Struggle over Harlem (Cambridge, MA: Harvard University Pres, 2017).

9. The connection between renewal and governance comes through more strongly in the urban political science and sociology literature. See, as examples, Robert Dahl, *Who Governs: Democracy and Power in an American City* (New Haven, CT: Yale University Press, 1961); Keyes, *The Rehabilitation Planning Game*; John R. Logan and Harvey L. Molotch, *Urban Fortunes: The Political Economy of Place* (Berkeley: University of California Press, 1987); and Clarence N. Stone, *Regime Politics: Governing Atlanta, 1946–1988* (Lawrence: University Press of Kansas, 1989). These works, however, flatten the ways racism and racial exclusion shaped power and governance. More recent work on community development and governance addresses some of these concerns: Marwell, *Bargaining for Brooklyn*; Mary Pattillo, *Black on the Block: The Politics of Race and Class in the City* (Chicago: University of Chicago Press, 2007); and Levine, *Constructing Community*.

10. Yanni Tsipis and David Kruh, *Building Route 128: Images of America* (Charleston, SC: Arcadia, 2003), 177.

11. Sam Bass Warner, *Streetcar Suburbs: The Process of Growth in Boston, 1870–1900* (Cambridge, MA: Harvard University Press, 1962); Henry C. Binford, *The First Suburbs: Residential Communities on the Boston Periphery, 1815–1860* (Chicago: University of Chicago Press, 1985).

12. "Of All of Callahan's Highways, Route 128 Seems to Be 'It,'" *Boston Globe*, July 22, 1951; "Industries Interested in Locating Plants along New Route 128," *Boston Globe*, September 29, 1951.

13. As quoted in Tsipis and Kruh, *Building Route 128*, 117; United States Commission on Civil Rights, Massachusetts Advisory Committee, *Route 128: Boston's Road to Segregation*, a joint report by the Massachusetts Advisory Committee to the US Commission on Civil Rights and the Massachusetts Commission against Discrimination (Washington, DC: US Commission on Civil Rights, 1975), 3. For more on the rise of Route 128 and its impact on local and national politics and liberalism, see Geismer, *Don't Blame Us*.

14. Of the ninety-nine firms along Route 128 in 1957, seventy-seven had moved their headquarters from Boston, contributing to an estimated eighteen thousand new jobs in the suburbs. US Commission on Civil Rights, *Route 128*, 38; Alexander J. Bone, "Economic Impact Study of Massachusetts Route 128," prepared for the Massachusetts Department of Public Works, by the Transportation Engineering Division Department of Civil and Sanitary Engineering Department of Massachusetts Institute of Technology (Cambridge, MA: MIT, 1958), i–ii; Everett J. Burtt Jr., *Labor Supply Characteristics of Route 128 Firms*, Research Report No. 1-1958, Federal Reserve Bank of Boston, Vertical File (VF), Graduate School of Design (hereafter GSD), Harvard University, 12.

15. Susan Rosegrant and David R. Lampe, *Route 128: Lessons from Boston's High-Tech Community* (New York: Basic Books, 1992), 80; James C. O'Connell, *The Hub's Metropolis* (Cambridge, MA: MIT Press, 2013), 153; Geismer, *Don't Blame Us*, 21–22.

16. Jackson, *Crabgrass Frontier*; Lizabeth Cohen, *A Consumers' Republic: The Politics of Mass Consumption in America* (New York: Random House, 2003).

17. Ira Katznelson, *When Affirmative Action Was White: An Untold History of Racial Inequality* (New York: Norton, 2005), chap. 5.

18. Cambridge, Massachusetts, was an exception. US Commission on Civil Rights, *Route 128*, 9. For a deeper history, see Paige Glotzer, *How the Suburbs Were Segregated: Developers and the Business of Exclusionary Housing, 1890–1960* (New York: Columbia University Press, 2020).

19. US Commission on Civil Rights, *Route 128*.

20. US Commission on Civil Rights, *Route 128*, 39.

21. Geismer, *Don't Blame Us*, 24; O'Connell, *The Hub's Metropolis*, 174.

22. Lily Geismer, "Good Neighbors for Fair Housing: Suburban Liberalism and Racial Inequality in Metropolitan Boston," *Journal of Urban History* 39 (October 2012): 454–77.

23. Historians repeatedly frame the whiteness of suburbia as a product of local and federal political economy. See Jackson, *Crabgrass Frontier*; Sugrue, *The Origins of the Urban Crisis*; Cohen, *A Consumers' Republic*; Self, and Sugrue, "The Power of Place"; Robert O. Self, *American Babylon: Race and the Struggle for Postwar Oakland* (Princeton, NJ: Princeton University Press, 2003); and Kevin M. Kruse, *White Flight: Atlanta and the Making of Modern Conservatism* (Princeton, NJ: Princeton University Press, 2005).

24. On the changing demographics of Boston in the postwar period, see King, *Chain of Change*; Gerald Gamm, *Urban Exodus: Why the Jews Left Boston and the Catholics Stayed* (Cambridge, MA: Harvard University Press, 1999); Lawrence J. Vale, *Reclaiming Public Housing: A Half-Century of Struggle in Three Public Neighborhoods* (Cambridge, MA: Harvard University Press, 2002); and Geismer, *Don't Blame Us*.

25. James N. Gregory, "The Second Great Migration: A Historical Overview," in *African American Urban History: The Dynamics of Race, Class and Gender since World War II*, ed. Joe W. Trotter Jr. and Kenneth L. Kusmer (Chicago: University of Chicago Press, 2009), 20. For more on the Great Migration, see, for example, James Grossman, *Land of Hope: Chicago, Black Southerners, and the Great Migration* (Chicago: University of Chicago Press, 1989); and Isabel Wilkerson, *The Warmth of Other Suns: The Epic Story of America's Great Migration* (New York: Vintage, 2011).

26. Rheable M. Edwards, Laura Morris, and Robert Coard, "The Negro in Boston," 1963, Government Documents (hereafter GD), Boston Public Library (hereafter BPL), 13. On migration from the Caribbean to Boston, see Violet Showers Johnson, *The Other Black Bostonians: West Indians in Boston, 1900–1950* (Bloomington: Indiana University Press, 2006).

27. Whitney M. Young Jr., *Task Force Report on a Preliminary Exploration of Social Conditions and Needs in the Roxbury-North Dorchester GNRP*, for Action for Boston Community Development, June 1961, BRA 2231, GD, BPL, 7.

28. Edwards, Morris, and Coard, "The Negro in Boston," 16; US Commission on Civil Rights, *Route 128*, 21.

29. Edwards, Morris, and Coard, "The Negro in Boston," 13E.

30. Edwards, Morris, and Coard, "The Negro in Boston," 3. Also James Oliver Horton and Lois E. Horton, *Black Bostonians: Family Life and Community Struggle in the Antebellum North* (New York: Holmes & Meier, 1979); Stephen Kantrowitz, *More than Freedom: Fighting for Black Citizenship in a White Republic, 1829–1889* (New York: Penguin, 2012).

31. Edwards, Morris, and Coard, "The Negro in Boston," 12E–13E; Warner, *Streetcar Suburbs*, 66.

32. Edwards, Morris and Coard, "The Negro in Boston," 13A.

33. Historians (and activists at the time) reject the notion that northern segregation was not de jure, noting the legal and policy basis of segregation in housing, education, and employment. My purpose in using this language is to differentiate the kind of openly segregated facilities characteristic of the South from those of the North. Thomas Sugrue, *Sweet Land of Liberty: The Forgotten Struggle for Civil Rights in the North* (New York: Random House, 2008), offers a useful synthesis of this history. Much of this research comes from the field of urban history and through the lens of individual cities. See Jeanne F. Theoharis and Komozi Woodard, eds., *Freedom North: Black Freedom Struggles Outside the South, 1940–1980* (New York: Palgrave Macmillan, 2003); Martha Biondi, *To Stand and Fight: The Struggles for Civil Rights in Postwar New York City* (Cambridge, MA: Harvard University Press, 2006); Matthew Countryman, *Up South: Civil Rights and Black Power in Philadelphia* (Philadelphia: University of Pennsylvania Press, 2007); Michael Woodsworth, *Battle for Bed-Stuy: The Long War on Poverty in New York City* (Cambridge, MA: Harvard University Press, 2016); Brian Purnell, Jeanne Theoharis, and Komozi Woodard, eds., *The Strange Career of Jim Crow North* (New York: New York University Press, 2019). On activism in Boston, see Jeanne Theoharis, "'We Saved the City': Black Struggles for Educational Equality in Boston, 1960–1976," *Radical History Review* (Fall 2001): 61–93; Jennifer Hock, "Bulldozers, Busing, and Boycotts: Urban Renewal and the Integrationist Project," *Journal of Urban History* 39, no. 3 (May 2013): 433–53; and Karilyn Crockett, *People before Highways: Boston Activists, Urban Planners, and a New Movement for City Making* (Amherst: University of Massachusetts Press, 2018). For a firsthand account of activism, see King, *Chain of Change*.

34. The 1950 census showed that median income for African Americans was $1,567, while for whites that figure was $2,075. Edwards, Morris, and Coard, "The Negro in Boston," 11–13E, 54. Inequality in Boston's public schools was made famous by Jonathon Kozol in *Death at an Early Age: The Destruction of the Hearts and Minds of Negro Children in the Boston Public Schools* (Boston: Houghton Mifflin, 1967).

35. Edwards, Morris, and Coard, "The Negro in Boston," 16.

36. *Discrimination in Housing in the Boston Metropolitan Area*, report of the

Massachusetts Advisory Committee to the US Commission on Civil Rights, December 1963, 3.

37. Young, *Task Force Report*, 35–37.

38. Theoharis, "'We Saved the City.'"

39. US Commission on Civil Rights, *Route 128*, 37.

40. "Mayor John B. Hynes Outlines New Tax Plan for City of Boston," speech delivered at Boston College School of Business Administration, October 26, 1954, BRA 3548, GD, BPL. Detailed accounts of Boston's renewal history include Lawrence W. Kennedy, *Planning the City upon a Hill: Boston since 1630* (Amherst: University of Massachusetts Press, 1994); and O'Connor, *Building a New Boston*.

41. Summary analysis of City of Boston and County of Suffolk, Auditing Department Annual Reports, Fiscal Years 1939, 1946–1965, GD, BPL.

42. Gerald E. Frug and David Barron, "Boston Bound: A Comparison of Boston's Legal Powers with Those of Six Other Major American Cities," Policy Brief, Rappaport Institute for Greater Boston, December 2007, https://www.hks.harvard .edu/sites/default/files/centers/rappaport/files/boston_bound.pdf.

43. Mayor James Michael Curley—famous for his rise through machine politics and for winning reelection while under federal indictment for mail fraud—tried to manipulate municipal finances by keeping assessments inflated beyond market value while granting abatements to those willing to pay his political cronies legal fees to contest the assessments. O'Connor, *Building a New Boston*, 77–78.

44. Sociologists have described this pressure as "the growth machine." Harvey Molotch, "The City as Growth Machine: Toward a Political Economy of Place," *American Journal of Sociology* 82, no. 2 (September 1976): 309. Also, Logan and Molotch, *Urban Fortunes*.

45. "Mayor John B. Hynes Outlines New Tax Plan," 5.

46. Alexander Von Hoffman, "A Study in Contradictions: The Origins and Legacy of the Housing Act of 1949," *Housing Policy Debate* 11, no. 2 (2000): 309.

47. The notable exception was New York development czar Robert Moses, who jumped at federal monies for slum clearance. See Robert Caro, *The Power Broker: Robert Moses and the Fall of New York* (New York: Knopf, 1974).

48. The Housing and Home Finance Agency (hereafter HHFA) in charge of federal renewal grants defined the workable program by outlining seven categories against which it would evaluate municipal proposals requesting renewal funds. They dealt with housing safety, the administration of renewal programs, and the people living in housing slated for renewal. HHFA, "How Localities Can Develop a Workable Program for Urban Renewal," Revised December 1956, VF, GSD, Harvard University, 2.

49. Kennedy, *Planning the City upon a Hill*, 159.

50. Wendell E. Pritchett, "The 'Public Menace' of Blight: Urban Renewal and the Private Uses of Eminent Domain," *Yale Law and Policy Review* 21, no. 1 (2003): 3–4.

51. "Mayor John B. Hynes Outlines New Tax Plan," 7; Boston Housing

Authority, "The New York Streets Project Report, Preliminary," Urban Redevelopment Division, June 1952, BRA 2646, GD, BPL, 3.

52. Boston Housing Authority, "The New York Streets Project Report," 9.

53. Boston Housing Authority, "The New York Streets Project Report," 8.

54. "Mayor John B. Hynes Outlines New Tax Plan," 7; Boston Housing Authority, "The New York Streets Project Report," 2.

55. Edward Bernard Murphy, "Preliminary Appraisal of Marketability and Reuse Values West End Area, Boston, Mass," BRA 2643, GD, BPL, 9. The renewal plan for the West End originally called for 58 percent of the new housing to be high-rent housing, 28 percent low or middle income, and 14 percent rehabbed or retained housing. Boston Housing Authority, "The West End Project Report: A Redevelopment Study," 32.

56. Boston Housing Authority, "The West End Project Report," 33, 48; Lawrence J. Vale, *From the Puritans to the Projects: Public Housing and Public Neighbors* (Cambridge, MA: Harvard University Press, 2007), 275–77.

57. Gans, *Urban Villagers*, 3–4.

58. King, *Chain of Change*, 20–21.

59. King, *Chain of Change*, 19.

60. For examples of this ambiguity, see HHFA, "How Localities Can Develop a Workable Program for Urban Renewal." These debates certainly presaged the conflicts over defining "maximum feasible participation" under the War on Poverty discussed in chapter 2.

61. For a longer discussion of "no citizen participation" in the West End, see William C. Loring Jr., Frank L. Sweester, and Charles F. Ernst, *Community Organization for Citizen Participation in Urban Renewal*, prepared for Massachusetts Department of Commerce, 1957, 12–15.

62. Vale, *From the Puritans to the Projects*, 275.

63. See, for example, oral histories from UMass Boston, "Decent Place to Live" Collection, which parallel J. S. Fuerst with Bradford D. Hunt, *When Public Housing Was Paradise: Rebuilding Community in Chicago* (Westport, CT: Praeger, 2003).

64. For a study of where West Enders moved, see Chester Hartman, "The Housing of Relocated Families," in Wilson, *Urban Renewal*, which notes the "shotgun" pattern of wide relocation around the region (295).

65. Digital Scholarship Lab, "Renewing Inequality," in *American Panorama*, ed. Robert K. Nelson and Edward L. Ayers, accessed May 4, 2021, https://dsl.richmond.edu/panorama/renewal.

66. Hartman, "The Housing of Relocated Families," 313; Vale, *From the Puritans to the Projects*, 301–3.

67. Initial assessment of the 1950s renewal program found mixed results. By 1964, all parcels in the New York Streets project area had been leased or sold, with an estimated $20 million spent by private developers, outpacing the public-sector investment of $7 million. City officials estimated that investments had nearly

doubled the potential tax revenue from the fifteen-acre area and touted the project as "proof that renewal can serve as a vehicle for private industrial and commercial development." On the other hand, the relocation of thousands of families placed new strains on the low-income public and private housing markets and the neighborhoods that housed them. Boston Redevelopment Authority, "New York Streets, Fact Sheet 1964," May 7, 1964, BRA 3181, GD, BPL.

68. US National Commission on Urban Problems, *Building the American City: A Report by the U.S. National Commission on Urban Problems* (Washington, DC: US Government Printing Office, 1968), 165.

69. "Proceedings Redevelopment Section, Conference on Working Problems in Urban Renewal," February 1956, East Lansing Michigan, VF, GSD, Harvard University, 1.2.

70. The effective tax rate increased to $101 per thousand from the 1949 rate of $56.80 per thousand. Kennedy, *Planning the City upon a Hill*, 168. On the impact of bond ratings for cities, see Destin Jenkins, *The Bonds of Inequality: Debt and the Making of the American City* (Chicago: University of Chicago Press, 2021).

71. O'Connor, *Building a New Boston*, 147.

72. By 1967, municipal taxes accounted for an average one-half of the funds needed to support municipal services and administration. Federal and state aid, along with non-tax revenue sources filled the other half of the coffers. US National Commission on Urban Problems, *Building the American City*, 6.

73. Jacobs, *Death and Life of Great American Cities*; Gans, *Urban Villagers*.

74. Karilyn Crockett connects urban renewal in Boston to the political activism of anti-highway protests and Black power organizing in *People before Highways*, and Lawrence J. Vale connects the political aftermath of urban renewal to the implementation of the HOPE VI program in *After the Projects: Public Housing Redevelopment and the Governance of the Poorest Americans* (New York: Oxford University Press, 2018).

75. As quoted in Boston Redevelopment Authority, "BRA Annual Report, 1962," GD, BPL, 36.

76. Murray B. Levin, *The Alienated Voter: Politics in Boston* (New York: Holt, Rinehart and Winston, 1960), 1.

77. Levin, *The Alienated Voter*, 2.

78. Levin, *The Alienated Voter*, 14.

79. "Mayor Reports on 'Operation Revival,'" *City Record* 52, no. 16 (April 16, 1960). Collins's "New Boston" sounded an awful lot like Hynes's vision for the city, with commitments to keep taxes low and property values high and to use land usage policies to increase the financial stability of the city. Kennedy, *Planning the City upon a Hill*, 175.

80. Cohen, *Saving America's Cities*, 148, 12, 29.

81. "Mayor Collins Tackles Urban Redevelopment," *City Record* 52 no. 5 (January 30, 1960); "Redevelopment Authority Considers 10 Area Planning Applications

Preliminary to Request for Federal Funds," *City Record* 52, no. 44 (October 29, 1960).

82. Edward Logue, speech to Boston College Seminar, reprinted in "Urban Development Prospects as Seen by Edward Logue," *City Record* 52, no. 16 (April 16, 1960); Cohen, *Saving America's Cities*, 11, 207.

83. Cohen, *Saving America's Cities*, 149. Logue raised the federal investment in Boston without assuming an equal burden on the municipal budget. He negotiated to let future capital investments in renewal areas count toward the city's renewal contribution, effectively lowering the burden of renewal on the municipal ledger. He also convinced the state to contribute substantially to the renewal efforts downtown by agreeing to split the remaining costs charged to the city. Kennedy, *Planning the City upon a Hill*, 174.

84. John Collins, "Mayor's Statement," in "The 90 Million Dollar Development Plan," reprinted in *City Record* 52, no. 39 (September 24, 1960).

85. Collins also maintained a cozy relationship with business elites known as "the Vault" who met regularly at the Boston Safe Deposit and Trust Company to steer the renewal process. O'Connor, *Building a New Boston*, 147, 167–68; Cohen, *Saving America's Cities*, 161.

86. A staff of eighty in 1961 ballooned to 498 by 1967. Kennedy, *Planning the City upon a Hill*, 175. On Logue's faith in experts, see Cohen, *Saving America's Cities*, 11–12, 108.

87. Cohen, *Saving America's Cities*, 74–75.

88. On Boston's organizational landscape, see Keyes, *The Rehabilitation Planning Game*; Gamm, *Urban Exodus*; and Deutsch, *Women and the City*. On block clubs more generally, see Amanda I. Seligman, *Chicago's Block Clubs: How Neighbors Shape the City* (Chicago: University of Chicago Press, 2016).

89. Chester Rapkin, "The Seaver-Townsend Urban Renewal Area: A Section of the Roxbury-North Dorchester General Neighborhood Renewal Plan Area," January 1962, BRA, GD, BPL, 37–39; Hock, "Bulldozers, Busing and Boycotts."

90. "How Localities Can Develop a Workable Program for Urban Renewal," HHFA, revised December 1956, VF NAC 1613.5u, GSD, 11; see also Loring, Sweester, and Ernst, *Community Organization*, 8.

91. Keyes, *The Rehabilitation Planning Game*, 54. For a longer discussion of renewal in the South End, see chapter 3.

92. Edward Logue to Paul Ylvisaker, June 14, 1960, Grant 62-457, Reel 2634, Ford Foundation Records (hereafter FF), Rockefeller Archive Center (hereafter RAC), New York.

93. David Wallace to Paul Ylvisaker, December 1, 1960, Grant 62-457, Reel 2634, FF, RAC.

94. Boston Community Development Program, press release, March 21, 1961, Grant 62-457, Reel 2633, FF, RAC; Action for Boston Community Development, "Origins of ABCD," 3.

95. Action for Boston Community Development, "Agreement of Association," June 25, 1962, Grant 62-457, Reel 2633, FF, RAC.

96. Keyes, *The Rehabilitation Planning Game*, 114.

97. Chester Rapkin, "The Washington Park Urban Renewal Area: An Analysis of the Economic, Financial, and Community Factors That Will Influence the Feasibility of Residential Renewal," December 1961, BRA 2492, GD, BPL, 24–27; Hock, "Bulldozers, Busing, and Boycotts," 436. On the movement of Boston's Jewish community institutions to the suburbs, see Gamm, *Urban Exodus*.

98. Incorporation papers, as quoted in Freedom House, "25 Years: It's a Beginning, 1949–1974," May 1974, box 2, folder 6, Collection M101, Metropolitan Council for Educational Opportunity, Inc. records (hereafter METCO), NU. See also Otto Snowden and Muriel Snowden, "Citizen Participation," *Journal of Housing*, no. 8 (1963): 435–39.

99. Snowden and Snowden, "Citizen Participation," 435.

100. Freedom House, "25 Years."

101. Seligman, *Chicago's Block Clubs*, 3.

102. "Coffee Hour," April 20, 1954, box 26, folder 798, Collection M16, Freedom House Inc. records (hereafter FH), NU; "Community Coffee Hour," February 21, 1956, box 26, folder 802, FH; "The Story of the Freedom House Coffee Hour," box 26, folder 794, FH; "Community Coffee House," October 22, 1959, box 26, folder 803, FH; "Coffee Hour," December 1, 1959, box 26, folder 803, FH.

103. "Coffee Hour" November 12, 1959, box 26, folder 803, FH. Also, "Report of the Committee of the Proposed Freedom House Forum," October 26, 1953, box 26, folder 792, FH.

104. Boston Redevelopment Authority, "Your New Washington Park: A Bold Program in Urban Renewal," BRA 2472, GD, BPL.

105. Rapkin, "The Washington Park Urban Renewal Area," 9.

106. Muriel Snowden to Friend, April 9, 1959, box 26, folder 803, FH.

107. Emphasis in original. Muriel Snowden to Friend, April 9, 1959.

108. "Sunday at 8," March, 24, 1963, box 26, folder 821, FH; Hock, "Bulldozers, Busing, and Boycotts," 435.

109. Rapkin, "The Washington Park Urban Renewal Area," 19–20.

110. Otto Snowden, telegram to Mayor John F. Collins, September 22, 1960, Northeastern Digital Repository, http://hdl.handle.net/2047/D20235131.

111. As quoted in Freedom House, "25 Years."

112. Keyes, *The Rehabilitation Planning Game*, 163–68.

113. Freedom House, press release, May 13, 1958, box 26, folder 814, FH; "Sunday at 8," October 29, 1961, box 26, folder 819, FH.

114. Rapkin, "The Seaver-Townsend Urban Renewal Area."

115. Snowden and Snowden, "Citizen Participation," 437.

116. "Report on the Examination of the Accounts of the Boston Redevelopment Authority from October 4, 1957 to February 25, 1963," reprinted in US House of

Representatives, "Hearings Before the Subcommittee on Housing of the Committee on Banking and Currency," 90th Cong, 1st Sess., on H.R. 8068 a Bill to Amend and Extend Laws Relating to Housing and Urban Development, and for Other Purposes, April 1967, 443–44; Anthony J. Yudis, "Authority Spending More Cash—Time," *Boston Globe*, February 12, 1962.

117. Image caption in Freedom House, "25 Years," 11.

118. Muriel Snowden, "Planning with People: Finding the Formula," Boston College Seminar, April 23, 1963, box 26, folder 825, FH.

119. Snowden and Snowden, "Citizen Participation," 438.

120. As quoted in Keyes, *The Rehabilitation Planning Game*, 170.

121. Anthony J. Yudis, "Reaction For and Against Renewal Startles BRA," *Boston Globe*, July 1, 1962.

122. Yudis, "Reaction For and Against Renewal."

123. For a longer discussion of the debates, see Keyes, *The Rehabilitation Planning Game*, 170–88.

124. Snowden and Snowden, "Citizen Participation," 438.

125. Anthony J. Yudis, "Citizens Offer Renewal Plan: Let's Get On With It, Say Washington Park Leaders," *Boston Globe*, December 19, 1962.

126. For example, Muriel Snowden penned a letter to the editor of the *Boston Globe* to counteract a negative article calling Washington Park an "ugly crater." Muriel Snowden, "What People Talk About: A Further Look," *Boston Globe*, October 27, 1965.

127. Snowden, "Planning with People;" emphasis in original.

128. "Sets 'What's Right' Tone: Bostonians Proud of Hub—Collins," *Boston Globe*, March 13, 1963; Snowden and Snowden, "Citizen Participation," 438.

129. Anthony J. Yudis, "Cuts in FHA Red Tape Vowed," *Boston Globe*, May 11, 1963; "Sets 'What's Right' Tone"; Anthony J. Yudis, "Collins Blasts 'Political Minded' Foes of Urban Renewal," *Boston Globe*, April 24, 1963; Daniel J. O'Brien, "Round About," *Boston Globe*, April 28, 1963; "Boston Renewal Exhibit Set for Opening Today," *Boston Globe*, April 5, 1964.

130. "Boston Renewal Exhibit."

131. Anthony J. Yudis, "Amazed—Enthusiastic—Challenged: New Boston Looks Good to Visiting City Planners," *Boston Globe*, April 12, 1964.

132. Snowden and Snowden, "Citizen Participation," 437; Muriel Snowden, *Black Women Oral History Project, Interview with Muriel S. Snowden*, January 21, October 30, and November 20, 1977, Schlesinger Library, Radcliffe College, Harvard University, 63.

133. Hock, "Bulldozers, Busing, and Boycotts," 439–40.

134. Keyes, *The Rehabilitation Planning Game*, 227.

135. Hock, "Bulldozers, Busing, and Boycotts," 446–47.

136. NAACP Boston Branch, *NAACP Community Info* 1, no. 6 (April 27, 1963), box 3, folder 18, Collection M94, Phyllis M. Ryan papers, NU.

Chapter 2

1. Action for Boston Community Development, "Origins of ABCD," 1965, ABCD 65.3, GD, BPL. For a detailed history of ABCD's early years that emphasizes the organization's pursuit of funding, see Stephen Thernstrom, *Poverty, Planning, and Politics in the New Boston: The Origins of ABCD* (New York: Basic Books, 1969).

2. Ed Logue to Paul Ylvisaker, June 14, 1960, Grant 62-457, Reel 2634, FF, RAC.

3. David Wallace to Paul Ylvisaker, December 1, 1960, Grant 62-457, Reel 2634, FF. Ylvisaker challenged Logue more directly, too. See Paul Ylvisaker to Edward Logue, October 4, 1960, and Paul Ylvisaker to Edward Logue, June 20, 1960, Grant 62-457, Reel 2634, FF.

4. Lester W. Nelson, undated memo to Paul Ylvisaker, Grant 62-457, Reel 2634, FF.

5. David Hunter to "PY et al," July 5, 1960, Grant 62-457, Reel 2634, FF.

6. Anthony Yudis, "Ouster Report Stirs ABCD," *Boston Globe*, January 22, 1965.

7. Morris frames this alignment as a product of the New Deal, from which emerged "a new voluntary sector based on the provision of specialized, professional services that complemented the material provision of the public sector." Morris, *The Limits of Voluntarism*, xvi, xli–xlii. See also Cebul and Williams, "Really and Truly a Partnership," on public-private partnerships during the New Deal.

8. A first wave of scholarship affirmed this popular notion of big-government liberalism in the 1960s, including works by observers and historians. See, as examples, Sar A. Levitan, *The Great Society's Poor Law: A New Approach to Poverty* (Baltimore: Johns Hopkins University Press, 1969); James L. Sundquist, *Politics and Policy: The Eisenhower, Kennedy, and Johnson Years* (Washington, DC: Brookings Institution, 1968); James T. Patterson, *America's Struggle against Poverty, 1900–1994* (Cambridge, MA: Harvard University Press, 1981, 1994); Allen J. Matusow, *The Unraveling of America: A History of Liberalism in the 1960s* (New York: Harper & Row, 1984); John Morton Blum, *Years of Discord: American Politics and Society, 1961–1974* (New York: Norton, 1991); and James T. Patterson, *Grand Expectations: The United States, 1945–1974* (New York: Oxford University Press, 1996). Newer works frame liberalism as expanding government authority in certain policy areas while remaining purposefully anemic or reliant on the private sector in others. These seeming tensions have been particularly apparent in histories of housing, immigration, incarceration, and welfare policies, in which rights and protections simultaneously expanded while also reinscribing inequalities based on gender, race, ethnicity, and sexuality. Brent Cebul, *Illusions of Progress: Business, Poverty, and Liberalism in the American Century* (Philadelphia: University of Pennsylvania Press, forthcoming); Chappell, *The War on Welfare*; N.D.B.

Connolly, *A World More Concrete: Real Estate and the Remaking of Jim Crow South Florida* (Chicago: University of Chicago Press, 2014); Hinton, *From the War on Poverty*; Kohler-Hausman, *Getting Tough*; Kornbluh, *The Battle for Welfare Rights*; Nadasen, *Welfare Warriors*; Orleck, *Storming Caesars Palace*; Annelise Orleck and Lisa Gayle Hazirjian, eds. *The War on Poverty: A New Grassroots History* (Athens: University of Georgia Press, 2011); Taylor, *Race for Profit*. See also Cebul, Geismer, and Williams, *Shaped by the State*. Gerstle, *Liberty and Coercion*, roots expansions of federal power in the Supreme Court rather than in the executive or legislative branches (chap. 9).

9. INCITE! organized a conference in 2000 where activists and scholars together developed the concept of the "non-profit industrial complex," drawing on theories of the military- and prison-industrial complexes. The volume resulting from the conference defined it as "a system of relationships between the State (or local and federal governments), the owning classes, foundations, and nonprofit-NGO social service and social justice organizations" (xiii). INCITE!, *The Revolution Will Not Be Funded*.

10. For alternative proposed structures, see Mark Fortune, "Task Force Report on Planning for Human Need: An Aspect of Total Community Development," BRA 3539.6, GD, BPL; Thernstrom, *Poverty, Planning, and Politics*, 28–29.

11. ABCD's incorporation as a nonprofit organization situated it in the private sector, but close ties to city government infused a degree of publicness into it. Thernstrom's account refers to ABCD as a "halfway house between the private and public sectors." Thernstrom, *Poverty, Planning, and Politics*, 86.

12. As quoted in Thernstrom, *Poverty, Planning, and Politics*, 16.

13. Albert Boer, *The Development of USES: A Chronology of the United South End Settlements, 1891–1966* (Boston: United South End Settlements, 1966), 36–41.

14. O'Connor, *Poverty Knowledge*, 104, 117, 124, and see more generally chaps. 4 and 5.

15. Edward Logue to Paul Ylvisaker, June 14, 1960, Grant 62-457, Reel 2634, FF.

16. Thernstrom, *Poverty, Planning and Politics*, 61.

17. For more on the Ford Foundation, see Alice O'Connor, "Community Action, Urban Reform"; Alice O'Connor, "The Ford Foundation and Philanthropic Activism," in *Philanthropic Foundations: New Scholarship, New Possibilities*, ed. Ellen Condliffe Lagermann (Bloomington: Indiana University Press, 1999), 169–94; Gregory K. Raynor, "The Ford Foundation's War on Poverty: Private Philanthropy and Race Relations in New York City, 1948–1968," in O'Connor, *Philanthropic Foundations*, 195–228; and Ferguson, *Top Down*.

18. Edward Logue to Paul Ylvisaker, June 14, 1960, Grant 62-457, Reel 2634, FF; Paul Ylvisaker to Edward Logue, June 20, 1960, Grant 62-457, Reel 2634, FF.

19. For the origins of this approach in foreign development work, see Immerwahr, *Thinking Small*.

20. O'Connor, "Community Action," 595–96.

21. Thernstrom, *Poverty, Planning, and Politics*, 175.

22. As quoted in O'Connor, "The Ford Foundation and Philanthropic Activism," 170.

23. Hinton, *From the War on Poverty*, chap. 1.

24. O'Connor, "Community Action," 611. The committee consisted of representatives from the attorney general's office, the Department of Labor, and the Department of Health, Education, and Welfare. For an overview, see Gayle Olson-Raymer, "The Role of the Federal Government in Juvenile Delinquency Prevention: Historical and Contemporary Perspectives," *Journal of Criminal Law and Criminology* 74, no. 2 (Summer 1983): 578–600.

25. Richard Cloward and Lloyd Ohlin, *Delinquency and Opportunity: A Theory of Delinquent Gangs* (Glencoe, IL: Free Press, 1960). On the influence of this theory on the Ford Foundation and the president's committee, see O'Connor, *Poverty Knowledge*, 127–31; Hinton, *From the War on Poverty*, 35–40.

26. Morris, *The Limits of Voluntarism*, 164–68.

27. Juvenile Delinquency and Youth Offense Control Act of 1961. For draft versions of the bill, see box 7, folder 8, Richardson White Jr. Personal Papers, John F. Kennedy Presidential Library (hereafter JFKL), Boston. For more on the president's committee's grantmaking, see Hinton, *From the War on Poverty*, 39–49.

28. Action for Boston Community Development, "Agreement of Association"; Thernstrom, *Poverty, Planning, and Politics*, 170–71.

29. On the pressures to seek funding and the uncertainty of government funding, see Morris, *The Limits of Voluntarism*, 187–92.

30. Boston Community Development Program, press release, March 21, 1961, Grant 62-457, Reel 2634, FF.

31. O'Connor highlights the deep intellectual and social connections between the president's committee and the Ford Foundation, highlighting the "cadre of predominantly male academic and foundation experts" as a distinguishing feature of 1960s-era poverty interventions. O'Connor, *Poverty Knowledge*, 125, also chap. 5.

32. The failure of the War on Poverty to address structural economic issues has been a long-standing critique, articulated forcefully in histories of the welfare rights movement. See Chappell, *The War on Welfare*; Nadasen, *Welfare Warriors*; Orleck, *Storming Caesars Palace*; Orleck and Hazirjian, *The War on Poverty*; Andrew Pope, "Making Motherhood a Felony: African American Women's Welfare Rights Activism in New Orleans and the End of Suitable Home Laws, 1959–1962," *Journal of American History* 105, no. 2 (2018): 291–310.

33. Christopher Lydon, "A Big YEA for Youth," *Boston Globe*, August 4, 1963.

34. Lydon, "A Big YEA for Youth."

35. "Boston Gets Federal Aid to Help Jobless Youth," *Boston Globe*, September 12, 1963.

36. Notes on Meeting of Demonstration Project Panel, January 8–9, 1962, box 1, folder 1, Eleanor Charwat Personal Papers, JFKL.

37. Grants would be evaluated on several criteria: comprehensiveness of the proposal; participation of public and private agencies; local financial investment; transferability of the program; and plans for evaluation and research. President's Committee, "Summary of Federal Anti-Delinquency Program," Grant 62-457, Reel 2634, FF.

38. Notes on Meeting of Demonstration Project Panel; "administratively unsound" in Sanford Kravitz to Henry Saltman, July 6, 1962, Grant 62-457, Reel 2634, FF.

39. Action for Boston Community Development, "Report to the Ford Foundation for the Period Ending September 30, 1963," Grant 62-457, Reel 2633, FF.

40. The Federal Delinquency Program Objectives and Operations under the Presidents' Committee on Juvenile Delinquency and Youth Crime and the Juvenile Delinquency and Youth Offense Control Act of 1961, November 1962, box 1, folder 4, Eleanor Charwat Personal Papers.

41. Demonstration Projects Technical Advisory Panel, November 30, 1962, box 4, folder 13, Daniel Knapp Papers, JFKL. Of the grant, $900,000 was earmarked for administration, and $1 million would be held in a development fund for special projects to be distributed to ABCD if Ford Foundation staff considered the projects of possible national importance for replication elsewhere. Grant award letter to Charles Schotland, August 31, 1962, Grant 62-457, Reel 2632, FF.

42. Anthony Yudis, "Boston Gets $1.9 Million," *Boston Globe*, September 9, 1962.

43. As quoted in Uncle Dudley, "Boston Is First Again," *Boston Globe*, September 10, 1962.

44. Memorandum on the Youth Development Program of the Boston Youth Opportunities Project, Grant 62-457, Reel 2634, FF.

45. In many ways, this was an updated model of the "scientific charity" movement that began in the late nineteenth century to apply the rationality of science to social problems and to coordinate local efforts through casework, research, and monitoring. Katz, *In the Shadow of the Poorhouse*, 68–87.

46. Action for Boston Community Development, "A Report on ABCD Activities, to the Ford Foundation and the President's Committee on Juvenile Delinquency and Youth Crime, September 1963–August 1964," Grant 62-457, Reel 2633, FF, 6.

47. Action for Boston Community Development, "Report to the Ford Foundation," Appendix D.

48. Thernstrom, *Poverty, Planning, and Politics*, 50–51.

49. Thernstrom, *Poverty, Planning, and Politics*, 164–70.

50. Clifford Campbell, Michael Svirdoff, and Homer Wadsworth, memo to Paul Ylvisaker, December 21, 1965, Grant 62-457, Reel 2634, FF.

51. Action for Boston Community Development, "Report to the Ford Foundation," 41–42.

52. Action for Boston Community Development, "Report on ABCD Activities," 251.

53. Action for Boston Community Development, "Report on ABCD Activities," 18.

54. Action for Boston Community Development, "Report on ABCD Activities," 141.

55. Edward Meade Jr., memo to Paul Ylvisaker, December 21, 1965, Grant 62-457, Reel 2633, FF.

56. Action for Boston Community Development, "Report on ABCD Activities," 9–16.

57. Massachusetts State Advisory Committee to the United States Commission on Civil Rights, "Report on Racial Imbalance in the Boston Public Schools," January 1965, https://archive.org/details/reportonracialim00unit; Massachusetts State Board of Education, "Because It Is Right—Educationally: Report to the Advisory Committee on Racial Imbalance and Education," April 1965, box 1, folder 16, Phyllis M. Ryan papers; William H. Ohrenberger, "A Statement of Policy and Recommendations on the Subject of Racial Imbalance and Education in the Boston Public Schools," June 1965, box 1, folder 38, Phyllis M. Ryan papers.

58. Massachusetts State Advisory Committee, "Report on Racial Imbalance."

59. "Collins Says Hub Ready with Firm Rights Stand," *Boston Globe*, June 21, 1963. Thernstrom notes the political benefits Collins gained via ABCD "to symbolize the city's concern for social . . . renewal" but ignores the racial context. *Poverty, Planning, and Politics*, 172.

60. As examples, William Fripp, "Racial Issues, Here and in South," *Boston Globe*, May 24, 1963; Ian Forman, "Schools for the New Boston—IV Aching Problem of Desegregation," *Boston Globe*, June 5, 1963; Ian Forman, "A New School Life in Roxbury," *Boston Globe*, July 21, 1963; William Fripp, "Growing Pains Face Boston Schools Today," *Boston Globe*, September 5, 1963; Ian Forman, "Logue Initiated School's Test," *Boston Globe*, October 23, 1963. On housing, Anthony J. Yudis, "Progress Report: Both Optimism and Pessimism," *Boston Globe*, November 28, 1963; Jean Dietz, "Plenty of Jobs for Service Corps," *Boston Globe*, February 9, 1964; Jean Dietz, "Columbia Point . . . and a Bold Idea," *Boston Globe*, January 9, 1965.

61. Action for Boston Community Development, "Report on ABCD Activities," iii; Adam R. Nelson, *The Elusive Ideal: Equal Educational Opportunity and the Federal Role in Boston's Public Schools, 1950–1985* (Chicago: University of Chicago Press, 2005), 37.

62. Action for Boston Community Development, "Report on ABCD Activities," iii.

63. "March on Boston Demands Bring Progress," *COREspondent*, May 16, 1965, box 2, folder 2, Frank J. Miranda Papers (M112), NU; Jean Dietz, "Anti-Poverty Group Off to Washington to Fight Freeze-Out," *Boston Globe*, October 26, 1965; "Melvin H. King," *Boston Globe*, October 27, 1965.

64. Massachusetts State Advisory Committee, "Report on Racial Imbalance;" Massachusetts State Board of Education, "Because It Is Right;" Ohrenberger, "A Statement of Policy and Recommendations."

65. Office of Economic Opportunity, Narrative History, vol. 1, part 1, box 1, folder: Volume I, Part I, Narrative History, Administrative History, Presidential Papers of Lyndon Baines Johnson (hereafter LBJL), Austin, TX, 19. The program served as an intellectual template as well. Morris, *The Limits of Voluntarism*, 166–67.

66. David L. Hackett, memo to Charles L. Schultze, January 22, 1963, box 1, folder 5, Legislative Background, Economic Opportunity Act, LBJL.

67. Action for Boston Community Development, "Report on ABCD Activities," 342.

68. "Why Should Conservatives Support the War on Poverty," circulated May 26, 1964, box 25, folder: WE 9 Poverty Program, 5/16/64–6/10/64, White House Central Files, WE 9, LBJL.

69. Sar A. Levitan, "The Community Action Program: A Strategy to Fight Poverty," *Annals of the American Academy of Political and Social Science* 385 (September 1969): 70.

70. Historians frequently note the tensions and contradictions essential to mid-century liberalism; see, in particular, Connolly, "The Strange Career of American Liberalism."

71. Katz, *In the Shadow of the Poorhouse*, ix–x. There was also continued skepticism about this approach and tension between the traditional charitable establishment and the War on Poverty. Morris, *The Limits of Voluntarism*, 172–84.

72. "Draft Specifications," December 28, 1963, Legislative Background, box 1, folder 5, Economic Opportunity Act.

73. "Why Should Conservatives Support the War on Poverty."

74. As examples, Smith and Lipsky, *Nonprofits for Hire*, and Salamon, *Partners in Public Service*.

75. Title II, Sec. 201 and 202 (a)4, Economic Opportunity Act of 1964.

76. Direct aid programs of Medicare and Medicaid as well as amendments to social security and Aid to Families with Dependent Children represented key, if insufficient, expansions of protections for those experiencing poverty. See Chappell, *The War on Welfare*; Tani, *States of Dependency*. Even then, some dollars under the social security amendments of 1967 made their way through nonprofit organizations. Morris, *The Limits of Voluntarism*, 194–205.

77. Charles E. Gilbert and David G. Smith, "Emerging Patterns of Federalism in Health, Education, and Welfare," prepared for the annual meeting of the American Political Science Association, September 6–10, 1966, New York, p. 6, box 4, folder: "Gilbert-Smith Federalism Paper," Office Files of Frederick M. Bohen, LBJL.

78. Laurence E. Lynn Jr., "Social Services and the State: The Public Appropriation of Private Charity," *Social Service Review* 76, no. 1 (March 2002): 67.

79. That this phrase became such a contentious one took the authors by

surprise. Daniel P. Moynihan, *Maximum Feasible Misunderstanding: Community Action in the War on Poverty* (New York: Free Press, 1969). Historians have since explored how poor people harnessed the mandate to bring needed resources and political power to their communities. See, in particular, Orleck and Hazirjian, *The War on Poverty*.

80. Economic Opportunity Act 1966, Section 203; Economic Opportunity Act 1967, Section 202c3 and 202c4.

81. Economic Opportunity Act 1966, Section 209, Section 205 (1).

82. Endicott Peabody to Lyndon Johnson, August 3,1964, box 25, folder: WE 9 Poverty Program, 7/21/64–9/30/64, White House Central Files, WE 9, LBJL.

83. Action for Boston Community Development, Minutes of Special Meeting of Executive Committee of Board of Directors, February 15, 1965, Grant 62-457, Reel 2634, FF. Collins also highlighted ABCD in testimony before Congress as the president of the American Municipal Association. "Collins Makes Plea for War on Poverty," *Boston Globe*, February 25, 1964.

84. Action for Boston Community Development, "Poverty Indices by Boston GNRPs," 1964, BRA Folio 166, GD, BPL, Table 1.2.

85. Wilfred C. Rodgers, "Boston in Front Line of LBJ Poverty War," *Boston Globe*, February 23, 1964.

86. "Poverty Programs Get Boost," *Boston Globe*, March 25, 1965; "ABCD Receives $473,839," *Boston Globe*, May 16, 1965.

87. Data collected from National Archive and Records Administration, "Access to Archival Databases (AAD)," http://aad.archives.gov/aad/series-list.jsp?cat =GS30. Records about Community Action Program Grants and Grantees, created 7/1/1964–9/30/1981 from Record Group 381. As the number of grants increased, so did the average grant size—from an average of $49,565 in 1965 to $213,115 in 1967. Summary of Receipts, Expenditures and Fund Balances, Year Ended Dec. 31, 1964, in Action for Boston Community Development, "Action for Boston Community Development, Inc. Accountants' Report," Financial Statements, December 31, 1964, Grant 62-457, Reel 2634, FF. Of that $7 million in grants, $4.7 million came from the Office of Economic Opportunity, $1.5 million from the Department of Labor, and $600,000 from the Department of Health, Education, and Welfare. Grant Request—Public Affairs, Paul Ylvisaker to McGeorge Bundy, May 6, 1966, Grant 62-457, Reel 2633, FF.

88. Yudis, "Ouster Report"; Anthony J. Yudis, "ABCD Troubles Far Reaching," *Boston Globe*, January 26, 1965; "ABCD Answers Charges," *Boston Globe*, November 18, 1965; "Charge Collins Using ABCD as Racial Lever," *Boston Globe*, July 15, 1965; "ABCD: Tottering Child or Walking Colossus," *Boston Globe*, August 8, 1965; "U.S. Probers Freeze Hub Poverty Funds," *Boston Globe*, November 18, 1965; "ABCD Fund Probe Due for Expansion," *Boston Globe*, November 22, 1965.

89. Clifford Campbell to Paul Ylvisaker, December 2, 1964, Grant 62-457, Reel 2634, FF.

90. Kiernan Bracken, memo to Paul Ylvisaker, June 25, 1965, Grant 62-457, Reel 2633, FF.

91. Kieran Bracken, memo to Paul Ylvisaker, November 29, 1965, Grant 62-457, Reel 2633, FF.

92. Eric Hanson to Louis Winnick, September 28, 1965, Grant 62-457, Reel 2633, FF.

93. Laurie B. Green, "Saving Babies in Memphis: The Politics of Race, Health, and Hunger during the War on Poverty," in Orleck and Hazirjian, *The War on Poverty*, 174.

94. Office of Economic Opportunity Administrative History, box 1, folder Volume I, Part I, Narrative History, 98–99.

95. John C. Thomas, "U.S. Probers Freeze Hub Poverty Funds," *Boston Globe*, November 18, 1965.

96. "ABCD Answers Charges," *Boston Globe*, November 18, 1965.

97. Robert Kenney, "Early Thaw for ABCD Funds Likely," *Boston Globe*, November 19, 1965.

98. Joseph Slavet to Paul Ylvisaker, November 10, 1965, Grant 62-457, Reel 2633, FF.

99. Joseph Slavet to Paul Ylvisaker, August 24, 1965, Grant 62-457, Reel 2632, FF.

100. Joseph Slavet to Paul Ylvisaker, August 24, 1965, Grant 62-457, Reel 2632, FF.

101. Robert Coard to Sibohan Oppenheimer-Nicolau, December 26, 1972, Grant 62-457, Reel 2633, FF.

102. Charles Stewart and Kieran Bradley, memo to Paul Ylvisaker, April 28, 1966, Grant 62-457, Reel 2633, FF.

103. ABCD opened a third skill training center in the fall of 1968 with funds from the Ford Foundation, which the US Department of Labor later reimbursed. "Report on Ford Expenditures, the Period Beginning December 1968 and Ending November 1969," February 17, 1970, Grant 62-457, Reel 2633, FF.

104. In August 1965, for example, Slavet asked Ford to backdate a grant of $300,000 to the multiservice centers from the original May 1, 1965, to March 15, 1965, in order to cover expenses of over $35,000 as the funds from the Department of Health, Education, and Welfare were less than anticipated. Joseph Slavet to Paul Ylvisaker, August 24, 1965, Grant 62-457, Reel 2632, FF.

105. Standard grant procedures required ABCD to return unexpended funds to the Ford Foundation at the end of the grant period. Siobhan Oppenheimer-Nicolau to Robert Coard, April 24, 1974, Grant 62-457, Reel 2633, FF. ABCD responded that returning the foundation's money "without resolving these still outstanding audit reports could severely impair this Agency's ability to function in the future." Robert Coard to Williard Hertz, March 27, 1974, Grant 62-457, Reel 2633, FF.

106. Bryant Rollins, "Give Authority More and . . . ," *Boston Globe*, March 13, 1965, 7.

107. Orleck and Hazirjian, *The War on Poverty*.

108. Robert L. Levey, "A Mile of Marchers," *Boston Globe*, April 24, 1965; Robert B. Kenney, "Demonstrators Hand Mayor 15-Point Plan," *Boston Globe*, April 24, 1965.

109. "Area Voting Set in War on Poverty," *Boston Globe*, July 27, 1965.

110. David B. Wilson, "ABCD Leader Raps U.S. Poverty Fight," *Boston Globe*, November 30, 1965.

111. Ray Richard, "The Poor Show the Way," *Boston Globe*, September 2, 1966.

112. Janet Riddell, "Disillusionment Impedes Poverty Election Turnout," *Boston Globe*, November 27, 1965.

113. Janet Riddell, "Anti-Poverty Election May Be Postponed," *Boston Globe*, September 25, 1966.

114. Jean Dietz, "U.S. to Probe Hub Poverty Program," *Boston Globe*, June 26, 1965.

115. Jean Dietz, "Residents Say U.S. Will Probe ABCD," *Boston Globe*, October 28, 1965; "SNAP to Press for Atty. Williams OK," *Bay State Banner*, October 30, 1965; Action for Boston Community Development, "Neighborhood Profile: Roxbury-No. Dorchester," 1967, BRA 2293, GD, BPL.

116. As quoted in Jean Dietz, "Residents Say U.S. Will Probe ABCD," *Boston Globe*, October 28, 1965.

117. Action for Boston Community Development, "Neighborhood Profile: Roxbury-No. Dorchester."

118. Quoted in Elizabeth Weymouth, "BRA Chief Critical of War on Poverty," *Boston Globe*, November 25, 1965.

119. Office of Economic Opportunity Administrative History, box 2, folder: Volume II—Documentary Supplement Chapter I, 156.

120. Office of Economic Opportunity Administrative History, 156–57, and quote from bureaucrat as cited in footnote on p. 157.

121. As quoted in Lynn, "Social Services and the State," 68, 63.

122. Thernstrom similarly points to ABCD's adaptability as the characteristic that kept funding coming in the door without accomplishing much on the other side. Thernstrom, *Poverty, Planning and Politics*, 46, 166. My emphasis here is on the political desirability of that characteristic and the structural embedding of it in urban governance.

Chapter 3

1. "South End Resignation Called Off," *Boston Globe*, February 4, 1965; "Melvin H. King," *Boston Globe*, October 27, 1965.

2. "Everybody Wins," *Bay State Banner*, February 4, 1967; as quoted in Melvin B. Miller, "Mel King Reinstated to USES as Director of Community Project," *Bay State Banner*, February 4, 1967.

3. Miller, "Mel King Reinstated."

4. King had run unsuccessfully for the Boston School Committee in 1961, 1963, and 1965. Jeremiah Murphy, "King Gets New Job with Old Employer," *Boston Globe*, January 31, 1967.

5. "Everybody Wins."

6. On national-level politics and policy, see Jill Quadagno, *The Color of Welfare: How Racism Undermined the War on Poverty* (New York: Oxford University Press, 1994); Michael K. Brown, *Race, Money, and the American Welfare State* (Ithaca, NY: Cornell University Press, 1999); and Chappell, *The War on Welfare*. Similar dynamics played out at the local level, too, as African Americans saw clear connections between movements for poor people, welfare rights, and civil rights. For examples, Charles Payne, *I've Got the Light of Freedom: The Organizing Tradition and the Mississippi Freedom Struggle* (Berkeley: University of California Press, 1995); Susan Youngblood Ashmore, *Carry It On: The War on Poverty and the Civil Rights Movement in Alabama, 1964–1972* (Athens: University of Georgia Press, 2008); Self, *American Babylon*; Sugrue, *Sweet Land of Liberty*; Orleck, *Storming Caesars Palace*; Orleck and Hazirjian, *The War on Poverty*; and Woodsworth, *Battle for Bed-Stuy*.

7. This statement applies to a variety of communities traditionally excluded—particularly ethnic and immigrant communities—who similarly turned to community organizations as a long-standing strategy of survival. For examples during the War on Poverty, see chapters by Marc S. Rodriguez, Adina Black, William Clayson, and Karen Tani, in Orleck and Hazirjian, *The War on Poverty*; also Sonia Song-Ha Lee, *Building a Latino Civil Rights Movement* (Chapel Hill: University of North Carolina Press, 2016).

8. Erica Kohl-Arenas provides one of the strongest analyses of how funding shaped social movements in her study of philanthropic support of the farmworkers movement in California in *The Self Help Myth*.

9. Clemens, *Civic Gifts*, 9.

10. Benjamin Soskis, "A History of Associational Life," in Powell and Bromley, *The Nonprofit Sector*, 32–35, 57–59. See also Theda Skocpol, Ariana Liazos, and Marshall Ganz, *What a Mighty Power We Can Be: American Fraternal Groups and the Struggle for Racial Equality* (Princeton, NJ: Princeton University Press, 2006).

11. Elisabeth Clemens, "Nonprofits as Boundary Markers: The Politics of Choice, Mobilization, and Arbitrage," in Powell and Bromley, *The Nonprofit Sector*, 197–200. Scholarship in sociology and political science on the relationships between nonprofit organizations and social movements has greatly informed my thinking. Useful overviews include chapters by Elisabeth Clemens, David Suarez, and Breno Bringel and Elizabeth McKenna, in Powell and Bromley, *The Nonprofit Sector*. See also Sidney Verba, Kay Lehman Schlozman, and Henry E. Brady, *Voice and*

Equality: Civic Voluntarism in American Politics (Cambridge, MA: Harvard University Press, 1995); Theda Skocpol, *Diminished Democracy: From Membership to Management in American Civic Life* (Norman: University of Oklahoma Press, 2013).

12. As examples, Theda Skocpol, *Protecting Soldiers and Mothers: The Political Origins of Social Policy in the United States* (Cambridge, MA: Harvard University Press, 1992); Gordon, *Pitied but Not Entitled*; Dorothy Sue Cobble, *The Other Women's Movement: Workplace Justice and Social Rights in Modern America* (Princeton, NJ: Princeton University Press, 2003); Tomiko Brown-Nagin, *Courage to Dissent: Atlanta and the Long History of the Civil Rights Movement* (New York: Oxford University Press, 2011); Megan Ming Francis, *Civil Rights and the Making of the Modern American State* (New York: Cambridge University Press, 2014).

13. Danielle Allen, "A Forgotten Black Founding Father," *The Atlantic*, February 10, 2021.

14. Adelaide M. Cromwell, *The Other Brahmins: Boston's Black Upper Class, 1750–1950* (Fayetteville: University of Arkansas Press, 1994).

15. Deutsch, *Women and the City*, 19.

16. Boer, *The Development of USES*, 30.

17. Deutsch, *Women and the City*, 19–20. Evelyn Brooks Higginbotham speaks to the power of spaces made of and for Black women and their activism in *Righteous Discontent: The Women's Movement in the Black Baptist Church, 1880–1920* (Cambridge, MA: Harvard University Press, 1993). Verba, Schlozman, and Brady note this intergenerational nurturing of civic skills as a key feature of voluntary associations in *Voice and Equality*, 4.

18. Melnea A. Cass, Oral History Interview for *The Black Women Oral History Project*, February 1, 1977, OH-31, Schlesinger Library, Harvard University, Cambridge MA, 59.

19. Cass, *Black Women Oral History Project*, 82.

20. Jeanne Theoharis has written several pieces on Ruth Batson's activism. See "'We Saved the City,'" as well as chapters in Theoharis and Woodard, *Freedom North*, and in Jeanne Theoharis and Komozi Woodard, eds., *Groundwork: Local Black Freedom Movements in America* (New York: New York University Press, 2005).

21. King, *Chain of Change*, 32–25, 80.

22. David Greenstone and Paul E. Peterson, *Race and Authority in Urban Politics: Community Relations and the War on Poverty* (New York: Russell Sage Foundation, 1973), 28, 32; Orleck and Hazirjian, *The War on Poverty*, 17.

23. "Extra," *Bay State Banner*, April 2, 1966, 1.

24. Louis Kaufman, "Civil Rights Leaders Won't Back Bennett as ABCD Director," *Boston Globe*, April 10, 1966.

25. 1967 Amendments to the Economic Opportunity Act, Public Law 90-222, Section 211c.

26. ABCD Progress Report, October 1967, Grant 62-457, Reel 2634, FF.

27. Statement by Doris Graham, Hearings Before the Subcommittee on Employment, Manpower, and Poverty of the Committee on Labor and Public Welfare (hereafter Hearings), United States Senate, 90th Cong., 1st Sess. on Examining the War on Poverty, Part 15, Boston, June 1, 1967, 4518.

28. Jean Dietz, "Residents Say U.S. Will Probe ABCD," *Boston Globe*, October 28, 1965.

29. "CAPs Approved by Governor," Grant 62-457, Reel 2634, FF; ABCD Progress Report, October 1967, Grant 62-457, Reel 2634, FF. Recipients included small neighborhood day care centers, the Boston Public Schools, the Harvard Graduate School of Education, and the neighborhood Area Planning Action Councils. National Archives, "Access to Archival Databases (AAD)," http://aad.archives.gov/aad/series-list.jsp?cat=GS30.

30. Ford Review Committee Report, June 22, 1967, Grant 62-457, Reel 2634, FF.

31. Ford Foundation, "Ford Development Operating Fund, Period Ending 11/30/70," Grant 62-457, Reel 2633, FF.

32. Crystal R. Sanders, *A Chance for Change: Head Start and Mississippi's Black Freedom Struggle* (Chapel Hill: University of North Carolina Press, 2016); Claire Dunning, "New Careers for the Poor: Human Service and the Post-Industrial City," *Journal of Urban History* 44, no. 4 (2018): 669–90.

33. "Community Development Council and Neighborhood Action Center—Report of the Director, December 1966," in Hearings, 4645.

34. Graham, Hearings, 4518.

35. Statement by Betty Meredith, Hearings, 4521.

36. For another example, see Orleck, *Storming Caesars Palace*.

37. "Leaderless SNAP Oks ABCD Pact," *Boston Globe*, November 23, 1965.

38. "The War on Poverty," *Bay State Banner*, October 16, 1965, 4; "ABCD Delays So. End Program," *Bay State Banner*, October 9, 1965, 1; as quoted in "Protest ABCD Decision: South End Rallies behind Atty. Williams," *Bay State Banner*, October 23, 1965.

39. "CAPs Approved by Governor."

40. "Professional Staff Assignments," July 6–August 20, 1965, box 25, folder 766, FH; Morris, *The Limits of Voluntarism*, 183.

41. "Sponsors' Guidelines: Project Head Start—Boston," undated, box 25, folder 767, FH.

42. "ABCD Head Start Programs, Agreement with Sponsor," June 1965, box 25, folder 765, FH.

43. Rheable Edwards to Phillip Snowden, June 2, 1965, box 25, folder 765, FH.

44. Rheable Edwards to O. Phillip Snowden, April 29, 1965, box 25, folder 765, FH.

45. Notes, "Operation Head Start—Boston," May 27, 1965, box 25, folder 765, FH; Minutes, "Project Head-Start—Boston," June 8, 1965, box 25, folder 766, FH.

46. Rheable M. Edwards, memo to All Sponsors of Head Start Classes, July 7, 1965, box 25, folder 766, FH.

47. Fran Litman, memo to Leo Burke, May 19, 1965, box 25, folder 767, FH; Minutes, "Project Head-Start."

48. Freedom House, Requisition No. 2, August 10, 1965, box 25, folder 767, FH; Freedom House, Requisition No. 3, August 20, 1965, box 25, folder 767, FH.

49. Meredith, Hearings, 4521. See also statements by James Duffy, Barbara Searcy, and George Bennett in Hearings.

50. Statement by George Bennett, Hearings, 4508; emphasis in original.

51. Statement by Leroy Boston, Hearings, 4606–7.

52. Action for Boston Community Development, "Report on ABCD Activities."

53. Joseph Slavet to Henry Saltzman, December 14, 1964, Grant 62-457, Reel 2633, FF; Joseph Slavet to Paul Ylvisaker, April 28, 1965, Grant 62-457, Reel 2633, FF; Joseph Slavet to Paul Ylvisaker, November 10, 1965, Grant 62-457, Reel 2633, FF.

54. "The Natural History of a Professional Reform Organization: Roxbury Multi-Service Center," box 1, folder 5, Collection M109: Roxbury Multi-Service Center records (hereafter RMSC), NU.

55. "Birds Eye View," box 1, folder 5, RMSC.

56. "Agency History," box 1, folder 5, RMSC.

57. "Brief Report on Roxbury Multi-Service Center for 1967," box 1, folder 5, RMSC.

58. "A Crucial Decision," *Bay State Banner*, March 25, 1967.

59. "An Anecdotal History, 1964–1984," box 1, folder 6, RMSC.

60. Hubie Jones, The HistoryMakers A2004.203, interviewed by Robert Hayden, October 14, 2004, The HistoryMakers Digital Archive, session 1, tape 3, stories 6–8.

61. "Report of Operations," February 1966, box 1, folder 7, RMSC.

62. "Report on 1967," box 1, folder 5, RMSC.

63. "Brief Report on the Roxbury Multi-Service Center for 1968," box 1, folder 5, RMSC.

64. "A Report on Roxbury: The Night of June 2," prepared by the Commission on Church and Race, Massachusetts Council of Churches, box 10, folder 86, James P. Breeden Collection (ML59), Dartmouth College Archives and Special Collections. For more on the welfare rights movement, see Nadasen, *Welfare Warriors*, and Orleck, *Storming Caesars Palace*.

65. Hubert E. Jones, "Forward" board minutes, July 1970, box 2, folder 28, RMSC.

66. Hinton, *From the War on Poverty*, 125.

67. National Advisory Commission on Civil Disorders, *Report of the National Advisory Commission on Civil Disorders* (Washington, DC: NACCD, 1968), 150–55. See also 329n97.

68. National Advisory Commission on Civil Disorders, *Report of the National Advisory Commission on Civil Disorders*, 288.

69. National Advisory Commission on Civil Disorders, *Report of the National Advisory Commission on Civil Disorders*, 295.

70. Roxbury Multi-Service Center, Annual Report: 1969, box 2, folder 14, RMSC; Board Minutes, October 1970, box 2, folder 31, RMSC; "Outline of Proposal for Spanish MSC," box 2, folder 32, RMSC.

71. Ana Maria Rodriquez Diamond, "Statement before U.S. Civil Rights Commission," Board materials, June 1971, box 2, folder 41, RMSC.

72. Board Minutes, July 1970, box 2, folder 28, RMSC; Board Minutes, April 1971, box 2, folder 39, RMSC.

73. Roxbury Multi-Service Center, "Brief Report on the Roxbury Multi-Service Center for 1968," box 1, folder 5, RMSC.

74. Roxbury Multi-Service Center, "Brief Report on the Roxbury Multi-Service Center for 1968."

75. Roxbury Multi-Service Center, Annual Report: 1969; Task Force on Children Out of School, *The Way We Go to School: The Exclusion of Children in Boston* (Boston: Beacon, 1970).

76. Roxbury Multi-Service Center, "1964–1985: An Anecdotal History," May 1984, box 1, folder 6, RMSC.

77. Jacquelyn Dowd Hall, "The Long Civil Rights Movement and the Political Uses of the Past," *Journal of American History* 91, no. 4 (March 2005): 1233–63; Peniel Joseph, *The Black Power Movement: Rethinking the Civil Rights–Black Power Era* (New York: Routledge, 2006).

78. "Proposal for the Development of RMSC, 1969–1974," box 1, folder 68, RMSC.

79. On Black power as a local movement, see as examples Komozi Woodard, *A Nation within a Nation: Amiri Baraka (Le Roi Jones) and Black Power Politics* (Chapel Hill: University of North Carolina Press, 2000); Self, *American Babylon*; Donna Murch, *Living for the City: Migration, Education and the Rise of the Black Panther Party in Oakland, California* (Chapel Hill: University of North Carolina Press, 2010); Goldstein, *The Roots of Urban Renaissance.*

80. Roxbury Multi-Service Center, Annual Report: 1969.

81. Board Minutes, January 1970, box 2, folder 22, RMSC; Board Minutes, May 1970, box 2, folder 26, RMSC.

82. Board Minutes, May 1970, box 2, folder 26, RMSC.

83. "Sav-more Newsletter," February 1970, RMSC Board Materials, box 2, folder 23, RMSC.

84. Roxbury Multi-Service Center, Annual Report: 1969.

85. Hubie Jones to Friend, January 1970, box 2, folder 22, RMSC.

86. Board Minutes, April 1970, box 2, folder 24, RMSC.

87. "OEO Submission, CAP 81, Narrative Summary," Board Materials, July 1970, box 2, folder 28, RMSC.

88. Board Minutes, April 1970, box 2, folder 24, RMSC.

89. Board Minutes, May 1970, box 2, folder 26, RMSC.

90. Board Minutes, June 1970, box 2, folder 27, RMSC.

91. Roxbury Multi-Service Center, "Position on Continuation of the War in Vietnam," Board Minutes, May 1970, box 2, folder 26, RMSC; Cappy Pinderhughes to Friend, August 5, 1971, Board materials, August 1971, box 2, folder 43, RMSC.

92. Board Minutes, September 1971, box 2, folder 44, RMSC.

93. On the connections between Black power and community development, see Tom Adam Davies, "Black Power in Action: The Bedford-Stuyvesant Restoration Corporation, Robert F. Kennedy, and the Politics of the Urban Crisis," *Journal of American History* (December 2013): 736–60; Ferguson, *Top Down*; Goldstein, *The Roots of Urban Renaissance*; Brian Purnell, "'What We Need Is Brick and Mortar': Race, Gender, and Early Leadership of the Bedford-Stuyvesant Restoration Corporation," and Julia Rabig, "'A Fight and a Question': Community Development Corporations, Machine Politics and Corporate Philanthropy in the Long Urban Crisis," both in *The Business of Black Power: Community Development, Capitalism and Corporate Responsibility in Postwar America*, ed. Laura Warren Hill and Julia Rabig (Rochester, NY: University of Rochester Press, 2012).

94. Jim Vrabel, "A Citizen and a Celtic," *Bay State Banner*, April 12, 2011.

95. King, *Chain of Change*, 111.

96. In a paper prepared for the United South End Settlements, a Cambridge firm recommended that the neighborhood agency form a "development corporation to function as a stimulus and an agency for the development of new and rehabilitated housing." "General Statement to Consider the Formation of a Development Corporation to Assist in Urban Renewal Programs in the South End District of Boston," Statement prepared by James L. Harris, Harris and Freeman, Inc. for the United South End Settlements, March 1963, BRA 1909, GD, BPL, 1–3. See also chap. 5.

97. Woodsworth, *Battle for Bed-Stuy*, 232.

98. Cohen, *Saving America's Cities*, 221–26.

99. Lower Roxbury Community Corporation, "The Future of Lower Roxbury Is Happening Now!" box 1, folder 5, Collection M106: Lower Roxbury Community Corporation records (hereafter LRCC), NU; Ronald Bailey, Diane Turner, and Robert Hayden, *Lower Roxbury: A Community of Treasures in the City of Boston*, for LRCC by the Department of African American Studies at Northeastern University (Roxbury, MA: Afro Scholar Press, 1993), chap. 3.

100. Bailey, Turner, and Hayden, *Lower Roxbury*, 20, 23–26, 33.

101. "Articles of Incorporation," June 30, 1966, box 1, folder 2, Collection 0023: Urban Planning Aid, University of Massachusetts at Boston Archive and Special Collections Boston, Massachusetts (hereafter UMass). See also Crockett, *People before Highways*; Luce, "The Lower Roxbury Community Corporation vs. BRA," August 1968, box 1, folder 20, Collection 70: Roots of the Rainbow Exhibit Collection (hereafter RR), UMass; Charles "Chuck" Turner, The HistoryMakers A2005.080, interviewed by Robert Hayden, March 25, 2005, The HistoryMakers Digital Archive, session 1, tape 3, stories 10–11.

102. Alan Lloyd Wilson, "The Effect of the Funding Environment on Community Based Development Organizations" (master's thesis, Department of Urban Studies and Planning, Massachusetts Institute of Technology, 1982), chap. 2.

103. Lower Roxbury Community Corporation, "The Future of Lower Roxbury Is Happening Now!"

104. *Voice* (newsletter) 1, no. 1 (August 17, 1968), box 1, folder 9, LRCC.

105. LRCC won a memorandum of understanding with the mayor and BRA in 1967 that allocated fifteen acres of renewal land for low-income housing development. "Washington Park Urban Renewal Bulletin," undated, box 1, folder 8, LRCC; "Memorandum of Understanding," undated, box 1, folder 20, RR.

106. Board Minutes, May 15, 1969, box 1, folder 1, LRCC; Tom Nutt, memo to LRCC Board, May 15, 1969, box 1, folder 1, LRCC.

107. "LRCC Landscape Fund Drive," box 1, folder 5, LRCC.

108. Board Minutes, September 12, 1972, box 1, folder 4, LRCC.

109. See, for example, Minutes, Meeting with John Warner, January 13, 1970, box 1, folder 2, LRCC.

110. Notes on the meeting at St. Stephens Parish Hall, January 28, 1968, box 17, folder 83, Collection M111: Inquilinos Boricuas en Acción records (hereafter IBA), NU.

111. They also demanded that land taken by the BRA as part of the renewal effort be "turned over to the community to operate and maintain." "Parcel 19 News," October 1968, box 6, folder 27, IBA.

112. Bylaws, Emergency Tenants' Council of Parcel 19, Inc., box 17, folder 69, IBA.

113. Emergency Tenants' Council, Preliminary Development Proposal, November 10, 1969, box 48, folder 17, IBA.

114. Terence J. Farrell to Israel Feliciano, March 4, 1970, box 48, folder 17, IBA; John D. Warner, memo to BRA, December 4, 1969, box 48, folder 17, IBA; "represents" in Boston Redevelopment Authority, press release, December 10, 1969, box 48, folder 18, IBA.

115. "Villa Victoria" clipping from *La Comunidad, Design, Development and Self-Determination in Hispanic Communities* (National Endowment for the Arts, 1982), box 6, folder 23, IBA.

116. Emergency Tenants' Council, Preliminary Development Proposal.

117. Charles E. Claffey, "Tenants Unite to Save South End," *Boston Globe*, March 31, 1970.

118. Of Latinos living in the South End of Boston in 1968, 77 percent of households had migrated from the countryside or small towns in Puerto Rico; 11 percent of males and 11 percent of females had an education beyond the tenth grade; 52 percent of male heads of household could not read or speak English, and 59 percent of male heads of households held regular employment. Mario Luis Small, *Villa Victoria: The Transformation of Social Capital in a Boston Barrio* (Chicago: University of Chicago Press, 2004), 24.

119. As an example, Matthew Edel, Peter Bohmner, and Charles Fenton, "A Projection of Costs for the Community Self-Determination Program," MIT Department of Economics, reprinted July 16, 1968, *Congressional Record*, 22140.

120. Economic Opportunity Act 1966, Public Law 89-794, November 8, 1966, Title I, Part D.

121. The Community Self-Determination Act of 1968, S. 3875, S. 3876, H.R. 18709, 90th Cong., 2nd Sess. (1968), section 2; National Advisory Commission on Civil Disorders, *Report of the National Advisory Commission on Civil Disorders*, 153, 155, 217.

122. Hill and Rabig, *The Business of Black Power*.

123. "The Circle Inc. Plans Expansion," *Bay State Banner*, December 24, 1970.

124. "For the Last Sixteen Years . . . ," undated, box 6, folder 23, IBA.

125. "Boston's Neighborhood Development and Employment Agency (NDEA)," undated, BRA 3812, GD, 23.

126. Boston Black United Front, "Statement of Demands," box 1, folder 6, Boston Black United Front Records, Roxbury Community College Archive, Boston; "United Front's 21 Demands to Business, Government," *Boston Globe*, April 9, 1968. See also Crockett, *People before Highways*.

127. Boston Black United Front, "United Black Appeal," box 24, folder 1, Boston Black United Front Records.

Chapter 4

1. "Kevin White for Mayor," *Boston Globe*, November 6, 1967.

2. J. Anthony Lucas, *Common Ground: A Turbulent Decade in the Lives of Three American Families* (New York: Knopf, 1985), profiled Hicks, "The Chairwoman," in his epic account of busing. Scholars emphasize, too, the roles of race, gender, and class identities in her politics, including Ronald P. Formisano, *Boston against Busing: Race, Class, and Ethnicity in the 1960s and 1970s* (Chapel Hill: University of North Carolina Press, 2012); Matthew F. Delmont, *Why Busing Failed: Race, Media and the National Resistance* (Berkeley: University of California Press, 2016), 81–91; Elizabeth Gillespie McRae, *Mothers of Massive Resistance: White Women and the Politics of White Supremacy* (New York: Oxford University Press, 2018), 224–27.

3. Hicks became a national figure too. Delmont, *Why Busing Failed*, 83, 89, 193–97.

4. This pushes against Suleiman Osman's "decade of the neighborhood" by highlighting the policy apparatus that underwrote this version of governance. Suleiman Osman, "The Decade of the Neighborhood," in *Rightward Bound: Making American Conservative in the 1970s*, ed. Bruce J. Schulman and Julian E. Zelizer (Cambridge, MA: Harvard University Press, 2008), 106–27.

5. My discussion of White's powers as dependent on higher tiers of government is informed by Paul E. Peterson, *City Limits* (Chicago: University of Chicago Press, 1981), and Gerald E. Frug, *City Making: Building Communities without Building Walls* (Princeton, NJ: Princeton University Press, 1999).

6. Quote from Sara Davidson, "New York's 'Little City Halls' Taking on Crucial Importance," *Boston Globe*, September 24, 1967; Eric A. Nordinger, *Decentralizing the City: A Study of Boston's Little City Halls* (Cambridge, MA: MIT Press, 1972), 36–37; National Advisory Commission on Civil Disorders, *Report of the National Advisory Commission on Civil Disorders*, 153.

7. David Nyhan, "Kevin White Is Now Dean of Nation's Mayors," *Boston Globe*, October 2, 1977.

8. David Ellis, "White Tours City, 'Hears' Citizens," *Boston Globe*, March 14, 1969.

9. Kevin H. White, "Neighborhood Services Department," position paper, June 8, 1967, referenced in Robert Healy, "Who Inherits Collins Vote?" *Boston Globe*, June 12, 1967.

10. As quoted in Nordinger, *Decentralizing the City*, 53.

11. Nordinger, *Decentralizing the City*, 52.

12. Ken Hartnett, "At Age 5, Little City Halls Earn Their Keep," *Boston Globe*, July 23, 1973.

13. "Liberal or Conservative? It Depends," *Boston Globe*, August 22, 1971.

14. Quoted in Nordinger, *Decentralizing the City*, 54; David R. Ellis, "East Boston's 'Little City Hall' Eases Resident's Cut-Off Feelings," *Boston Globe*, July 28, 1968; "Dorchester Gets 3d Little City Hall," *Boston Globe*, October 4, 1968.

15. National Advisory Commission on Civil Disorders, *Report of the National Advisory Commission on Civil Disorders*, 153.

16. David W. Davis, letter to the editor, *Boston Globe*, September 26, 1969.

17. Nordinger, *Decentralizing the City*, 230.

18. Rev. Walter J. Dron, letter to the editor, *Boston Globe*, October 20, 1969; Margo Miller, "Chinatown Finds a New Voice," *Boston Globe*, January 7, 1979.

19. Christopher Lydon, "The Men around Kevin White," *Boston Globe*, March 9, 1969.

20. Bernard J. Frieden and Marshall Kaplan, *The Politics of Neglect: Urban Aid from Model Cities to Revenue Sharing* (Cambridge, MA: MIT Press, 1975).

21. US Advisory Commission on Intergovernmental Relations, *Fiscal Balance in the American Federal System*, vol. 1 (Washington, DC: Government Printing Office, 1967), 147, 151, as quoted in Frieden and Kaplan, *The Politics of Neglect*, 15.

22. Frieden and Kaplan, *The Politics of Neglect*, 3.

23. Similar concerns about government inefficiency motivated many of Carter's urban policies as well as his interest in devolution and faith in private entities such as nonprofits. Thomas J. Sugrue, "Carter's Urban Policy Crisis," in *The Carter Presidency: Policy Choices in the Post–New Deal Era*, ed. Gary M. Fink and Hugh Davis Graham (Lawrence: University Press of Kansas, 2008).

24. Elisabeth Clemens, "Lineages of the Rube Goldberg State: Building and Blurring Public Programs, 1900–1940," in *Rethinking Political Institutions: The Art of the State*, ed. Ian Shapiro, Stephen Skowronkek, and Daniel Galvin (New York: New York University Press, 2006), 380–443.

25. The literature on Model Cities is limited, though summarized in Bret A. Weber and Amanda Wallace, "Revealing the Empowerment Revolution: A Literature Review of the Model Cities Program," *Journal of Urban History* 38, no. 1 (2012): 173–92. See also Mandi Isaacs Jackson, *Model City Blues: Urban Space and Organized Resistance in New Haven* (Philadelphia: Temple University Press, 2008). The classic text is Charles Haar, *Between the Idea and the Reality: A Study in the Origin, Fate and Legacy of the Model Cities Program* (Boston: Little, Brown, 1975).

26. Robert Mitchell and Norman Beckman, "A Framework for Demonstration Projects in Metropolitan Planning and Effectuation," Staff paper no. 2, December 1965, box 1, Legislative Background: Model Cities, LBJL.

27. Chester Rapkin and Grace Milgram, "A Framework for Center City Demonstration Projects," Staff paper no. 1, December 1965, box 1, Legislative Background: Model Cities.

28. Hans Spiegel, "Employing Local Residents in Project Areas," Staff paper no. 8, December 1965, Legislative Background: Model Cities; Dunning, "New Careers for the Poor."

29. Demonstration Cities and Metropolitan Development Act of 1966, Public Law 89-754, November 3, 1966.

30. US Department of Housing and Urban Development, *Program Guide: Model Neighborhoods in Demonstration Cities* (Washington, DC: Government Printing Office, 1967).

31. The final report recommended six cities with population over 500,000, ten with population between 250,000 and 500,000, and fifty cities with population below 250,000. *Task Force Report: Proposed Programs for the Department of Housing and Urban Development*, as reprinted in Haar, *Between the Idea and the Reality*, 292–308.

32. Demonstration Cities and Metropolitan Development Act of 1966. HUD emphasized the need for metropolitan-wide participation, noting that poor neighborhoods needed "bridges—not walls." This recognized the embeddedness of poor neighborhoods in larger political economies but also enabled Model Cities funding to underwrite activities outside the Model Neighborhood. As a result, Seattle spent 70 percent of its Model Cities funds in places outside the Model Neighborhood, whereas Boston spent 70 percent inside the neighborhood. David Rogers, "Boston Model Cities Program—What 'Models' Did It Build?" *Boston Globe*, August 20, 1975.

33. Frieden and Kaplan, *The Politics of Neglect*, 56–57.

34. Elliot Friedman, "Model City Drive Starts," *Boston Globe*, April 8, 1967.

35. Demonstration Cities and Metropolitan Development Act of 1966.

36. Elliot Friedman, "Asks People's Voice Heard in Model City," *Boston Globe*, April 21, 1967; Anthony Yudis, "The Model City Snag—Who Speaks for the Residents," *Boston Globe*, April 23, 1967.

37. Anthony Yudis and Elliot Friedman, "Council, Collins to Duel on Model City Today," *Boston Globe*, April 26, 1967.

38. Text of the resolution as reprinted in "Citizens to Control Model City, Await $240,000 from Washington," *Bay State Banner*, May 6, 1967.

39. "Atkins at Council," *Bay State Banner*, April 29, 1967.

40. "Employee Guidebook," undated, box 117A, Model Cities Administration Papers (hereafter MCA), Boston City Archives (hereafter BCA), Boston. At the time of my research, the MCA collection was unprocessed and, as a result, my box designations indicate their location as of 2015. As stated by Daniel Richardson and quoted in Janet Riddel, "Model City Residents Meet," *Boston Globe*, December 11, 1967.

41. Outlet Newsletter, August 1972, box 106A, MCA.

42. "Boston Model City Program: The 4th Year, Directory of Services," undated, box 119B, MCA.

43. Anthony Yudis, "Many Model City Applications Just Make Federal Deadline," *Boston Globe*, May 7, 1967. Application to HUD for a Grant to Plan a Comprehensive City Demonstration Program, April 27, 1967, box 117A, MCA.

44. "Boston's Model City: A Progress Report," box 117A, MCA.

45. "Manpower Planning for Model City Program in Boston," undated, box 14, folder: City of Boston, Mass; Programs and Data, Office Files of Frederick M. Bohen.

46. "Model Neighborhood Proposal: A Summary of the Application to the Department of Housing and Urban Development for a $240,000 Planning Grant," April 1967, box 141A, MCA.

47. "Comprehensive Demonstration Program," October 15, 1968, box 13A, MCA.

48. Model Neighborhood Board, "The New Federalism and the Future for Community Development," February 23, 1974, box 119A, MCA.

49. "Paul Parks," Oral History, 2009, Collection 165: Lower Roxbury Black History Project, NU.

50. "BMCP: Program Status Report," February 15, 1972, box 117B, MCA.

51. "Model City Administration: Status List as of June 13, 1973," box 27A, MCA.

52. "BMCP: Program Status Report," April 15, 1970, box 92A, MCA.

53. "Contract Status List," October 1970, in the Boston Model City Program Quarterly Status Report, box 140A, MCA.

54. "Model City Administration."

55. "Inter-Office Communication Re: Contracts, Federated Dorchester," October 2, 1973, box 113B, MCA.

56. "La Alianza Hispana, Inc. Report Period: August 1, 1972–September 30, 1972," box 106A, MCA.

57. "Application to the Department of Housing and Urban Development for a Grant to Plan a Comprehensive City Demonstration Program, 27 April 1967," box 117A, MCA.

58. Professional Services Contract — La Alianza, undated, box 120B, MCA.

59. "Boston Model Neighborhood Board," 1972, box 113B, MCA.

60. Department of Housing and Urban Development, *A Policies and Procedures Manual for a Local Model Cities Program*, Model Cities Management Series Bulletin No. 5 (Washington, DC: Government Printing Office, 1971).

61. As examples, William Braucher, memo to Bertram Walker, October 1, 1974, box 62B, MCA; John A. Bulliner to Iris Thompson, February 16, 1972, box 146A, MCA; Ann E. Stokes, memo to Executive Committee, February 27, 1975, box 62B, MCA.

62. See box 92A, MCA.

63. For a complete list, see "Contract Status List, October 1970."

64. See Boston Model Neighborhood Board: Quarterly Statistical Summary, 1972, box 12B, MCA.

65. Professional Services Contract — La Alianza.

66. Paul Parks to Commissioner Joseph E. Curtis, April 26, 1973, box 151A, MCA.

67. "Community Development Evaluation Series No. 10: The Federal Grant Process — An Analysis of the Use of Supplemental and Categorical Funds in the Model Cities Program," US Department of Housing and Urban Development, August 1972.

68. James Jennings, "Urban Machinism and the Black Voter: The Kevin White Years," in *From Access to Power: Black Politics in Boston*, ed. James Jennings and Mel King (Cambridge, MA: Schenkman Books, 1986), 81.

69. Hinton notes that by 1968, "the carceral state had already begun to metastasize" to include social programs thanks to legislation in 1965. Elizabeth Hinton, "'A War within Our Own Boundaries': Lyndon Johnson's Great Society and the Rise of the Carceral State, *Journal of American History* 102, no. 1 (June 2015): 102. See also Hinton, *From the War on Poverty*; Kohler-Hausman, *Getting Tough*.

70. As quoted in Flamm, *Law and Order: Street Crime, Civil Unrest, and the Crisis of Liberalism in the 1960s* (New York: Columbia University Press, 2007), 42.

71. Flamm, *Law and Order*, 51–52.

72. "The Overshadowing Issue," *Time*, August 2, 1968.

73. Nancy E. Marion, *A History of Federal Crime Control Initiatives* (Westport, CT: Praeger, 1994), 240.

74. In 1975 the Mayor's Safe Streets Act Advisory Committee reorganized and renamed itself the Mayor's Office of Criminal Justice (MOCJ). The records of both agencies were consolidated at the Boston City Archives into the MOCJ collection, which was unprocessed at the time of my research in 2013.

75. Matthew Storin, "U.S. Grants State $5.4 Million to Aid Local Crime Fighting," *Boston Globe*, January 19, 1970; Matthew Storin, "$9.4m Slated to Help State

Fight Crime," *Boston Globe*, November 11, 1970; "U.S. to Spend $18 M for Mass. Crime War," *Boston Globe*, July 15, 1971.

76. The mayor's office oversaw only 3 percent of the city's law enforcement budget and therefore held much less sway over municipal agencies whose diversified funding streams insulated against change. "Functions of the Agency," box 3, Mayor's Office of Criminal Justice records (hereafter MOCJ), BCA; "Introduction," Criminal Justice Development Agency, Grant Award Documents, 1974, box 5, MOCJ.

77. Lawyers Committee for Civil Rights under Law, "Law and Disorder III: State and Federal Performance under Title I of the Omnibus Crime Control and Safe Streets Act of 1968," 75, in Hearing Before the Subcommittee on Criminal Laws and Procedures of the Committee of the Judiciary (US Senate), June 5 and 6, 1973; Donald B. Manson to Robert Kane, September 2, 1975, box 14, MOCJ.

78. Mike Grace, memo to Don McGowan, May 26, 1976, box 14, MOCJ.

79. "The Planning Process," ca. 1975–76, box 14, MOCJ.

80. "Statement of Strategy for 1976," submitted to Massachusetts Committee on Criminal Justice, May 9, 1975, box 14, MOCJ.

81. "The Planning Process"; Donald B. Manson to Robert Kane.

82. Donald B. Manson to Robert Kane.

83. Donald B. Manson to Robert Kane.

84. "Crime: What to Do about It?" *Bay State Banner*, June 4, 1970.

85. "Sav-More Security Program: Attitudinal Study," 1971, box 6, MOCJ; "Text of Kenneth I. Guscott's Statement," Press Conference Minority Police Recruitment, September 1, 1972, box 2, MOCJ.

86. "Statement of Strategy for 1976," May 9, 1975, box 14, MOCJ.

87. Annual Report of Sav-More Community Security Program, December 1972–73, box 4, MOCJ.

88. South End Security Program, box 3, MOCJ.

89. "Crime Fighting the Neighborly Way, or (How to Stay Ahead of the Rip-Off Artist)," undated, box 6, MOCJ.

90. "Blacks Recommend Changes to DiGrazia," *Bay State Banner*, February 1, 1973; "Statement of Strategy for 1976."

91. "High Crime Security Area—Bromley Heath Community Patrol Subgrantee Quarterly Report, January–March 1973," August 1973, box 2, MOJC; "Interim Report Bromley Heath Community Patrol," undated, box 2, MOCJ; "Narrative," September 1974, box 5, MOCJ.

92. See Bromley Heath Community Security Grantee Reports, box 4, MOCJ.

93. "Boston Public Housing Security Program," July 16, 1974, box 9, MOCJ.

94. "The Planning Process."

95. Donald B. Mason to Robert Kane.

96. Linda Katz to Floyd Cully, November 22, 1976, box 15, MOCJ.

97. "Commodity Receipt," SNAP Security Program, box 3, MOCJ; "Work Plan," January–June 1974, box 3, MOCJ; Linda Weiss, memo to Walter Jabzanka,

August 28, 1973, box 3, MOCJ; Linda Weiss to William Shabazz, August 28, 1973, box 3, MOCJ.

98. R. A. Whittington to William Shabazz, September 20, 1973, box 3, MOCJ.

99. National Advisory Commission on Criminal Justice Standards and Goals, *Community Crime Prevention* (Washington, DC: US Government Printing Office, 1973); "Boston Public Housing Security Program."

100. Anne Kirchheimer, "Crime Fight Won, Their Funds Run Out," *Boston Globe*, December 31, 1975; Anne Kirchheimer, "Bromley Heath Patrol Gets HUD Grant," *Boston Globe*, February 13, 1976; Anne Kirchheimer, "Bromley Patrols Near End," *Boston Globe*, October 1, 1976.

101. Annual Report of Sav-More Community Security Program.

102. Robert J. Kane, memo, August 21, 1975, box 14, MOCJ.

103. "The Planning Process."

104. "A Call for Leadership," *Boston Globe*, June 26, 1976.

105. State Senator Bill Owens quoted in Nyhan, "Kevin White Is Now Dean"; Hubert E. Jones, "Introduction" in Jennings and King, *From Access to Power*, 4.

106. Tess Bundy, "'Revolutions Happen through Young People!': The Black Student Movement in the Boston Public Schools, 1968–1971," *Journal of Urban History* 43, no. 2 (2017): 273–93.

107. Jeremy Wolff, "A Timeline of Boston School Desegregation, 1961–1985," Civil Rights and Restorative Justice Project, Northeastern University School of Law.

108. As examples, "Woman Burned to Death by Assailants in Roxbury," *Boston Globe*, October 4, 1973; "Man Stoned, Dies; Two Injured as Violence Hits Columbia Pt.," *Boston Globe*, October 5, 1973; Ken Hartnett and Bob Sales, "Anger and Fear—A Bomb Boston Must Defuse," *Boston Globe*, October 7, 1973; Al Larkin, "Hub Community Leaders Move to Ease Tensions, "*Boston Globe*, October 7, 1973; Nils Bruzelius, "Boston Cab Driver's Body Found in Roxbury," *Boston Globe*, October 7, 1973.

109. Boston High School Crisis Response Program, LEAA Application, June 24, 1971, box 3, MOCJ.

110. Revised Work Plan, "Boston High School Crisis Response Program," box 3, MOCJ.

111. Draft, "School Crisis Prevention and Response: Outline of an LEAA grant proposal," 1973, box 20, folder 66, Collection M130: Citywide Educational Coalition records (hereafter CEC), NU.

112. Edward W. Brooke, telegram to Donald E. Santarelli, July 12, 1974, box 12, MOCJ.

113. Roxbury Community Crime Prevention Program, Quarterly Report, April–June 1976, box 15, MOCJ.

114. Dee Prim, memo to Joe Tasby, November 1, 1973, box 6, MOCJ.

115. Annual Report of Sav-More Community Security Program.

116. Annual Report of Sav-More Community Security Program.

117. Ron Hutson and Katherine Kennedy, "School Desegregation in Boston and the Emerging Black Leadership," *Boston Globe*, November 17, 1974; Marvin Pave, "Jamaica Plain Marches against Violence," *Boston Globe*, October 21, 1974; Ken Boatwright, "Hyde Park Working for Peaceful School Year," *Boston Globe*, August 24, 1975.

118. Hutson and Kennedy, "School Desegregation in Boston."

119. "History and Future of the City-Wide Educational Coalition," undated, box 6, folder 13, CEC.

120. Annual Report of Sav-More Community Security Program; Daily Log, October 3, box 22, folder "Daily Incident Logs," Kevin H. White Mayoral Records, BCA; Roxbury Community Crime Prevention Program, Quarterly Report, April–June 1976, box 15, MOCJ; Ken O. Botwright, "All-Black Police Unit Opposed," *Boston Globe*, November 20, 1971.

121. Daily Log, September 20, 1974, box 22, folder "Daily Incident Logs," Kevin H. White Mayoral Records.

122. Daily Log, September 16, 1974, box 22, folder "Daily Incident Logs," Kevin H. White Mayoral Records.

123. Sav-More Community Security Program, Quarterly Report, January–March 1975, box 11, MOCJ.

124. "Key Witness in Pratt Murder Trial Surrenders to Boston Policemen," *Boston Globe*, September 21, 1973.

125. Daily Log, September 21, 1974; D-Street Community Development Program, Program Report July 1973–September 1974, box 4, MOCJ.

126. D-Street Community Development Program, Program Report.

127. D-Street Community Development Program, Program Report.

128. See letters in box 5, folder 42, CEC.

129. Emphasis in original. Request for a Planning and Development Grant, box 5, folder 60, CEC.

130. Request for a Planning and Development Grant.

131. Nyhan, "Kevin White Is Now Dean."

132. As quoted in Nyhan, "Kevin White Is Now Dean."

133. As quoted in Nyhan, "Kevin White Is Now Dean."

134. Richard Nixon, "Special Message to the Congress on Special Revenue Sharing for Urban Community Development," March 5, 1971, online at Gerhard Peters and John T. Woolley, *The American Presidency Project*, http://www.presidency.ucsb.edu/ws/?pid=3339.

135. Nixon, "Special Message to the Congress."

136. Gerald R. Ford, "Remarks on Signing the Housing and Community Development Act of 1974," August 22, 1974, online at Peters and Woolley, *The American Presidency Project*, http://www.presidency.ucsb.edu/ws/?pid=4620.

137. Paul R. Dommel et al., *Decentralizing Community Development* (Washington, DC: Brookings Institution for the Department of Housing and Urban Development, 1978).

138. The President's Task Force on Model Cities, *Model Cities: A Step Towards the New Federalism* (Washington, DC: Government Printing Office, August 1970); John Herbers, "Nixon Endorses Model Cities Aid with Local Rule," *New York Times*, September 11, 1970; John Herbers, "Nixon Drops Plan to Cut Off Funds for Model Cities," *New York Times*, February 28, 1971.

139. Statement of Amy Totenberg, Education/Instruction, Hearings Before the Committee on Banking, Housing and Urban Affairs, US Senate, 94th Cong., 2nd Sess., Oversight on the Administration of the Housing and Community Development Act of 1974, August 23–26, 1976, 323.

140. Mayor's Office of Public Service, "Departmental Descriptions, City of Boston, Kevin White, Mayor," Spring 1976, BRA 4067, GD, 46.

141. Community Planning and Development, Office of Evaluation, "Citizen Participation: Experience and Trends in Community Development Block Grant Entitlement Communities," US Department of Housing and Urban Development, 1977; Richard P. Nathan et al., *Block Grants for Community Development* (Washington, DC: Brookings Institution for the Department of Housing and Urban Development, 1977), 483.

142. Christopher B. Carlaw, "The 1977 Community Development Block Grant Program for the City of Boston, by Program and by Neighborhood," April 1977, BRA 3522, GD; CDBG, Grantee Performance Report IV: 1975–1979, BRA 3421, GD.

143. Jennings, "Urban Machinism," 70.

144. Nathan et al., *Block Grants for Community Development*, 498.

145. Carlaw, "The 1977 Community Development Block Grant Program."

146. Jennings, "Urban Machinism," 57.

147. Kim Phillips-Fein, *Fear City: New York's Fiscal Crisis and the Rise of Austerity Politics* (New York: Metropolitan Books, 2017).

148. CDBG, Grantee Performance Report IV.

149. Jennings notes that even with the limitations of a mayor's power, "the *structural* position of the mayor's office can give the occupant opportunities to initiate political decisions that begin to favor the interests of the powerless." Jennings, "Urban Machinism," 59.

150. Jennings, "Urban Machinism," 81–82.

151. Sugrue, "Carter's Urban Policy Crisis," 144–45.

Chapter 5

1. Robert Chandler, memo to File, August 30, 1972, Reel 1444, Greater Boston Community Development Grant 700636 (hereafter GBCD), FF.

2. Meeting minutes, written in English, note an effort to be more welcoming to Spanish-speaking residents. Emergency Tenants' Council Development Council, Minutes, May 28 1970, box 15, folder 64, IBA.

3. Robert B. Whittlesey, *Social Housing Found* (self-pub., Toplink, 2018), chap. 1.

4. Whittlesey, *Social Housing Found*, 87–90; Robert Whittlesey, *The South End Row House and Its Rehabilitation for Low-Income Residents*, Report on Low-Income Housing Demonstration Project (Mass LIHD-3) (Boston: South End Community Development, 1969), 9–11; R. Allen Hays, *The Federal Government and Urban Housing: Ideology and Change in Public Policy* (Albany: State University of New York Press, 1995), 101–3. On the role of nonprofits in housing development, see Alexander Von Hoffman, *House by House, Block by Block: The Rebirth of America's Urban Neighborhoods* (New York: Oxford University Press, 2003), and Avis C. Vidal, "Housing and Community Development," in *The State of Nonprofit America*, 2nd ed., ed. Lester M. Salamon (Washington, DC: Brookings Institution Press, 2012), 266–93.

5. Whittlesey, *Social Housing Found*, 125; "A Proposal to the Ford Foundation in Request of Funding for a Three-Year Period for Greater Boston Community Housing, Inc.," March 30, 1970, Reel 1444, GBCD, FF.

6. Greater Boston Community Development, "An Interim Report and Proposal for the Second and Third Years' Operations and Funding," Reel 1444, GBCD, FF, 15–16.

7. Mitchell Sviridoff, memo to McGeorge Bundy, September 11, 1970, Reel 1444, GBCD, FF.

8. Whittlesey, *Social Housing Found*, 126.

9. Though focused on Cleveland, Michael McQuarrie similarly points to "institutional innovations" in community development as central to emergent patterns of urban governance in the 1970s and 1980s. McQuarrie, "Nonprofits and the Reconstruction of Urban Governance."

10. Harvey Molotch, "The City as a Growth Machine: Toward a Political Economy of Place," *American Journal of Sociology* 82, no. 2 (September 1976): 309–32; John R. Logan and Harvey L. Molotch, *Urban Fortunes: The Political Economy of Place* (Berkeley: University of California Press, 1987).

11. Nonprofits had been involved in housing production and management for decades, as churches and labor unions in particular sought to provide basic and affordable shelter for those in need. On the European origins of these housing cooperative models, see Daniel T. Rodgers, *Atlantic Crossings: Social Politics in a Progressive Age* (Cambridge, MA: Harvard University Press, 1998), 191, 467, 475–77; Robert E. Tolles, *A Decent Place to Live* (New York: Ford Foundation, 1971).

12. "Limited Dividend Sponsorship," April 13, 1970, box 17, folder 85, IBA; ETC Rehabilitation Contract for a Limited Dividend Venture, December 29, 1970, box 17, folder 85, IBA; William Waldrom, memo prepared for ETC Development Corporation Board, April 20, 1970, box 15, folder 64, IBA.

13. Lawrence J. Vale has told the story of public housing in Boston several times; see *From the Puritans to the Projects*, *Reclaiming Public Housing*, and *After*

the Projects. Though not about Boston, Rhonda Williams's work remains essential. See Williams, *The Politics of Public Housing.*

14. "List of Legislation for '72–'73," box 2, folder 28, RR.

15. Mel King and Samantha George, "The Future of Community: From Local to Global," in *Beyond the Market and the State: New Directions in Community Development,* ed. Severyn T. Bruyn and James Meehan (Philadelphia: Temple University Press, 1987), 220.

16. King helped build this coalition from his Wednesday Morning Breakfast Group, which functioned as his policy shop to debate ideas, draft legislation, and connect people with backgrounds in research, activism, and planning. The group included economists and urban planners from MIT and representatives from the federally funded research group, the Center for Community Economic Development. On the anti-highway movement in Boston, see Crockett, *People before Highways.*

17. Mitchell Sviridoff, memo to McGeorge Bundy. See also Robert Powell Sangster to Langley Keyes, August 6, 1973, Reel 1444, GBCD, FF.

18. Lewis S. W. Crampton to Bob Whittlesley, August 10, 1973, Reel 1444, GBCD, FF.

19. Ronald F. Ferguson and Helen F. Ladd, "Massachusetts," in *The New Economic Role of American States: Strategies in a Competitive World Economy,* ed. R. Scott Fosler (New York: Oxford University Press, 1988), 34.

20. Massachusetts Executive Department, "An Economic Development Program for Massachusetts," August 1976, 6; emphasis in original.

21. Michael Dukakis and Rosabeth Moss Kanter, *Creating the Future: The Massachusetts Comeback and Its Promise for America* (New York: Summit Books, 1988), 47. Lily Geismer details Dukakis's interest in investment, a knowledge economy, and the local technology industry. See Geismer, *Don't Blame Us,* esp. chap. 10.

22. Ferguson and Ladd, "Massachusetts," 37–38; Pierre Clavel, *Activists in City Hall: The Progressive Response to the Reagan Era in Boston and Chicago* (Ithaca, NY: Cornell University Press, 2010), 40–41; King, *Chain of Change,* 202.

23. Chapter 40F, "An Act Creating the Massachusetts Community Development Finance Corporation," Massachusetts General Court, Senate No. 1604, Section 2, 1975.

24. Though authorized in 1975, the CDFC had not yet received its authorized financing from a $10 million state bond by early 1976. The initial legislation required a separate bill to issue the state bond, which got held up for over a year. Jonathan Fuerbringer, "The State and the Capital Supply," *Boston Globe,* March 26, 1977.

25. S. Donald Gonson, "CDFC a State Agency," letter to the editor, *Boston Globe,* April 30, 1979; Chapter 40H, "An Act Establishing the Community Economic Development Assistance Corporation," Massachusetts General Court, Chapter 498, Section 1, 1978.

26. Massachusetts Executive Office of Communities and Development, "The Community Enterprise Economic Development Program," August 1984.

27. Karl Seidman, "A New Role for Government: Supporting a Democratic Economy," in Bruyn and Meehan, *Beyond the Market and the State*, 202.

28. Rebecca K. Marchiel, *After Redlining: The Urban Reinvestment Movement in the Era of Financial Deregulation* (Chicago: University of Chicago Press, 2020), 124.

29. Greater Boston Community Development, "The Annual Report," November 1971, Reel 1444, GBCD, FF.

30. In 1983 LISC added a program for rural CDCs. Local Initiatives Support Corporation, "A Review of LISC Program Activities, June 1980–December 1982," Grant 08000010, Reel 5487, Frames 2100-1, FF.

31. Geoffrey Faux, *CDCs: New Hope for the Inner City*, Report of the Twentieth Century Fund Task Force on Community Development Corporations (New York: Twentieth Century Fund, 1971), 4.

32. Grant Action, July 28, 1971, LISC, Grant 07190480, Reel 4979, Frame 1934, FF.

33. "Program Action, No: 719-480," LISC, Grant 07190480, Reel 4979, Frame 1855, FF; Rachel Wimpee, "The Economics of Empowerment: The Civil Rights Origins of Program-Related Investments" (working paper, University of Southern California Conference on Philanthropy and Public Policy, March 14–16, 2019). The extent to which this program targeted minority neighborhoods is uncertain. See Ferguson, *Top Down*. Also, Hill and Rabig, *The Business of Black Power*.

34. Tolles, *A Decent Place to Live*. See Taylor, *Race for Profit*, on why these seeming failures of the state and market were, in fact, by design.

35. Tolles, *A Decent Place to Live*.

36. On field building in philanthropy, see Paul Brest and Hal Harvey, *Money Well Spent: A Strategic Plan for Smart Philanthropy*, 2nd ed. (Stanford, CA: Stanford University Press, 2018), 235–37.

37. Tolles, *A Decent Place to Live*.

38. Patricia Rosenfield and Rachel Wimpee, "The Ford Foundation: Constant Themes, Historical Variations," (Sleepy Hollow, NY: Rockefeller Archive Center, 2015), 15; Alice O'Connor, "Bringing the Market Back In: Philanthropic Activism and Conservative Reform," in Clemens and Guthrie, *Politics and Partnerships*, 122–25.

39. Rosenfield and Wimpee, "The Ford Foundation."

40. LISC: Boston Annual Report, December 1982, Grant 08000010, Reel 5488, Frames 847-865, FF.

41. Recommendation for Grant Action, May 17, 1984, LISC, Grant 08000010, Reel 5488, Frame 2277, FF.

42. Local Initiatives Support Corporation, "Operating Guidelines for Programs of the Local Initiatives Support Corporation," Grant 08000010, Reel 5488, Frame 1093, FF; LISC: Boston Annual Report, December 1982.

43. Local Initiatives Support Corporation, "Operating Guidelines."

44. Local Initiatives Support Corporation, "A Statement of Policy for the Programs of the Local Initiatives Support Corporation," March 12, 1981, Grant 08000010, Reel 5488, Frame 1090, FF.

45. Local Initiatives Support Corporation, "A Statement of Policy."

46. Local Initiatives Support Corporation, Memorandum: Evaluation Plan for LISC, January 3, 1983, Grant 08000010 Reel 5487, Frame 02205, FF.

47. Other top-ranking destinations for LISC funds were California, Chicago, and the South Bronx. This mix of states, cities, and neighborhoods as designated areas of concentration make comparisons between areas difficult.

48. Local Initiatives Support Corporation, "Status of Donor Funds, December 31, 1983," Grant 08000010, Reel 5487, FF.

49. In comparison to other areas of concentration, Boston ranked third for LISC support, outpaced only by California and Chicago. Local Initiatives Support Corporation, "Summary of Approved Program Actions," December 31, 1984, Grant 08000010, Reel 5488, Frame 12, FF.

50. Seidman et al., "From Urban Renewal to Affordable Housing Production System: Boston Mayors and the Evolution of Community Development Corporations in Boston," April 2016, Community Innovators Lab, MIT Department of Urban Studies and Planning, 12–14.

51. Local Initiatives Support Corporation, "A Statement of Policy."

52. Community Development Finance Corporation, "CDFC Handbook," undated, likely 1978, Mass.CFI.2i; C73, UMass Library, 1; Rachel G. Bratt, *Rebuilding a Low-Income Housing Policy* (Philadelphia: Temple University Press, 1989), 269.

53. Community Development Finance Corporation, "CDFC Handbook," 1, 6.

54. Kirk Scharfenberg, "Bottom Line: Public Benefit," *Boston Globe*, April 5, 1980.

55. In Community Development Finance Corporation, "Third Annual Report," October 1980, GD, Library at the University of Massachusetts at Amherst (hereafter UMA).

56. "Chairman's Letter," in Community Development Finance Corporation, "Third Annual Report," 1.

57. Cheryl Devall, "Codman Sq. Residents, Friends Proudly Open 'Our Market,'" *Bay State Banner*, May 31, 1979.

58. "Our Market: The Wrong Assumptions Led to Failure," *Boston Globe*, September 18, 1983.

59. Community Development Finance Corporation, "Third Annual Report," 1. Also, Community Development Finance Corporation, "CDFC Handbook," 1. Governor Dukakis's successor, Edward King, had little interest in community development, letting several board seats on CEDAC and CDFC remain vacant and effectively halting grantmaking and technical assistance. Advocates then founded

the first statewide association of CDCs in 1982 to lobby for the reallocations of funding. The organization, the Massachusetts Association of Community Development Corporations, benefited from Dukakis's reelection in 1982. Scharfenberg, "Bottom Line." Massachusetts Association of Community Development Corporations, "CDCs: Making the Difference in Your Community," undated, BRA 5001, BPL.

60. "Our Market: The Wrong Assumptions."

61. Nancy Nye, "Six Years Later: The Experience of the Massachusetts CDFC," *Entrepreneurial Economy* 2, no. 9 (March 1984): 12.

62. Local Initiatives Support Corporation, "Summary of Approved Program Actions."

63. Local Initiatives Support Corporation, "Summary of Approved Program Actions."

64. Norbone Berkeley Jr. to Isaacson, Ford, Webb, & Miller, March 1, 1985, LISC Grant 08000010, Reel 5488, Frame 1398, FF.

65. Local Initiatives Support Corporation, "Status Report or Program Actions Approved by LISC," August 15, 1983, Grant 08000010, Reel 5487, Frame 01942, FF.

66. Local Initiatives Support Corporation, Loan Portfolio as of November 30, 1982, Grant 08000010, Reel 5487, Frame 2161–93, FF. LISC staff only lent below 7 percent interest "in extraordinary cases." Local Initiatives Support Corporation, Portfolio Analysis, Grant 08000010, Reel 5487, Frame 2161–93, FF. By 1985, the percentage of funds on housing development loans increased to 66 percent. Local Initiatives Support Corporation, "Summary Fact Sheet for the Period June 1, 1980–June 30-1985," Grant 08000010, Reel 5487, Frame 2457–59, FF.

67. Local Initiatives Support Corporation, Program Portfolio Analysis, Grant 08000010, Reel 5487, Frame 2165, FF.

68. Local Initiatives Support Corporation, Program Portfolio Analysis.

69. Local Initiatives Support Corporation, "Summary Fact Sheet."

70. Norbone Berkeley Jr. to Isaacson, Ford, Webb, & Miller.

71. Norbone Berkeley Jr. to Isaacson, Ford, Webb, & Miller.

72. LISC: Boston Annual Report, December 1982; Recommendation for Grant Action, August 14, 1986, Grant 08000010, Reel 5487, Frame 2246–64, FF.

73. Robert D. Lilley, "The LISC Public-Private Partnership," *Response by the Center for Corporate Public Involvement*, 12 no. 3 (May 1983), Grant 08000010, Reel 5488, Frame 570, FF.

74. Logan and Molotch, *Urban Fortunes*, 1.

75. Total Studio Report, MIT, "From the Ground Up: A Strategy for the Dudley Street Neighborhood," (1981), box 2, folder 8, Collection M55: La Alianza Hispana Papers (hereafter LAH), NU.

76. In each of its projects, LISC sought to leverage private and public-sector funds by using its monies to fill critical gaps. As a result, LISC materials regularly boasted high leverage ratios, noting that the ratio of outside investments to LISC

investments in LISC-sponsored housing construction topped forty-three-to-one, and rehab projects at seventeen-to-one in 1982. Local Initiatives Support Corporation, "LISC Investments Compared with Total Project Costs as of 11/30/82," Grant 08000010, Reel 5487, Frame 2174, FF, RAC.

77. On cities as at the forefront of a neoliberal policy agenda, see Dávila, *Barrio Dreams*; Weaver, *Blazing the Neoliberal Trail*; Andrew J. Diamond, *Chicago on the Make* (Berkeley: University of California Press, 2020); Andrew W. Kahrl, "The Short End of Both Sticks: Property Assessments and Black Taxpayer Disadvantage in Urban America," in Cebul, Geismer, and Williams, *Shaped by the State*, 189–217; and Diamond and Sugrue, *Neoliberal Cities*.

78. "Neighborhood Improvement Program for the City of Boston, 1975," January 27, 1974, BRA 2316, BPL.

79. Notably, the city employed this strategy only for funding low-income neighborhoods, preferring direct aid mechanisms to homeowners or investments in public infrastructure such as sidewalks, lighting, and security in neighborhoods such as Beacon Hill, where "the housing stock is basically sound and the real estate market is healthy." Office of Program Development, "Neighborhood Improvement Program, 1978–1979," BRA 2316 1978/79, BPL.

80. "Neighborhood Improvement Program." On the changing nature of Democratic politics, especially in Massachusetts, see Geismer, *Don't Blame Us*.

81. In a 125-page report, the word *stabilize* or *stability* appears eighteen times, and the word *confidence* appears twenty-five times. See, as examples, 2–5, 7–8. Office of Program Development, "Neighborhood Improvement Program."

82. Geismer, *Don't Blame Us*, chap. 10.

83. Norman Krumholz and Pierre Clavel, *Reinventing Cities: Equity Planners Tell Their Stories* (Philadelphia, PA: Temple University Press, 1994), 131.

84. Krumholz and Clavel, *Reinventing Cities*, 132.

85. Between 1980 and 1983, around nine thousand rental units in Boston were converted into condominiums, of which 60 percent were outside the downtown area. Thomas F. McCormack, "The Implementation of the Boston Housing Partnership" (master's thesis, Department of Urban Studies and Planning, Massachusetts Institute of Technology, 1985), 7–8; Boston Housing Partnership, "The Boston Housing Partnership, Inc. Program Summary, 1983–1985," BRA 4611, BPL.

86. Joseph Slavet, "Housing Issues in Boston: Guidelines for New Policy and Program Perspectives" (condensed version of a working paper prepared for the Boston Committee, Inc., Boston Urban Observatory, March 1983), 36–38.

87. Seidman et al., "From Urban Renewal," 25.

88. Peter Medoff and Holly Sklar, *Streets of Hope: The Fall and Rise of an Urban Neighborhood* (Boston: South End Press, 1994), 11–12.

89. Medoff and Sklar, *Streets of Hope*, 3.

90. James P. Brady, "Behind the Burning of Boston," *Boston Globe*, October 23, 1983; Michael K. Frisby, "Arson Report Cites Two Hub Areas," *Boston*

Globe, March 12, 1986. See also Dylan Gottlieb, "Hoboken Is Burning: Yuppies, Arson, and the Postindustrial City," *Journal of American History* 106, no. 2 (September 2019): 390–416.

91. Quoted in Medoff and Sklar, *Streets of Hope*, 2.

92. Directors Report, March 10, 1981, box 3, folder 32, LAH; Housing Survey, May 1, 1981, box 4, folder 25, LAH.

93. Housing Survey, May 1, 1981.

94. Proposal for Section 8 Assisted Moderate Rehabilitation by Alianza Hispana submitted to BHA, July 10, 1981, box 4, folder 26, LAH.

95. Proposal for Section 8 Assisted Moderate Rehabilitation.

96. Director's Report, January 14, 1981, box 3, folder 32, LAH.

97. Nelson Merced, "La Alianza Hispana, Inc. 1984 Annual Report," March 1985, box 2, folder 11, LAH.

98. Director's Report, January 14, 1981.

99. Director's Report, November 12, 1981, box 2, folder 6, LAH.

100. Seidman et al., "From Urban Renewal," 18–19; McQuarrie, "Nonprofits and the Reconstruction of Urban Governance," 245; Goldstein, *Roots of Urban Renaissance*, 138.

101. Joseph Ornsteen and Alianza Hispana, Purchase and Sale Agreement, 1981, box 4, folder 25, LAH.

102. Bob Engler, memo to Alianza Hispana, Inc., May 21, 1982, box 4, folder 25, LAH.

103. Thomas Block to Nelson Merced, February 17, 1982, box 4, folder 26, LAH.

104. Proposal for Section 8 Assisted Moderate Rehabilitation by Alianza Hispana.

105. Minutes, November 12, 1981, box 2, folder 6, LAH; Paul Tsongas to Margery Luening, October 5, 1982, box 4, folder 28, LAH; John Sullivan to Nelson Merced, June 16, 1982, box 4, folder 26, LAH; Sandra Rosenblith to Nelson Merced, May 17, 1984, box 4, folder 33, LAH.

106. Thomas Block to Mark Breen, December 13, 1983, box 4, folder 31, LAH.

107. The package GBCD put forward also included buildings being renovated by CDCs in Codman and Egleston Squares. Massachusetts Moderate Rehabilitation Project, "Project Summary," November 8, 1982, box 4, folder 27, LAH.

108. Richard A. Marks to Melvyn Colon and Arne Abramson, September 6, 1984, box 5, folder 1, LAH.

109. Executive Office of Communities and Development, "The Community Enterprise Economic Development Program: A Survey of CEED Funded CDC Activities 1979–1983," August 1984, GD, UMA; Massachusetts Community Development Finance Corporation, "Annual Report," 1983, GD, UMA.

110. Goldstein, *The Roots of Urban Renaissance*, esp. chap. 5; Gottlieb, "Hoboken Is Burning," 399–400; Marchiel, *After Redlining*.

111. Not all of it was designated as affordable housing, nor are there proper estimates for how many units would have been built in the absence of the mechanisms developed from the mid-1970s to the mid-1980s. Seidman et al., "From Urban Renewal," 34.

112. On the tensions and transformation of the Democratic Party, see Geismer, *Don't Blame Us*; Timothy J. Lombardo, *Blue-Collar Conservatism: Frank Rizzo's Philadelphia and Populist Politics* (Philadelphia: University of Pennsylvania Press, 2018).

113. King, *Chain of Change*.

114. Mel King for Mayor, "News Release: King Campaign Launches 'Rainbow' Offensive," October 29, 1983, box 2, folder 34, RR; Mel King for Mayor pamphlet, box 2, folder 29, RR; Melvin H. King to Michael Liu, August 1, 1983, box 1, folder 37, Collection M163: Chinese Progressive Association records (hereafter CPA), NU.

115. Seidman et al., "From Urban Renewal," 21–22.

116. Boston Redevelopment Authority, "Fact Book," 1982, BRA 3756, BPL.

117. "Boston's Neighborhood Development and Employment Agency," undated, BRA 3812, BPL.

118. Boston Foundation, "There at the Beginning," 2004, Gov Doc. X1 BOF04/1, BPL.

119. Godfrey M. Hyams Trust, press release, July 31, 1985, Grant 08000010, Reel 5488, Frame 102, FF.

120. For a concise summary of the LIHTC, see Alex F. Schwartz, *Housing Policy in the United States*, 2nd ed. (New York: Routledge, 2006), 103–24.

121. McQuarrie, "Nonprofits and the Reconstruction of Urban Governance;" Sarah Snyder, "Tax Credits Turn Low-Income Housing into Moneymaker," *Boston Globe*, January 17, 1988.

122. Neal R. Peirce and Carol F. Steinbach, *Enterprising Communities: Community-Based Development in America, 1990* (Washington, DC: Council for Community-Based Development, 1990), 35.

123. Massachusetts Association of Community Development Corporations, "The Impact of Tax Reform on Community-Based Development: A One Day Conference," BRA 5127, BPL.

124. Peirce and Steinbach, *Enterprising Communities*, 32; Whittlesey, *Social Housing Found*, 243–45.

125. "Paul S. Grogan" Recommendation for Grant Action, August 14, 1986, Grant 08000010, Reel 5487, Frame 02270–72, FF.

126. Paul Grogan to Barron Tenny, January 25, 1988, LISC, Grant 08000010, Reel 5487, Frame 2414, FF.

127. Dukakis and Kanter, *Creating the Future*, 171.

128. As quoted in Alexander Reid, "A 19-Year Struggle Succeeds: South End 'Tent City' Housing Project Nears Completion," *Boston Globe*, July 21, 1987.

129. Edward Quill, "Copley Place Plan Protested," *Boston Globe*, November 20, 1979; Boston Redevelopment Authority, "Copley Place: Urban Development Action Grant Application," April 1980, BRA 4811, BPL; Kirk Scharfenberg, "Prosperity: Who Profits?," *Boston Globe*, February 9, 1980; Jane Adams, "Hosing, Not Parking, Say S. End Protestors," *Boston Globe*, April 29, 1981.

130. Boston Redevelopment Authority, "Tent City: A Development Proposal for Parcels 11A and 11B," Urban Development Action Grant Application, November 30, 1984, BRA 2626, BPL; Elizabeth Siefel, memo to Robert Embry, October 24, 1980, box 28, folder: Copley Place, Collection 60: South End Project Area Committee Records, UMass; "Tent City: A Development Plan Emerges," box 28, folder: Tent City, South End Project Area Committee Records.

131. Boston Redevelopment Authority, "Tent City: A Development Proposal for Parcels 11A and 11B," 5.

132. Alexander Reid, "Applications to Be Taken for Tent City," *Boston Globe*, August 9, 1987; Patricia Wen, "Many Applicants Said to Find Tent City Too Expensive," *Boston Globe*, July 15, 1987.

133. Doris Sue Wong, "2,000 Show for Affordable Housing: Tent City Project Offering 203 Units," *Boston Globe*, August 14, 1987.

134. For a discussion of this critique, see Peirce and Steinbach, *Enterprising Communities*, 22. Goldstein notes ideological changes about economic integration as at times aligning with these financing pressures. Goldstein, *Roots of Urban Renaissance*, 226–27.

135. Avis C. Vidal, *Rebuilding Communities: A National Study of Urban Community Development Corporations* (New York: Community Development Research Center, New School for Social Research, 1992), 118.

136. Housing development won more financial support for CDCs across all sources of potential funding: local government, foundations, banks, and corporate lenders. Vidal, *Rebuilding Communities*, 117–18.

137. Snyder, "Tax Credits Turn Low-Income Housing."

Chapter 6

1. Boston Persistent Poverty Project (hereafter BPPP), *In the Midst of Plenty: A Profile of Boston and Its Poor*, Boston Foundation, December 1989, X1/BOF/89/1, BPL, 9.

2. Though he often attributed the phrase to President John F. Kennedy, Reagan used it as a justification for his own supply-side economic agenda. For example, Ronald Reagan, "Remarks in Denver, Colorado, at the Annual Convention of the National Association for the Advancement of Colored People," June 29, 1981, accessed online December 2020, *The American Presidency Project*, https://www.presidency.ucsb.edu/node/247463.

3. On the long 1980s as a period of urban crisis, see Daniel T. Rodgers, *Age of Fracture* (Cambridge, MA: Harvard University Press, 2011); Kimberly Phillips-Fein, *Fear City: New York's Fiscal Crisis and the Rise of the Age of Austerity* (New York: Metropolitan Books, 2017); Holtzman, *The Long Crisis*.

4. Helen Ladd and Julie Boatright Wilson, *Proposition 2½: Explaining the Vote*, Research Report R81-1, Kennedy School of Government Urban Planning Policy Analysis and Administration, Harvard University, April 1981; Helen Ladd and Julie Boatright Wilson, "Tax Limitations in Massachusetts" (working paper prepared for the National Institute of Education, Kennedy School of Government, Harvard University, January 1982). Also, Lawrence Susskind, ed., *Proposition 2½: Its Impact on Massachusetts* (Cambridge, MA: Oelgeschlager, Gunn & Hain, 1983).

5. Jerome Rothenberg and Paul Smoke, "Early Impacts of Proposition 2½ on the Massachusetts State-Local Public Sector" (working paper 317, Department of Economics, Massachusetts Institute of Technology, April 1983), 2. On the tax revolt in California, see especially Self, *American Babylon*.

6. Smith and Lipsky, *Nonprofits for Hire*, 6–11, 207–9; Lester M. Salamon and Alan J. Abramson, *The Federal Budget and the Nonprofit Sector* (Washington, DC: Urban Institute Press, 1982).

7. As quoted in "Text of the Dukakis Inaugural Address," *Boston Globe*, January 7, 1983; Kevin White, Office of Intergovernmental Relations, *Challenge of the 1980s: Solving Community Problems through Public/Private Partnerships*, 1983, M3/B16 FR 83/1, BPL.

8. Public-private partnerships are often framed as a hallmark of neoliberal governance. See Harvey, *A Brief History of Neoliberalism*, 47; Brown, *Undoing the Demos*, 128. On their promotion by Democrats, see Cebul, Geismer, and Williams, *Shaped by the State*; Weaver, *Blazing the Neoliberal Trail*, 118; Diamond, *Chicago on the Make*; Diamond and Sugrue, *Neoliberal Cities*.

9. Scholars of neoliberalism and of the state have largely replicated this ambiguity in their use of the term. Freeman and Minnow's *Government by Contract* focuses on for-profit partners, whereas Katz's *In the Shadow of the Poorhouse* and Salamon's *Partners in Public Service* discuss nonprofit ones. Scholars of neoliberal urbanism, particularly in case studies, offer more specificity with both for-profit and nonprofit partners, confirming the value of grounded histories of neoliberalism that Diamond and Sugrue call for in their introduction to *Neoliberal Cities*, 2. See also, for examples, the chapters in Diamond and Sugrue, *Neoliberal Cities*. Similar ambiguity follows the term *privatization*.

10. These examples widen the array of foundations that actively encouraged public-private partnerships beyond those avowedly committed to free market principles. See Alice O'Connor, "The Privatized City: The Manhattan Institute, the Urban Crisis, and the Conservative Counterrevolution in New York," *Journal of Urban History* 34, no. 2 (January 2008); Steven Teles, *The Rise of the Conservative*

Legal Movement: The Battle for Control of the Law (Princeton, NJ: Princeton University Press, 2008).

11. Michael McQuarrie, "Race, Participation, and Institutional Transformation: Black Politics in Cleveland, 1965–2010," in Diamond and Sugrue, *Neoliberal Cities*, 189, 199.

12. Boston Municipal Research Bureau, "Boston's Personnel Reduction Program: Good Effort after One Year Should Be Maintained," February 26, 1982, X1 BMR S3 82-3, BPL.

13. Boston Municipal Research Bureau, "Boston's 1981 Personnel Reduction Program: A Second Look after Six Months," September 16, 1981, X1 BMR S3 81-10, BPL.

14. In the first year after Proposition 2½, Moody's bond rating service downgraded twenty-eight cities and towns in Massachusetts at the same time that interest rates climbed. Joan FitzGerald, "Mass. Cities and Towns Selling Bonds Again," *Boston Globe*, August 1, 1982; Rothenberg and Smoke, "Early Impacts of Proposition 2½." Also, Jenkins, *The Bonds of Inequality*.

15. Raymond L. Flynn and Financial Analysis Research Group, *Boston in Transition: A Financial Analysis* (Boston: John McCormack Institute of Public Affairs, University of Massachusetts, ca. 1984), 1-45. Between 1976 and 1980, lower-income communities in Massachusetts lost an average of $19.91 per capita in federal aid, while higher-income areas gained an average $2.36 per capita. Rothenberg and Smoke, "Early Impacts of Proposition 2½," 43.

16. Walter Robinson, "The Proposition 2½ Ax Swings in Many Directions," *Boston Globe*, January 27, 1987; Walter Robinson, "King to Unveil $6.39b Budget," *Boston Globe*, January 28, 1981.

17. Marvin Pave, "User Fees Help Make Up for Prop. 2½," *Boston Globe*, January 7, 1984.

18. As quoted in Peter Cowen, "White Priority: Safe Streets for All," *Boston Globe*, November 8, 1979; "Confronting the Racism in Boston," *Boston Globe*, October 5, 1979; "Boston's Racial Problems Are Real . . . ," *Boston Globe*, November 23, 1979.

19. Al Larkin, "3 Teens Charged in Football Shooting," *Boston Globe*, October 1, 1979.

20. "A Program for Racial Peace," *Boston Globe*, April 7, 1980.

21. City of Boston, "Making Room: Comprehensive Policy for the Homeless" December 1986, M3/B16/ESC/S2/1986, BPL; Katz, *In the Shadow of the Poorhouse*, 296.

22. Michael B. Katz, ed., *The "Underclass" Debate: Views from History* (Princeton, NJ: Princeton University Press, 1993).

23. Claudia K. Norris, *On-the-Job Training and the Private Industry Council: A Technical Assistance Guide*, Report for the Employment and Training Administration, Department of Labor, September 1980, 3.

24. Kevin H. White, letter in "The Boston Private Industry Council: A New Partnership," in Subcommittee on Employment Opportunities, Committee on Education and Labor, House of Representatives, March 1980, 96th Cong., 2nd Sess., 489.

25. Prepared Statement on HR 6796, Legislation to Revise and Reauthorize Title VII of the Comprehensive Employment and Training Act by Catherine N. Stratton, Executive Director, the Boston Private Industry Council Before the Subcommittee on Employment Opportunities, Committee on Education and Labor, US House of Representatives, March 1980, 96th Cong., 2nd Sess., 494.

26. William S. Edgerly, letter in "The Boston Private Industry Council," 490.

27. Norris, On-the-Job Training, 10.

28. Donald Lowery, "Locally, the Concern Mounts: Federal and City Budgets Deal a Blow to Summer Workers," Boston Globe, March 22, 1982; Hinton, From the War on Poverty, 222–30.

29. Susan Trausch, "A Return to the Old-Time Volunteer," Boston Globe, January 31, 1982.

30. David Warsh, "The Great Summer Jobs Hunt," Boston Globe, April 15, 1980.

31. Kirk Scharfenberg, "Filling the Jobs Gap: Don't Look to Business," Boston Globe, May 16, 1981.

32. Peter Mancusi, "Odd Couple: City Youth, Summer Job," Boston Globe, June 19, 1981; Donald Lowery, "Locally, the Concern Mounts: Federal and City Budgets Deal a Blow to Summer Workers," Boston Globe, March 22, 1982; Donald Lowery, "Summer Jobs Program Turns to Private Sector," Boston Globe, March 24, 1982.

33. Robert B. Kenney, "A Gloomy Summer Job Forecast for Massachusetts," Boston Globe, May 30, 1982. "Providing More Summer Jobs," Boston Globe, June 17, 1983; Marvin Pave, "Youths' Summer Job Outlook Brightens," Boston Globe, April 26, 1983.

34. Susan Trausch and Stan Grossfeld, "The Professorial Banker," Boston Globe, August 28, 1977.

35. Jan Wong, "Business Extra: King of the Hill," Boston Globe, December 6, 1983; Doug Bailey, "Edgerly Leaves on a High Note as Marshall Carter Steps In," Boston Globe, June 23, 1992.

36. "In Brief," Boston Globe, October 27, 1982.

37. Research and Policy Committee of the Committee for Economic Development, Public-Private Partnership: An Opportunity for Urban Communities (New York: Committee for Economic Development, February 1982), 1.

38. As quoted in Muriel Cohen, "Hub Leaders Challenged to Make a Better City," Boston Globe, June 9, 1982.

39. Donald Lowery, "Leaders Discuss Boston Problems," Boston Globe, July 15, 1982.

40. Cohen, *Saving America's Cities*, 161–64, 181–85.

41. As quoted by William S. Edgerly, "A New Direction for Boston," *Boston Globe*, January 18, 1983.

42. Suleiman Osman, *The Invention of Brownstone Brooklyn: Gentrification and the Search for Authenticity in Postwar New York* (New York: Oxford University Press, 2012); Sylvie Tissot, *Good Neighbors: Gentrifying Diversity in Boston's South End* (New York: Verso, 2015).

43. Hispanic Office of Planning and Evaluation, "Hispanic Youth in Boston: In Search of Opportunities and Accountability," no. 21, Frieda Garcia Papers (unprocessed), NU, 36.

44. Hillel Levine and Lawrence Harmon, *The Death of an American Jewish Community: A Tragedy of Good Intentions* (New York: Free Press, 1992); Medoff and Sklar, *Streets of Hope*, 25–27; Gamm, *Urban Exodus*, 42–55.

45. For a popular version of this critique, see Ananad Giridharadas, *Winners Take All: The Elite Charade of Changing the World* (New York: Knopf, 2018).

46. William S. Edgerly, "Partnership That's Working," *Boston Globe*, July 12, 1983.

47. Committee for Economic Development, *Public-Private Partnership*, 2, 5.

48. White, *Challenge of the 1980s*.

49. See National Commission on Excellence in Education, *A Nation at Risk: The Imperative for Reform*, An Open Letter to the American People, A Report to the Nation and Secretary of Education (Washington, DC: US Government Printing Office, April 1983).

50. Spotlight Team, "Boston Public Schools: Their Plight and Future," *Boston Globe*, June 20–July 4, 1982, box 28, folder 20, METCO.

51. As cited in William Greider, "Business, Schools Join Forces on Jobs," reprinted from *Rolling Stone* magazine in *Boston Globe*, February 20, 1983.

52. Hispanic Office of Planning and Evaluation, "Hispanic Youth in Boston," 25–26, 33.

53. As quoted in Kenneth R. Rossano, "The Public Schools: Essence of State," *Boston Herald*, March 1, 1983, box 43, folder 4, METCO.

54. "Reforming Boston's Schools," *Time*, March 7, 1983, box 7, folder 26, Collection M159: Carmen A. Pola papers (hereafter CAP), NU.

55. As quoted in "Reforming Boston's Schools;" Eleanor Farrar, "The Boston Compact: A Teaching Case," Center for Policy Research in Education, July 1988.

56. "Tri-Lateral Council for Quality Education: A Partnership Organization," box 7, folder 32, CAP.

57. Muriel Cohen, "Boston Compact Putting Youths to Work," *Boston Globe*, September 9, 1983. Certainly the notion that schools prepare future workers was not itself new; see Cristina Groeger, *The Education Trap: Schools and the Remaking of Inequality in Boston* (Cambridge, MA: Harvard University Press, 2021).

58. "The Boston Compact: Executive Summary," March 1983, box 7, folder 32, CAP.

59. Kenneth J. Cooper, "Boston Compact Draws Fire from Blacks on School Board," *Boston Globe*, September 30, 1982.

60. Farrar, "The Boston Compact," 9–11.

61. Farrar, "The Boston Compact," 11; Cooper, "Boston Compact Draws Fire."

62. As quoted in Farrar, "The Boston Compact," 14.

63. As an example, Greater Boston Civil Rights Coalition, "Responses of Candidates Re: Recommendations for Education," 1983, box 7, folder 21, CAP.

64. "The Boston Compact: Executive Summary," emphasis in original.

65. Eleanor Farrar and Anthony Cipollone, "The Business Community and School Reform: The Boston Compact at Five Years," National Center on Effective Secondary Schools, March 1988, 9.

66. Rushworth M. Kidder, "Boston's Public Schools: Signs of Change from Negative to Positive," *Christian Science Monitor*, October 4, 1982, box 43, folder 1, METCO.

67. Farrar and Cipollone, "The Business Community and School Reform," 8.

68. The Boston Plan for Excellence in the Public Schools, "SEED: Spreading the Word," BRA 4092, BPL; "The Boston Plan for Excellence," M3/B16 SD 89/2, BPL.

69. Farrar and Cipollone, "The Business Community and School Reform," 1–2.

70. Greider, "Business, Schools Join Forces"; "Reforming Boston's Schools."

71. Greider, "Business, Schools Join Forces."

72. "The Boston Compact: Executive Summary."

73. Peggy Hernandez, "Seven Cities to Duplicate Hub School's Compact," *Boston Globe*, February 20, 1987.

74. As quoted in William G. Miller, "British Try Out a Boston Idea," *Boston Globe*, November 1, 1987; Steven Erlanger, "Hub Takes Lesson Plan on Schools to London," *Boston Globe*, December 6, 1986. See Weaver, *Blazing the Neoliberal Trail*.

75. Farrar, "The Boston Compact," 29.

76. Private Industry Council, "Boston Compact Placement Status Report," November 1985, box 6, folder 28, RMSC.

77. Hispanic Office of Planning and Evaluation, "Hispanic Youth in Boston," 38.

78. See Hispanic Office of Planning and Evaluation, "Hispanic Youth in Boston."

79. Sarah Snyder, "Business to Schools: We Want Results," *Boston Globe*, October 25, 1988.

80. Patricia Wen, "Business Leaders Won't Renew School Pact til Progress Seen," *Boston Globe*, December 10, 1988.

81. Muriel Cohen, "Some Critics of Boston Schools Find Pace of Change Too Slow," *Boston Globe*, May 19, 1992; Thomas C. Palmer, "Will Legislature Expand School Choice?" *Boston Globe*, December 6, 1992; Joan Vennochi, "Dangerous Liaisons," *Boston Globe*, March 12, 1993; Peter J. Howe, "Education Reform Loses Luster on the Hill," *Boston Globe*, April 22, 1993.

82. "Report of the Special Committee on the Homeless," Chairman Thomas M. Menino, December 3, 1985, box 34, folder 20, Kip Tiernan papers, Schlesinger Library, Harvard University.

83. City of Boston, "Making Room: Comprehensive Policy for the Homeless."

84. Between 1980 and 1985, the proportion of Boston renters paying over half their income for housing nearly doubled to 21 percent. City of Boston, "Making Room."

85. "Pine Street Inn Shows New Home," *Boston Globe*, October 1, 1979; Christina Robb, "Taking Care: The Women at Rosie's Place," *Boston Globe*, October 28, 1979; Jean Dietz, "Mental Patients Flood Pine St.," *Boston Globe*, August 21, 1980; Timothy Dwyer, "Boston's Streets Are Their Home," *Boston Globe*, July 20, 1981; Ellen L. Bassuk, "Addressing the Needs of the Homeless," *Boston Globe*, November 6, 1983. This reflected a national uptick in coverage. In addition to increased newspaper articles, Michael Katz credits the publication of two books—Ann Marie Rousseau's *Shopping Bag Ladies: Homeless Women Speak about Their Lives* (New York: Pilgrim, 1982) and Ellen Baxter and Kim Hopper's *Private Lives, Public Spaces: Homeless Adults on the Streets of New York City* (New York: Community Service Society of New York, Institute for Social Welfare Research, 1981)—with bringing homelessness onto the national stage. Katz, *The Undeserving Poor*, 193.

86. Anthony J. Yudis, "Seventy Buildings to Be Restored," *Boston Globe*, February 10, 1985.

87. McCormack, "The Implementation of the Boston Housing Partnership," 14.

88. Boston Housing Partnership, "Initial Material Describing the Partnership's Demonstration Rehabilitation Program," February 1983, BRA 4608, BPL. As an exception, Boston's linkage program required developers to contribute to the city's housing trust fund. Pierre Clavel, *Activists in City Hall*.

89. Boston Housing Partnership, "Board of Directors," January 1985, BRA 4619, BPL.

90. Boston Housing Partnership, "Program Summary," BRA 4612, BPL. The participation of race leaders on the Boston Housing Partnership board is largely consistent with Lester Spence's argument about the "neoliberalization of black politics." Lester K. Spence, "The Neoliberal Turn in Black Politics," *Souls* 14, no. 3–4 (2012): 139–59; Mary Pattillo, "Race, Poverty, and Neighborhood Planning in Chicago from the New Deal to Neoliberalism," in Diamond and Sugrue, *Neoliberal Cities*, 14. On CDCs as "representative," see Levine, *Constructing Community*.

91. McCormack, "The Implementation of the Boston Housing Partnership," 22.

92. McCormack, "The Implementation of the Boston Housing Partnership," 24–25, 50.

93. Local Initiatives Support Corporation, "Summary of Approved Program Actions," December 21, 1984, Grant 08000010, Reel 5487, Frame 2476, FF.

94. As quoted in McCormack, "The Implementation of the Boston Housing Partnership," 24.

95. McCormack, "The Implementation of the Boston Housing Partnership," 38.

96. As quoted in McCormack, "The Implementation of the Boston Housing Partnership," 49.

97. McCormack, "The Implementation of the Boston Housing Partnership," 42.

98. Yudis, "Seventy Buildings."

99. Joan Vennochi, "'Partnership' to Rehabilitate Housing Yields First Results and Draws Praise," *Boston Globe*, May 12, 1985.

100. Ross Gelbspan, "Mutual Interest: Boston's Corporate-Public Alliances Provide New Opportunities, Offer Models for Other Cities in Era of Shrinking Federal Role," *Boston Globe*, November 10, 1986.

101. Anthony J. Yudis, "Outlook for Boston: A Boom," *Boston Globe*, January 11, 1981.

102. Peter Drier, "Redlining Cities: How Banks Color Community Development," *Challenge* (November–December 1991): 15–23.

103. As an example, display ad 29, *Boston Globe*, May 20, 1986; Andrew Dabilis, "Fund for the Homeless Passes $400,000 Mark," *Boston Globe*, December 6, 1984; Paul Hirshon, "Yuppies Try to Bolster Their Image by Helping Out Boston Charities," *Boston Globe*, May 12, 1987; John Robinson, "To Have and Have Not: Mobilizing to Help the Homeless," *Boston Globe*, April 5, 1985; Carol Flake, "Ship Ahoy for a Cause," *Boston Globe*, June 20, 1986.

104. Ronald Reagan, "Inaugural Address," January 20, 1981; *Goals for Boston* (newsletter) 5, no. 1 (Spring 1987), BRA 4258, BPL.

105. As examples, Richard J. Margolis, "Will the Patient Live?" *Foundation News* (September/October 1985), box 2, folder 8, Collection M178: Grants Management Associates records (hereafter GMA), NU; Alan Lupo, "Change Is in the Air along Dudley Street," *Boston Globe*, February 17, 1985.

106. As quoted in Margolis, "Will the Patient Live?"

107. Newell Flather, Notes, summer 1984, box 2, folder 10, GMA.

108. Flather, Notes.

109. "In Search of Community: A Strategic Planning Conference in Boston's Dudley Square Neighborhood," July 1984, box 5, folder 32, GMA; Boston Redevelopment Authority, "Dudley Square Plan: A Strategy for Neighborhood Revitalization, Briefing Book Draft," December 17, 1984, box 5, folder 18, GMA; Ian Menzies, "A Clash over Dudley Sq.," *Boston Globe*, March 12, 1985.

110. Ad Hoc Community-Wide Meeting Committee Report, January 30, 1985, box 5, folder 7, GMA.

111. See Ad Hoc Community-Wide Meeting Committee Reports for December 5, 1984; December 12, 1984; January 4, 1985; January 16, 1985; January 30 1985; February 13, 1985, box 5, folder 7, GMA.

112. Medoff and Sklar, *Streets of Hope*, 54.

113. As quoted in Margolis, "Will the Patient Live?" 38. Medoff and Sklar quote Coleman slightly differently: "Who the hell are you people and what do you want? . . . Who is Riley? Why should we trust you?" Medoff and Sklar, *Streets of Hope*, 53.

114. "The Dudley Street Neighborhood Initiative: An Overview," January 1985, and "The Dudley Street Neighborhood Initiative: An Overview," revised March 1985, box 5, folder 34, GMA.

115. Dudley Street Neighborhood Initiative, "Draft Proposal to the Riley Foundation," August 16, 1985, box 2, folder 11, LAH; Medoff and Sklar, *Streets of Hope*, 85–86.

116. Dudley Street Neighborhood Initiative, "Draft Proposal to the Riley Foundation;" also "The Dudley Street Neighborhood Initiative Revitalization Plan: A Comprehensive Community Control Strategy," prepared by DAC International, Inc., September 1987, BRA 2521, 1, BPL.

117. "Request for Proposals—Comprehensive Plan of Development," *Boston Globe*, August 10, 1986; Medoff and Sklar, *Streets of Hope*, 96.

118. Jacobs, *Death and Life of Great American Cities*, 311.

119. Medoff and Sklar, *Streets of Hope*, 116.

120. As quoted in Medoff and Sklar, *Streets of Hope*, 125.

121. Medoff and Sklar, *Streets of Hope*, 123.

122. Anthony J. Yudis, "$3 Billion in Projects Changing the Cityscape," *Boston Globe*, November 11, 1984.

123. As quoted in Medoff and Sklar, *Streets of Hope*, 134.

124. As quoted in Medoff and Sklar, *Streets of Hope*, 110; Peter S. Canellos, "Neighborhood Hopes to Wield Eminent Domain," *Boston Globe*, October 28, 1988.

125. The actual transfer of property to the newly incorporated land trust, Dudley Neighbors, Inc., took several more years.

126. As quoted in Medoff and Sklar, *Streets of Hope*, 144.

127. Proposal by Peter Medoff and Holly Sklar for completion of *Breaking Ground*, Reel 6832, Frame 0134, DSNI, Grant 09150126, FF; Recommendation for Delegated-Authority Grant, September 26, 1990, Reel 6832, Frame 0151–55, DSNI, Grant 09150126, FF. See also Medoff and Sklar, *Streets of Hope*.

128. Bailey, "Edgerly Leaves on a High Note."

129. As quoted in David Osborne and Ted Gaebler, *Reinventing Government: How the Entrepreneurial Spirit Is Transforming the Public Sector* (New York: Penguin Books, 1992), 36.

130. As quoted in Medoff and Sklar, *Streets of Hope*, 144.

131. Osborne and Gaebler's *Reinventing Government* promoted "catalytic government" and became a basis of Clinton's policy agenda.

Chapter 7

1. Raymond L. Flynn, "America Ready to Go: Rebuilding America's Cities Together, A Recommendation to the Clinton Administration and the New Congress," 1992, BRA 3502, BPL, 47.

2. Flynn, "America Ready to Go," 1.

3. Flynn, "America Ready to Go," 3.

4. Flynn, "America Ready to Go," 1, 2.

5. Flynn, "America Ready to Go," 4, 63; Michael E. Porter, "The Competitive Advantage of the Inner City," *Harvard Business Review* (May–June 1995); Goldstein, *The Roots of Urban Renaissance*, 247–49.

6. Flynn, "America Ready to Go," 1, 127.

7. Economic Development and Industrial Corporation, City of Boston, "Investing in Human Development Promoting Economic Self-Sufficiency," November 1991, M3/B16/EDIC 91/5, BPL.

8. Jacqueline Trescott, "Lessons of Her Father," *Washington Post*, April 27, 1985.

9. Melinda Marble and Martella Wilson Taylor, "Efforts to Combat Poverty in Boston: A Brief History, 1960–1990," June 26, 1990, box 15, folder 46, Collection M127: Persistent Poverty Project Records (hereafter PPP), NU, 24.

10. Ange-Marie Hancock, *The Politics of Disgust: The Public Identity of the Welfare Queen* (New York: New York University Press, 2004); Chappell, *The War on Welfare*, chap. 5.

11. BPPP, *In the Midst of Plenty*, 9.

12. BPPP, *To Make Our City Whole: A Report of the Strategy Development Group of the Boston Persistent Poverty Project*, Boston Foundation, 1994, X1/BOF/94/1, BPL, 9.

13. Katz, *The "Underclass" Debate*. See also William Julius Wilson, *The Truly Disadvantaged: The Inner City, The Underclass, and Public Policy* (Chicago: University of Chicago Press, 1987).

14. Anna Faith Jones, opening remarks in "The Persistent Poverty Project: Teresa Amott Seminar Five," Boston Foundation, June 14, 1990, X1/BOF/90/1, BPL.

15. BPPP, *To Make Our City Whole*.

16. BPPP, "Summary of Community-Based Focus Groups," undated, box 8, folder 26, CPA.

17. Marilyn S. Johnson, *The New Bostonians: How Immigrants Have Transformed the Metro Region since the 1960s* (Amherst: University of Massachusetts Press, 2015).

18. "1:1 Community Fabric," undated, box 8, folder 26, CPA.

19. BPPP, *To Make Our City Whole*, 22.

20. BPPP, *To Make Our City Whole*, 5.

21. Spence, "The Neoliberal Turn in Black Politics," 143, 150.

22. BPPP, *To Make Our City Whole*, 37. Though not explicitly stated, this framework around community building was inspired in part by the rise of social capital theories, especially Robert D. Putnam, "Bowling Alone: America's Declining Social Capital," *Journal of Democracy* 6, no. 1 (1995): 65–78.

23. Thomas Menino to Friend, February 1994, in BPPP, *To Make Our City Whole*.

24. "Current Status of Healthy Boston," May 5, 1993, box 16, folder 84, PPP; Meeting Agenda, June 3, 1993, box 16, folder 74, PPP.

25. Flynn, "America Ready to Go," 128.

26. My use of the word *game* here draws on Keyes, *The Rehabilitation Planning Game*, esp. 6–7.

27. Don Aucoin, "Flynn Declares He Is Running for a 3d Term," *Boston Globe*, July 28, 1991.

28. Department of Health and Hospitals, "Schools, Hospitals, Housing Join Quest for Healthy Boston," news release, August 7, 1991, box 16, folder 74, PPP.

29. "The Healthy Boston Initiative," undated, box 2, folder 24, LAH.

30. Economic Development and Industrial Corporation, "Investing in Human Development."

31. Michael McGrath, "Note from the Editor," *National Civic Review* (Winter 2013): 3.

32. As quoted in Diana Markel, "Comprehensive Planning and Collaborative Action: Neighborhood Coalitions in Boston" (master's thesis in city planning, Massachusetts Institute of Technology, May 1996), 30.

33. Department of Health and Hospitals, "Schools, Hospitals, Housing Join Quest."

34. Department of Health and Hospitals, "Schools, Hospitals, Housing Join Quest;" "The Healthy Boston Initiative;" "What Is Healthy Boston," undated, box 20, folder 8, RMSC.

35. "The Healthy Boston Initiative."

36. "What Is Healthy Boston."

37. Markel, "Comprehensive Planning and Collaborative Action," 5.

38. Markel, "Comprehensive Planning and Collaborative Action," 5.

39. City of Boston, "Health Boston Initiative: Building Community Coalitions, Pilot Program Planning Grant: Overview," revised November 26, 1991, box 16, folder 82, PPP, 8–10; "The Healthy Boston Initiative."

40. "The Healthy Boston Initiative;" "What Is Healthy Boston."

41. "Meeting of Ad-Hoc City Officials: Discussion of Healthy Boston," meeting minutes, September 17, 1991, box 16, folder 80, PPP.

42. South End/Lower Roxbury Coalition, minutes, March 26, 1992, box 12, folder 17, IBA. In *After the Projects*, Lawrence Vale connects the infrastructure of nonprofit organizations created in resistance to urban renewal to the politics and implementation of HOPE VI in cities around the United States.

43. "Healthy Boston Initiative: List of Approved Coalitions," July 14, 1992, box 20, folder 8, RMSC.

44. While today we are more accustomed to LGBTQ+ as an inclusive acronym, entities at the time described here used GLBT as a descriptor, and my writing here retains that preferred acronym. Healthy Boston Coalition for Gay, Lesbian, Bisexual, and Cross-Gender Youth, Needs Assessment, 1992–1993, box 1, folder 48, Collection 107: Boston Alliance of Gay and Lesbian Youth Records (hereafter BAGLY), NU.

45. "Healthy Boston Coalition for Gay, Lesbian, BiSexual, and TransGender [*sic*] Youth," undated, box 1, folder 49, BAGLY.

46. "The Coalition for Gay, Lesbian, Bisexual and Transgender Youth," undated, box 1, folder 49, BAGLY.

47. "Applauds" in Maura Pensakr to Theodore Landsmark, June 3, 1994, box 2, folder 1, BAGLY; "secure relationships," in Coalition for Gay, Lesbian, Bi-Sexual and TransGender Youth, "Healthy Boston Initiative: Moving Toward Sustainability, FY95 Request for Coalition Operating Grant," May 1994, box 2, folder 1, BAGLY.

48. Grove Hall Healthy Boston Coalition, "Grove Hall Today: A Time for Renewal," 1994, box 11, folder 41, RMSC, 21–22.

49. Project RIGHT Collaborative, "Job Description: Community Organizer," undated, box 11, folder 23, RMSC.

50. Grove Hall Healthy Boston Coalition, "Grove Hall Today," iii.

51. Grove Hall Healthy Boston Coalition, "Grove Hall Today," ii.

52. Grove Hall Healthy Boston Coalition, "Grove Hall Today," v.

53. South End/Lower Roxbury Healthy Boston Coalition, Action Plan—Draft, May 16, 1994, box 12, folder 17, IBA; Newsletters, Egleston Square Coalition, 1993, box 16, folder 81, PPP. Sociologist Patrick Sharkey argues that the presence of nonprofit organizations—both those directly related to violence prevention and those pursuing other goals—contributed to what he calls the "great crime decline" in American cities during the 1990s. Patrick Sharkey, *Uneasy Peace: The Great Crime Decline, the Renewal of City Life, and the Next War on Violence* (New York: Norton, 2018), 50–55. Also, Patrick Sharkey, Gerard Torrats-Espinosa, and Delaram Takyar, "Community and the Crime Decline: The Causal Effect of Local Nonprofit Formation on Violent Crime," *American Sociological Review* 82, no. 6 (2017): 1214–40. For a more critical take on the role of nonprofits, see Laurence Ralph, *Renegade Dreams: Living through Injury in Gangland Chicago* (Chicago: University of Chicago Press, 2014).

54. Christopher Winship, "End of a Miracle? Crime, Faith, and Partnership in Boston in the 1990s," in *The Long March Ahead: African American Churches and Public Policy in Post–Civil Rights America*, ed. R. Drew Smith (Durham, NC: Duke University Press, 2004), 171–92.

55. On the Boston Miracle, see Anthony Braga, David Kennedy, E. J. Waring, and Anne Piehl, "Problem-Oriented Policing, Deterrence, and Youth Violence: An Evaluation of Boston's Operation Ceasefire," *Journal of Research in Crime and Delinquency* 38, no. 3 (2001): 195–226; Christopher Winship, Anthony Braga, and David Huearu, "Losing Faith? Police, Black Churches, and the Resurgence of Youth Violence in Boston," *Ohio State Journal of Criminal Law* 6, no. 1 (Fall 2008): 141–72. For a more popular take, see David M. Kennedy, *Don't Shoot: One Man, a Street Fellowship, and the End of Violence in Inner-City America* (New York: Bloomsbury, 2011), or "God vs. Gangs: What's the Hottest Idea in Crime Fighting: The Power of Religion," *Newsweek*, June 1, 1998.

56. Healthy Boston Violence Prevention Initiative, meeting minutes, October 18, 1994, box 2, folder 2, BAGLY.

57. "Addendum 1, History of the South End Teen Empowerment Project," undated, box 12, folder 17, IBA; South End/Lower Roxbury Healthy Boston Coalition, "Action Plan, Second Draft," March 26, 1994, box 12, folder 17, IBA.

58. Healthy Boston Violence Prevention Initiative, meeting minutes, October–December 1994, box 2, folder 2, BAGLY.

59. Quotes from "Update City-Wide Peace Campaign," undated, box 2, folder 2, BAGLY; Newsletters, Egleston Square Coalition, 1993, box 16, folder 81, PPP.

60. "Healthy Boston: The Next Phase: A Concept Paper," March 21, 1996," box 2, folder 1, BAGLY.

61. Letter to Coalition Coordinators, October 7, 1994, box 3, folder 34, Collection M136: Sociedad Latina, Inc. records, NU.

62. Boston Healthy Start Initiative, "Service Delivery Sub-Contracts Awards," undated, box 3, folder 33, Sociedad Latina, Inc. records; Charter School Application Submitted to Commonwealth of Massachusetts Executive Office of Education for Federated Dorchester Neighborhood House, 1994, UMass Amherst Library, Mass EDI.2: C38/Neigh; Charter School Application Submitted to Commonwealth of Massachusetts Executive Office of Education for Egleston Community Charter School, 1995, UMass Amherst Library, Mass EDI.2: C38/1995/Egleston.

63. "Request for Proposal for Evaluation of Healthy Boston," May 13, 1993, box 16, folder 79, PPP.

64. Healthy Boston Coalition Training and Technical Assistance, notes, November 6, 1992, box 16, folder 76, PPP.

65. Miller et al., "Healthy Boston Evaluation: Preliminary Findings," June 19, 1995, box 16, folder 83, PPP, 5, 11.

66. "Healthy Boston: The Next Phase: A Concept Paper."

67. Stephen A. Borrelli, "Finding the Third Way: Bill Clinton, the DLC, and the Democratic Platform of 1992," *Journal of Policy History* 13, no. 4 (2001): 429–62; Lily Geismer, "Agents of Change: Microcredit, Welfare Reform, the Clintons, and Liberal Forms of Neoliberalism," *Journal of American History* 107, no. 1 (June 2020): 107–31.

68. Dávila, *Barrio Dreams*, 4.

69. Empowerment Zones Signing Ceremony, January 17, 1994, C-Span, https://www.c-span.org/video/?53817-1/empowerment-zones-signing-ceremony&start=99.

70. City of Boston, "Boston Works: Partnerships for a Sustainable Community," June 1994, BRA 2630, BPL, 20–21.

71. As quoted in "Healthy Boston/BRA Meetings: Empowerment Zone," March 1994, box 5, folder 8, CPA.

72. BPPP, *In the Midst of Plenty*, 23.

73. Chinatown Coalition, meeting minutes, April 14, 1994, box 5, folder 8, CPA.

74. Chinatown Coalition, meeting minutes, March 9, 1995, box 5, folder 8, CPA. See also Andrew Leong, "The Struggle over Parcel C: How Boston's Chinatown Won a Victory in the Fight against Institutional Expansionism and Environmental

Racism" (working paper, Institute for Asian American Studies, September 22, 1997).

75. Chinatown Coalition, meeting minutes, March 9, 1995; Chinatown Coalition, meeting minutes, May 5, 1994, box 5, folder 8, CPA.

76. Thomas M. Menino to Honorable Henry G. Cisneros, June 27, 1994, in City of Boston, "Boston Works."

77. City of Boston, "Boston Works," 22.

78. City of Boston, "Boston Works," "not experts," 3, 8; "deep-rooted," 180.

79. Andrew Cuomo and Dan Glickman, *What Works! In the Empowerment Zones and Enterprise Communities*, vol. II (Washington, DC: US Department of Housing and Urban Development and US Department of Agriculture, 1998), i.

80. Weaver, *Blazing the Neoliberal Trail*, 16, 19.

81. Goldstein, *The Roots of Urban Renaissance*, 245.

82. "Empowerment Zone/Enterprise Community Program Status and Funding," undated, box 5, folder 9, CPA; Robert Keough, "The Death and Life of an Empowerment Zone," *CommonWealth*, Winter 1998; Donald Sykes to Linda Haar, December 30, 1994, box 5, folder 9, CPA.

83. Henry Cisneros to Thomas Menino, December 21, 1994, box 5, folder 9, CPA.

84. "Focal Points for 9/30/95," box 5, folder 10, CPA; "Proposal for 'Immigrants Create Jobs' Press Event," box 8, folder 5, CPA; Beverly Wong to Community Member, May 9, 1996, box 5, folder 5, CPA.

85. Chinatown Coalition, "Updates," March 1996, box 5, folder 5, CPA.

86. Vale, *After the Projects*, chap. 7.

87. James Jennings, "The Empowerment Zone in Boston, Massachusetts, 2000–2009: Lessons Learned for Neighborhood Revitalization," *Review of Black Political Economy* 38, no. 1 (2011): 63–81; See Goldstein, *The Roots of Urban Renaissance*, chap. 6, for a discussion of Empowerment Zone funding in Harlem and the use of tax credits by CDCs to attract large retail stores to the neighborhood.

88. Krippner, *Capitalizing on Crisis*; Brown, *Undoing the Demos*, 131–32.

89. Jennings, "The Empowerment Zone in Boston," 67, 74, 78.

90. James Jennings, *Community-Based Nonprofits and Neighborhood Distress in Boston, Massachusetts*, report prepared for the Barr Foundation, February 2009, https://sites.tufts.edu/jamesjennings/files/2018/06/reportsCommunityBasedNon profits2009.pdf.

91. Peter R. Orsazg et al., "Developing Effective Place-Based Policies for the FY 2011 Budget," memorandum for the Heads of Executive Departments and Agencies, August 11, 2009, M-09-28, https://obamawhitehouse.archives.gov/sites /default/files/omb/assets/memoranda_fy2009/m09-28.pdf.

92. Jeremy R. Levine and William Julius Wilson, "Poverty, Politics, and a 'Circle of Promise': Holistic Education Policy in Boston and the Challenge of Institutional Entrenchment," *Journal of Urban Affairs* 35, no. 1 (2013): 7–24.

93. "The Dudley Street Neighborhood Initiative: Application for Planning Grant from the Promise Neighborhoods Program," 2010, https://www2.ed.gov /programs/promiseneighborhoods/2010/narratives/dudleystreet.pdf.

94. US Department of Housing and Urban Development, "Creating Choice Neighborhoods: Boston's Critical Community Improvements," Choice Neighbor-hoods Promising Practice Guides, Issue Brief No. 1, https://www.hud.gov/sites/docu ments/CNPPGUIDE-BOSTON.PDF.

95. Crosby, Schlessinger, Smallridge with Bryant Associates for the Fairmount Greenway Task Force, "The Fairmount Greenway Concept Plan," March 2011, https://fairmountcollaborative.org/2016/wp-content/uploads/2016/08/Fairmount-Green way-Concept-Plan-2012_-reduced.pdf. See also Levine, *Constructing Community*.

Conclusion

1. Natalie Homes and Alan Berube, *City and Metropolitan Inequality on the Rise, Driven by Declining Incomes* (Brookings, January 14, 2016).

2. Ana Patricia Muñoz et al., "The Color of Wealth in Boston," Federal Re-serve Bank of Boston, March 25, 2015. Also, Boston Redevelopment Authority Research Division, "Boston Citywide Plan: Trends in Poverty and Inequality," Oc-tober 2015; Boston Indicators Project, "A Great Reckoning: Healing a Growing Divide," June 2009.

3. Emily Zimmerman et al., *Social Capital and Health Outcomes in Boston*, Technical Report (Center on Human Needs, Virginia Commonwealth University, September 2012), https://societyhealth.vcu.edu/media/society-health/pdf/PMReport _Boston.pdf; Story Hinckley, "Egleston Square: A City Divided in Life and Death," *The Scope Boston*, December 7, 2018, https://thescopeboston.org/704/projects /washington-street-egleston-square/?utm_campaign=coschedule&utm_source =twitter&utm_medium=bostonfdn.

4. Clayton M. Christensen et al., "Disruptive Innovation for Social Change," *Harvard Business Review* (December 2006): 96.

5. For a contemporary account of the tension between systems and structures, see Giridharadas, *Winners Take All*, 94–98. For a proposed means of shifting to-ward structural change in foundation giving, see Villanueva, *Decolonizing Wealth*, and the work of Solidaire, accessed August 2019, www.solidairenetwork.org.

6. Jennings, "Community-Based Nonprofits."

Index

Greater Boston Community Development, 147, 149–50, 152, 154, 158, 162; fundraising of, 170–71, 177, 196–97
Great Migration, 5, 29–30
Great Society, 6, 66, 68, 96, 121. *See also* War on Poverty
Green and Blue program, 229
Grogan, Paul, 174, 176
Grove Hall, 15, 227, 237–38

Hackett, David, 67
Haitian community, 226
Hall, Prince, 83
Hampton, Fred, 100
Harlem Children's Zone, 240–41
Harriet Tubman House, 83–84
Harris, Barbara, 217
Harvard University, 2, 42, 70, 118, 261n6, 271n6
Head Start, 87, 89–91
health care, 87–88, 121, 126, 222, 235, 243. *See also* Boston Department of Health and Hospitals; Healthy Boston
health insurance, 13
Healthy Boston, 212, 220–30, 233, 240. *See also* Egleston Square Coalition; youth violence; Grove Hall; Upham's Corner Coalition
Hernandez, Jorge, 198
Hicks, Louise Day, 113–14
Hispanic Office of Planning and Evaluation, 217
homelessness, 2, 197, 200, 210
homeownership, 28–29, 238, 264n28
Honeywell, 187, 194
HOPE VI housing program, 237, 324n42
hospitals, 6, 22, 68, 144, 185; and nonprofits, 222; work in, 191
housing, 95, 99, 101, 103, 107, 117; cooperatives, 306n11; cost of, 244, 320n84; development of, 147–49, 158, 164, 168, 174, 178–79; funding for, 126, 128, 155; market for, 165–66, 171–72, 177; and neoliberalism, 180, 200; and publicprivate partnerships, 196, 210; and race, 185. *See also* affordable housing; Boston Housing Partnership; community development corporations (CDCs); public housing; real estate
Housing Act of 1949, 34

Housing and Community Development Act of 1974, 142
Housing and Home Finance Agency, 47, 275n48
Houston, Julian, 217
Hunter, David, 53
Huntington, Samuel, 118
Hyde Park, 143–44, 165
Hyams Trust, 174–76, 227
Hynes, John, 33–35, 37–39, 49

identity politics, 82, 99, 220, 248. *See also* ethnicity; gender; race
"I Have a Dream" Coalition, 226
immigrants, 8, 29–31, 144, 213, 290n7; neighborhoods of, 35; poverty among, 216. *See also* migrants
immigration, 31, 216, 281n8
INCITE!, 282n9
inequality, 4, 9–10, 14, 16–17, 19; in Boston, 242–45; in education, 194; end of, 96; in governance, 216; in housing, 178; and nonprofits, 250; persistence of, 22–23, 181–82, 210, 238–39, 269n56, 281n8; in social services, 64, 112. *See also* education; poverty; race; segregation
Inquilinos Boricuas en Acción, 109, 160–62, 164, 198. *See also* Emergency Tenants' Council; Villa Victoria

Jabzanka, Walter, 133
Jacobs, Jane, 6, 38
Jamaica Plain, 118, 123, 159, 165–66
Jewish community, 31, 43, 70
Jewish Community Relations Council, 217
Jim Crow, 5, 29, 96; in northern states, 30
John F. Kennedy Multi-Service Center, 110
John Hancock Mutual Life Insurance, 157, 193–94, 197
Johnson, Lyndon, 6, 8, 10–11, 21, 53, 77; crime policy of, 129–30; and devolution, 114, 119; liberalism of, 176; and Model Cities, 120, 142; War on Poverty of, 66–68. *See also* Great Society; War on Poverty
Jones, Anna Faith, 214–15
Jones, Hubie, 94–100, 111, 136, 198, 217, 249
Jones, William, 198

South End Community Security Program,
132–33
South End Neighborhood Action Program,
88–89
South End Project Area Committee, 145
Spillane, Robert, 192
state government, 115, 119, 152–53. *See also*
Massachusetts
State Street Bank, 186, 188, 193
St. Marks Center, 63, 85
Stratton, Catherine, 186
suburbanization, 20, 26–27, 29, 33, 51. *See
also* Route 128; white flight
Sun Belt, 27, 142
Sviridoff, Mitchell, 199

Task Force on Out of School Children, 98,
136
Tax Reform Act of 1969, 265n32
Tax Reform Act of 1986, 175
Taylor, Rita, 76
tech sector, 22, 166, 191, 212, 235, 243;
and housing prices, 181, 189. *See also*
hospitals; Massachusetts Miracle;
universities
Temporary Aid for Needy Families. *See* Aid
to Families with Dependent Children
tenant management corporations, 18
Ten Point Coalition, 228
Tent City Corporation, 177–78
Thatcher, Margaret, 232
Tocqueville, Alexis de, 49
Tri-Lateral Council for Quality Education,
192
Truman, Harry, 34
Trump, Donald, 239

unemployment, 58, 185–87, 195, 231. *See also*
Private Industry Councils
unemployment insurance, 8, 13
United Black Appeal, 111
United Community Services, 111
United Kingdom, 1, 195, 232
United South End Settlements, 41–42, 59,
63, 80–81, 84; and Healthy Boston, 222;
and urban renewal, 102, 295n96. *See
also* Community Assembly for a United
South End; King, Mel; South End
United States Commission on Civil Rights,
29, 32
United States Congress, 2, 33–34, 37, 68, 90

United States Department of Health, Education, and Welfare, 73, 283n24, 288n104
United States Department of Housing
and Urban Development (HUD), 47,
120, 126–27, 134, 142, 299n32; Choice
Neighborhoods program, 241; private
partnerships of, 199
United States Department of Labor, 2, 63,
73, 186, 283n24, 288n103
United States government, 1, 3, 262n9,
266n36; crime policy of, 129; economic
policy of, 5; education policy of, 98; expansion of, 54, 120–21; as granting agency,
11–12, 40, 53, 56, 60, 70, 73–74, 241; housing policy of, 28, 142, 154; and neoliberalism, 17–18, 236, 242; partnerships of,
211–13; as philanthropist, 77–78; social
policy of, 8–10, 16, 57, 66–69; urban policy
of, 6–7, 19–21, 23, 26, 34, 231–32, 266n37;
welfare programs of, 101. *See also* Bush,
George H. W.; Bush, George W.; Clinton,
Bill; Community Development Block
Grants; Empowerment Zone/Enterprise
Communities; Ford, Gerald; grantmaking; Great Society; Johnson, Lyndon;
Kennedy, John F.; Model Cities program;
Nixon, Richard; Obama, Barack; urban
renewal; War on Poverty; welfare state
United States State Department, 94
United Way, 111
universities, 6, 22, 28, 42, 68, 144. *See also*
Harvard University; Massachusetts
Institute of Technology
Upham's Corner Coalition, 224
Upper Roxbury, 43–44, 48, 51. *See also*
Washington Park
"urban crisis," 7, 9–10, 14, 21, 31, 264n21;
and law enforcement, 135; management
of, 245; in the 1980s, 181; politics of, 54,
128; and renewal, 51. *See also* urban
renewal
Urban Enterprise Zones, 212
urban governance, 4–9, 14–16, 244–45;
and CDCs, 149–50, 172; community
participation in, 26, 40, 50, 79, 97–98, 151;
diversity in, 214; inequality in, 250; and
neoliberalism, 18–19, 164, 182, 212; nonprofit neighborhoods in, 21–22, 101, 129,
208, 230, 247; nonprofits in, 55–56, 61,
66, 83, 110, 123, 289n122; public-private
partnerships in, 191; racial politics of, 92,